Mr. Burkitt and Africa

Mr. Burkitt and Africa

by Bernard Glemser

THE WORLD PUBLISHING COMPANY
New York and Cleveland

Published by The World Publishing Company
2231 West 110th Street, Cleveland, Ohio 44102

Published simultaneously in Canada by
Nelson, Foster & Scott Ltd.

First Printing—1970

Library of Congress Catalog Card Number: 70–112435
Printed in the United States of America

WORLD PUBLISHING
TIMES MIRROR

To
V.C.G.

Contents

Introduction

Every now and then something of importance occurs in the scientific world that is more than a scientific event pure and simple, and finds its best expression as a story. Scientific discovery is not entirely a matter of laboratory glassware and sophisticated instruments, of progressing in a series of precise steps from *a* to *b* to *c*. Human beings are involved, and the jump from *a* to *b*, or from *b* to *c*, may be accompanied by spectacular emotional fireworks, by tragedy, comedy, and misunderstandings more appropriate to a novel than a technical paper. One example that comes to mind is *The Double Helix*, by Dr. J. D. Watson, an account of how he and two fellow scientists solved the problem of the structure of DNA, the cellular substance which has been called "the very stuff of life." The discovery, which earned the three men a Nobel Prize, is described in detail in every modern textbook of biology. The *story*, though, is something else. It is full of mischief, uncertainty, decision, indecision; and its central characters are remarkably vivid (who can forget the opening sentence: *I have never seen Francis Crick in a modest mood*, or the mysterious and doomed Rosalind Franklin?).

This book is the story of a series of medical discoveries which began in 1957 and are still continuing. The story's central character is an Irish surgeon, Denis Parsons Burkitt, who early in his life committed himself to work among the people of Africa, and who eventually "happened" to come upon and identify a form of cancer that afflicts many African children. He then set off on a safari of ten thousand miles, with two devoted missionary friends, and literally tracked down the peculiar circumstances in which this tumor occurred. This, though, is only the first part of the story; for Denis Burkitt then went on to discover means for curing the cancer in a significant number of cases.

Whenever any writer announces that he is going to give an account of a cure for a particular form of cancer, the reader should promptly assume an attitude of hard disbelief. Cures for cancer, unfortunately, are exceedingly rare—unless, that is, the cure is accomplished in the conventional manner by means of surgery or radiotherapy. The work of Denis Burkitt and his colleagues, however, has become one of the cornerstones of contemporary cancer research, and it is being followed up by experts all over the world. In a book called *Man Against Cancer* I described Mr. Burkitt's appearance before an audience of cancer specialists (the actual occasion was an address he gave in 1967 at the Sloan-Kettering Institute for Cancer Research in New York): "He has a decided military bearing—the result, perhaps, of his five years of service in the British Army, or of having grown up in Enniskillen, Northern Ireland, which is renowned (he will tell you proudly) as the home of two great regiments. His voice has an Irish lilt, and he cannot resist making a joke or two as he tells about his work in Kampala, Uganda.

"Then the color slides come on the screen. About half are photographs of his African children, with grotesquely distorted faces or swollen bodies, resulting from the tumor which has been given his name. *But each color slide showing a child with a tumor is followed by another color slide showing the same child without a tumor*—cured by a handful of pills or a single injection. The last color slide shows a long line of these children, attired in their bright East African robes, standing in a sunny little street and gazing solemnly at the camera. They are clear-eyed and, as far as any human being can tell, in perfect health." It is not surprising that these photographs invariably bring Mr. Burkitt an ovation.

But an account of the discovery and treatment of a particular form of cancer scarcely sounds like enthralling fireside reading. The reader is herewith assured that it is one of the most remarkable stories in the history of medicine; that it is neither painful nor depressing; and that all the people who participate in the story, without exception, are highly dedicated and highly motivated. Many of the principal characters, indeed, are men of deep religious faith; and although this may be surprising in an age of disbelief and cynicism, it is true to say that if the religious element had been absent the story would have been absent, too. The sequence of discoveries described in this book would not, and probably could not, have occurred, and medical science would have been much poorer in consequence.

A number of scientists helped me most generously in the preparation of this book, and I owe them a profound debt of gratitude. They include Mr. Burkitt himself (who gallantly withstood numerous lengthy and exhausting interviews, and answered a multitude of letters); the Rev. Dr. Hugh C. Trowell; Dr. E. H. Williams; Mr. Peter Clifford; Dr. Dennis H. Wright; Professor M. A. Epstein; Dr. Gilbert Dalldorf; Professor George Klein; Dr. Jan Stjernswärd; Dr. G. B. de Thé; Dr. Malcolm Pike; Dr. Thomas M. Bell; Dr. J. L. Ziegler; Dr. Gertrude Henle and Dr. Werner Henle (in whose laboratories I also had the pleasure of talking to Miss Elaine Hutkin). I am particularly grateful to Professor Sir Ian McAdam for permission to quote from a personal letter; and I am happy indeed to have Mr. Burkitt's permission to print extracts from his diary of the long safari. Several scientists who played an important part in the story were not interviewed, to my great regret, because circumstances prevented our meeting: they include Professor M. S. R. Hutt, Professor J. N. P. Davies, Professor A. J. Haddow, and Dr. C. A. Linsell. I must thank the renowned photographer Fritz Henle for permission to reproduce the portrait of Dr. Werner Henle (his brother) and Dr. Gertrude Henle, as well as the photograph of the charming young scientists who worked on the Burkitt–infectious mononucleosis project, and I am very grateful to the Medical Superintendent of Mulago Hospital, Dr. Y. B. Semambo, for sending me the aerial photograph of the magnificent new hospital buildings. I owe thanks, also, to Dr. Daniel H. Connor, Chief of the Infectious Diseases Branch of the Armed Forces Institute of Pathology in Washington, D.C., for his lively photograph of Denis and Mrs. Burkitt.

Conversations were recorded in New York, Philadelphia, and Grand Rapids; in London, Birmingham, and Salisbury, England; in Nairobi, Kenya; in Kampala, Entebbe, and Arua, Uganda. Once again, the engineer in charge of the recording equipment was my wife, Violetta Constance Glemser.

Mr. Burkitt and Africa

1

View over a Lake

Uganda, at the present time, has only one international airport. It is on the shore of Lake Victoria and it is called Entebbe-Kampala, because it serves both towns.

Kampala, the capital of Uganda, is twenty-one miles away, almost due north, but it is in hilly terrain—the town itself sprawls over seven hills—and jet planes cannot approach it. The airport, therefore, is a few minutes' drive from the center of Entebbe, originally the seat of British government in Uganda and still described as the country's administrative capital. But Uganda is relatively small; its area is about 91,000 square miles, approximately the same as Oregon or Wyoming or the United Kingdom, and it really does not need two capitals. As a result, Entebbe is gradually being divested of its governmental responsibilities, and it now has the appearance of a ghost town. Nothing very much seems to happen from day to day; the atmosphere is relaxed; the pace of life is slow and dreamy.

The main shopping area is unattractive. The shops are

3

dull, small, crowded, poorly lit. The places to visit are the zoo; the Botanical Gardens, which has a fine stand of rain forest; and—if you have an invitation and are interested in virology— the East African Virus Research Institute. Otherwise there is nothing of great interest. A war memorial, a bank, a post office—nothing wildly exciting.

However, not far from the war memorial is a fine old hotel, the Lake Victoria, where the visitor can while away his time in comfort. It has a swimming pool; there are numerous tables on the lawn, shaded by big umbrellas, where you can enjoy a leisurely afternoon tea; and it is a jumping-off place for safaris to many of the famous game parks—Kagera, Serengeti, Murchison Falls National Park—or to the snowcapped Mountains of the Moon.

Before dinner you can sit on a broad and pleasant balcony drinking waragi, which is distilled from bananas and can be ordered with or without banana flavor. It is the national drink; it is delicious and seems to be nonintoxicating; and it costs only a few pennies.

Below you is an electrical contraption on a tall iron standard, which attracts and kills marauding insects, electrocuting them with a harsh crackle. Beyond, you look across a beautifully manicured golf course; and beyond this, about half a mile away, is the lake. Victoria Nyanza is the second-largest freshwater lake in the world, covering nearly 27,000 square miles (the largest is Lake Superior, covering nearly 32,000 square miles); it is 250 miles long from north to south, and 150 miles wide, and Scotland would fit into it nicely.

In the evening light it looks exceedingly beautiful. The water is smooth, blue-gray, enticing, and it spreads like an ocean right across the horizon. There are a great many islands on it, with pretty names— Sagitu Island, Lolui Island, Mwama Island, Zinga, Buvu, Lulamba, Serinya, Kalangala,

Bwendero, and countless more. If you arrived here in daylight, flying across the lake from Nairobi, you will have seen many of them from the air, and you must have thought how romantic they look, with their palm trees and unspoiled beaches. It would be wonderful, you may have told yourself, to sail to Dwaji Island or to explore the fabulous Sese Islands. You might even sail to Jinja and discover for yourself the source of the Victoria Nile.

Africa. Enchanted Africa. Mysterious Africa.

But there is something curiously wrong with this picture. Speak to the two friendly and helpful ladies in the hotel travel bureau and they will tell you—most regretfully—that they cannot arrange any excursions for you on Victoria Nyanza: there is no longer an excursion steamer. And when you go up to the balcony and look out across that enormous expanse of water you will observe that it is almost totally lifeless—at least in terms of human life. Far out, perhaps, there may be a few fishing boats; closer in, at the Entebbe Club, there are a few—very few—small sailboats tied up to moorings.

This is strange. You know that anywhere in Europe, in North America, in Japan, in Australia, a similar expanse of water would be teeming with human beings. There would be sailboats tacking all over the place, and motorboats going much too fast, and water-skiers, and fishermen, and young women splashing each other, because all water sports are joyous and have the power to dispel the dark clouds of the spirit.

Not here. Here man is pointedly absent. There are no dainty sailboats, no noisy motorboats, no children's voices, not even a crying baby. When you become aware of the emptiness and the silence it is alarming, and baffling. The friendly ladies in the travel bureau will explain it in a single word: *bilharzia.*

Most medical historians spare only a few lines for Theodor Bilharz. He was a German helminthologist (that is, a scientist who studies worms); he lived from 1825–62; he discovered the tiny worm, or blood fluke, that was named for him in 1852.

Bilharzia is a parasite, and one of the most dangerous known to man. It lives its life in a very specific cycle. First, it is harbored in the fleshy body of a certain kind of freshwater snail. At some stage in its development it leaves the snail, and for about forty-eight hours it is a free-swimming tadpole-shaped organism. It may now come in contact with a human being who is bathing or wading in the water, walking along a wet beach, or sitting in apparent security in a boat. The organism attaches itself to its new host by means of suckers, enters through the skin, and is carried to various organs where it mates, and then proceeds to produce as many as a thousand eggs a day. Extensive damage is done to the bladder and the lower part of the colon (some authorities believe that bilharzia may be responsible for cancer of the bladder). Meanwhile, great numbers of eggs are passed in the victim's urine; they hatch, seek out their special freshwater snails, and begin the cycle anew. The disease caused by bilharzia is known as bilharziasis, or—a term preferred by many authorities—schistosomiasis.

According to Dr. G. C. Coles, of the Department of Zoology at Makerere University College, Kampala, bilharzia infests virtually all the lakes and streams of Uganda. In a statement printed in the Uganda *Argus* of December 1, 1968, under a banner headline: WARNING: BILHARZIA IS A KILLER, Dr. Coles states, "In view of the prevalence of bilharzia and the fact that in many areas little is known about its distribution, the best advice for people is to avoid all contact with water in rivers, streams, pools and lakes." In the West Nile District alone, it is estimated that 200,000 people have the disease.*

This is only part of the story as it concerns the African continent. All along the Victoria Nile, all along the Albert Nile and the White Nile and the Blue Nile, over a course of 3,500 miles to Cairo and, ultimately, to the great Delta of the Nile discharging into the Mediterranean, the populations are subject to bilharzia infection, and it is the severe organic damage inflicted by the parasite that debilitates these people. They are literally drained of energy, and thus incapable of doing the work that would lead them out of poverty. The development of irrigation programs, indispensable to an expanding economy, only brings bilharzia closer to more and more human beings.

The obvious solution is to eliminate the freshwater snails, which are essential to the life cycle of bilharzia. Unfortunately, even if this were feasible (in some African nations the cost would be more than the total national income) it might disturb the entire ecology of tropical and North Africa. All that can be done is to provide treatment for people suffering from the disease; but again, any full-scale treatment for the millions of men, women, and children at present infected is far beyond the resources of the available medical services.

And bilharzia is only one of Africa's health problems.

* The well-known zoologist, explorer, and television personality Jack Paar reports seeing a sign on the banks of a lake in Uganda: WARNING: SWIMMING IN THIS LAKE IS SUICIDE.

The light on majestic Victoria Nyanza is a little less bright now; and this is the time of day when the mosquitoes become active, dancing in their trillions on the fringes of the lake. But you have no need to worry unduly about them. You have been taking your anti-malaria pills regularly, and before you flew here you had all the requisite inoculations: smallpox, yellow fever, typhoid, paratyphoid, cholera, tetanus, and perhaps polio. You are, indeed, in far better shape to resist infection than most of the Africans who live here. Not many of them have ever had an inoculation of any kind.

It is a curious fact that the African is now almost totally secure from attack by the wild and savage animals that are supposed to surround him. Few Africans today, even those living in the bush, see a lion from one year to the next; and very few—adults or children—go to make a lion's dinner. Any sensible leopard stays as far from man (Man the Coatmaker) as possible; the threat from rampaging elephants is not excessively high; crocodiles in most areas are, by and large, a tourist attraction, although one would be rash to tempt them; snakes are troublesome but by no means as severe a menace as they are in India.

One of the major threats to the African, unfortunately, comes from physical violence: heads are bashed in, throats are slit, poison is slipped into the family beer. Broken bones, knife wounds, infected bites (*human* bites), fill the emergency wards of every African hospital.

But by far the greatest threat arises from forms of life the African never sees: viruses, bacteria, protozoa, in a tremendous variety of forms, causing a staggering variety of illnesses.

To list them all would be depressing in the extreme. Naming just a few will be sufficient to give some idea of the fearful burden of disease carried by the African people, sapping their vitality and thwarting their progress.

First and foremost is malaria—massive, inescapable malaria. In tropical Africa this is primarily a disease of children, who are subject to repeated infection almost from birth. If the child survives, and passes through adolescence, some sort of immunity or resistance to malaria often develops.

There is amebic dysentery, also a deadly disease of childhood. Bilharziasis is also common among children. There are yaws, and hookworm, and filariasis (which, among other things, causes elephantiasis). There is trypanosomiasis, or sleeping sickness, spread by the tsetse fly. There is onchocerciasis,* another parasitic infection, spread by the bite of the black fly, which may cause blindness and complete or partial deafness: vast areas of Africa have been abandoned by man because of this pestilence, after the people have endured mass blindness for generations. There is leishmaniasis, or kala-azar, or dumdum fever, yet another parasitic infection, transmitted by sandflies. There are tuberculosis, venereal disease, leprosy, smallpox, yellow fever. There are numerous kinds of fungus infection, some extremely serious.

The total outcome is grim. In most African nations, half of all the children die before they reach the age of five. At the other end of the scale, you see very few Africans, male or female, with white hair, for only 10 percent live beyond the age of forty. In general, the African does not live long enough to succumb to heart disease or cancer, the leading causes of death in Western man, and the reason is that, for the most

---

* This is usually pronounced *onco-ser-sý-asis*. "Onchocerca" means barbed tail and refers to the parasite's method of attaching itself to its victim; "asis," like "osis," simply means a medical condition or state.

part, heart disease and cancer make their appearance in the fifth and sixth decades of the life span. There are exceptions to this generalization (some forms of cancer are prevalent in certain parts of Africa, rare in the West); but on the whole it is the communicable diseases that menace and encircle the African, those diseases that are firmly established in his environment, that thrive in tropical heat and humidity and in the conditions of poverty.

Disease, then, is the major problem of the mass of human beings in Uganda, and Kenya, and every other African nation. The Ugandan government spends one-tenth of the national income on health services—the World Bank, which has a say in such matters, will not approve spending more—and this is simply not enough to pay for the medical resources to cope with the situation.

In these circumstances it is remarkable that a disease now called Burkitt's lymphoma, accounting for only a few hundred lives a year (not in any single country but over a large part of tropical Africa) should have attracted the interest of scientists all over the world. "In the total context of disease in Africa," Mr. Burkitt once observed, "it is only an infinitesimal fleabite." But a fleabite of a special kind, and of special importance.

Forerunners

The outside world has responded to the African's particular vulnerability in many different ways throughout the centuries: slavery, colonialism, exploitation, pillage, murder. There has also been—and it deserves to be remembered—another kind of response: compassion, a form of giving, as against the many forms of taking.

This is an age that regards with suspicion the motives of any white man who went to Africa uninvited, and many people dismiss (or condemn) the early missionaries as fanatics who served to open the way for all the evils of imperialism, who kept the African in subjugation by threatening him with eternal hellfire while the traders and colonists stripped the continent of its wealth. The picture is untrue, and we do these men a profound injustice if we judge them in such distorted terms.

Two of the early African missionaries have a place in this book. Their influence is indirect, but it is nevertheless vital. The first, of course, is David Livingstone, a man of incredible

resolution and spiritual force. He has perplexed all his biogra-
phers; in some respects he is completely incomprehensible to
modern readers; yet, as you follow him year by year, his
accomplishments, his mistakes, his failures, his strength, fill
you with awe. He is elemental.

Most of us have forgotten what poverty and hardship
really mean, and it is worth recalling how men made their
way in the world a century and a half ago. Livingstone was
born in Blantyre, Scotland, in 1813. At the age of ten he was
put to work in a cotton factory. Out of his first week's wages
he bought a Latin grammar, and somehow or other he mem-
orized it sentence by sentence as he tended the spinning
jennies. His workday was from six o'clock in the morning until eight at night; when he finished he hurried on to evening
classes, which lasted until ten o'clock, and when he arrived
home—a single room served for the entire family: father,
mother, and four other children—he continued to read until
midnight. He was at last prepared to enter college in Glas-
gow when he was twenty-three, and began studies in chemistry, medicine, Greek, and divinity. There, he wrote later,
"in the glow of love which Christianity inspires, I soon resolved to devote my life to the alleviation of human misery;
and therefore set myself to obtain a medical education in
order to be qualified for that enterprise." He completed his
medical studies in London and was accepted (not altogether
with enthusiasm) by the London Missionary Society. His
hope was to be sent to China. The Directors of the Society
intended to send him to the West Indies. Eventually it was
agreed that he should go to Africa.

He went out as a missionary doctor, but fairly soon his
attitude hardened. In a letter to one of his tutors, the Rev.
Richard Cecil, he wrote: "I did not at first intend to give up
all attention to medicine and the treatment of disease, but

now I feel it my duty to have as little to do with it as possible. I shall attend to none but severe cases in future, and my reasons for this determination are I think good. The spiritual amelioration of the people is the object for which I came, but I cannot expect God to advance this by my instrumentality if much of my time is spent in mere temporal amelioration." He believed fervently that the immortal souls of those who had not accepted the Christian gospel would perish in the Great Assize—the Last Judgment; thus the saving of souls became his primary purpose. It was then that he began his travels in southern Africa, pressing north into what he called —and what was in fact—the dark interior: territory which had not been explored by any Europeans, where Christianity was totally unknown. "It was the dream of the imperialist Cecil Rhodes, a generation later," writes Dr. George Seaver in his biography of Livingstone, "that the uncolonized portion of the map of South Africa, from the Cape to the Zambesi, should be painted red for Britain. It was the dream of the missionary David Livingstone that the whole continent should be painted white for Christ."

His journeys extended from the Cape northward, deep into the Congo and almost to the equator; and from Quelimane on the Indian Ocean right across Africa to Luanda on the Atlantic Ocean. It is estimated that he explored one-third of the continent, at a time when it was largely a blank space on the map, and he filled in the geographical details with extraordinary accuracy. Ultimately, the urge to explore unknown Africa, to press on and on, overshadowed the missionary impulse; but his greatest passion, inflamed by the atrocities of the Portuguese and Arab slavers, was to put an end to the slave trade. "The sights I have seen, though common incidents of the (slave) traffic, are so nauseous that I always strive to drive them from memory. . . . The slaving scenes come back unbidden, and make me start up at dead of night, horrified by their vividness." And in a letter to the *New York Herald,* asking for aid to end the traffic in slaves, he concluded, "All I can say in my solitude is, may Heaven's rich blessing come down on everyone—American, English, Turk—who will help to heal this Open Sore of the World." The words are engraved on his tomb in Westminster Abbey.

The effect of Livingstone upon the young men and women of his time is indescribable. Sixteen years after he first went to Africa he returned home for a visit. He spent six months writing his great *Missionary Travels,* a book of nearly 700 pages, which instantly ran through nine printings; and he then toured the country, giving talks to large audiences, receiving acclamation everywhere. Dr. Seaver writes: "He was on the crest of a tremendous wave of public enthusiasm which happily coincided with a wave of national prosperity. He was already an established hero. In the eyes of his countrymen nothing comparable with his achievements had occurred since Drake sailed round the world. His sudden disclosure of the resources, both human and material . . . was spectacular, and henceforth Central Africa became a focus of national interest—political, mercantile, and missionary."

Livingstone's message to those who cheered his accomplishments was fierce and direct: "Do you carry on the work which I have begun. I leave it with you." Nothing more needed to be said.

The last journeys of Livingstone ended in tragedy. He died in 1873, after fearful hardships, searching—mistakenly—for the four mysterious fountains which he believed might be the source of the Nile. Henry Morton Stanley, who had found him virtually dying two years earlier at Ujiji on Lake Tanganyika, set himself to carry on Livingstone's work. He marched into Africa with a small army of followers, reached Lake Victoria, made his way up the eastern side of the lake, survived encounters with hostile tribesmen (and hippos); and in due course met Mutesa, ruler of the largest kingdom of Uganda. (The name of the country is Uganda; the name of this ancient kingdom is Buganda; the name of a native of Buganda is Muganda, and the plural is Baganda; anything relating to Buganda is Kiganda; the name of the language is Luganda.)

A famous dispatch from Stanley, printed in the London *Daily Telegraph* in November 1875, testifies to his powers of persuasion. It reads, in part: "I have indeed undermined Islamism so much here that Mutesa is determined henceforth, until he is better informed, to observe the Christian Sabbath as well as the Moslem Sabbath, and the great captains have unanimously consented to this. . . .

"But oh, that some pious, practical missionary would come here! What a field and harvest ripe for the sickle of civilization. Mutesa would give him anything he desired—houses, land, cattle, ivory, etc.; he might call a province his own one day. It is not the mere teacher that is wanted here. The Bishops of Great Britain collected, with the classic youth of Oxford and Cambridge, would affect nothing by mere talk with the intelligent folk of Uganda. It is the practical Christian tutor who can teach people how to become Christians, cure their diseases, construct dwellings, understand and exemplify agriculture and turn his hand to anything, like a sailor—this is the man who is wanted. Such a man if he could be found, would become the Saviour of Africa. He must be tied to no one church or sect, but profess God and His Son and the moral law, and live a blameless Christian, inspired by liberal principles and charity to all men, and devout faith in Heaven. He must belong to no one nation in particular, but the entire white race. Such a man Mutesa, King of Uganda, Usoga, Unyoro and Karagwe—a kingdom three hundred and sixty geographical miles in length by fifty in breadth—invites to repair to him. He has begged me to tell the white men that if they will only come to him he will give them all they want. Nowhere is there in all the Pagan world a more promising field for a mission than Uganda. . . .

"Here, gentlemen, is your opportunity—embrace it! The people on the shores of the Nyanza call upon you!"

Within a few weeks, £24,000 ($120,000, an immense sum in 1875) had been subscribed for a mission to the court of Mutesa, and volunteers began to hurry out to embrace the opportunity. They found to their bewilderment that Stanley had allowed himself to be hypnotized by his own eloquence. The welcome they had been promised was not forthcoming. They were constantly harassed, a number of them were brutally murdered, many were killed in the civil wars that seemed to go on endlessly in Central Africa; and many, inevitably, died of disease. The result, of course, was that the missionary fervor only increased.

In November 1896, twelve missionaries sent out by the Church Missionary Society began a safari from Mombasa, on the east coast, to Kampala. One of the men in the party was Albert Ruskin Cook, a young doctor; there were two women, one of them Miss Katherine Timpson, whom Cook later married.

The journey took eighty-four days. The twelve missionaries marched more than 700 miles, through forests, swamps, desert, and over mountains. Wild animals were a serious threat. In many places the natives were openly hostile. The white men and women came down with dysentery, a terrible affliction in such primitive conditions; the carriers came down with the usual tropical diseases.

On the very first day that the party entered Uganda, at Ngogwe, halfway between Jinja and Kampala, Dr. Cook treated 226 patients.

It was only a foretaste of what awaited him. Unlike Livingstone, Cook's purpose in coming to Africa was to organize a medical mission and hospital. His concern was to heal the bodies of the Africans, as a first step toward saving their immortal souls; and he set to work in a shed with a mud floor, transforming it into a serviceable hospital in which he could see patients and perform operations, with Katherine as his nurse to administer anesthetics and apply dressings. Soon a larger hospital was built, consisting of two huts, each with six beds. Later he moved to a more ambitious hospital with fifty beds, described as "the finest building in Uganda, shaped like a double Greek cross, 120 feet long and 40 feet across at the widest part."

Livingstone, crying out passionately about the Open Sore of the World, was referring to the vicious slave traffic in Central Africa; but the term could be applied literally to the great lake and the territory surrounding it. Before the arrival of Albert and Katherine Cook there were no medical facilities at all in the whole of Uganda, except an ineffectual mission dispensary. The healers of the sick were the witch doctors or muttering old sorceresses. The average man (Rousseau's "noble savage") was generally in a wretched state of health, riddled with disease, weakened by malnutrition, ignorant, and oppressed by murderous tyrants whose forces of law and order consisted of regiments of executioners. The average man's wife had her first pregnancy at the age of about twelve, was exhausted by successive pregnancies until she was in her early twenties, and then literally withered away into premature old age.

Dr. Cook's little hospital was besieged by patients every day. That was not enough for him. First on foot, later on the first bicycle seen in Uganda, he went to tend the sick in outlying villages, and the people gathered in crowds to be examined and receive medication. *Everybody* seemed to be sick. On one trip, accompanied by the irresistible Katherine, he tended more than five thousand patients and performed fifty major operations. On another occasion he set out for a district where smallpox was raging and inoculated three thousand people—more than eight hundred in a single day.

This was a man truly devoted to the noble practice of medicine. His duty was to heal the sick, and he did all that was possible in utterly primitive conditions. Many of the tropical diseases were not yet understood by medical scientists; and early in his career, for example, Dr. Cook was forced to look on helplessly as an epidemic of sleeping sickness killed more than a quarter of a million Baganda. In 1916, during World War I, the Cooks and a few trained doctors, helped by some medical assistants, had to deal with the simultaneous outbreak of four epidemics: smallpox, cerebrospinal meningitis, choleraic dysentery, and—most serious of all—bubonic plague.

Gradually the truth became clear: the Baganda people were facing extinction. Statistics for a seven-year period, from 1914 to 1920, showed only 68,000 births, against 97,000 deaths and 7,000 stillbirths. Infant mortality was appallingly high: Jack Cook, Albert's brother, found that 70 percent of infants died before they were a week old. In one district, births for that seven-year period were 16,000, while deaths—including stillbirths—totalled 31,000. Albert and Katherine Cook, by establishing hospital services, by training African medical assistants and midwives, by persuading the government to take action against venereal disease, by encouraging education programs, may well have saved the Bagandan nation.

Cook's biographer, Brian O'Brien,* describes him as he was seen by a contemporary: "A quiet, yet stubborn man, medium height, chunky and quick moving. Red beard, mild blue eyes, and a very nice sense of humor. . . . He had a nerve of iron; he'd take risks that would make your blood run cold. When he was called, he set off, no matter where; through elephant country with no protection whatever, down the lake in a canoe that leaked like a basket or through neck-deep swamps that crawled with snakes. He was absolutely without fear. He believed that God had sent him to do a job and his logical scientific mind made it impossible to think God would let anything interfere with that job."

The passion with which Albert and Katherine Cook did their work (on the allowance given to married missionaries of £15—$75—a month) inevitably undermined their health. They were worn down, writes O'Brien, by the long journeys, the crowds of patients, drenching rains, the night chills of the mountains and the sweltering heat of the swamps. "They both suffered recurring bouts of malaria. Katherine frequently collapsed with blinding headaches, and insomnia made her nights a dread. The doctor's leg, swollen to twice its normal size by phlebitis (the result of typhoid contracted from a patient) tormented him incessantly; chronic dysentery, held in check by morphine, drained his strength." In

* *That Good Physician: The Life and Work of Albert and Katherine Cook of Uganda.* London: Hodder and Stoughton, 1962.

1938, Katherine died of encephalitis, after a severe attack of malaria. Albert Cook lived until 1951, loved and respected by the people of Uganda. He had been knighted some twenty years earlier, thus joining the small, distinguished group of missionary knights; but at his death he received an even more signal honor. Watched by grieving crowds, his coffin was carried by the great chiefs of Buganda to the cathedral on Namirembe Hill; and there, in a grave lined with royal bark cloth, he was buried beside his dear Katherine. It was the only royal funeral ever accorded to a white man in Uganda.

It is unlikely that he felt he had done anything unusual or remarkable. After Cook's death an African wrote: "The arrival of Sir Albert Cook fifty years ago was the greatest event as far as the progress of my country was concerned." But for Albert Cook himself the key to all his conduct was doing, as well as he could, the work that had been mapped out for him. Only a fool would argue that he was mistaken in his beliefs.

After a particularly arduous safari, treating patients who were suffering from sleeping sickness, leprosy, blackwater fever, hydrocele—the whole gamut of tropical disease—he wrote in his journal: "Is it any wonder that we magnify our office, and that we love this happy work with an ever growing affection; and conversely, is it not amazing that from our overstocked profession at home, so few—pitifully few, considering the respective needs—Christian doctors come out?" It is reminiscent of Livingstone's challenge, *Do you carry on the work which I have begun. I leave it with you.* And, as with Livingstone, Cook's message did not go unheeded.

Making of a Surgeon

Denis Parsons Burkitt was born in February 1911, in Enniskillen, Northern Ireland, the county town of Co. Fermanagh. It lies on Lough Erne, not very far from Donegal Bay, which opens onto the Atlantic Ocean; and it has the distinction of being the only town in the world to have two regiments named after it. The population is about eight thousand.

The Burkitt family traces its ancestry to the Norman invasion of Ireland. Midway in the family history, one of its members married a daughter of Oliver Cromwell (who is considered by many Irishmen to be a monster of satanic proportions). A certain independence of mind is also evident in Denis Burkitt's maternal forebears. His mother came from County Cork; *her* father, an architect who designed the handsome Cork courthouse, was offered a knighthood by the British government and turned it down, declaring that he preferred to live and die as plain Mr. Hill and wanted nothing else.

James Parsons Burkitt, father of Denis, was one of seven children. *His* father, also a man of independent spirit, was a Presbyterian minister in a totally Catholic environment in the west of Ireland, and it is not surprising that he lived in considerable poverty. No doubt as a result of their upbringing, each of his five sons did remarkably well. One went to India in the Civil Service and became a Resident, corresponding to Governor of a State. One went to Guatemala and did valuable work on ancient monuments. Another became Senior Engineer in the Punjab, and was later associated with the Aswan Dam project, for which he was decorated by the British government.

Another of the five sons, Roland Wilks Burkitt, went out to Nairobi in 1911 when, according to his biographer, "it was but a wood-and-iron dorp scattered over the plains."[*] He was highly qualified, being a Fellow of the Royal College of Surgeons of Ireland, and for many years he was the town's only private practitioner.

"A very remarkable man was my Uncle Roland," Denis Burkitt once said of him, obviously with great pride: "He was an eccentric man, but people who stand for something very specific in rather perverse society are bound to be considered eccentric if they have a centre different from the society in which they live. He was a man of the *utmost* standard of morals: if he thought the Governor (of Kenya) had done anything wrong he would tell him so instantly." And again: "My Uncle Roland was an absolutely fearless man for what was right. He was a tremendous student of Scripture, but rather *anti* the established church. He started a little Sunday

---

[*] *Under The Sun: A Memoir of Dr. R. W. Burkitt, of Kenya,* by J. R. Gregory. 119 pages. This was privately printed in Kenya and is undated.

meeting in Nairobi, which in a different form still goes on today, fifty years later."

Roland Burkitt was clearly larger than life. He might have sprung fully armed from one of the novels of Joyce Cary: a blunt and vigorous man, supremely confident in himself and with little patience for the rest of the world. Some of the methods of treatment he introduced were new, and he applied them so thoroughly and ruthlessly that among the settlers of Nairobi he was known as "Kill or Cure Burkitt." He believed, for instance, that cold packs—or better still, cold baths—were helpful in treating patients with high fever. "During the influenza epidemics and in the malarial seasons," writes his biographer, Dr. Gregory, "Burkitt had patients all over the town in cold baths, under wet sheets, being sprayed with watering cans or merely being sponged. . . . Woe betide the relative or nurse who abandoned treatment before the desired result was achieved, but some people were not above setting an African servant on watch to give warning of the doctor's approach, so that a comfortable bed could be abandoned for the bathroom. Prominent and worthy citizens, in response to a warning from the watcher, could be seen rushing in their pelts along passages to the bathroom and plunging into a cold bath, while the doctor's Ford car chugged up to the house. . . . If a thought struck him in the middle of the night that some point had been overlooked or some other line of treatment was desirable, he would not hesitate to get up and drive off to his patient, arousing the whole household to achieve his object. A very sick patient could be quite certain that Burkitt would arrive to see him between five and six in the morning."

One of the best tales illustrating his belief in cold treatment for fever concerns a very big woman living some distance out in the country. "He found her with a very high temperature," Dr. Gregory writes. "He decided to bring her into hospital in Nairobi. Her relatives wanted to wrap her in blankets, afraid she would get cold, but Burkitt refused. Instead, he insisted that she should travel naked in the back of his open Ford car. On the way in, he stopped and took her temperature. He found it was dropping, so he took off his coat and wrapped it around her. As the story goes, the patient eventually reached the hospital dressed in all of Burkitt's clothes, while he arrived naked. When I plied him with this story, a twinkle came into his eye as he said, 'Ah, Gregory! People are apt to exaggerate.'"

What few of his patients knew was that he had a passion for his work: "New methods would be studied until he had mastered the minutest detail. He would come away (from visits to London) after weeks of watching the leading surgeons, satisfied and delighted if he had learned one new "tip," and what he knew was at the disposal of all those who wished to learn. His generosity in this respect knew no bounds."

But he had very fixed ideas, says Gregory, on how women should dress and behave: "He considered that women should wear long dresses. When it became fashionable for women to don frocks that stopped above the knees, he inaugurated a preaching campaign against them. He would look at a woman's knees in a fixed way and cause her much embarrassment by saying, 'A woman's knees are very ugly. You should cover them up.' . . . Mrs. Burkitt was a particularly beautiful woman, tall, slender, graceful and well featured. . . . She met what she considered to be an impossible situation by having her dresses fitted with two belts, one of which enabled her to wear them long to please her husband, and one which held them up to the fashionable length to please the dictates of fashion. It caused immense amusement to her friends to see her skirt being lengthened the moment Dr. Burkitt appeared on the scene."

On the other hand, he was a man to be trusted. "He would put everything else aside to go where he thought he was most needed. In those days calls came from great distances over two or three hundred miles away, and in wet weather, over bad roads, they could be nightmare journeys. Every detail for getting his car through swampy patches had to be dealt with, and medical equipment to meet all emergencies had to be taken. . . . On occasion he travelled into the Northern Frontier of Kenya, which in those days was a five days' journey, to bring in a hunter who had met with an accident and had fractured a thigh. He travelled hundreds of miles into Tanganyika Territory at the request of his colleagues to see desperately ill patients and, if necessary, he would transport them back to Nairobi in his car, spending days on the journey."

Eccentric? Perhaps so. But one would like to see a little more of this eccentricity in contemporary medical practice.

James Burkitt, the second in age of the five sons, was the only one to stay home. He became county surveyor in Fermanagh and was responsible for all the county roads and for the building of several bridges. He had a "little hobby" (according to his son Denis) which none of the family took seriously: birdwatching. Now, birdwatching is a hobby that few non-birdwatchers are inclined to take seriously; furthermore, James Burkitt chose to study, in particular, the robins in his ten-acre garden—the sprightly, lovable little robin redbreast who for countless years has appeared on Christmas cards as a symbol of good cheer and good will toward all men—and nobody could take *that* very seriously. But James Burkitt became the world authority on robins. He was the first naturalist to band birds so that their individual behavior could be studied and recorded; and, consequently, he was able to plot for the first time the territory inhabited—and so jealously guarded—by each bird. He showed that far from being happy, good-natured little creatures, male robins are pugnacious bullies. Each robin was allotted a number; its location in the garden was marked on a map; its movements were followed minutely; and its history was recorded on long foolscap pages, written in an unusually fine Italian hand. The great ornithologist David Lack named him as one of the seven men who have contributed most to the understanding of bird behavior (among the other six were Edmund Selous and Julian Huxley), a distinction that came as a surprise to his family, which had never realized he was such an authority.

He, too, was a man of deep Christian faith; and this—unlike birdwatching—he successfully imparted to his children. Perhaps something of the birdwatching habit was also imparted; in another form it may have played an important part in Denis Burkitt's later development, leading him to become a careful and astute observer and a patient keeper of records. Denis has acknowledged this influence in a typical manner: "I feel very much that anything one has accomplished is due to what one has received, in two senses. First of all, at birth, through inheritance from both parents. Secondly, what one receives through life." The point is made in a text from Corinthians, framed and hanging on the wall of his London office: *What do you possess that was not given you? If then you really received it as a gift why take the credit to yourself?* In the Authorized King James Version the text reads: *For who maketh thee to differ from another? and what hast thou that thou didst not receive? Now if thou didst receive it why dost thou glory, as if thou hadst not re-*

ceived it? It is a simple argument that blunts the edge of conceit.

At school (as he recalls it now) Denis Burkitt was poor to mediocre at everything except mathematics. An undistinguished child, according to his own account.

When he was eleven years old he suffered an accident which had severe effects later on: "Several boys were throwing stones. One of the stones hit me in the eye."

He wore glasses at the time. The glasses were broken, and he lost his right eye. There were no immediate psychological results—the accident worried his parents more than it worried him. He was in a hospital for five weeks, and he remembers most vividly the great joy of being presented with a steam engine as compensation, *a real, working steam engine,* something to delight any boy. And eventually he received a fine blue matching glass eye, so perfectly made that few people recognize it for what it is.

Upon his release from the hospital, his mother sent him and his brother Robin (eighteen months younger than Denis) to a preparatory school in Anglesey, North Wales. Three years later the boys went on to Cheltenham, and four years later they were admitted to the University of Dublin.

At this point certain elements not commonly found in accounts of contemporary medical science become more and more important. Relatively few scientists today are willing to ascribe their achievements to Divine Guidance, or Divine Will, or Divine Plan. Here there is a fundamental and vitally important difference: the principal character in this narrative, and some others who appear later, are convinced of the immanence of God; they have complete faith in His guidance, complete trust in His goodness, absolute reliance that He will heed their prayers and that His word will be made clear to them; and their conduct in all things is rooted in the Christian ethic. For the reader with similar religious beliefs no further explanation is necessary. For the reader without any deep religious beliefs no further explanation is possible. But whichever way he leans, it will be an interesting exercise for the reader to test his beliefs or nonbeliefs against what occurs in the story from now on.

Denis Burkitt was eighteen years old when he went to Dublin University, and he and his brother were firmly—passionately—committed to one idea: they would do anything, anything in the world, except become doctors. Robin, therefore, started to study modern languages; Denis, therefore, started to study engineering; and both ended as surgeons.

Engineering was enjoyable enough, but it aroused no great enthusiasm in Denis's heart or mind. He did not excel in it, he found his first year colorless, and he made few friends. But the change to medicine did not come about as a result of consultations with any secular advisers: "I attribute it to a spiritual committal to follow what was God's will for me. . . . I made it very much a matter of prayer, and the more I prayed about it the more I felt an overwhelming conviction that God was calling me to make this change. It was made clear to me that medicine was what I was meant to be doing. I had no doubts about it at all. For a time I found it difficult to pluck up the courage to switch over my career, but I felt I must do it. I had asked for guidance, and if I turned back and took what seemed to be an easier way I would always blame myself."

He was now set for two years of pre-clinical studies, and then three years of clinical work. With a foundation of spiritual assurance and a new sense of direction, he moved up from being a mediocre engineer to third or fourth from the top in his medical courses. He was wholly gripped by medicine—"thrilled by it," he says, "thrilled all the way through."

Now, also, he met the people who were to prove—after his family—the greatest formative influence in his life: a group of men at the university who had a faith that governed completely their behavior, their motives, and their thought.

This group originated with three men who returned to study medicine at Dublin University after the First World War and who, in Denis Burkitt's words, "had come into a personal experience of what faith in Christ could mean in their lives." One was Patrick Kerr Dixon, who eventually went out to found a hospital in the Congo and died there; the second was C. P. Martin, who eventually went to McGill University as Professor of Anatomy; the third was David Torrens, who remained in Dublin and became Professor of Physiology and Dean of the Medical School.

These men did not arise, so to speak, as a result of spontaneous spiritual generation. They were inspired by a still larger and more influential group which had its beginnings in Cambridge at the end of the last century, when a very strong movement of dedicated Christians was centered around seven men who were either Blues* or noted scholars and who went out to serve as missionaries in China. The powerful influence of the Cambridge Seven spread to other universities in Britain, resulting in the Intervarsity Christian Fellowship which, in turn, has had a far-reaching international impact. In later years Denis Burkitt was to meet members of these groups wherever he traveled; and the common

---

* Blues are athletes who have won the distinction of wearing their university color: light blue for Cambridge, dark blue for Oxford.

bond, the shared faith and understanding, were of enormous value.

The changeover from engineering to medicine occurred in 1930, when Denis was nineteen years old; and it is interesting, for the sake of perspective, to look back on the scene as it was then. The economic crisis leading to the Great Depression had already occurred in the United States, with grim repercussions all over the world. A couple of years earlier the first Five-Year Plan had been inaugurated in Russia; in many countries—Germany and France, particularly—the international communist movement, encouraged by the widespread economic distress, seemed to be gathering sufficient strength to challenge the shaky capitalist system. Writers such as George Bernard Shaw and H. G. Wells, who offered a sort of utopian socialism as a cure for the world's ills and at the same time advocated rebellion against middle-class morality, had profoundly affected the minds of large numbers of young men and women troubled by the breakdown of established values. Sigmund Freud and D. H. Lawrence, following other paths through the wilderness, offered solutions that seemed on the whole merely to add new problems to the old ones.

Denis Burkitt's path at that time was over a different mountain. "In those days," he comments, "I was much more narrow in my faith than I am today. Youth is always rather intolerant. I never went to the theatre, I hardly ever went to the cinema, I did not dance. And yet I can see that there was a value to it, because we channeled ourselves, we steered away from the groups who accepted everything. To some extent, in life only what is narrow is forceful and effective. A river that becomes wider and wider is likely to turn into a swamp, whereas a narrow river has force and power and direction. And I think that people often use the word *narrow* in a derogatory sense when they apply it to religious beliefs, but no athlete is going to get to the Olympic Games unless he stays in strict training and no scholar is going to get to the top unless he stays clear of time-wasting dissipation."

The Dublin group held meetings once a week; speakers came to address the group; friends outside the group were invited "to be helped in the same way that we had been helped." Members of the group met to confirm and enlarge their experience, to help each other, and there was always a clear understanding between these men that if they were to be of any real value in the world they must go out to the man in need. But, Burkitt insists, everything ultimately is based on the personal dealings between a man and God: "I have always in my life put more emphasis on personal daily devotion than outward church attendance—on a daily search for communion with God. I learned this in college, with my college friends, and I've kept it up ever since. Every morning, even now, when my wife and I get up we make ourselves our morning tea, and I bring morning tea to the family; and we then have half an hour or so just sitting up in bed, for prayer, for thought, for Bible reading, and so on. It gives me time to get orientated, and I've found it of immense value."

At the end of five years he passed out second in his class. There were two jobs as house surgeons available at his teaching hospital and he would have been glad to accept one of them in order to stay in Dublin; but one went to the man who was top of the class, the other to a man who had been captain of the football team and who had played for Ireland and who, in his own special way, could be said to have done much for the hospital.

Ireland could not offer an abundance of jobs and Burkitt,

like most of his class, went to various house jobs in England. A curious period followed. He went to Chester, in the west of England, as house surgeon for six months, then back for six months to his teaching hospital in Dublin. Then he shot up north to Preston, in Lancashire, where to widen his experience he "did" eyes, as well as ear, nose, and throat surgery. Then, feeling the need for higher qualifications, he went down to Poole, in Dorset, as Senior Resident Officer, a position somewhat senior to house surgeon. Then, having saved some money, he left hospital work for six months and went up to Edinburgh, where with one of his best and oldest friends, Guy Timmis, he found lodgings with full board at two guineas a week (about ten and a half dollars, a sum that he and Timmis considered to be scandalously exorbitant, if not downright extravagant).

In due course the two men took the examination for Fellow of the Royal College of Surgeons. "I passed," he says, "and Guy failed. It should have been the other way about." But now he could put the magic letters F.R.C.S.E. after his name (the *E* standing for Edinburgh); and from now on he was entitled to be addressed—as surgeons in Britain are traditionally addressed—as Mr. Burkitt. For Dr. Timmis there were few regrets. He went out to Africa in the government service, and today he runs a leper colony in Tanzania.

Mr. Burkitt Goes
to Sea

Young Mr. Burkitt—the year was 1938 and he was no more than twenty-seven years old—had now reached a turning point in his life. He had his F.R.C.S.E. in his pocket. The question was, what should he do with it, what use should he make of it? The Royal College of Surgeons does not hand out its Fellowships lightly or indiscriminately. You may have superlative medical talents, you may be a great healer, but that is far from enough. The Fellowship is awarded to a man only when the Royal College of Surgeons is fully satisfied that he meets its standards as a surgeon, and for no other reason.

Thus, acquiring his Fellowship meant, among other things, that his market value had gone up substantially. He could quite reasonably look forward to better and more lucrative appointments. Given a few years to establish himself, he could anticipate a comfortable income, a comfortable life. Successful surgeons are the maharajahs of medicine. They are the darlings of the income tax collector, they are revered by the people who sell Rolls-Royce limousines. And, of course, if a surgeon is good, if he knows his job thoroughly, if he can go inside the human body with confidence and take care of a perilous situation, he deserves every penny of his fee. It is better for the patient to give up his bank balance than to give up the ghost.

But Burkitt was still powerfully influenced by his college friends, by the special nature of his college experiences. There was a vast need among less fortunate people overseas for precisely those services he was fitted to offer, and he knew it too well. The call was strong. It had not yet crystallized, it was not yet specific, but it pressed upon him and he was not sure what to do about it. He needed time to think and time to pray. And finally, in typically Burkitt fashion, he signed as ship's surgeon on a cargo ship, the *Glen Shiel* of the Blue Funnel Line, and he sailed off to Manchuria.

The voyage, out and back, lasted five months. No more than twelve passengers may be carried on a cargo ship, but most of the time the *Glen Shiel* carried none at all. The crew was Chinese, and Burkitt had little to do in his official capacity beyond pulling a few teeth. There was a minimum of social activities, and he was left alone to think, to read, to seek some solution to his problem.

In certain respects it was precisely what a great many other young men were doing in those troubled years. Few of them had Denis Burkitt's qualifications. They signed up on cargo ships as deck hands, as anything, in order to get away and think, and seek adventure, and find a meaningful way to live. Young men today have the same urge: for some reason they have difficulty thinking at home, they are convinced that they will think more clearly five thousand miles away. Today, though, things have changed; the maritime unions are not particularly sympathetic toward young men who want to work their passage to foreign parts for the purpose of thinking, and something rather valuable has been lost.

The trip to Manchuria remains vividly in Burkitt's memory. The *Glen Shiel* sailed through the Mediterranean to Haifa; then to Port Said and through the Suez Canal to Port Taufiq; across the Arabian Sea to Colombo; then to Penang and Singapore; up the South China Sea to Hong Kong, and on to Shanghai and Dairen.

When he returned his mind was firmly made up about one thing: it would be impossible for him to join what he called "the surgical rat race" at home. He was one step nearer his ultimate destination.

The details of his future commitment still remained to be worked out in his mind. Meanwhile, he had a living to earn, and he went to Plymouth as Resident Surgical Officer.

Here two things happened which he could not possibly have anticipated. The first was the outbreak of World War II, which caused him considerable anxiety—he was unable to decide what to do, whether to leave Plymouth or stay on for another six months after completing his first tour of duty. "And again, as my custom was, I prayed about it; and again, as has happened to me in certain critical times in my life, a verse of Scripture stood out and seemed to be a message to me. I remember it well. It was a verse that says, *And be thou there until I bring thee word*—the words spoken by the Lord when he appeared in a dream to Joseph and told him to go down into Egypt with Mary and the Infant Jesus. It meant to me, *Stay where you are until you're told to move.* So I stayed on and [this was the second unexpected happening]

I met a nurse named Olive Rogers whom I eventually married. That, then, was *very* crucial in my life."

In 1940, after the evacuation of the British forces from Dunkirk, he volunteered for the army. They did not need more surgeons, and he was turned down. He then applied to the Colonial Office, specifying that he would like to work in West Africa and explaining that he wanted to go out there "with a Christian motive." Again he was turned down, this time for the reason, on paper, that he had lost an eye and therefore did not have enough sight for surgical work. The more likely explanation, he realized later, was that his motive alarmed the authorities. In those days the Colonial Service preferred men who were good company, who would fit in, who could hold their drink like gentlemen. Missionary types were suspect.

"Two days after the Colonial Office rejected me, I was reading the account in Exodus of the Israelites coming to the Red Sea; and their way was barred—they could not cross. And God said to Moses, *Speak unto the children of Israel, that they go forward,* in spite of the fact that they faced what seemed to be a total and impassable barrier. I felt that it was right for me: even though I had been turned down I was sure the way would open up again, just as it opened up for Moses. And I applied once more to the army, and I was accepted."

The next two years were spent in England. Then, on July 28, 1943, at a time when he was attached to an army hospital near Southampton, he took 48 hours' leave and married Olive. "We couldn't get a car, we couldn't get petrol, so we went away on our honeymoon by bus, straphanging all the way because the bus was full. When we arrived at the bus station in Midhurst, Sussex, we had to walk three miles to the hotel, carrying our suitcases, because there were no taxis."

Many honeymoon couples encounter troubles of this order, war or no war; they are part and parcel of traditional honeymoon procedure, nerve-racking at the time but acquiring a patina as the years go by, so that they ultimately take their place as gay and touching recollections of one's youth and innocence. But the essential factor in this honeymoon was that Denis Burkitt had found a wife who fully understood and fully shared his beliefs. In view of what developed later this was of paramount importance, and he has expressed it with great force: "I would not even have considered choosing a life partner with whom I did not feel a unity at that deeper level. In looking for a wife that was the first and absolute requirement, before anything else. I realize now how exceedingly little we knew each other, yet how exceedingly much I found in her which I did not know was there then. Again, to me, it is an example of how, if in these matters one seeks God's will, one gets abundant blessings out of it."

Then, almost at once, he was posted overseas. Denis and Olive Burkitt were separated for the first two and a half years of their married life.

He still wanted to go to West Africa. The army posted him to East Africa. It was as if, wishing to go to New York, he were taken instead to California, three thousand miles away. The point is of some importance in a review of Denis Burkitt's career: he did not choose East Africa; he was *sent* there, he *found* himself there. He served first in Kenya, later in neighboring Somaliland; and his duty as surgical officer was to look after African troops. For a while he was in Ceylon, then in Singapore.

The most significant event in his overseas service occurred when, on a local leave, he went to stay with friends in Uganda. Here, finally, he felt he had found his place. The physical features of the country, its scenery, its climate, pleased him; furthermore, it was largely an *African* country rather than a *settler* country—the difference, before independence, was important. His friends seemed to be making a strong impact upon the people, in both a spiritual and a material sense; and he met Africans who impressed him very deeply with their dedication, their honesty, their positive Christian approach to life. He felt impelled to help, to lend a hand here, to do whatever he could for these people, and when he arrived home in 1946 the feeling was strongly rooted. His calling, specifically, was to return to Uganda and work there. Once again, in his own words, he experienced the certainty that this was God's will, this was what he was destined to do. It could not be ignored.

It could not be ignored, but there was another factor to be taken into account. During his absence Olive had continued working as a Sister in a hospital in Eastbourne. Now the war was over. Major Burkitt had returned from distant lands and had resumed his former identity as Mr. Denis Burkitt, a Fellow of the Royal College of Surgeons (Edinburgh); and Olive Burkitt, like any young wife, was longing to settle down, to have a home of her own, to raise a family. She had not the slightest desire to go to Uganda; it was the last place in the world she would have chosen. Her inclination was to settle down in England; and her husband was tempted to throw everything to the winds and settle down with her.

For both partners it was a difficult time. In the end he was unable to turn away from what was so strongly implanted in him: the absolute necessity to follow his calling. The question, ultimately, was not one of deciding rationally what was the best course of action in the given circumstances. It was the infinitely more formidable question of heeding God's will—whatever God's will happened to be and no matter what it involved. That, in all his actions, *must* be the deciding factor.

A new application was made to go out in the Colonial Service, and after five years as a surgeon in the army he could hardly be turned down on the grounds of inadequate sight. But he was asked rather pointedly by the head of the Colonial Office if he was prepared to do anything they requested of him; he answered yes, feeling that if he said he would only do surgery it would be a mockery of his belief that he had a vocation to work in Africa. The point, in his mind, was of considerable importance. "If you say you have a vocation—a calling, a summons to the service of God—and then lay down stipulations, it's rather hypocritical. So I told them, *I'm not much good at anything except surgery, but I'll try to do whatever you ask.*"

He was accepted. He was then informed that he would be leaving for Africa in six months; and he was also informed that his wife could not accompany him. In those days, so soon after the war, there was a shortage of housing, and Colonial Service officers simply had to wait until accommodation for their families became available. So, after being separated for two and a half years, Denis and Olive Burkitt, with their first child on the way, were faced with another separation for an unspecified length of time. "I had to say goodby to her again," Denis Burkitt recalls, "and it was one of the most difficult things I've ever had to do."

5

Bush Surgeon

The sea journey in 1946 took about a month. The route was becoming familiar to Burkitt: across the Bay of Biscay, through the Straits of Gibraltar into the Mediterranean, passing Malta and Crete on the way to Port Said, through the Red Sea and the Gulf of Aden, and down the Indian Ocean to Mombasa, the chief port of Kenya. Mombasa is hot, humid, steamy, and it still carries memories of the centuries of horror when it was a center of the Arab trade in ivory and slaves. It is prosperous today, with a population of 150,000; ten minutes in a cabin cruiser will take visitors to some of the most exciting deep-sea fishing in the world; its harbor is picturesque, its waterfront is picturesque, its people are picturesque; but it is tainted—it cannot shake off the past as Buchenwald will never shake off the past.

Postwar scarcities prevailed here, too. Burkitt, coming ashore after his month at sea, could not get a room for the night and slept in the lounge of a small hotel. Early in the morning—the first morning of his new life in Africa—he walked out of the hotel into the bush for a few minutes of solitude and prayer.

Then he went by train to Nairobi. One of his companions, not by choice, was a senior Colonial Service officer who was so drunk that the African stewards had to carry him to bed. Burkitt vividly remembers the man emptying his bladder on the carriage floor: "And I remember saying to myself, If this is the example England gives to Africa, may God help me to give something different." He had always abstained from drinking; this experience affected him deeply and strengthened his resolve to stay away from alcohol.

From Nairobi he went to Kampala, and then in a small pick-up truck to his station: Lira, the principal town of Lango District, which stretches north from an immense complex of lakes, rivers, and marshes. The district immediately to the west, Bunyoro, includes the Murchison Falls National Park and extends to Lake Albert and the Congo frontier; the district to the north, Acholi, reaches to the Sudan.

As the crow flies, Lira is about a hundred and fifty miles from Kampala, but the crow is presumed to go in a straight line across all the rivers and swamps, across Lake Kioga and Lake Kwania, whereas a small pick-up truck has to travel in an arc, skirting the lakes and crossing the Victoria Nile by ferry at Atura, thus adding about seventy miles to the distance. Burkitt had already spent more than a year in East Africa, and the town was scarcely any different from the mental picture he had formed of it before his arrival. The Indian population lived in its own quarter, the bazaar; the Africans for the most part lived outside the town itself; the Europeans lived in red-tiled or corrugated-iron houses around the golf course and the all-important club. No building was more than a single story high. The surrounding country was absolutely flat; the roads were of the usual red mud, bordered by tall elephant grass, and ran perfectly straight for miles on end. There was none of the lushness one associates with tropical Africa, no rain forest, no wild outbursting vegetation. Here the most common tree was the rather drab Borassus palm, which rattles in the breeze as if its leaves are made of tin, and has a swelling on its trunk as if it is permanently pregnant. Virtually all the large wild animals had been killed or driven away.

It was very backward when Burkitt first went there. "Out in the bush," he says, "most people still wore animal skins. They grew cotton, and lived on millet and sorghum and sweet potatoes; and they were very friendly." For a couple of days he was put up in a rest house. Then he was given his own house, and on the day he moved into it an African came to see him and said he would like to be Burkitt's houseboy. His name was Yusufu, and he remained with the Burkitt family for the next twenty years, until they left Uganda. His portrait, painted by one of the hospital sisters, hangs today in the dining room of the Burkitt's home in England.

Olive joined him, with their first child, Judy, six months later. Denis went to Mombasa to meet her. "She'd had a terrible journey coming out. The conditions were like a troopship. There were thirteen mothers and children in one cabin, all going down with various infectious fevers, and she thought she would never get our daughter off the boat alive. We came back most of the way by train, but the last part of the trip was in the pick-up truck; and she told me later that she was horrified to see that I had such a big staff just for myself. In those days, of course, it was a kindness to the people to take them on as staff. I had a cook, and a boy to help the cook, and a houseboy, and a boy to work in the garden; and when Olive came I engaged an ayah for her."

It was a pleasant life, despite the primitive conditions. "The toilet was just a bucket, emptied every day by an ox-wagon. We carried in the water for the bath in a four-gallon drum. The light was an Aladdin lamp, or a hurricane lamp. And we were very happy. It would never have done to have started in Kampala and then gone upcountry. It's far easier in life to begin with simple living and go on to something better, than to go the other way. . . . One didn't work excessive hours under those circumstances. We reported to the hospital at about eight o'clock in the morning. We took an hour for lunch, and finished work at about half past four. We were always on call, because there was nowhere to go." In addition to the medical officer there was the usual establishment, found on most upcountry stations: the agricultural officer, the forestry officer, the police officer, and the District Commissioner, each with his own little office and his own house. Altogether there were perhaps a dozen European families. Prisoners from the local jail kept the golf course spick and span, and the District Commissioner was looked upon as a sort of Great White Father of the area. Relations between the administration and the people were excellent. At no time was there any element of resentment, of hostility, of danger. The whites followed the traditional mode of colonial life: wives gathered for coffee in midmorning, returned home for lunch with husbands, regrouped for afternoon tea and tennis, went to the club afterward. It has been described in novels a thousand times, and each time you read about it you wonder how the people survived the process of going around and around in a circle.

For Burkitt (and this was undoubtedly true also for his

colleagues in their particular fields) boredom was the very least of his problems. At that time, England had a statistical ratio of one doctor for every thousand people. In Lira, assisted by a single African doctor, Burkitt looked after a population of considerably more than a quarter of a million. He was responsible for public health in the entire district. He was responsible for the schools. He was responsible for the hospital administration. And he was responsible, of course, for surgery. No cars were available when he first went out: he traveled everywhere by bicycle or, in special circumstances, by ambulance. Eventually he acquired his trusty Ford pick-up truck, which was ten years old and notable for having virtually no brakes. "But since the country is entirely flat," he says, quite reasonably, "and since every road is entirely straight, and since, also, there is no traffic, the pick-up truck was fairly safe because one always had a mile or so in which to glide to a stop."

The central hospital in Lira had a hundred beds, but scattered around Lango District there were about a dozen sub-dispensaries staffed by medical orderlies. Once a week Burkitt would go on safari, visiting them. "That was why I chose a pick-up truck. I would find among the patients at the sub-dispensaries some who definitely needed hospital treatment, and I would pile them in the back of the truck and bring them to the hospital. Then, when I went out again, I would fill up the back of the truck with patients who were ready to go home, and return with another truckload of patients who needed operations. At the same time I'd carry out drugs and any other supplies the dispensaries needed."

Occasionally he took Olive with him on safari overnight, and apart from almost being eaten to death by mosquitoes she survived these experiences very well. Later, she learned that the country around Lira was highly malarial. The climate was not too hot for Europeans: the temperature rarely went above 88°, never went below 72°. Given a refrigerator, which the Burkitts could not obtain in Lira because of postwar shortages, life would have been unshadowed. Even without a refrigerator they were happy and content.

In his first year at Lira, Burkitt increased the number of operations from seventeen to more than 600. By and large, the people were debilitated by chronic malaria, by hookworms, and by all the other infections and parasites that afflict the African in the bush. They were highly susceptible to tuberculosis and meningitis. Most of them were anemic. Hernias were common, due to three factors: incompetent surgery at birth, which leaves the child with a defective, protuberant navel; poor diet, both for children and adults, which results in a distended abdomen; and the picturesque habit of carrying heavy loads on the head, which puts great pressure on the spinal column, the pelvic muscles, and the abdominal wall. A great many of Burkitt's cases were hydroceles, a collection of fluid in the testicles often resulting in enormous distention. This, because he had to treat it so often, led to his first venture into geographic pathology—the study of the manner in which disease is affected by climate and geographical location; and he came up with a remarkable finding—in the eastern part of his district one man in three suffered from hydrocele, while in the western part the incidence dropped to 1 percent. This finding was never followed through, and why hydrocele should occur in such a peculiar pattern remains obscure. Fortunately (in a sense), hernias and hydrocele require what Burkitt terms "short" operations. Whenever possible he had to concentrate on procedures and treatment "where one is able to do the most good with the minimum expenditure of time, material and effort, because the circumstances are such that it is only possible to touch the fringe of all that needs to be done."

Injuries of various kinds helped to fill the hospitals and dispensaries. Mostly they were the outcome of fights—the free use of knives, pangas, bludgeons, and other simple weapons readily available in the bush. Severe bite wounds were frequent, and it is a remarkable fact that the hospital treated eight victims of human bites for every snakebite victim. Human bites can be exceedingly dangerous, even lethal, because of infection; on the other hand, there are few highly poisonous snakes in Uganda and snakebite deaths are relatively infrequent.

The Lira experience was to prove of immense value to Denis Burkitt. It strengthened his confidence in himself: when, a dozen times a day, you are confronted with decisions that mean life or death, you *must* have confidence in yourself, in your own values, your own judgment, otherwise you collapse inwardly, and probably outwardly, too. It gave him, also, an understanding of the problems faced by all upcountry doctors, in both government and mission hospitals. He had been in their shoes. He was one of them; and they could trust him.

The Colonial Office presumably had the right to send him anywhere they pleased. Fifteen months after he arrived in Lira they exercised their prerogative. In January 1948, he received a telegram informing him that he was posted to Mulago Hospital in the capital, Kampala.

The reasons for the transfer were perfectly valid (and even if they were not, Burkitt would still have had to comply with his orders). Mulago Hospital, which grew from the primitive hospitals started by Sir Albert Cook, was the center of the government hospital system in Uganda. Late in 1947 the senior surgeon had retired and returned to England, and as a consequence all surgery in the hospital was being done by the one surgeon who remained, Professor Ian McAdam. The pressure of work proved so great that he fell ill with an acute duodenal ulcer and a message was hastily sent to Burkitt requesting him to come down to Mulago and take over.

Mulago Hospital, named for the hill on which it stands, was then a collection of miscellaneous buildings, for the most part huts, which had grown up over the years in a fairly haphazard way. Hut was simply added to hut when a particular need arose. The war had curtailed any further growth, but by 1948 the hospital was enlarging its facilities once again. Separate units were formed for surgery, medicine, and gynecology, and in due course there was to be a further subdivision into what was probably the most important of all services for the African community, pediatrics.

In some ways Burkitt was not sorry to be transferred. Looking back on the time he spent in Lira, he felt duly grateful for being given the opportunity to turn his hand to so many different things. But his chief skill was as a surgeon, "and I had, perhaps, the selfish hankering to get back to surgery altogether. Not that I was particularly competent as a surgeon. . . . But I knew more about surgery than anything else."

The work load was far heavier than it had been at Lira. At the beginning there were only two qualified surgeons— McAdam and Burkitt, assisted by five or six junior doctors (today the surgical staff is more than sixty). The encouraging and exciting aspect of the situation when Burkitt arrived was that Mulago was growing in every sense, and it continued to grow: "I had the privilege and opportunity of growing with it. If you find yourself linked to a growing place, you are carried up with it as it grows. If you link up with a place that is going down, you tend to go down with it. From that point of view I was very fortunate." Within a couple of years a Department of Surgery was formed, and Sir John Croot was appointed Professor of Surgery. The medical side, with separate wards and facilities, was headed by a man whom Burkitt calls the best-known doctor in East Africa at that time, Dr. H. C. Trowell.

For ten years Burkitt worked at Mulago Hospital, heading one of the three surgical units—Professor Ian McAdam and Sir John Croot headed the other two—when, without any forewarning, the direction of his life was decisively changed. It was as if he were in a boat going up a broad river, and suddenly the boat turned away from the main stream and continued up a branch of the river he had never seen before. The actual event was nothing more than a common occurrence in the daily routine. Something of the same sort happened all the time.

One day—nobody can recall the precise date—Dr. Hugh Trowell asked Denis Burkitt if he would be kind enough to look at a patient in Ward One of the old Mulago Hospital.* There was nothing unusual about the request, there was no emergency. It was ordinary procedure—one doctor asking another doctor for an opinion. "I can't remember whether I

---

* A brief explanation may avoid confusion. The old Mulago Hospital is "the collection of huts" referred to earlier, although the main building was comparatively elaborate—a pavilion-type colonial structure, surmounted by a graceful little clock tower, looking rather like a primitive Howard Johnson's restaurant. The new Mulago Government Hospital, built to replace it, is one of the most impressive hospitals in the world, a striking example of modern hospital design.

was the surgeon on duty, or whether he just said to me in passing, *Denis, would you look at this patient for me*. Ward One was the children's ward, and we both had patients in it."

The patient Dr. Trowell asked Burkitt to look at was a boy aged about five. An ordinary small boy. What made him different from other small boys was that he had swellings in all four quadrants of his jaws—that is, swellings on both sides of the upper jaw, and swellings on both sides of the lower jaw.

The little boy's name was Africa. His parents gave him the name out of love and pride, perhaps, or because they could not think of any other name to give him. Other people in other lands might be called Walter Scott, or William Henry Ireland, or John Philip Holland; but this child's name was Africa, and he was undoubtedly very frightened at finding himself in Ward One of the old Mulago Hospital.

The best-known doctor in East Africa could not explain those four symmetrical jaw swellings; nor could the surgeon whose opinion had been requested. They could be sure of only one thing: little Africa would not live very long.

"Ever since I came to Mulago in 1948 we—the other medical officers and myself—had seen tumors of the jaws in children," Denis Burkitt now says. "They were cancers. We cut them out.

"But this boy had swellings on both sides of both jaws, which was unusual. I didn't think it was a tumor—it made no *sense* as a tumor, because nobody is likely to have four tumors at once. It didn't make sense as an infection, either.

"I examined him very carefully, made some notes, and took some photographs—I always carried two cameras, one for black and white and one for color photographs. Afterwards I discussed the case with Hugh Trowell, and I told him I didn't know what it was. We had tissue sent out for section (that is, for examination under the microscope) but this didn't help us very much; and we just felt—Hugh and I— that we didn't know the diagnosis. This isn't as peculiar as it sounds. It happens often. One is frequently meeting things one can't pin down.

"In a country like England you can turn to all sorts of experts for their opinion and advice, but in Uganda in those days there weren't many experts to whom we could turn. There were conditions which you recognized because you saw them fairly frequently: you knew, *This is this* by what it looked like, or what it felt like, but you had no name for it. You couldn't say exactly *what* it was until somebody found an organism, or detected something or other, that caused it.

"And the jaw condition on this little boy, Africa, was just one of the queer, unidentified things we came across. It was interesting. But neither Hugh Trowell nor I could say with certainty what it was."

Then, only a few weeks later, when he was visiting the district hospital in Jinja, on the northern shore of Victoria Nyanza, fifty miles from Kampala, he happened to glance out of the window of one of the wards; and there, on the grass, was another child with a fat, swollen face. Burkitt hurried outside and found that he was not mistaken. "It was just the same as the mouth of the little boy I had seen in Mulago Hospital. I took photographs again, and I made notes. And I began thinking about these things seriously."

So, early in 1957, the drama began.

Interlude:
A Different Pyramid

Hugh Carey Trowell takes a place at the very outset of the Burkitt story by virtue of a few concerned words spoken to a colleague. The results were to be startling. But Dr. Trowell also has a place of his own in the history of medicine in East Africa, and his contributions to the well-being of millions of human beings are of tremendous importance.

London, not Dublin, was Hugh Trowell's background. He trained at St. Mary's Hospital from 1923 to 1928, did house jobs for a year, and experienced the spiritual call to go out to Africa. The wise men he consulted urged him to be sensible. He was told: *You have a great future here.* And he was solemnly warned: *The hospitals are very bad out there. You will be unable to do any decent work, and you will go with loose women, and you will take to drinking whisky, and after twenty years you will come home a total wreck.*

He married the day after he finished his house jobs. His

wife, Margaret, was a student at the Slade School of Art in Bloomsbury: she shared his beliefs, religious and humanitarian. Soon after they were married Hugh went out to Kenya in the Colonial Medical Service and was posted to a new hospital upcountry, about sixty miles from Nairobi—so new and primitive that there was not even a road leading to it. His wife accompanied him, and in this wilderness their first child was born.

Patients were few, for the simple reason that the Africans were utterly terrified of the white newcomers who—it was well known—ate the livers and other organs of anyone foolish enough to go to them for treatment. In addition to a lack of patients there was a lack of drugs, a lack of equipment, a lack of facilities, and Dr. Trowell (who can now look back and comment gently, "I was probably a difficult youngster") criticized the authorities so sharply that he expected to be sent home. The authorities, however, seemed impressed by the young man's spirit. After six months he was recalled to Nairobi and put in charge of a new project for training African medical orderlies, which raised quite unexpected problems—"the orderlies all thought they were going to be doctors the day after they started their training, and they went on strike because we wouldn't issue them stethoscopes."

He remained in Nairobi for nearly six years, and during this time he became aware of an unusual disease of children —not the disease that aroused Denis Burkitt's interest several years later but something else. He has written a searing account of it: "No one wanted the old K.A.R. [King's African Rifles] Hospital in Nairobi, so I was given it. In sullen mood I went into the corrugated iron building; it was dark, it was full of bed lice, the children were all crying, but many of them had brown hair although they were African babies and many of them had swollen legs with edema. On walking through the ward at night, lit by one hurricane lantern, one would hear the low moan of the children dying; we did not know why they were dying, but it was Kwashiorkor. So there, as far as I am concerned, it all started. The 400-bedded hospital had one water tap; during all my six years it never had a microscope; no African could speak English; we could not even examine urine, stool, or blood slide in the hospital, everything went to a laboratory situated over a mile away. We only knew that when the baby developed black spots on the skin it was going to die. Then one day I surprised my wife by saying that I felt fairly certain I was dealing with a new disease. Its outstanding sign was the brown hair, the swollen legs of edema, but this is where the trouble started. There are so many causes for edema, all sorts of heart diseases, kidney diseases and blood diseases caused edema. Might not some recognized disease be there and missed? You could miss a lot, believe me, in the old Ward Five of the Nairobi K.A.R. Hospital."

It was indeed a new disease, and a particularly fearsome one. Unknown to Trowell then, an English missionary doctor in West Africa, Cicely Williams, had observed the same conditions in the children in her hospital, and it was she who one day learned from one of her nurses that the disease was called kwashiorkor. Cicely Williams asked, "What does 'kwashiorkor' mean?" The nurse explained, "It means the sickness that the older child gets when the next baby is born." And, according to Dr. Ann Dally in her biography, *Cicely: The Story of A Doctor*, Cicely Williams exclaimed, "My God, I believe that's the explanation." She had remembered the psalm: *I refrain my soul, and keep it low, like a child that is weaned from his mother: yea, my soul is even as a weaned child.*

The work of Cicely Williams and Hugh Trowell and,

later, other doctors, was to lead to the understanding of what the World Health Organization called "the most widespread and severe nutritional disorder known to medical science." It has become only too familiar in recent years as a result of the ghastly war fought between the Nigerians and the Biafrans. Those children with the fleshless skulls and bloated abdomens are in the terminal stage of kwashiorkor, and it is no longer the weaning disease but the disease of relentless and disgraceful fratricide.

In reasonably peaceful tropical areas it is due to protein deficiency, often the result of a child being weaned because the mother is again pregnant, and being put on a diet which contains insufficient protein to meet the demands of early growth. In tropical areas ravaged by war, it is still due to a lack of protein, as a result of deliberate starvation, of unforgiveable human viciousness.

In 1935 Hugh Trowell and his family left Kenya for Uganda, and he took up new duties at Mulago Hospital. "It had some ten wards built of corrugated iron," he says. "The floors were mud, the roofs were grass. By the time I arrived these had more or less been replaced by huts with concrete floors. There were facilities for doing post mortems, a small laboratory where blood slides for malaria could be prepared; but you couldn't do any advanced biochemistry such as tests for blood proteins or blood sugar."

In Kenya there had been a rigid belief that no African could become a doctor; at best, he could only reach the level of a male nurse. Uganda was rather more enlightened, a legacy of the teaching of Sir Albert Cook and other medical missionaries. The mission hospitals, consequently, had gone ahead and were training what was vaguely termed "a doctor kind of person," more advanced than male nurses or medical orderlies but still far from a qualified physician.

"It was a very pleasant tropical setting," Dr. Trowell recalls. "African nationalism had not yet come to the fore. We weren't overwhelmed by large and complex instruments. Most of us had some disease we were chasing—mine was kwashiorkor. The white community remained apart, but some of us felt this shouldn't continue indefinitely, and we started to entertain some of the Africans in our home—it was slightly nerve-racking because if we were caught we would have been in serious trouble. The Africans couldn't speak English, and even if you were able to engage them in conversation you would have had to talk about goats, and crops, and the things that interested them.

"Early on it was difficult to get the Africans into the hospitals. We would go out into the markets, and we would take medicines with us and give them to the people; we'd leave the car in the market and if somebody was very ill we'd tell them to go and sit in the car so that we could examine them a little more carefully. They were very suspicious. They thought we were poisoning them. They had their own system of medicine—witch doctors who were not only medicine men but holy men of a sort, having great power: power over life and death."

During this time Margaret Trowell was marking out her own path. She had become very interested in the African's potential for art, and more or less as a hobby she had begun to give art lessons on the back veranda of her home. In due course this grew into a full-fledged art school. Her husband says of her: "In a strange way she released their artistic powers. She said to the Africans, *No, don't copy us, just have fun with paint and paper and get on with your own things.* She was also in charge of the museum; she collected African masks, and carvings, and weapons, and wrote about them, making us realize that they were really great works of art in their own right and that they should be a source of pride and inspiration to the African people." Today, Margaret Trowell is recognized as one of the outstanding authorities on African art and her books are known all over the world. As a tribute to her work, the art school in Makerere College was given her name when she retired—the Margaret Trowell School of Fine Art.

The discovery of kwashiorkor was not instantly acclaimed as a triumph of medicine. In West Africa, Cicely Williams became seriously ill as a result of her intensive study of the problem, and eventually accepted an appointment in Southeast Asia (where she was imprisoned by the Japanese during the war in the Pacific and suffered bitter hardships, including prolonged starvation, a subject on which she was a world authority). Hugh Trowell, in East Africa, was unable to define the problem in his own mind, and, hampered by inadequate scientific facilities, was assailed by people "who thought I was taking the thing too far."

Then, during World War II, Professor Harold Himsworth, at the time Professor of Medicine at University College, London, was asked by the British government to describe what diseases would occur in the British Isles if Britain lost the war. There was nothing academic about this exercise. Nazi submarines were taking an enormous toll of British shipping, destroying vast amounts of the imported foodstuffs that were essential to Britain's survival; and Nazi strategy, clearly, was to starve the British people into submission.

Since Britain could not import enough meat and would be unable to catch enough fish, and since most of her cattle would be killed so that pastures could be ploughed up for wheat, Himsworth could be certain that there would be a shortage of protein.

The first step, obviously, was to investigate the effects of protein shortage.

He induced protein malnutrition in rats and found that in addition to the expected symptoms—loss of weight, physical weakness, and so on—the liver of these animals was invaded and seriously damaged by excessive amounts of fat. Hugh Trowell, learning of Himsworth's work, sent him specimens of liver tissue taken from children who had died of kwashiorkor, showing similar evidence of excessive fatty deposits; and, in Trowell's words, Himsworth became very excited. His experimental disease, induced in rats in England, was actually occurring in human beings in East Africa, and he had a decisive answer to his question, at least as far as it affected young children. If Britain lost the war, the resultant shortage of protein would cause severe malnutrition and this could be expected to bring about a widespread condition similar to tropical kwashiorkor.

The mechanism of the disease was still unknown and there was no theory to account for its strange effects. Giving protein-rich foods to a child suffering from severe kwashiorkor would not necessarily change the course of his illness. You could virtually pour good food into him and he would still die. Why was protein starvation largely irreversible? Why couldn't a starved child be restored to health if he was given ample amounts of the proteins and vitamins he had been denied?

The answer was found by chance (or by the good fortune that seems to attend certain people) soon after World War II came to an end. Britain then had large stocks of powdered milk left over, and Trowell, through the Colonial Office, ordered supplies to be sent to him in Kampala to feed his kwashiorkor patients.

When the supplies arrived, Trowell's assistant came to him in great agitation and informed him that instead of powdered *whole* milk he had been sent *skimmed* milk.

At this, Hugh Trowell—normally the mildest and gentlest of men—flew into a tremendous rage. He was convinced that the bureaucrats in London were attempting to foist on him something they wanted to get rid of: processed milk, which had little nutritional value. But it appeared that the substitution might well have been arranged by higher authorities, for the children dying of kwashiorkor actually *thrived* on skimmed milk, and many of the symptoms of their disease were reversed. It was marvelous; and it seemed to make no sense. The children rejected whole milk, with its high nutritional value, but they willingly accepted skimmed milk.

Now, skimmed milk is milk from which the cream has been removed. Cream is largely butterfat. The digestion of fats, proteins, and starches is dependent upon the special secretion manufactured by the pancreas, which is called the pancreatic juice. This was the clue to the problem: kwashiorkor, among other things, causes the pancreas to become defective, so that there is a reduction in the activity of the pancreatic juice. Because of this failure the sick children were unable to digest whole milk with its high fat content, and the fat was deposited in the liver. Fat-free skimmed milk, on the other hand, provided the children with the nourishment they needed so desperately and gave them hope of a speedy recovery.

So kwashiorkor, which throughout the history of mankind must have affected the destinies of untold millions of human beings, ceased to be a mystery, although it still remains a severe problem. But, unquestionably, the work of

Cicely Williams and Hugh Trowell will in due course benefit the inhabitants of every tropical nation in the world. They were the true pioneers, the first not just to *see* the problem but to *observe* it. The solution seemed to come by accident, yet on this score it is worth recalling C. G. Jung's dictum: *There are no accidents.*

In 1947 the British government was disturbed by reports of serious unrest among porters working on the railways in East Africa, and a board of inquiry was set up to look into the situation. Dr. Trowell was appointed to review the medical aspects. He found that the porters' living conditions were wretched, and he reported in the strongest terms that changes were essential, the men must be fed better, must be given better housing, must be given some hope for the future. "I was appalled," he says, "by their aggressive, rebellious spirit; and this was in fact the beginning of the trouble that erupted as the Mau Mau movement a year or so later."

There was a bonus. While he was traveling to Nairobi on this mission he first met Denis Burkitt. "We were in the same carriage on the train. We merely talked for a few hours, but Denis made quite an impression on me. I thought, This is a very keen man. We didn't discuss it much but I recognized him to be a sincere Christian and I recognized, too, that he would have what I call a warm attitude to the Africans. Not everybody out there had it. He certainly would be one of those who would be humane and fair."

So a friendship began. As far as medical history is concerned its most significant moment occurred ten years later when Denis Burkitt entered Ward One of the old Mulago Hospital at Dr. Trowell's request to examine a little boy named Africa.

Like other physicians, Trowell had occasionally seen this

condition in the past. Once, in 1935, when he was on safari
to the islands of Lake Victoria, inspecting the population for
evidence of sleeping sickness, he came across a little boy
with "lumps" on the jaws. "I can't remember much about it
except that I thought it was a peculiar complaint, and I told
the boy, *I can't treat you here, you must come back to
Mulago with me.* I didn't know what the disease was, because
it wasn't one lump, which might be called an ordinary cancer,
but several lumps. Vaguely, at the back of my mind, was the
knowledge that the children out here had these lumps: one
encountered them from time to time, one would ask surgeons
to see them but nobody could throw much light on the
trouble. When another case turned up in 1957 I asked Denis
to look at it. I don't think I asked him in any deliberate way
—it was just his turn to see surgical cases that week. Later, I
remember him saying, *If you see any more of these cases, do
let me know;* and I think we saw two or three of them in the
next few months."

When Burkitt was posted to Mulago Hospital in 1948 he
was still, in the professional sense, a young man. In order of
seniority he was the third, or junior, member of the surgical
team, and he was not expected to do the more elaborate and
difficult surgical operations. His experience was of a different
order from that of Professor Croot or Professor McAdam,
both of whom came to Mulago after long connections with
English teaching schools: John Croot had served for many
years in the Department of Surgery at Bristol, Ian McAdam
—a very forceful personality—had made a great name for
himself at Edinburgh.

"Denis Burkitt," Trowell says, "was rather quiet and un-
assuming, not at all the conventional picture of an incisive
and purposeful surgeon. But when my son needed an operation—it wasn't anything major—I was glad Denis performed

it. If you had asked him, soon after he came to Mulago, *Are you ever going to be the Professor of Surgery here?* he would have said, *Oh, no, no. I'm very happy to be at Mulago Hospital, working with Africans, helping to train them, and so on. But Ian McAdam and the others are ahead of me.*

"The point is that he had, and still has, a great capacity to *pursue.* It's a temperamental gift which also links on to his religious beliefs. He was never obtrusive about his religion, he would never buttonhole people or indulge in great and elaborate theological discussions, and he had a great respect for anybody whose views differed from his: he was very charitable in his dealings with others."

Hugh and Margaret Trowell left Kampala in 1958 to return home. His work on kwashiorkor had resulted in extraordinary difficulties and in quite unexpected repercussions. For example, Communist agents attempted to contact him, hoping they could persuade him to say that kwashiorkor in Africa was due to colonialism, despite the established fact that the disease had been occurring for untold centuries throughout the tropics and elsewhere. (It was common in the Middle Ages, before the agricultural revolution in Europe; and there is a statue in a Florentine church which shows the Infant Christ with the big potbelly and swollen legs that are typical of the disease.) Trowell says, "We started by looking at the apex of an enormous pyramid. We didn't know how far down the base of the pyramid was, but in the end we began to realize that the majority of children in some parts of Africa and tropical Asia and tropical America have (at least) a mild degree of this disease. For a time we couldn't get agreement with the pathologists that this was a disease in its own right, so we couldn't find out why our children were dying; we couldn't get agreement with the biochemists, so we couldn't cure the thing. Now, looking back, I think that any idea—if it's really big—must be baptized with cold water. If the infant survives its baptism, it will thrive. . . .

"We have to ask why, in the world's history, the wheat eaters, or the cereal eaters, or those who had milk and meat, were able to create civilizations, whereas the people who had yams and cassava and all the other protein-deficient foods were unable to produce a civilization. I began to see that civilizations seldom arose in the tropics because the people failed to solve two problems: how to store calories, and how to get protein-rich food to growing children. Today this is possible, not by labeling any tropical food as bad, for they are all good and reflect the beneficence of Creation, but by adding other foods which can be stored, and are easily cooked, and are rich in protein.

"For me, it all started with babies crying in the night."

After his arrival in England he retired from medicine; he took holy orders, and he is now the Rev. Dr. Hugh Carey Trowell, vicar of Stratford-sub-Castle, in Salisbury. He has earned his place in history; and he can look at Denis Burkitt with understanding and with affection. "I know Denis terribly well," he says. "But if anybody had told me, *This is a man who is going to make a discovery of international importance,* I should have said no. He was too quiet, too modest. And I would have been wrong. The gifts which really land a major thing are humility, and perseverance, and seeing things fresh, and perhaps not taking a too exalted view of your own capacities. And, nearly always, the great discoveries start with just a tin can and a piece of string."

7

Invitation to a Safari

The doctors in Mulago Hospital could not save little Africa. In Jinja Hospital they could not save the other little boy who was suffering from the same disease. And so their parents came for them, in deep distress, bringing them great masses of fresh flowers, and carried them away to be laid to rest in the proper place and in the proper manner. It is a sight you see every day in any African hospital: the grieving parents in their best clothes, the motionless little body, the masses of flowers. Too many children die in Africa, of too many diseases.

The outcome was always the same, it was absolutely inevitable: all children with this peculiar disease, marked by heavily swollen jaws, died within six to twelve weeks after the illness became apparent. No drug—except to some slight extent the deadly war gas, nitrogen mustard—slowed the course of the disease. Surgery—and by its nature it was harsh and disfiguring surgery—gave only a brief respite. Young children between the ages of, say, two and ten grow at an astonishing rate. If by some terrible mischance they develop a malignancy it will grow as fast as the child's general rate of growth, and often a great deal faster. These jaw tumors grew very rapidly indeed. They doubled themselves in about forty-eight hours, and a young child could not live with them for more than about three months.

But why had a disease with such unmistakable symptoms failed to attract attention until 1957? Was it a new disease which was only now afflicting human beings; or was it a disease that had suddenly begun to occur with greater frequency; or had it, up to this time, been overlooked?

Anybody who has lived in Africa, even briefly, will have been touched by the tenderness that African parents show their children. The ancient social system works very well in this respect: families stay together, children are prized and receive infinite love from father and mother and all the other members of the particular group in which they live.

In these circumstances, the jaw tumors are not likely to be ignored. They first manifest themselves by loosened teeth, swollen and painful gums. Then, because of their rapid growth, the tumors become larger and more evident, and the child begins to suffer serious discomfort. The alarmed parents would then set out to seek help, if necessary walking twenty, thirty, or even fifty miles to the nearest hospital. Buses now run between the larger towns in East Africa and bicycles are abundant; but often, in the more remote areas, people have no money for a long bus ride and they walk from one place to another, plodding along the side of the red mud roads in single file. A woman taking her sick child to a hospital many miles away may carry him in her arms, at the same time carrying another child on her back or feeding at her breast, and balancing a bundle of her possessions on her head.

Over the years, then, most children with jaw tumors reached a hospital. They were seen by doctors or by nurses or by medical orderlies. They received treatment. They died. And this has been going on for a very long time. Sir Albert Cook had described the condition in his notebooks, calling it a sarcoma—a term used for a certain type of tumor. "Sarcomas are common in Africa," he wrote in 1902, "particularly sarcomas of the jaw." Hugh Trowell had seen them, first on Lake Victoria, later at Mulago; and other doctors in East Africa had seen them and drawn attention to them without arousing any great interest.

As for Denis Burkitt, during his fifteen months at Lira he must certainly have encountered a case or two, and quite certainly he encountered several cases during the years he was at Mulago. Somehow or other these cases did not arouse him, they did not produce any great inner excitement. He himself says, "I *must* have been seeing the tumor in those first ten years in Africa, but we weren't recognizing it. There's a great difference between seeing a thing and observing a thing, and unless you actually look for it, it can pass you unnoticed."

What occurred to Denis Burkitt, then, was no sudden vision, no sudden flash of inspiration, nothing as dramatic and immediate as Sir Isaac Newton's apple falling in the orchard. After ten years, so he says, he woke up to something that had been there all along. One has to remember, though, that Burkitt maintained a heavy schedule of surgery, that he had to concern himself with the endless details which are an inescapable part of hospital routine, and that he took his responsibility toward his patients very seriously: he cared about them, he worried about them.

Yet it is clear that the child in Ward One of Mulago Hospital and the child playing on the grass outside Jinja Hospital rarely left his thoughts. He could have left the problem where it was, of course, merely noting that he had run across something unusual—symmetrical swellings on both sides of the upper and lower jaws; but his interest was stirred, he was compelled to go on.

The first step was to examine the records of all children who had been treated at Mulago for jaw tumors.

Next, he went over the records of all children who had been treated for tumors of any kind.

And, as new patients with the disease came to the hospital, he looked at them more closely.

As a rule, a malignant growth originates in one particular place in the body. In other words, it will at first involve only a single site, it will have a single focus. For example, it may first appear in a kidney, as an almost imperceptible colony of malignant cells, and there it will continue to grow to an appreciable size. This—the original growth—is known as the primary tumor; and a primary tumor alone can often be treated successfully by surgery or radiotherapy.

As the tumor grows, unfortunately, some malignant cells may migrate to other parts of the body, to a lung, perhaps, or to the liver; and they may initiate new growths, which are known as secondary tumors. When a malignancy spreads in this fashion it becomes exceedingly serious because treatment is far more difficult.

Burkitt uncovered a strange state of affairs in these children with the jaw tumors. "When I examined them more carefully I found that whenever we had a jaw tumor *there would be another tumor elsewhere*. The jaw tumor was not an isolated occurrence. There might also be tumors of the long bones, or of the thyroid, the kidneys, the ovaries, and so on."

The significance of this finding was that *the same disease* could appear in many different forms. It might manifest itself as a jaw tumor. But it might manifest itself without involving the jaws at all. It might first become apparent as an abdominal tumor, or as an ovarian tumor, or as a kidney tumor; nevertheless, these were all manifestations of the same disease, coming to the surface at different places in different children. And when more than one tumor was found in a child, they were all part of what might be called a multiple or multifocal tumor.

In the past each of these tumors had been classified as a separate entity. Now, with the recognition that they were all the same tumor—no matter where they first showed up—an accurate identification became possible. For a time it was thought that they might be neuroblastomas, but two of Burkitt's colleagues, Professor J. N. P. Davies and Dr. G. T. O'Conor, showed that the strange multiple tumor was a form of lymphoma.*

---

* The terms "neuroblastoma" and "lymphoma" need, and deserve, a rather more detailed explanation.

A *neuroblastoma* is a tumor arising from early forms of nerve cells. It frequently originates in one of the adrenal glands (which sit like a cap over each kidney) and may spread from there to the cranium, the liver, lungs, lymph nodes, and bones.

A *lymphoma* is a malignancy affecting the lymphatic system, which consists of lymphatic vessels, lymph nodes, and lymphoid (or lymphatic) tissue.

The *lymphatic system* is a circulatory system similar in many ways to the circulating blood system. It carries the lymph,

"In those days," Burkitt says, "we used to have a staff meeting on Saturday mornings, when the physicians and surgeons and gynecologists met together and one of them would present for discussion any special work he was doing. It was at one of these Saturday morning meetings in Mulago Hospital that I first presented this information about a tumor of

---

which bathes all the tissues of the body. Lymph is a transparent liquid, resembling blood plasma, containing varying numbers of white blood cells and a few red blood cells.

The *lymphatic* vessels branch throughout the body like the blood vessels. They are somewhat fragile, with thinner walls than the veins.

Lymph nodes are small bean-like structures composed of a mesh, or network, of tissue containing fixed white blood cells (as distinct from the free-moving white blood cells in the circulating blood). The network within a lymph node acts as a filter, trapping any solid particles that may have entered the lymph, and engulfing harmful organisms such as bacteria. In many infections, the lymph nodes become swollen and painful, and can be felt as "glands" under the angle of the jaw, under the armpits, or in the groin, but they are also found in the inner side of the knees and the elbows, and in great profusion in the linings of the digestive tract, the liver, the respiratory passages, and the cavity containing the heart.

Lymphoid tissue is composed of a network similar to the lymph nodes and acts in much the same way. The tonsils and the adenoids are composed of lymphoid tissue; so is much of the spleen, the thymus and the appendix.

Lymph nodes and lymphoid tissue form a vital part of the body's defense against infection. They compose the *reticuloendothelial system*, which simply means the system of networks lining the interior surface of the blood vessels, lymph vessels, and cavities in the bone marrow, the spleen, the liver, and other organs.

the jaw with deposits in other parts of the body. Everyone was very interested."

At the end of 1957, Dr. George Oettlé visited Kampala, and by good fortune Denis Burkitt met him and thus had an opportunity to talk to him.

George Oettlé was an outstandingly brilliant young man. At the time of this meeting he was (at the age of thirty-six) Director of the Cancer Research Unit of the National Cancer Association of South Africa, at the South African Institute for Medical Research, and he had done remarkable work on various malignancies that seem to occur with uncommon frequency in some regions of Africa—cancer of the liver, for example, and cancer of the esophagus.*

He was obviously just the man to be consulted about the strange tumor that had caught Burkitt's attention. "I met him

* What is of particular interest is that, like Denis Burkitt and other people in this story, he was deeply religious. A few words by a colleague, Professor J. F. Murray, deserve to be quoted: "Critical to a degree, he used his brilliant mind to test and evaluate every statement he encountered and every set of facts uncovered in the course of his research. Nothing irritated him more than loose or slovenly thinking, and he delighted in the application of logic to the assessment of his research findings. . . . He had a profound knowledge of the Bible and was a man of deep and unshakeable faith in the Providence of God. Despite his brilliant mind, his great scientific achievements, and his research ability he was a humble and lovable man. . . . No one could be long in the presence of George Oettlé without realizing that this was a man whose every thought and action was coloured and determined by Christian love and faith."

George Oettlé died in November 1968, after emergency heart surgery. His contribution to medical science was immense. A further reference to him will be found on p. 233, in Mr. Burkitt's diary.

at the hospital," Burkitt says. "I showed him my photographs and slides. I said, *I am interested in this problem,* and I told him what I was doing about it and asked for his ideas. He was interested in the histology (that is, the microscopic structure of the tissues of the tumor) and he was interested in the cases."

Oettlé was interested for a good reason. When he finished looking at the photographs and slides he told Burkitt, simply but with authority, that this tumor did not occur in South Africa.

Most people would have accepted it as a straightforward statement of fact: *This tumor does not occur in South Africa.* But once again Burkitt reacted in his own characteristic way; he mulled over Oettlé's comment and began to ask himself some new questions.

The distance from Kampala to Johannesburg, as the crow flies, is about 1,800 miles, and the crow would have to fly over a number of different countries—from Uganda over Tanzania, Zambia, Mozambique, Rhodesia, and Botswana, skirting the Congo and Malawi. It would also fly over the great expanse of Lake Victoria, Lake Tanganyika, and (if it lost its bearings slightly) Lake Nyasa. It would miss the snowcapped, cloud-covered Mountains of the Moon, but it would have to cross the Muchinga Mountains, and it would see numerous great rivers—the Ruaha, the Luangwa, the Zambesi, the Limpopo, and many others. There would be all kinds of terrain— marshes, hills, forests, veldt.

Now, Burkitt said to himself, if the tumor occurs commonly (or relatively commonly) here in Uganda, and it does not occur at all some two thousand miles away in South Africa, *where does it stop?*

Clearly it had to stop somewhere between Uganda and South Africa. There had to be a line (he called it *an edge*) dividing tumor territory from non-tumor territory. *Here,* children could have the disease; *there,* children did not have the disease. If such an edge could be found it would be of great interest, of superlative interest, because it might provide some clues to this tumor—environmental clues, hereditary clues, dietary clues, anything.

And, as it happened, *Where does it stop?* turned out to be one of the most stimulating questions in medical history.

Burkitt then took an immense step forward, and boldly applied for a grant to support his research. Cancer research is a costly business, and tens or hundreds of thousands of dollars may be required to start a project and keep it going. Burkitt obtained his grant: the impressive sum of £15 (about forty dollars). He used it for printing and mailing 1,200 leaflets illustrated with his own photographs of children with the tumor. "We obtained addresses from everybody we could. Then we sent the leaflets to government and mission doctors throughout Africa, with a little questionnaire asking, *How long have you worked in your hospital, and have you seen this condition?*"

This preliminary work, as he calls it, went on for about three years. "It was a part-time hobby, because I was employed full time as a government surgeon. But, at a guess, I might have had three to four hundred replies from different parts of Africa. Whenever I spoke at a conference I would get addresses from people. I would meet Dr. Brown, who knew Dr. Smith, who worked at such and such a place, and I would write to him. It wasn't all done at once, and the answers came in dribs and drabs."

At the end of the three years something valuable had been accomplished. On the wall of his office hung several maps. The information provided by the doctors who answered his questionnaire was plotted on these maps by means of colored pins. "We couldn't afford fourpence each [4¢] for mapping pins," Burkitt says, "so I painted the heads of drawing pins myself in different colors to distinguish the different tumors."

The colored drawing pins showed that there was a belt right across equatorial Africa where this children's tumor was common. There was also a sort of tail hanging down East Africa from Kenya to Mozambique.

So the tumor had a pattern of its own. It was obeying certain laws. It was not a haphazard occurrence.

A map may provide an immense amount of information, but it is only a special kind of document. A painted drawing pin is only a kind of symbol, and it cannot talk to you in detail about what it represents. The obvious thing for Denis Burkitt to do next was to go out and look at the situation himself, and he began to plan a trip which—he hoped—would clarify the mystery. "I said to myself, we have to find an edge. If we can find an edge to the belt, that might be the place to look for some environmental factor related to the tumor."

There was little point looking for an edge north of the belt: here one entered the bleak, unpopulated areas of the Sudan and Ethiopia. Due east and due west, the tumor belt went all the way to the sea. In the Congo medical services had been hopelessly disrupted, and any European might find himself in trouble. The best hope was the tail hanging down from the eastern end of the belt, a thickly populated area with many hospitals.

At the outset he fancied that he would buy a secondhand Volkswagen and drive down to South Africa alone, visiting hospitals on the way. After he had given this some thought he realized that it would be much too tiring, and that companionship was essential on such a long trip.

One of his best friends, Dr. E. H. (Ted) Williams, director of a mission hospital near Arua, in northeast Uganda, happened to be visiting Kampala, and Burkitt asked him if he would be prepared to join the safari.

Dr. Williams was not at all happy about it. He was due to go on leave to England; there were various family complications; and he replied, "I don't know if I can, Denis." Burkitt said, "I wish you would," and Dr. Williams returned to Arua, thought about it, then wrote to Burkitt saying he would go. Mrs. Williams would travel to England by herself and stay there while her husband went on safari to South Africa.

"But I felt," Burkitt says, "that there ought to be three people, because if you invite only one, and he drops out through sickness or for some other reason, you are left alone and the whole thing collapses. If there are two others, and one has to return home, you can still continue."

The third man to be invited was Cliff Nelson, a Canadian. He had been in government medical service in Uganda, and when his contract expired he joined Dr. Williams' mission (the Africa Inland Mission, which is predominantly American, with headquarters in Brooklyn).

So, with a full complement, Burkitt settled down to planning the safari in detail.

The Long Safari

The immediate plans called for a safari of no less than ten thousand miles. The immediate problem was how to pay for it. Again, good fortune came to Denis Burkitt's aid. One day Sir Harold Himsworth (who had been knighted since the war, when he and Hugh Trowell communicated in high excitement about protein deficiency, and was now Director of the Medical Research Council in London) walked into Burkitt's office and asked him about his current work. Burkitt described the projected trip to South Africa. Sir Harold asked, "How much money do you need?" Burkitt was taken aback: "Very tentatively—I was afraid to ask for too much— I said I was terribly anxious, if it was at all possible, to get together about £100 [$280] for this safari. And Sir Harold said, *I think I'll make it £150.* But then, when he went back to England he sent me £250."

This was Burkitt's third research grant. He had originally received £15 from government funds and then another £10, all of which had long since been spent on leaflets and postage stamps, not to mention drawing pins. With £250 from Sir Harold Himsworth, Burkitt must have felt he had come into a fortune, and he forthwith commissioned Dr. Williams to try to find a suitable secondhand car.

Now, Dr. Ted Williams has an affinity—among other affinities—for mechanical things: for shortwave radios, and cameras, and plumbing fixtures, and—particularly important at this juncture—cars. He understands these dumb objects, and it is very possible that they are aware that he understands them, for they tend to respond to him. And one of the reasons Denis Burkitt was eager to have his company on the safari (among other reasons) was Ted Williams' magic way with automobiles. "He could change a big end bearing," Burkitt says with pride, "while you were having a cup of coffee. He could do anything to a motor car in any circumstances; and that, of course, is invaluable." To which Dr. Williams retorts, "Not true. Just typical Burkitt blarney."

The Simba were on the rampage in the Congo; mission hospitals were being burned down, missionaries were being slaughtered. One member of the Africa Inland Mission in the Congo was fortunate enough to get away unharmed and managed to reach Ted Williams' hospital just across the border in northern Uganda. He was driving a 1953 Ford Jubilee stationwagon—an American model, with left-hand drive—which had already covered some 45,000 miles of the indescribably appalling Congo roads. Dr. Williams was able to acquire it for £250.

The Jubilee was then given a thorough overhaul and two spare tires were attached to the roof. Since car thieves are just as active in Darkest Africa as elsewhere—perhaps even more so—Dr. Williams followed his usual practice of installing a secret ignition switch. Later, somewhere in the middle of Tanzania, after a day's drive during which they passed a total of two cars, one of which was wrapped around a tree, the Jubilee suddenly stopped dead. Dr. Williams' secret ignition switch had let him down; and apart from a flat tire at nine thousand miles and a loose flywheel ring that had to be hit with a hammer every so often, this was the sole mechanical failure of the entire trip.

The preliminary planning was very thorough. The safari would take ten weeks. A daily schedule was drawn up, giving the time of arrival and departure for each stop. All arrangements for overnight accommodations were made well in advance of their departure. Spare parts were collected for anything that, in Dr. Williams' expert opinion, might break down. As for medical supplies: "We took enough to look after ourselves," Burkitt says, "and we used to joke with each other and say, after all, we ought to be pretty safe medically: we were three doctors, laden down with medical equipment, making a beeline from one hospital to the next. But I don't think we had to use any of the medicine."

The safari started on October 7, 1961. In ten weeks, exactly as they had planned, they covered ten thousand miles, journeyed through twelve countries, and visited fifty-seven hospitals.*

The route is given here: for the record, for those who enjoy armchair travel, and for those who enjoy the bark and growl of African place names. Some of the smaller villages may not be found in the average atlas, and some will be found only with difficulty—if at all—on the large-scale Shell or Michelin touring maps.

---

* A factor of considerable importance to Denis Burkitt was that the Director of Medical Services at Mulago Hospital, Dr. William Davis, graciously (and wisely) recognized the ten weeks not as leave but as a period of duty.

From Kampala, Burkitt and Ted Williams drove south down the west shore of Lake Victoria to Bukoba; then to Ndolage; then, picking up Cliff Nelson, to Kibondo. Then to Kasulu, where they turned west and made a loop around to Kigoma and Ujiji, the meeting place of Stanley and Livingstone on Lake Tanganyika.

They then drove down an utterly desolate, tsetse-infested part of Tanzania to Mpanda; next to Sumbawanga; then to Abercorn, in Zambia.

Here once again they turned westward in a loop that took them to Fort Rosebery and back to the main road at Kasama. They doubled back to Abercorn, and bore east and south to Karonga on Lake Malawi (Lake Nyasa on maps that are more than a few years old).

Then to Livingstonia; Fort Jameson; Lilongwe; and Blantyre, where Burkitt spoke at a meeting and performed some operations.

The next stage, south from Blantyre, was extremely difficult. They had planned to drive southwest to Salisbury, but this proved impossible: the Zambesi was too low and the ferry across it had stopped running. They then drove due south, mostly over dirt roads, to Dona Ana, where they put the stationwagon on a goods train and crossed the Zambesi over what was then the longest bridge in the world. They resumed driving, thought they were lost (because their map was wrong), tried in vain to find their direction by a compass, which none of them could read, tried to find their direction by the moon, which gave them no information because it was directly overhead, and continued to drive all night until by good luck rather than intent they reached Beira, on the coast.

After a rest they turned westward to Umtali; up to Salisbury; then south to Fort Victoria and the Zimbabwe ruins, which John Gunther describes as "among the most formidable and mysterious in the world." They continued south, over Breit Bridge into Rhodesia, then through the Kruger National Park to Lourenço Marques, and westward again to Johannesburg, where they were greeted by George Oettlé.

They returned over the Breit Bridge once more, to Bulawayo; east to Wankie and Livingstone; up to Lusaka, through Broken Hill to Kitwe; then northeast across Zambia through Mpika and on to Mbeya; then up to Itigi, in the midst of more desolation, where the car had to be loaded on to a train (booked six months ahead) because the road marked on the map does not actually exist; to Tabora, where the car was unloaded; then on to Kola Ndoto (beside the Williamson diamond mines), where Cliff Nelson was working; and then to Mwanza, on the south shore of Lake Victoria. By boat, then, to Kisumu; and, finally, through torrential rain and floods, to Kampala.

At Lilongwe and Beira they saw children suffering from the tumor; but in general the hospitals they visited received no more than two or three cases a year, and it was therefore unlikely that on a given day Burkitt would find a child undergoing treatment. Some hospitals, of course, reported a much higher incidence of the disease: one, in Malawi, had admitted five patients in the preceding six months, while another in Tanzania had admitted six patients in three months. A pathologist in Lourenço Marques, Dr. Prates, had seen no less than forty children with the disease in the past four years, and he had assembled a remarkable collection of plaster models of some of these children, cast for him by the curator of the city museum. "An unusual form of medical witness," Burkitt calls this collection, and he was fascinated by it.

Everywhere he went, Burkitt gave lectures, held conferences with doctors, nurses, and medical assistants, explaining what had brought him so far and what he was seeking. The principal purpose of the safari was not simply to visit hospitals reporting the tumor but *to discover where each patient was living when the tumor first manifested itself.* The location of the hospital was of secondary importance: it might be ten, twenty, forty miles away. "We got a great deal of information from records," Burkitt says: "We were able to examine case sheets and find out where patients came from; and a doctor might tell us, *Yes, we have seen a number of these cases and they all came from that valley down there.*" And this was what Burkitt needed to know in order to establish the edge he was seeking: exactly where the tumor occurred. The safari was really a highly ambitious exercise in geographic pathology.

Several theories to explain the peculiar incidence of the tumor had already been put forward by various people. One theory was that the tumor belt across equatorial Africa, and the tail extending south, corresponded to areas of radioactivity. Another theory suggested that the tumor might be related to diet; and yet another theory implicated mineral deposits, or a *lack* of mineral deposits—such as molybdenum.

As the old stationwagon trundled down to Johannesburg a new idea emerged. The three men sitting together on the front seat of the Jubilee had an advantage denied to most scientists: time—long uninterrupted stretches of time, time to think and time to talk. "We discussed things as we went along," Burkitt says. "We were enjoying ourselves, and we'd talk about all the things we'd seen. I don't know who thought of it first, whether it was Cliff or Ted or me—although I imagine that Ted and Cliff probably made a much bigger contribution than I did—but we suddenly realized that we weren't finding *an edge* to the belt. *We were finding an altitude barrier.*"

What they had found was this: the tumor might be common in a particular area but—depending upon the locality—it stopped at a certain altitude.

Near the equator the tumor stopped at about 5,000 feet. *No cases occurred above this height.*

In Malawi (then Nyasaland), farther away from the equator, the altitude barrier was at 3,000 feet. *No cases occurred above this height.*

In Swaziland, still farther away from the equator, the altitude barrier fell to only 1,000 feet. *No cases occurred above this height.*

It was a remarkable finding, based entirely on the long careful process of establishing precisely where the tumor occurred. It was also a puzzling finding: why should a malignant tumor of human beings be dependent on *the altitude* at which those human beings lived?

Later, Burkitt wrote about this discovery, "In retrospect, I realize that relating the tumor to altitude was the result of the unhurried discussions possible on road travel but denied to the air traveler. I would almost certainly have missed the point had I traveled alone."

Back in Kampala there was, again, great interest in this new development. A human malignant tumor, a deadly human cancer, dependent upon altitude? Nobody had ever heard of such a thing, or even suspected such a thing. The ten thousand-mile safari in the old Jubilee stationwagon had proven to be more than worthwhile. Denis Burkitt, Ted Williams, and Cliff Nelson had contributed something original to medical science.

Their discovery was then taken a stage further by another of Burkitt's friends and colleagues, Professor A. J. Haddow, Director of the East African Virus Research Institute at Entebbe.

Haddow looked at Burkitt's findings and put another interpretation upon them. True, there was an altitude barrier. True, no cases occurred above a certain height, depending on the distance from the equator. But when the various altitudes were checked against the pattern of climate, Haddow showed that the altitude barrier was in fact *a temperature barrier, and the tumor did not occur where the temperature fell below about 60° F*. Therefore, where the temperature commonly fell below 60° F, children were unlikely to develop this tumor; where the temperature was commonly above 60° F the tumor was likely to occur. And this explained the strange business of altitude, for, obviously, the nearer you were to the equator the higher you had to go to reach the tumor-free zones where the temperature dropped below 60° F. Conversely, tumor-free areas, with a temperature below 60° F, were found at lower and lower altitudes the farther you traveled from the equator.

The excitement of discovery still ran high—perhaps even higher. Never before had a malignant tumor of human beings been related to climatic temperature. It was a milestone in geographic pathology.

"When we had reached that point," Burkitt says, "with such encouraging results, I felt a little more daring; and I asked if I could look around a little further. In fact, I asked if I could go to West Africa and see what was happening there. This was a short trip. I was there for only three weeks."

The same preliminary work had been done, of course:

mission and government hospitals had received Burkitt's questionnaires, letters had passed to and fro. And once more his characteristic method of investigation produced some striking and mysterious findings.

The tumor was common in the southern part of Nigeria.

But around Kano, a heavily populated area five hundred miles from Lagos, the tumor was exceedingly rare.

Something of the same sort happened in neighboring Ghana. The tumor could be found everywhere, except around Accra, on the coast.

And again Alex Haddow was able to provide an explanation.

This time the governing factor was rainfall. Government maps and statistical tables showed that in southern Nigeria and Ghana the annual rainfall is from 200 to 400 inches.

Kano, however, is close to the Sahara Desert, and it is in a local dry area (called by climatologists a rain shadow) with no more than 10 to 20 inches of rain a year.

Similarly, Accra is the driest part of the African coast, with an annual rainfall that is almost negligible.

The tumor had now been found to be dependent upon two factors: temperature and rainfall. It was a very unusual tumor indeed.

As a scientist one still had to be cautious. One could not, merely on the basis of two safaris, leap to conclusions. Some great matters were at stake here—insights, perhaps, into the mysteries of other forms of cancer.

So a third safari was planned, to the Republic of Rwanda; and for a number of reasons Burkitt's findings in Rwanda could be expected to settle the issues, one way or another.

Rwanda is one of the world's newest nations: until 1962

it was part of a sort of duplex nation, Rwanda-Urundi, under UN trusteeship administered by Belgium. It is approximately the size of Maryland, or Haiti, and it is the most densely populated country in Africa. It lies to the southwest of Uganda: the Republic of the Congo is to its west, and on the south is Burundi, which to the confusion of many Europeans was formerly Urundi. The Nile is considered to rise in the headwaters of Kagera River, which flows into Lake Victoria; and Rwanda is famous, additionally, for its giant Batusi (or Watusi), some of whom are more than seven and a half feet tall, and—at the other end of the human scale—its Batwa (or pygmies), most of whom are between four and five feet tall.

Essentially, Rwanda is a high plateau bristling with mountains, and with a great many beautiful lakes. John Gunther describes the road from Kisenyi to the capital, Astera (now Kigali), as "the most spectacular and dangerous I have ever traveled on." Lake Kivu, which forms part of the western border with the Congo, is typical of the region: it is 4,790 feet above sea level, and crocodiles (so the people living on the lakeshore say) cannot survive because the water is several degrees too cold for them.

In this high, heavily populated area, Burkitt could find no evidence of the tumor; no hospitals had seen it. Furthermore, many of the hospitals made a practice of sending specimens of tumor tissue to Mulago Hospital for identification, and Burkitt's tumor had never been reported. It simply did not occur at this altitude, where the temperature consistently falls below 60° F.

The story was different at Bujumbura, the capital of Burundi, about 250 miles from the equator on the extreme northeast corner of Lake Tanganyika. Bujumbura is comparatively low. Its altitude is only 2,625 feet and its climate is hot and humid. Here, sure enough, the tumor was found to occur. The pattern held good: Rwanda and Bujumbura, for all intents and purposes, clinched the argument.

We make use of maps of many different kinds: maps showing the physical features of some particular territory—its shape, its national boundaries, its cities and villages, its mountains and its lakes and its rivers; maps showing geological data, or population patterns, or vegetation, or mineral deposits; maps showing the incidence of various forms of disease.

The map in Burkitt's office, dotted with hand-painted drawing pins, summarized all the evidence he had gathered in East Africa, West Africa, Rwanda, and finally Bujumbura.

Professor Haddow could provide a similar map, but by different means. Burkitt describes how he did it: "Alex looked at my map and said to himself, *What must I do to Africa to get a map like that?* And he found that if he rubbed chalk all over a map of Africa and then wiped off those areas where the rainfall was below 30 inches and the temperature fell below 60° F, he was left with an almost exact duplicate of my tumor map, simply on these factors of temperature and rainfall." This, of course, corresponded to the findings so far.

But Haddow went a step further. He asked himself, *What other map of Africa would have a similar pattern, with such emphasis on the factors of temperature and rainfall?* The answer was (and it came fairly easily to Professor Haddow because he is an entomologist): *an insect map of Africa.*

As luck would have it, Burkitt and Haddow were unable to lay their hands on a map of African mosquitoes, but in an old book on tsetse flies they found a map which fitted Burkitt's tumor map almost exactly. This did not implicate the tsetse fly because in many regions it had been wiped out since the book was printed: the map merely served to demonstrate that one insect, at least, could be related to those factors of rainfall and temperature associated with the tumor.

So there was now a *hint*, a *possibility*, that the tumor might be related to some insect. One had to be exceedingly cautious when one expressed this idea because nothing had been proven. Burkitt and Haddow only had a *suspicion* of a relationship, nothing more.

But another piece of evidence was added to the jigsaw puzzle as the result of the outbreak in 1959 of a disease called o'nyong nyong fever. This epidemic was, indeed, so severe that it has found a place in medical history, like the great influenza epidemics of 1918 and 1957. The disease causes the patient to feel that all his bones are broken (it is similar to dandy or breakbone fever), but it is rarely fatal.

Burkitt has given a vivid description of the epidemic: "It started in northwest Uganda. It raged across northern Uganda, affecting 98 percent of the population, *but when it reached an altitude of 5,000 feet it stopped*. It went around Lake Victoria. It went into part of southern Uganda. It went into Tanganyika. And everywhere it seemed to stop at about the same level as the tumor."

What is most interesting about o'nyong nyong fever is that it is caused by a virus; and this virus is carried by a mosquito. Professor J. N. P. Davies had already pointed out to Burkitt that his tumor map resembled a yellow fever map; and yellow fever, too, is caused by a virus carried by a mosquito. And at temperatures below 60° F the yellow fever viruses are unable to replicate themselves.

Nobody dared to say that Burkitt's tumor was actually

caused by a virus carried by mosquitoes.* Conclusive evidence was lacking. The circumstantial evidence, though, was enough to arouse excitement not only in Kampala but all over the world.

So Mr. Burkitt and his good friends and colleagues, working with research grants amounting to £275, riding around in an ancient Ford Jubilee stationwagon, seemed to have hit some kind of a jackpot. Here, for the first time, was a form of cancer that had every appearance of being related to an infection. "Once this thing got going," Burkitt says, "it went like a bombshell. I often say to people that if a boy goes on a picnic, and boils an egg, and by mistake sets fire to the prairie, you don't scold him, because he only meant to boil an egg. I am rather like that boy, only the fire went in a different way, and I really don't deserve any more credit than the boy deserves blame. But the fire went up. And it went up very quickly."

* Scientists prefer to use the term "arthropod." The arthropods include the *crustaceans* (lobsters, crayfish, crabs, shrimps, water fleas, and barnacles), the *arachnids* (spiders, scorpions, ticks, and mites), and *insects*, which are the largest class of all. Certain viruses carried by arthropods are called arboviruses, a piece of scientific shorthand derived from "*ar*thropod-*bo*rne."

Interlude: You Cross the Nile at Pakwach

One of the most significant clues to Denis Burkitt's character is his capacity for friendship. In the course of conversation he refers to his friends constantly, with great pride and with great affection. Many of them, of course, are in some branch of medicine; many of them share his religious beliefs; many of them have shared his African experience. "We have a full house," he wrote in a recent letter, "more than our six bedrooms can hold. We are often like this, and we give thanks that we have a home to which folks can come." In little more than two years, six hundred of his friends came to visit, by invitation or, as he says, "by just turning up."

Dr. E. H. Williams, chief engineer on the great tumor safari, belongs to the large group of men and women whom Burkitt refers to, broadly, as his best friends. The two men first met in 1948, but Ted Williams had encountered various members of the Burkitt family much earlier.

"I was born in Nairobi," he explains. "My father was in the Civil Service, and he was a personal friend of Denis's Uncle Roland—the first practicing surgeon in East Africa and a very remarkable man. I grew up with William Burkitt, the son of the great Dr. Burkitt (as we used to call him), and I remember the doctor saying in my presence, when I was a boy, that the Burkitts could trace their ancestry back to the Norman invasion of Ireland. They are very strong characters, these Burkitts."

The same can be said of the Williams family. Very strong characters. Very remarkable men.

Kuluva Hospital, where Dr. Ted Williams and Dr. Peter Williams live with their families, is about eight miles from the little township of Arua, in northwest Uganda. It is so far to the north that it is close to the border of Uganda and the Sudan, and so far to the west that it is very close to the border of Uganda and the Congo. It is remote, very remote. Many maps show Arua simply as a dot, with no roads leading to it; but this has changed. There are roads now, bumpy but passable.

The easiest way to reach Kuluva Hospital is to rent a plane in Kampala and fly the three hundred miles to Arua. That, however, is a costly way to travel, and it is more sensible to rent a car. It is still more sensible to engage a driver with your rented car, for even in fair weather the roads are treacherous and you are likely to encounter some unexpected hazards.

Your first stop will be at Masindi, 130 miles from Kampala, where there is a fine old colonial hotel with broad verandas and well-kept grounds, and where you can enjoy a cup of exceptionally good Ugandan coffee. Linger and savor the brew, because the opportunity will not occur again. Then you drive north to the Murchison Falls National Park, and if you are new to Africa you must turn off to see the Falls. They are magnificent. At this point the Victoria Nile is constricted from about half a mile in width to a few yards, and the wild, foaming water then plunges about a hundred and fifty feet and pours on—full of crocodiles, and giant perch weighing a hundred pounds or more, and bilharzia—to enter Lake Albert at Fort Magungo.

Your second stop will be at Paraa Lodge, which is usually crowded beyond its capacity and where you may have to wait an hour or so for a rather indifferent sandwich and a bottle of soapy Ugandan beer. Elephant and hippo come right up to the lodge, and you are warned, a little ironically, not to feed them. But you would be unwise to skip Paraa because it, and Masindi, are the only hotels on your route: you have no other choice.

Murchison Falls National Park is vast—miles and miles and miles of boring scrub. There seem to be great numbers of elephants, and since the park is not fenced in you will see herds of them outside the park boundaries. To someone who is not elephant-obsessed they appear to be brooding, malevolent, mountainous gray hulks, inhabiting a world of their own. In a herd they look like a slightly animated Stonehenge. They require, as an item of diet, a mineral contained in the bark of the local trees, and you drive through extensive areas of the park which look as if they have been devastated by ceaseless bombardment: every tree has been stripped of its bark by the elephants, every tree is grotesquely dead, every branch is gaunt, yellow, leafless, and the scene is one of utter desolation. If you are a student of ecology or a subscriber to the *New Statesman* you might immediately assume that this is another tragic example of the way man rapes and ruins his environment; but, no. Nature has been raped and ruined here by her own pet pipe-nosed pachyderms.

At certain times of the year, too, you will drive through a succession of bush fires, set by the game wardens in order to burn off the old sour grass and bring up new grass, which will attract the park animals so that they can be seen and admired by tourists. It is an eerie experience, driving into a dense cloud of black smoke and crackling flame and coming out upon a screeching assembly of birds—huge marabou storks, demoiselle cranes, kites, even secretary birds, picking off the insects and small animals fleeing the fire. Scavengers. They resent you, and you soon learn to resent them.

When you leave the northern gate of the park you enter tsetse fly territory (and on your return trip some lackadaisical guards will flick the inside of your car with long whisks to make sure you have not acquired any of these pestiferous creatures, the carriers of sleeping sickness). Now you will see herdsmen riding bicycles and carrying nine-foot spears, terribly dangerous weapons with a broad spearhead at one end and a long, sharp spike at the other end; and if you ask your driver why the men carry these things he will tell you, "To defend themselves." "To defend themselves against what?" "Their enemies," the driver will say; but he may then admit that the spears are to kill any game that strays out of the park. It is forbidden, but the people have a desperate need for meat, and there are not enough game wardens to stop the poaching. So, day by day and night by night, the animals mysteriously vanish.

You cross the Nile at Pakwach. This is the Albert Nile, flowing out of Lake Albert, but indistinguishable from any other stretch of that ancient river. Chances are good that the ferry will have broken down, and you will have to wait patiently while repairs are made. You will not be alone. There will be a long line of trucks and safari cars, and there will be scores of poor Africans waiting with you, some of them striding up and down and abusing the government in passionate tones, because the government is supposed to be responsible for running the ferries. The Nile is broad, fast-moving, and it looks dirty, perhaps because it carries a great deal of mud, as well as sewage; and you are likely to be distressed by the Africans' general indifference to self-preservation—they wade into the dirty brown water, splash it over themselves to cool off, drink cupped handfuls of it, give it to their children to drink. You can understand why they suffer from a multiplicity of frightful diseases; the mystery is how any of them manage to survive.

Once across the river you are in the West Nile District of Uganda, which stretches—as its name implies—from the west bank of the Nile to the Congo border (on the west) and to the Sudan (on the north). It is a single government administrative unit, according to Dr. Williams, with a population of about half a million comprising four main tribes, and its area is slightly less than that of Wales. The scenery is a welcome change from the flat scrub of the national park: it is rather like the more picturesque sections of the Rhine Valley—lush and wooded, with sugarloaf mountains rising in the distance. Your driver will put on speed now, because he is uneasy in this territory on the other side of the Nile. He is among alien people whose language he cannot understand and who regard him with suspicion. From Pakwach it is some eighty miles to Kuluva Hospital, and despite the condition of the red-mud road he will cover the distance in less than an hour and a half. He will be unaware that this district has won a place in medical history, and at the back of his mind he will undoubtedly be asking himself why on earth you had to come to such a forsaken spot. Not Godforsaken. It is far from that.

Most of us exist within a small circle from which we rarely escape: certain rooms in a certain building in a certain street in a certain country. We may move from one place to another, but the change is usually insignificant. We do certain kinds of work and society rewards us with certain benefits: we have hot and cold running water and efficient disposal systems; we can obtain a variety of foods without having to carry nine-foot spears all the time; we are provided with numerous pleasures and luxuries—films, theaters, concerts, books, fine clothes, speedy automobiles; we have extensive medical facilities to care for our physical well-being, drugs to put us to sleep and drugs to wake us up. But at some time or another most of us become conscious of the smallness of our own particular circle, we are alarmed by its limitations, and we ask ourselves if this is why we were granted the miracle of life, merely to exist within such a tiny enclosure, devoid of any important challenge, devoid of spiritual or physical joy, devoid of adventure, devoid of beliefs. We wonder: What would it be like to break out of the little circle, to do work (unspecified) that will test all our muscles, to deny ourselves the enfeebling benefits and pleasures that society provides? Then, after agonizing over this prospect for a while, after some juvenile tantrums because Fate has treated us so badly, the circle quietly encloses us again and life goes on in the old settled way. We rarely escape. The traffic lights are *all* red; they remain red; and if they ever turned to green few of us would know what to do next.

The Kuluva story begins with a God-fearing wine merchant in the City of London, Mr. Hammond, who endowed several beds in the London Hospital (and made a practice of visiting them every Sunday afternoon to comfort the occupants). Among other good deeds, he became a godfather to Edward Hammond Williams and left him a legacy that helped to pay for the young man's medical education at St. Bartholomew's Hospital. Dr. Williams then went to the Mildmay Mission Hospital in the East End of London to complete his internship; here he met a nurse named Muriel Edith Mary Francis, whom he married.

In 1941 they sailed from England to Africa to begin life as missionaries. They were fortunate to arrive: the ship taking them to Cape Town narrowly missed being torpedoed by a Nazi submarine.

After three months of traveling, Ted and Muriel Williams boarded a paddle steamer on the Albert Nile and chugged upstream to Rhino Camp, in those days "a meagre collection of buildings, partly for the benefit of the East African Railways & Harbours and partly connected with a Cotton Ginnery," now a tourist landmark. They were met by two missionaries in a car named *The Yellow Peril* and driven to Arua, forty miles due west, the main mission station for the district.*

No *medical* missionaries had worked here up to this time. Dr. Williams and his wife began the venture with the barest

---

* Nobody can tell this story better than Dr. Williams himself, and much of this account is taken from a booklet written by him entitled "Probably *Not:* The Story of Kuluva," published by the Africa Inland Mission, 3 John Street, London, W.C.1, price 6d (about 6¢); unfortunately out of print. Here once more we encounter aspects of personal faith not too frequently found in descriptions of scientific discovery and accomplishment; but any reader whose chief concern is scientific enlightenment need not worry: there is plenty ahead.

minimum of equipment plus about £10 (then about $50) in funds.

"God sent a tremendous test to the faith of the two missionaries," writes Dr. Williams. "No gifts arrived to supplement the £10 capital and the meagre equipment already in hand. For three months the heavens seemed as brass, and the Faith Basis of the Mission meaningless. Nevertheless, a start was made. Two dilapidated one-room buildings were repaired, and fittings manufactured from packing cases. It seemed queer doing operations under a bare thatched roof with no protective ceiling. . . . In their home the two missionaries did not find things very thrilling: there was no glass in the windows, just a bamboo lattice; bare whitewashed walls, dusty floor, lots of white ants attacking suitcases and furniture nightly. . . . Then quite suddenly the Lord sent £50 for a car, and £300 for buildings, and other gifts which enabled much needed medical supplies to be ordered. An old car was bought for £27 10s [$137], some necessary spare parts purchased with the balance of the original gift; and this car did yeoman service for seven and a half years. . . . The element of doubt loomed large in the minds of the two missionaries. Outside observers, if asked if this venture would ever succeed, would no doubt have replied, 'Probably not.' Surely, the call, guiding and purpose seemed mistaken. Something was wrong somewhere."

What was wrong, perhaps, was human frailty: the lack of a few material things, such as money and equipment. But the first year passed, "and with it came the dawn of a new comprehension of the opportunity and challenge of the work. Soon a few small buildings were built. The doctor's wife would look after the bulk of the patients each morning, leaving a few for her husband to see in moments snatched from building operations. The afternoons were mostly spent in making window frames and hospital furniture.

"These," Dr. Williams says, "were busy and fruitful years, but not years of real expansion in the work. God's time for this had not yet come, though much was being learned, such as language, customs, people, building, car mechanics and a host of smaller things." Two daughters were born, Joy and Mollie, and Dr. Williams relates how one of them, only four years old, "slipped unnoticed into the operating theatre one day when an emergency operation for the amputation of a leg, to save the life of a little boy, was being performed. The atmosphere was tense, for it was touch and go. While the doctor's wife concentrated on giving the anesthetic, the doctor wielded knife and surgical saw with all speed, and the little girl's presence passed unnoticed until the amputation was completed. Then with a shock she was noticed. But she was merely sorry for the little boy and quite unmoved by an operation which would make the average adult go into a faint. Later, when it came to teaching the little boy to walk on crutches, the missionaries' child learned first, and then moved by her sympathy for the little boy's plight, she taught him herself."

After World War II, interest in the problem of leprosy in Africa (and elsewhere) grew considerably. Surveys showed unsuspected concentrations of leprosy victims, but at the same time the development of new drugs provided more effective treatment of the disease, which is caused by a microorganism similar to the tuberculosis bacillus.

"God also guided in the enlargement of the existing medical work in the West Nile to include leprosy, but this could not be attempted on the already overcrowded Arua station site. . . . One day a friendly chief was taken for a drive to look for a possible new site in the area under his jurisdiction. As the car was driven along a well-known stretch of land, an area of land on the right of the road suddenly seemed to take on a new significance. It was dominated by a hill, a well-known landmark, called Kuluva. Years later, piecing together the meaning of this name—"a place of strife"—and fragments of history, it seems clear that long ago a clan lived in this place who may have been from a tribe of iron-workers. Fragments of slag, the remains of an old hearth, and a primitive stone tool have been found to support this supposition. It appears that this clan, by its cruel and frequent raids on the clans around, earned their bitter hatred until one day they banded together and massacred the iron-workers. Since that time, the land had remained uninhabited, yet ready in the purpose of God for the Africa Inland Mission to occupy it decades later.

"Lease formalities for 200 acres took about a year to complete, and then one day beside the road thirty workmen were engaged to start developing the land. A road was begun, boundaries were demarcated, and work was started on a plantation of eucalyptus trees.

"It took five years to build Kuluva and develop its work. This is fairly rapid growth in Africa Inland Missionary history and is a wonderful indication of the Lord's provision and guidance. Building with bricks, mud mortar, eucalyptus poles and grass . . . between forty and fifty brick buildings, inexpensive and therefore not of too high a quality or degree of permanence, have been erected, using perhaps half a million bricks. . . .

"So bit by bit the work enlarged from the original thirty leprosy patients to a total of 350; from twelve hospital beds to forty; from 30,000 outpatient attendances a year to 70,000."

*   *   *

This was written by Dr. Williams in 1955, fourteen years after he and his wife stepped off the paddle steamer at Rhino Camp, with £10 in funds and a minimum of medical equipment.

The friendly chief who led them to Kuluva had driven south with them from Arua. Approached from this direction the "place of strife" was on the right. You, driving north from Kampala, will see the site on your left; and entering the hospital grounds by a sweeping semicircle of rough road, you will find that those two untried and inexperienced young missionaries have accomplished wonders. Kuluva is a miracle. Ted Williams has now lost count of the number of buildings he and his African workmen (recruited from neighboring villages) have erected: between fifty and sixty, he will tell you, or perhaps more. Various people have come to Kuluva to help: his brother Peter, also a doctor, specializing in ophthalmology, arrived in 1948. Soon after they were joined by their parents.*

* Dr. Williams writes, in a personal communication: "Our present staff at Kuluva consists of the following: Fourteen Ugandan dressers trained at Kuluva, two record clerks, and other ancillary workers, totaling about forty. There are two expatriate (non-Ugandan) doctors, brothers, and their wives, both registered nurses and midwives; three nursing sisters (the title given if they are both nurses and midwives), expatriate, for the hospital, two nursing sisters for the leprosy work, and one sister with special training in ophthalmology—my brother, of course, being trained in this specialty (we see a great deal of onchocerciasis). We also have an expatriate manager, and his wife, who does the accounts.

We have had perhaps 35 to 40 medical students here in the last nine years from England and America, of which perhaps a dozen have been Smith Kline and French Fellowship students. They seem to find the experience here stimulating and very worthwhile."

Every morning, before lunch, Dr. and Mrs. Williams see, on an average, some three hundred outpatients, and in the afternoons Dr. Ted performs operations. In the evenings, whenever necessary, he drives out to the villages to see those who are unable to leave their homes. Kuluva Hospital is the nearest hospital of any kind for twenty thousand people in the West Nile District. It has seventy-five beds today, and in part—but only in part—the problem of nursing is solved by having relatives come in to look after patients. In the past ten years Ted Williams has treated *seven thousand* leprosy patients, and two hundred and fifty live in villages all through the valley.

"We have always tried to have better equipment than buildings," he says. "A lot of the buildings are just sun-dried brick, and they should last about twenty years. Then we can pull them down and put up better buildings.

"But a major part of our job is to propagate our faith, and this is not a reason for practicing second-class medicine. We must practice absolutely first-class medicine; and with that goes the Christian message, which is all-important to us. Practicing first-class medicine today, though, isn't easy.

"Wherever you go in the world—even in an out-of-the-way place like this—the problems of hospitals are the problems of cost. Two-thirds of costs are wages, and we often wonder where mission hospitals will go in the future. Medical treatment gets more and more expensive. The equipment you need for tests gets more and more expensive. People who come out new to work here have no idea of economy—*what we mean by economy*. They're accustomed to all sorts of disposable things—disposable this, disposable that.

"Here, we use a disposable syringe for two months."

❂   ❂   ❂

Ted Williams' decision to become a missionary doctor can be traced directly to a child's book about David Livingstone, given to him when he was six years old and still one of his most precious possessions. Half a century after Livingstone's death his words still had the power to inspire boys and men to seek out the most inaccessible places in Africa, to bring light and hope into darkness. *Do you carry on the work I have begun. I leave it with you.*

What helped to make Ted Williams one of the leading figures in the Burkitt story can also be traced back to his boyhood: a passion for maps, acquired from his father, who was Chief Computer in the Kenya Survey Department, a title that denoted he was in charge of the mapping section. Many years later, stimulated by Denis Burkitt during the great tumor safari, Dr. Williams began to plot on large-scale maps all cases of Burkitt's lymphoma (and other malignancies, such as cancer of the liver) he encountered at Kuluva Hospital.

Obviously, if he only plotted where the disease was first reported, it would appear that all cases had occurred at the hospital itself (and absurd as it seems, this is the way statistics are assembled in some areas). The key factor is *where the child lived when he or she showed the first signs of the disease.* "It's easy for me," Dr. Williams says. "With every one of my cases, after I've treated the child I take him, or her, home myself. So I know exactly where that child came from. And this *detailed plotting* is of tremendous importance. It is something that should be done by all missionary doctors who live and work for a lengthy period in underdeveloped countries."

The reason is that virtually all underdeveloped countries are now in process of development. In most parts of Africa the pattern of life is changing with extraordinary speed. Until recently, for example, the population of a fairly remote region like the West Nile District was relatively stable. Few people ever traveled more than a few miles from the village where they were born, simply because the means for travel were unavailable. Even a cheap bicycle was far beyond the means of the average man.

Now there is a daily bus to Kampala, and it has been estimated that about thirty thousand West Nilers travel to Kampala every year. Furthermore, the government is building a magnificent bridge across the Nile at Pakwach, to carry a railroad as well as cars and bicycles and pedestrians, and the old, inefficient ferry will soon be forgotten. People will move freely from place to place in Uganda, as they do anywhere else in the world; and as a consequence, keeping track of any disease will become increasingly difficult.

"We have perhaps ten years left here in which to do the detailed mapping of cases of cancer," Ted Williams explains. "I don't know the precise significance of my plotting. But we can say with certainty that *there*, on that spot on the map, a case of some particular kind of cancer occurred. And some indication of the value of this work is that the East African Virus Research Institute is making a copy of every one of my maps, so that there will be two records in existence."

By pure luck he works in a district which has an unusually high incidence of Burkitt's lymphoma: two to four times higher than elsewhere in Uganda, and higher, possibly, than anywhere in the world. It is not lucky that so many West Nile children develop the disease; it *is* lucky, and perhaps providential, that Dr. Williams happens to be there and can do something useful about the disease—treating its victims and helping to find the means to put an end to it. And his observations, his thinking, the evidence of his maps, have attracted scores of cancer scientists to Kuluva. "There is a tremendous concentration of scientists in this district at the moment," he said at the end of December 1968. "Investigators from the (British) Imperial Cancer Research Fund have come up four times this year, and they've carried out biological surveys on six hundred children. The Director of the East African Virus Research Institute, Dr. G. W. Kafuko, has been up here five times this year doing malaria surveys. Entomologists from the Institute came once a month to supervise mosquito catching: for two years they caught mosquitoes every single night in different parts of the district, and up to the end of last year they did special mosquito catches at every single home where Burkitt's lymphoma has occurred. These mosquitoes were sent back on ice; they were typed (that is, classified); and they were then ground up and examined for viruses. We don't have anything very dramatic yet, but we've established a pattern of viruses that are carried by mosquitoes, and you can draw a map of the West Nile showing these factors."

The maps display other factors, too. South of Arua there is a large area which is of great interest because no cases of Burkitt's lymphoma have occurred in it—a so-called "negative" or "blank" area. "In this blank area of ours," says Dr. Williams, "there are hardly any cattle. Up north, where most cases of the tumor occur, there are lots of cattle."

"Or, again, in the blank area there are no eucalyptus trees. In the tumor area up north there are lots of eucalyptus trees.

"Or, another curious thing: I've mapped the way tobacco cultivation has increased in this district. The tobacco plant, as everybody knows, harbors certain viruses. And it's very interesting that there is an almost 100 percent correlation between where Burkitt's tumor has occurred in the last sixteen or seventeen years, and how it has widened out, and how tobacco cultivation has widened out.

"Then there's the charnockite theory. Charnockite is a peculiar kind of rock, and if you plot charnockite formations on a map and compare them with the occurrence of Burkitt's tumor, there is a similarity: so much so that the information has been sent to London for computer analysis. It may turn out to be a factor.

"None of these things, so far, mean anything in themselves. But one day they may provide an important clue, and I just keep my eyes open for them, that's all."

The first time Ted Williams saw a child suffering from Burkitt's tumor was in 1942, one year after he and his wife arrived in Arua. He took photographs and—like Denis Burkitt fifteen years later—found himself puzzled by the child's condition. He continued to see cases of the disease year after year, and they continued to puzzle him. "I can show you some notes I made on a case in 1953: I couldn't make out why the child had a tumor of its orbit (the eye socket) and a tumor of the abdomen. On another card, my brother has written, *What IS this peculiar cancer?* We sent tissue specimens to the laboratories, and they couldn't help us."

This was a period, in Ted Williams' opinion, when cancer research found itself in a blind alley. "Researchers were reading papers *to* each other, writing papers *for* each other, and getting nowhere.

"Then Denis Burkitt came along. The great thing about Denis was that first and foremost he was a clinician, actually working with patients in a hospital. He broke out of the normal pattern of research (which is generally carried on in a laboratory) by observing *as a clinician* a tumor occurring in several sites in children. He went outside the laboratory, again, to track this tumor down, to find where and how it occurred; then he passed this information on to the laboratory researchers so that they could define what the tumor was.

"What he did, in fact, was to alter the whole concept of research. He showed that the clinicians, particularly people who work for a long time in one place—as we missionaries do—are in a position to assemble a great deal of unique and extremely valuable information.

"I can say this for myself: For years, research was something one read about in scientific journals. It required a lot of expensive equipment, and one never thought that one could start any kind of useful research in a remote place like this. It was Denis Burkitt who put me (and many other people in similar situations) on to the idea that *the research material is right here where we're working.*"

Ted and Muriel Williams live in a sort of bungalow—the last building to be completed in their building program. The living room is large and low and comfortable, and filled with the warmth of the people who live in it. Dr. Ted sits in an old armchair, surrounded by books and papers and maps and photographs, and he is perfectly willing to talk to you half the night, until his voice cracks with tiredness.

He cannot predict the future of Kuluva Hospital, or even his own future. Eventually, he tells you, all medical services in Uganda will be nationalized, and it is probable that Kuluva will be taken over by the government. "We should realize that we may not be here in ten years' time in our present form. We get some money from the government now, but we often wonder when it will stop. The Ugandans, perhaps rightly, feel we shouldn't be earning money that should go to Ugandans."

Meanwhile the work goes on: the healing and comforting of the sick, the promulgation of faith, the various research projects, the maps, the endless asking of questions. And the great tumor safari is very fresh in his memory. He laughs in wonderment as he recalls it. "The total cost of that piece of research work," he says, "including buying the car, having it thoroughly overhauled before we started on the trip, then selling it for a lower price afterwards; including our meals and staying at rest houses (and, to our consternation, staying at the best hotel in Johannesburg when we arrived there because our friends had booked us into it); *the total cost* of that trip was £650.

"At the time it was about two thousand dollars; and that's what Smith Kline and French give one student on a fellowship to come here for ten weeks. There were three of us on that safari; and I would think that at £650 it's the cheapest piece of major research of this century."

10

Bombshell

We have to bear in mind that Uganda is, after all, a relatively small country. Its capital, Kampala, is a relatively small city, not very well known outside Africa. Mulago Hospital is the teaching hospital of East Africa and thus an exceedingly important institution, but few medical men in Europe or America are aware of its importance or even of its existence.

So it seems improbable that the scientific world would be wildly excited by the news that one of the surgeons—the third in order of seniority, to be precise—in distant Mulago Hospital, in Darkest Africa, had come upon an unusual tumor affecting only a few hundred children a year. True, as Burkitt said, "Once this thing got going it went like a bombshell"; the miracle is that the news actually reached the outside world, that there was an opportunity for it to *get going*, instead of being totally ignored, as so often happens. One thinks of the Abbé Mendel, working patiently in his monastery garden in Brünn: his Laws of inheritance were published in 1866 and 1869, and went unnoticed until they were discovered by the Dutch botanist De Vries in 1900. Or, on another order, one thinks of Alexander Fleming, who in 1928 discovered penicillin by a chance observation (it happened to be the chance observation of a genius) and then had to wait ten years for further investigation of his findings.

Scientists do not deliberately ignore each other's work. There is no conspiracy to prevent the spread of medical knowledge. The problem is simple: such a torrent of scientific papers pours out of medical centers all over the world that it is utterly impossible for any human being to keep up with what is going on even in his own special field. Unless a discovery is of obvious importance, the likelihood is that it will pass unnoticed. Or it may attract attention briefly and then disappear in the deluge of the next day's papers.

It is interesting, consequently, to see with what generosity Providence treated Denis Burkitt.

He first discussed the tumor informally, without a paper, at one of the Saturday morning staff meetings in Mulago Hospital.

"I first presented it *officially*," he says, "at the annual meeting of the East African Association of Surgeons, in January 1958, at Kampala."

The emphasis here is on *surgeons*, and this becomes more apparent in the next stage of the story, for Burkitt's first published article on the tumor was in the *British Journal of Surgery*, in 1959. "I wanted to publish in a surgical journal because I was a surgeon," he explains, "although some of my colleagues said I should have published in a journal of pathology." For once his colleagues were right and he was wrong.

"It was received with a complete lack of interest. It didn't strike a bell with anybody." *

The next paper was written in collaboration with J. N. P. Davies, Professor of Pathology at Makerere University College Medical School. It was published in 1961. If the first paper was printed in a surgical journal because Mr. Burkitt was a surgeon, one can predict with a fair degree of certainty where he would wish the second paper to be printed; and one would be absolutely right. It appeared in an Irish journal called the *Medical Press,* which had asked Burkitt for a contribution. "This paper," he says with a bright Irish smile, "created a *little* interest."

The third paper was written by Burkitt and Dr. G. T. O'Conor, another member of the Department of Pathology at Makerere. It, too, appeared in 1961, but this time Burkitt was on the right track. He chose the periodical *Cancer,* published in Philadelphia, which is read by cancer experts not only in the United States but internationally. The same issue carried another article about the lymphoma, written by Dr. O'Conor; and it was these two articles that really sparked interest in Burkitt's work. "After these papers came out," he says, "people said, *This is something.* There were leaders in *The New York Times,* and so on; and we were flooded with requests for reprints."

* Medical readers may like to know of Burkitt's other papers. They are given here with his comments: "A Simple Serviceable Artificial Leg" (*E. A. Med. J.,* 1953). *This is still being made sixteen years later.* "A Boot and Caliper Bank" (*E. A. Med. J.,* 1960). *This has been modified since.* "A Simple Crutch" (*B. Med. J.,* 1961). *This has been very rewarding and very widely used.* "Subcutaneous Phycomycosis" (with other authors: *B. Med. J.,* 1964). "Relics of Tradition" (*E. A. Med. J.,* 1965). *Very provocative.*

Altogether, a total of four papers, published in less than two years, made Burkitt's tumor known to cancer scientists all over the world.

And in this way the bombshell went off.

One can ask, Precisely why did the news of Burkitt's tumor produce such a strong reaction in the world community of cancer scientists? What, really, was so special, so significant, so unusual, about a disease that afflicts no more than a few hundred African children every year? What made Burkitt's tumor so much more exciting to cancer scientists than, say, cancer of the lung, which kills about sixty thousand people a year in the United States alone, or cancer of the stomach, which kills vast numbers of people in such widely separated countries as Japan and Chile and Finland and Austria?

The answers are remarkably interesting; but we have to arrive at them by a rather roundabout route. Some of the answers, indeed, can only be given when more of the Burkitt story has been told.

There is no need to stress the fact that cancer is a major problem of mankind. In most developed countries, where people have a span of life approaching the Biblical threescore years and ten, it is the second leading cause of death, after heart disease. We fear it because its effects are grim, and also because it seems to attack us without rhyme or reason (except where there is a clear relationship, as in cancer of the lung, which is for the most part directly associated with the smoking of cigarettes). At the time Burkitt began his investigations only one form of cancer, called choriocarcinoma, could be cured by means of drugs alone, in a certain percentage of cases. Other forms of the disease could be cured only by means of surgery or radiotherapy, when these techniques could be applied. In general, drugs were held to be palliative; they helped to suppress the disease, they helped to extend the patient's life, but they were not by themselves curative.

Cancer does not occur without rhyme or reason, of course. It is subject, like everything else, to the laws of nature, and although it has many mysterious aspects we can be fairly certain that sooner or later these mysteries will be solved. We cannot say when: perhaps within twenty-five years, perhaps not for two hundred and fifty years. If we can walk on the moon, if we can take close-up photographs of Mars, then we can learn what causes cells to behave abnormally. Meanwhile, every clue, every lead, is of value.

In effect the rational study of cancer began in 1915, when two Japanese scientists at the University of Tokyo, Professor K. Yamagiwa and Professor K. Ichikawa, were able to induce skin cancer in rabbits by dabbing the ears with coal tar. Dabbing the ears once, twice, a dozen times, was insufficient. The process had to be continued regularly for more than six months.

Fifteen years later, Sir Ernest Kennaway, working with several colleagues in London, found one of the substances in coal tar which causes skin cancer. Its name is uninspiring, but it is renowned in medical history: 3,4-benzpyrene.

The importance of these discoveries was that, for the first time, scientists had the means to study cancer in the laboratory. They could produce skin cancer in controlled tests on certain animals; they could follow the progress of skin cancer from the first tissue changes to the ultimate malignancy.

From this beginning, immense benefits have been won. We now know many causes of skin cancer—excessive exposure to sunlight is possibly the most serious; but, more significant than anything else, we have learned that cancer is not always an unmitigated disaster. In the United States some 110,000 cases of skin cancer are reported in a year. Of these, only about 5,000 will be fatal; 105,000 will be cured.

This high cure rate is easily explained. Skin cancer occurs on the outer surface of the body, where it is readily seen and can be effectively treated. The changes in the skin usually take place over a long period of time—as much as twenty to forty years—and they are not likely to be overlooked.

It would be wonderful if all cancers could be recognized as easily, and could be treated with the same degree of success. The obvious problem with cancers occurring below the surface of the body is that frequently they remain completely hidden from view: they do not even manifest themselves as a lump. The early changes take place "silently"—that is, they are painless and produce no symptoms; and in adults a malignancy may progress for a long time before it is diagnosed. Cancer of the stomach, for example, may take about twenty-five years to mature. A man may begin to smoke cigarettes at the age of sixteen, and cancer of the lung is not likely to manifest itself until he is in his forties. In certain other forms of cancer the induction time may be as long as fifty years.

The cancer researcher is thus faced with peculiar difficulties. Assume that he is investigating stomach cancer. The only effective treatment for this disease at present is surgery. *If we could learn what causes stomach cancer* we might then take steps to prevent it from occurring at all.

But how can the scientist go about the task of finding the cause of this particular malignancy? Where can he begin? First and foremost, he is faced with the fact that the disease matures very slowly, over a period of twenty-five years or so. He cannot *predict* that it will strike a certain person. He cannot *see* the early changes leading to the growth of the tumor. He is unable to acquire vital information about the individual's condition when these early changes began to occur—about diet, allergies, vitamin deficiencies, and a thousand and one other factors that might affect the malignant process.*

Probably the most perplexing of all forms of cancer are the lymphomas (which were described earlier) and leukemia.

The name "leukemia" means "white blood condition," and it is actually a generic term for a number of different kinds of cancer that for the most part affect the white blood cells. In the United States about fourteen thousand adults and children die of leukemia each year. One way of classifying the different forms is according to the length of time the patient lives after the disease is recognizable: *acute,* less than six months; *sub-acute,* up to about a year; *chronic,* more than a year.

Chronic leukemia is the form most common in adults. It develops very slowly, and may continue for three years or more. In some patients the disease can be controlled very well, and many cases have been reported of patients who have lived for ten years or more after their disease was first diagnosed.

Acute leukemia is the form most common in children, although it may also affect adults. Without treatment the course of the disease is often exceedingly rapid, but new

---

* This is purely a hypothetical example. Research has not been able to pinpoint the cause, or causes, of stomach cancer, but much has been learned about it indirectly. It is "associated" with diet—with an excessive intake of starchy foods such as rice or potatoes; it is also "associated" with an excessive intake of smoked foods. Other "associations" are pernicious anemia, vitamin A deficiency, and peptic ulcers. Obviously, research on stomach cancer is exceedingly difficult, and we may have to wait some time to learn how it is caused.

drugs and new techniques can now help to extend life very considerably.

In the past quarter of a century there has been a concentration of research on leukemia. Again and again, scientists appeared to be close to a cure for one form of the disease or another; again and again the hope has been frustrated. Most disappointing, leukemia in all its forms is still a total mystery. We know that it can arise from excessive exposure to radiation, and possibly from the action of certain chemicals, particularly benzene; but these can cause only a tiny fraction of all the cases of leukemia occurring throughout the world. We have to admit that the cause, or causes, of human leukemia are unknown; and yet there is widespread confidence today that we are close to finding *a cause*. The magic word is "viruses."

In 1908, fifty years before Denis Burkitt set off on his first tumor safari, two Danish scientists, Wilhelm Ellermann and Olaf Bang, transmitted leukemia from one chicken to another by injecting a fluid obtained by filtering blood and tissue that had been affected by the disease. The fluid contained no leukemic cells (and is therefore called a cell-free filtrate), and the scientists concluded that the "infectious agent" which passed from one chicken to the other in this fluid must be a virus.

There was little progress in leukemia-virus research for the next forty years. In 1951, Dr. Ludwik Gross of New York, following a lead provided by Dr. Gilbert Dalldorf, was able to induce leukemia in newborn mice by means of a cell-free filtrate obtained from mice suffering from leukemia. Again, the conditions of the experiment were such that the infectious agent could only be a virus.

Subsequently, researchers found more than two dozen

viruses related in some way to murine leukemia (that is, leukemia occurring in rats or mice, as distinct from avian leukemia, which occurs in fowl and other birds). Particles that have the *appearance* of viruses have been found in a variety of animals—cats, dogs, and cattle.

Scientists could now argue that since viruses cause certain kinds of leukemia in animals, there is a strong possibility that viruses might be the cause of certain kinds of leukemia in man; and, in fact, several scientists have reported seeing "virus particles" in human leukemic tissue examined with the electron microscope. But evidence of this sort is very difficult to assess. True, the viruses may be *in* the leukemic tissue. How can we prove, though, that these viruses *caused* the leukemia? The difficulty is that we cannot take these virus particles (even if we could obtain them in sufficient numbers) and inject them into human beings. If we attempted to do so, and if the virus particles actually caused leukemia in a human being, the experiment would be legally tantamount to murder, for to all intents and purposes acute leukemia is invariably fatal.

Burkitt and his colleagues supplied the breakthrough. Those two papers published in *Cancer* in 1961 must have seemed sensational to all scientists who had been working on the mystery of leukemia. There was still no absolute and final proof. Nothing was yet certain. But that remarkable company of men, Denis Burkitt and Ted Williams and Cliff Nelson and Jack Davies and Greg O'Conor, had come up with a human lymphoma which *appeared* to be dependent on certain factors of temperature and rainfall. From these findings arose the *suspicion* that some arthropod *might* be implicated as the carrier of an infectious agent which *played a part* in causing the disease; and the evidence *suggested* that the arthropod *might very well* be a mosquito; and that the infectious agent *might very well* be a virus.

Scientists, particularly cancer scientists, have to be exceedingly cautious. Unless the proof is absolutely indisputable they must guard any statement with multitudes of qualifying phrases. Nevertheless, there could be no mistaking the significance of Burkitt's tumor. If a virus seemed to be involved in this particular form of human lymphoma, a virus (but not necessarily the same virus) might be involved in some forms of human leukemia. And—to carry the thought a stage further, to its supreme conclus n—many diseases caused by viruses can be controlled by neans of vaccines.

It was tremendous news, when its implications were understood. With very good reason, it e ed in scientific circles (as Mr. Burkitt said) like a bombshell; and there were more bombshells to come.

Denis and Olive Burkitt.

The old pick-up truck
taking patients to
Lira Hospital.

The operating theatre
in Lira Hospital.

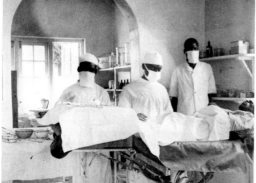

The magnificent new Mulago Hospital in Kampala, Uganda. The old
Mulago Hospital is visible near the top left-hand corner.

Old Mulago Hospital, Kampala.

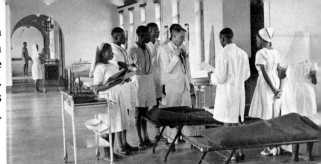

Dr. Hugh Trowell with some of his African medical students in the old Mulago Hospital. The photograph was taken in 1950.

Denis Burkitt.

Dr. Clifford Nelson, Dr. E. H. Williams, and D. P. Burkitt at the start of the long safari.

Torrential rains made roads virtually impassable on the last hundred miles of the long safari.

The "Lymphoma Belt"

━━━ Route of the
      long safari

● Areas where there are several cases.

△ Areas where the tumour is known to be common but where there is no
  specific documentation.

Dr. and Mrs. E. H. Williams in a busy section of Kuluva Hospital. In the background are medical assistants, patients, and relatives of patients who help with the nursing.

Dr. E. H. Williams (right), standing beside his Land Rover, looks across at Mount Wati in the West Nile District of Uganda. A remarkable cluster of twelve cases of Burkitt's lymphoma occurred here in 1966-67.

A group of twelve children (below), treated by Denis Burkitt, in total remission from Burkitt's lymphoma after chemotherapy.

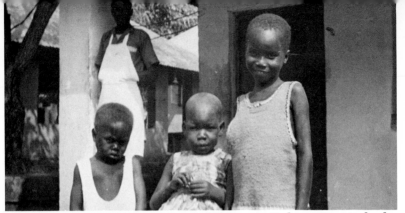

Three children at Kuluva Hospital who responded extremely well to a new method of treatment discovered by Dr. E. H. Williams, combining cytoxan (cyclophosphamide) with potassium iodide. The taller boy, on the right, was a very severe case: He had a jaw tumor, a spinal tumor which caused complete paralysis, a tumor in a leg bone, and later a tumor of the orbit of the eye. At the time the photograph was taken he had been in complete remission for twelve months.

Mr. Peter Clifford

Mr. Peter Clifford, of Kenyatta National Hospital, Nairobi, with a group of fifteen children, all of whom are in "total tumor regression" from Burkitt's lymphoma as the result of treatment by chemotherapy and, in some cases, immunotherapy. Some of the children still show signs of bony deformities, which can be expected to improve with time.

Dr. Dennis H. Wright
with his sixth child, Margaret,
who was born in Kampala in 1964.

Professor M. A. Epstein

A group of "immature"
EB virus particles in an infected
cell. The magnification of this
electron micrograph is 119,000.

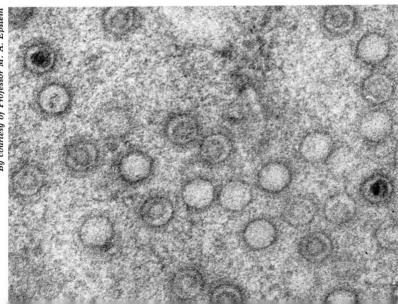

Drs. Gertrude and Werner Henle.

Dr. Werner Henle addressing the technical assistants who worked on the Burkitt-infectious mononucleosis project. They are, from left to right, Evelyn Walters, Elaine Hutkin, Theresa Berry, Angelika Patzel, and Marie Adams. Dr. Gertrude Henle stands listening in the background.

11

The African *Lymphoma?*

The air is clear in Kampala, the temperature is moderate, the streets are broad, the government buildings are dignified, and some of the better residential areas remind the American visitor of sections of Washington—the houses are set in spacious grounds, with delightful gardens. An English visitor might be reminded, perhaps, of one of his cathedral towns, Exeter, or Salisbury. In general, the city is placid. Nothing very much happens. Every evening the young Asians turn out in all their finery to parade along the main thoroughfare, Kampala Road; and every evening, also, precisely at sundown, an immense population of fruit bats flutters over the city to raid the orchards on Lake Victoria. The huge creatures fill the sky. There are millions of them. Then, at daybreak, they fly back to their roosts in Bat Valley, near the university.

One cannot claim that the city's quietude was greatly disturbed by Mr. Burkitt's bombshell. Few of its citizens were aware that anything noteworthy had occurred at Mulago Hospital or Makerere University College Medical School.

Insiders, however, were well aware of it. There was a great upsurge in activity, a great sense of excitement. One of the scientists who was in Kampala at the time, and who has since returned to take up an appointment at a large English university, said recently, "We were really under enormous pressure out there. Makerere is a small university, but with only one quarter of the staff that I now have here in England we were doing four or five times more work. I can remember working in the lab until nine, ten, twelve o'clock at night for several nights running."

Mr. Burkitt's safaris, in fact, had opened a door on a new and mysterious landscape. The next stage was to investigate in detail precisely what was taking place out there; and a number of new personalities now began to make their appearance, starting a series of extraordinary new expeditions of discovery. Among them was a young scientist working at the University of Bristol.

In 1960, Dennis H. Wright, an Englishman, faced a prospect that has dismayed young men in many countries since World War II: he was due to be called up for military service. Four years earlier he had qualified as an M.D., and he had been given deferments in order to work on a number of research projects. He was married; he had three children—two girls and a boy, aged four, two, and one; but there seemed to be little hope that he would be given any further deferment. National Service—the British equivalent of the American draft—was then petering out. The public mood in Britain was markedly unwarlike; the pomp and the trappings and the responsibilities of Empire were fast fading away; but the army—whatever its size and whatever its spirit—still needed medical officers.

Dr. Wright's unhappiness was at least twofold. He loved

his family and had an aversion to leaving home; and, further-more, his interests were somewhat removed from the field of general medicine. His field was pathology, and he had spe-cialized in histochemistry—the microscopic study of the chemistry of tissues and cells. A histochemist in the dwindling British army would have little hope of furthering his career, and Dennis Wright gloomily foresaw that in terms of what he could do best, his army service would be a waste of time.

At this point his life was changed by a simple and unex-pected remark. "The consultant hematologist* at Bristol, Dr. Alan Raper," he recalls, "had been the chief government pathologist in Uganda. He knew that my time was running out on the particular research I was doing, and one day he came to me and said, 'Why don't you go out to Uganda as a lecturer in the medical school?' At first this seemed like a completely mad proposition—I'd never thought of anything of the sort; but he pointed out that the Medical Recruitment Board might accept it as national service, in lieu of actually serving in the army. I wrote to them, and to my surprise they agreed."

So, some time later in 1960, Dennis Wright, twenty-nine years old, set off from London Dock on the *Rhodesia Castle* with his wife and three children, and sailed a familiar route around Gibraltar, through the Mediterranean to Port Said, Suez, Aden, Mombasa, and then by train to Kampala. At the railroad station he found that the entire Department of Pa-thology had turned out to greet him, a friendly gesture that caused him some embarrassment. In those days he used an electric razor, but there was no provision for such gadgets on the train, and he met his new colleagues for the first time

* A hematologist is a physician specializing in blood and the blood-forming tissues.

with three days' growth of whiskers sprouting all over his face.

The family settled into a house on a new college housing estate called Katalemwa, seven miles from Kampala. Progress had not spoiled Katalemwa. It was still rural, filled with masses of birds—and nowhere are the birds more entrancing than in Uganda. At night there were masses of fireflies—and nowhere is the night air softer or more deliciously fragrant. On the weekends, the drums of the hill tribesmen kept up an endless beat, and there was always the possibility of an encounter with a cobra or a mamba. "The problem of poisonous snakes isn't as severe as it is in India or Southeast Asia," Dr. Wright says, "but we had them. And one of my first postmortems was on a man who had died of snakebite."

The university staff, by force of circumstances, made up a tightly knit group. "There was an active social life. One frequently went out to dinner, and entertained people or gave parties in return. Our own social life tended to be less active because we had a young family and we enjoyed staying at home with the children rather than going out to a lot of parties. All the same, it was very pleasant. We didn't feel in any way cut off. In England, university staff tend to follow a nine-to-five routine, whereas in Africa we had an intimate contact all the time. We were all expatriates in a minority community, and we shared common problems and ambitions."

Mulago Hospital surprised him: "It was housed in an old pavilion-style building. I hadn't expected to see flowering trees between the wards, or the women in their gaily colored *basutes*." Some time later, when the Burkitt story aroused attention in the outside world, a London newspaper printed an artist's concept of the scene. Denis Burkitt was portrayed as a tall, thin, bony Colonial wearing a pith helmet, shorts, and knee-length stockings, and to underline his scientific qualifications the artist had given him a Van Dyke beard. Mulago Hospital appeared as a little bamboo hut; and Mr. Burkitt stood outside it, under a coconut tree, gravely inspecting an African child for signs of some deadly disease. "It wasn't like that at all," Dr. Wright comments.

But in 1960 few European or American scientists would have been impressed by the Department of Pathology in Makerere University College Medical School. It consisted of Professor J. N. P. Davies, two lecturers (one of whom was Dr. G. C. O'Conor) and the new arrival, Dr. Wright. Dr. O'Conor had come out in 1958 and was preparing to return to Washington, leaving the department with a staff of three pathologists.

It would have been an error to judge the department by its size. A great deal of work was being done, including a surprising amount of research. Professor Davies, for the first time in Uganda, had described a rare form of heart disease called endomyocardial fibrosis (a condition in which the lining and the muscles of the heart are affected by the formation of fibrous tissue. The disease has a high mortality rate and occurs commonly in young Africans in their second and third decades). Davies and O'Conor, jointly, had done extensive studies of malignant tumors—particularly lymphomas— in African children; they had then gone on to do important research on the pathology of the strange tumor discovered by Denis Burkitt.

Dennis Wright had the good fortune to become a member of this tiny, energetic unit. His official commitments at the outset were twofold. He was a lecturer in pathology in the medical school; he was also a pathology consultant to Mulago Hospital, doing post-mortems, looking at tissue sections, and so on. His involvement with Mr. Burkitt occurred almost against his own will.

"I had a room opposite Greg O'Conor's," he says. "My first recollections go back to the period when he and Denis Burkitt were working on the two papers which eventually appeared in *Cancer* in 1961. Denis is apt to talk in a very fast and excitable manner, and my impression was of a rather noisy man who used to appear all the time and chatter away to Greg.

"When Greg O'Conor left, I didn't have a special interest in the lymphomas. I was all set, then, to work with Jack Davies on endomyocardial fibrosis. The proportion of rare forms of heart disease is much higher in Africa than it is, say, in England, and the World Health Organization was greatly interested in the problem. In fact, they were planning to set up a scientific center in Kampala for the study of cardiomyo-pathys [diseases of the muscular tissues of the heart]: Jack Davies was to be the Director and I was to be the Deputy Director. But for various reasons Jack Davies decided to leave Africa, and the World Health Organization project fell through.

"Then, gradually, I began to develop more interest in the lymphomas—or, rather, this interest was thrust upon me.

"What happened was that wherever I turned I seemed to be confronted by lymphomas. Whenever I did a post-mortem it would turn out to be a lymphoma.

"Obviously, it was pure chance. But people began to comment on it. I remember Jack Davies looking at me in a rather strange way and saying, *You attract lymphomas.*

"If one analyzed it statistically, of course, one would un-doubtedly find that I just happened to run into a cluster of them at a particular time. But whatever the reason, they kept turning up and my interest in them kept growing.

"Then Jack Davies suggested that I ought to concentrate on lymphomas and do more research on them.

"Other people didn't agree. They said, *You'll just be wasting your time. It's all been done now. Greg O'Conor and Denis Burkitt have sorted it all out. What more is there to do?*

"And that, really, is where I started."

Lymphoma (like leukemia) is a generic term for several forms of disease that share certain features. "*Malignant lymphoma* is an American term," Dr. Wright explains. "British pathologists more often call them *the reticuloses.*" The most common are lymphosarcoma, reticulum cell sarcoma and Hodgkin's disease. They all tend to have what he calls "different behavior patterns," and they respond to different treatment in different ways.

"For example, Hodgkin's disease occurs throughout the world. It has similar manifestations everywhere. The diagnosis is made on an examination of sections of a lymph node. You will see a mixture of different kinds of cells, but there is one particular cell which is said to be diagnostic—it enables you to say that you are looking at Hodgkin's disease—called the Reed-Sternberg cell. If you have a lot of lymphocytes (white blood cells) and very few Reed-Sternberg cells it carries a much better prognosis (the outlook for the patient) than the other end of the spectrum where you have masses of Reed-Sternberg cells and very few lymphocytes."

Classifying a disease, placing it in its precise relationship to other similar diseases, is obviously of great importance in understanding and treating it. One can turn again to Hodgkin's disease: treated correctly at an early stage, it responds so successfully that many patients survive twenty-five years or more and often can be considered cured.

The earliest classification of Burkitt's tumor seemed to suggest, in Dr. Wright's words, "that it was just a curious manifestation of other lymphomas." Some cases were thought to resemble one kind of lymphoma; other cases appeared to resemble other lymphomas. At the outset, Dr. Wright set himself the task of deciding whether this was true; and although he could not foresee it, the outcome was to have a profound effect.

The standard procedure in identifying a lymphoma is this: the surgeon removes a lymph node from a patient, puts it in a bottle of formalin, and sends it to the pathologist.

The formalin, to some extent, shrinks the cells in the tissue.

Next, the pathologist removes the fixed* tissue from the formalin and dehydrates it in alcohol, causing more shrinkage of the cells. Finally, in order that it may be sliced conveniently for examination under the microscope, the tissue is put into molten wax which is at a very high temperature.

"It isn't surprising," Dr. Wright says, "that at the end of this procedure the cells have changed their shape. Of course, a pathologist becomes accustomed to these changes. Indeed, if you present him with tissue that hasn't been treated in this way he is likely to be confused."

Dr. Wright decided to turn to other techniques, a decision that eventually proved to be of critical importance. He attended the operating theater personally to collect tissue material; and instead of fixing the tissue in formalin, then dehydrating it in alcohol and immersing it in hot wax, he made use of a procedure called imprinting (and called by American pathologists *touch preparations*). "You take the fresh material before it is put into any fixative," Dr. Wright

---

* "Fixing" is defined as killing and hardening the tissue and cell elements so that they are preserved as closely as possible to their form in the living body. In practice, unfortunately, as Dr. Wright points out, distortion inevitably occurs.

says, "and cut it so that you have a freshly exposed surface. Then, very gently, you touch it onto a glass slide, and some of the cells will come off the cut surface and stick to the glass. You can then use whatever stain you choose: the cells will be spread out and much bigger than those seen in conventionally fixed preparations (because they haven't been shrunk and compressed) and it will be easier to see detail in them."

Dr. Wright's findings surprised everybody concerned with the tumor. Imprinting revealed that all cases of Burkitt's lymphoma were alike. They were not a mixture of different types of lymphoma. Furthermore, the malignant cells were not only similar and of a constant type: *they differed from the cells of any other form of malignant lymphoma.* *

In other words, Dennis Wright showed that the tumor was unique—the medical phrase is *a separate entity.*

* Students of biology may be interested in Dr. Wright's description of Burkitt's tumor as it is seen in an imprint preparation:

"Stained as a blood film with the Romanowsky stains, one would see what is obviously a very primitive cell. It has a rounded nucleus, although this is sometimes deeply cleft; it has three or four nucleoli and a sort of granular nuclear chromatin. It has a well-defined ring of cytoplasm which is intensely basophilic and stains intensely blue with Romanowsky dyes; and in this cytoplasm one can see vacuoles which—if you use the appropriate stain—you can show are fat vacuoles. This cell differs from the cell of any other form of lymphoma."

There have been frequent allusions to Burkitt's tumor showing under the microscope a "starry sky" appearance. Dr. Wright comments: "You have the actual tumor cell—a primitive lymphoid cell. Then you have a large non-malignant cell (called a histiocyte) which is reacting to the tumor. This disperses itself through the tumor tissue and gives the so-called starry sky pattern. It's a characteristic feature, but it is not specific."

More simply still: Burkitt's tumor was now shown to be a new disease.

The layman, understandably, would be perfectly content if no new diseases were discovered in this day and age. We already have more than enough. In the medical world, however, the discovery of a new disease—a separate entity—is an event of great importance.

It is worth repeating a few dates, to show how rapidly (in a relative sense) the story of Burkitt's tumor developed.

Denis Burkitt saw his first tumor patient, the little boy named Africa, in 1957. He first presented information about the tumor, officially, in January 1958. His first published paper appeared in 1959. Dennis Wright arrived at Makerere University College Medical School in 1960. Burkitt, Ted Williams, and Cliff Nelson set off on the long tumor safari in October 1961.

Medical science usually proceeds at a measured pace; but interest in Burkitt's work was so great that in February 1962 the International Union Against Cancer* held a conference in Paris, the theme of which was *Tumors of the Reticuloendothelial System in Africa*. In Dr. Wright's phrase, "it turned out to be a bit of a mixup." Although everybody accepted Burkitt's tumor as a malignancy, there was a lack of unanimity about its exact nature. (Dr. Wright's findings had not yet been published, and in fact were not published until the following year.) After a great deal of discussion it was decided to call Burkitt's tumor just that: Burkitt's tumor,

---

* The International Union Against Cancer is a nongovernmental voluntary organization with member organizations in sixty-seven countries. It is also known as L'Union Internationale Contre Le Cancer, or UICC. Its headquarters are in Geneva.

since any swelling or lump can justifiably be called a tumor. For the time being this became its official name; later the term Burkitt's lymphoma came into common use.

But another result of this conference was that Dennis Wright, at the age of thirty-two, became "the lymphoma man" in Uganda. He says, "After the Paris conference all cases of the tumor were referred to me. If a child died, I did the post-mortem; I received the biopsies not only of all cases of Burkitt's, but of all types of malignant lymphomas. Moreover, I was now in contact with a great many scientists outside Africa, and many of them subsequently played an important part in my work."

He had occasional difficulties adjusting to this role. "Sometimes," he says, "sitting at a conference in some country overseas, the chairman would announce, 'And tonight it is our good fortune to have with us the distinguished scientist, Dr. Dennis Wright, who has come from Africa to talk to us about Burkitt's lymphoma.' And I would think to myself, *Well, that's a surprise. I didn't know there's another Dennis Wright working on the lymphoma in Africa. I wonder what he's like.*"

Another name for the disease—not an official name, but one frequently used—was *the African lymphoma.* The pattern had been established so vividly: a belt across equatorial Africa, extending as a sort of tail down East Africa. Until 1960 the disease appeared to be uniquely African.

The tumor was then found to occur in the Territories of Papua and New Guinea, a discovery that caused a great deal of excitement. As in tropical Africa—which this region resembles climatically—the tumor comprised more than half of all childhood tumors. A little later it was also found to occur

in Brazil, again in similar conditions of temperature and rainfall.

In May 1964, Dennis Wright went home on leave with
his family. "We were staying with my wife's parents in Nor-
folk," he says. "And I left the family there, and went to visit
a number of hospitals."

All were in heavily populated areas: the Tumour Registry
in Liverpool; the Christie Hospital and Holt Radium Institute in Manchester; the Children's Hospital and Radiotherapy Centre in Sheffield; and the Hospital for Sick Children
in Great Ormond Street, London.

The purpose of his visit was to review all cases of malignant lymphoma (or, more precisely, *cases that had been diagnosed as lymphosarcomas*) occurring in children under fifteen years of age, going back as far as twenty years in some
instances; and he followed a very precise procedure.

He obtained, first, all the histological sections of these
cases—that is, the slides of the malignant tissue.

From these slides alone he selected those cases which, in
his judgment, were not lymphosarcomas (as they had been
diagnosed by the hospital pathologists) but instead showed
the features of Burkitt's lymphoma.

Then, having committed himself in this manner, he asked
to see the clinical notes detailing the history of each case, as
well as any other relevant material—post-mortem records,
photographs, and so on.

The results came as a shock to everyone concerned.

He found no cases of Burkitt's lymphoma in Liverpool.
In Sheffield, he found one *possible* case. In Manchester, of
thirty-two lymphomas, three were certainly Burkitt's, while
another three were uncertain. In Great Ormond Street, of
sixteen lymphomas, six were found to be Burkitt's. "They had
the typical clinical features of Burkitt's lymphoma," Dr.
Wright says. "It was very strange: they had sat in the rec-

ords all these years quite unnoticed. I became very excited, reading the descriptions of the multiple jaw tumors, the loosened teeth, the multiple visceral deposits—*typical cases of Burkitt's tumor in English children.*"

Altogether, there were not very many: nine cases, in a very large population, over a period of about twenty years.

Dr. Wright's investigations showed, of course, that Burkitt's lymphoma could be distinguished from any other lymphoma purely on the basis of the "histological criteria alone" —that is, the distinctive features visible in the tissue and cells.

But what caused much scratching of heads was coming across Burkitt's tumor in *Manchester,* of all places, and in *London,* of all places. What about Mr. Burkitt's findings that the disease occurred in certain specific conditions in tropical Africa (or New Guinea or Brazil), where there was heavy rainfall and the temperature never fell below 60° F? Gray old London and grimy old Manchester could hardly be less tropical. They are rainy, but not *so* rainy; and they tend to be cold most of the year.

And so the mystery deepened just a little more; and it deepened further as, in due course, cases were reported from the United States, from France, from Norway, even from Finland. Dennis Wright, traveling around the world two years later, found cases in India, in Thailand, in Singapore, in Hong Kong, in Australia. The African lymphoma obviously was not confined to Africa. True, only in New Guinea did it occur with the same frequency. Elsewhere, it was fifteen or twenty times less frequent.

But—and this was the cardinal point—*it occurred elsewhere.* Indeed, it seemed to occur virtually everywhere in the world, wherever scientists searched for it carefully enough; and there was good reason to wonder why.

12

Mr. Burkitt Tries Some Pills

It is possible to argue that Denis Burkitt was a fortunate man who happened to observe an unusual condition affecting a relatively small number of African children, who then paused long enough to ask himself some questions about this unusual condition, and thus happened to hit upon a new disease. Any one of a host of medical persons in East Africa might have spotted the tumor; and thus all it required was the knack of being observant, being inquisitive, being on the spot, plus a little good luck.

It is possible to argue next that a few physicians, surgeons, or pathologists, having become aware of this unusual condition, would have taken the step that followed: they would have gone to the trouble of printing more than a thousand leaflets describing the condition and would have sent them to virtually every government and mission hospital in

Africa, asking if anybody had seen this condition and, if so, would they please supply information about it.

It is then possible to argue, perhaps, that somebody would have taken the next obvious step: planning a scientific expedition, or safari, to investigate at first hand where, when and how this condition actually occurred, thus establishing it as the first malignant tumor in medical history that could be related to factors of altitude, temperature, and rainfall.

At this point, though, we have begun to stretch happenstance a little too far: we have really passed beyond the statistical possibilities of good luck. Dennis Wright expressed it well: "I think most of us would have sat back and thought, *There it is. It occurs in a belt across Africa. That's very interesting. Now let's wait, and in another ten years perhaps other people will write something about it. . . .* I can't think of anybody in medicine strictly comparable to Denis Burkitt. This was a firsthand, personal geographic search, on a vast scale. Most people would have thought it was too formidable a task altogether, that you should sit back and let the information come to you. But he went right out and *found* the information."

There is one other element in the Burkitt story, however, which raises it far beyond any statistical possibilities of good luck and equals in importance all the other aspects of his work as a benefit to humanity at large. That is: having discovered this tumor, having established where and how it occurred, having led the scientists of the world to the first human tumor that might well be related to a virus (or viruses, in various combinations), Mr. Burkitt proceeded to find the means *to cure* this tumor by means of pills—sometimes, in his own words, by just a handful of pills.

Since the condition he had discovered was a terribly

malignant form of childhood cancer, and since cancer is not easily cured, by pills or by any other means, Mr. Burkitt's story thus becomes unique.

We can survey, very briefly, the medical approaches to the treatment of a malignancy.

Altogether, four different methods are available. They may be used singly, or they may be combined; but in certain situations the use of a certain method may not be practicable.

The first of these methods of treatment, and the one most widely used, is surgery. If the malignancy is confined to a single site, and if the surgeon is able to remove it completely, there is good hope that the tumor may not recur.

The second method is radiotherapy. The radiotherapist focuses his rays on the tumor and, as in surgery, if the tumor is confined to a single site and can be completely destroyed there is hope that the patient may be cured. Radiotherapy is often used after surgery to destroy any small remnants of a tumor or to deal with secondary growths.

The third method is chemotherapy: treatment by means of drugs. In the lymphomas and leukemias where, from the outset, the disease is widely disseminated throughout the body, surgery cannot be used (except, in some lymphomas, to deal with localized tumors). Lymphomas such as Hodgkin's disease may be treated by radiotherapy; but in leukemia the physician has no alternative: he must make use of drugs. Unfortunately, in 1960, chemotherapy could cure only one form of cancer, choriocarcinoma, a strange tumor that occurs (rarely) during or after a pregnancy.

The fourth method of treatment is immunotherapy— making use of the patient's own immune defenses to act upon the malignancy. This seems to offer some hope for the future: in 1960 its clinical use was severely limited, and even at the present time its use is largely experimental.

Like other surgeons in East Africa, Mr. Burkitt had attempted to treat the tumor that bears his name by means of surgery. "It was useless and wrong," he said later. "Whenever we had a jaw tumor, we could find another tumor elsewhere. The jaw tumor was only one manifestation of a multiple tumor." So that removal of the jaw tumor only too often left other tumor masses in the child's body. Furthermore, the tumor grows with great rapidity: it doubles itself in forty-eight hours or less. Even heroic surgery—that is, surgery utilizing extreme measures—could not save a child's life.

The second of the methods used to treat cancer, radiotherapy, could not be employed at Mulago Hospital for the simple reason that it was not available. In 1960 no equipment for radiotherapy existed in Africa between Cairo, in the north, and Salisbury, Southern Rhodesia, more than three thousand miles to the south.* Yet, in due course, immense benefits were to arise from this lamentable situation.

Drugs had been used to treat some cases of the tumor, without any notable success. Here, again, we encounter special circumstances. Uganda is not a wealthy country. Burkitt's tumor is almost inconsequential compared to such widespread and economically damaging diseases as malaria

---

* The first radiotherapy unit to reach East Africa was installed at the end of 1968 in the Kenyatta National Hospital, Nairobi, a most generous gift to the people of East Africa from the people of Sweden. A large part of the credit for this gift goes to Professor George Klein, of the Karolinska Institutet, Stockholm, and his colleague, Professor J. Einhorn. One of the first patients to be treated was a boy, only ten years old, suffering from Hodgkin's disease.

and hookworm, and there was literally no money available to Burkitt and his colleagues for the purchase of experimental drugs. The situation was summed up by Professor M. A. Epstein: "In the context of the total medical background of an undeveloped territory, experimental drugs would have been a luxury, particularly since there was no indication that they would do any good."

As for immunotherapy, its potentiality lies in destroying the last few thousand malignant cells after the main bulk of the tumor has been destroyed by other means. The tumors seen in children with Burkitt's lymphoma were—in 1960 and today—totally beyond the scope of the immunologist.

Therefore, since surgery was rarely successful, since radiotherapy could not be employed because there was no equipment available (at least, in East Africa), and since nobody had achieved any success with drugs, Burkitt's tumor in 1960 was, to all intents and purposes, a wholly incurable disease.

Chemotherapy enters the Burkitt story in the way we have come to expect. Once more the sequence of events appears to depend on good fortune. There is no great Chemotherapy Program, there are no lengthy Chemotherapy Studies, not even one laboratory mouse, rat, hamster, or rabbit is involved. There is just another unexpected and almost unbelievable step forward.

What happened was that in January 1960 a number of scientists from the Sloan-Kettering Institute for Cancer Research in New York went out to Nairobi to treat various forms of cancer with new drugs and new techniques. One of the members of this group was Dr. Joseph H. Burchenal, an authority on cancer chemotherapy. The group as a whole was working at the Kenyatta National Hospital with Peter Clifford, Kenya's most eminent surgeon.

In the course of this visit Dr. Burchenal made a trip to Kampala and met Denis Burkitt at Mulago Hospital. Some time later Dr. Burchenal said in an interview, "I thought I had seen all childhood tumors in Memorial Hospital (New York) during the past twelve or fourteen years, but I had never seen anything like these tumors. Actually, it turned out later on, when I went through the records, that I had seen some cases which might be considered to be what we now call Burkitt's lymphoma, but we had not recognized them as such,"—a state of affairs in no way surprising, and reminiscent of Dennis Wright's discoveries in Manchester and London.

The outcome of the meeting was that Dr. Burchenal gave Mr. Burkitt a drug called methotrexate, and advice on how it should be administered. Subsequently another Sloan-Kettering scientist, Dr. Herbert F. Oettgen, came out to East Africa and, in Burkitt's words, "guided me a lot in those early days."

Then, undoubtedly to everybody's astonishment, the drug treatment began to show results. A brief paragraph in the Seventh Biennial Report of the Sloan-Kettering Institute, for the years 1959–61, gives what is probably the first indication that the group in East Africa had observed something unusual: "Methotrexate is being used in the treatment of round cell sarcoma of the face in African children in Nairobi and Kampala. Definite regression has been seen in some of the tumors, and it appears that the prolongation of survival time may have been achieved."

Almost from the outset it was apparent that the tumor, in Burkitt's words, was "incredibly amenable to treatment," and the official statement, *It appears that prolongation of survival time may have been achieved,* was too modest. Prolongation of survival time in the lymphomas and leukemias is usually reckoned in months; but *six years* after he began to use chemotherapy Mr. Burkitt could declare, "Some of the first patients we ever treated are still alive and well and, I believe, cured." Some of them were still alive and well *nine* years later.

The nub of the matter, the reason for all the excitement, is that before Dr. Burchenal and Mr. Burkitt met in 1960 only one form of cancer could be cured by chemotherapy: choriocarcinoma. Two scientists, Dr. Roy Hertz and Dr. Min Chiu Li, working in 1956 at the National Institutes of Health in Bethesda, Maryland, had treated a hundred and ten women suffering from choriocarcinoma with methotrexate, and thereby had made medical history: five years later, seventy of these women were still in remission from the disease and were considered to be cured.

But the treatment of choriocarcinoma is very severe. The drug must be administered in amounts that come close to causing general poisoning of the patient. This, in fact, has always been considered to be essential in the treatment of cancer by drugs: the maximum dosage the patient can tolerate has to be given to ensure that the greatest possible number of malignant cells are destroyed.

Burkitt's experience was different. He says, "The experts told me to treat my patients very heavily, with numerous courses of the drug, but several factors prevented me from doing this. I had a lot of other things to do—I had a whole surgical unit on my hands—and so I wasn't treating patients anything like as intensively as the experts recommended. Just the same, my patients did remarkably well. . . . The initial response was dramatic. If we had relatively small tumors, we saw them disappear. If they were bigger tumors they would partially disappear: we would keep treating them and they would keep recurring. . . . We didn't know our real results for some time because although we had initial success with

so many of our patients, they went away and never came
back to the hospital. They might still be alive—we don't
know. We had no follow-up program then (that is, keeping
a record of the patient's progress after treatment). We'd
started something, with no idea where it was going to lead;
and we just allowed the patients to go home, and lost touch
with them."

Two of these children remain clearly in Burkitt's memory.
They are identified as numbers in a series—J95 and J76; and
this is how it is convenient for them to appear in the official
records, *J* indicating a jaw tumor. But in real life J95 was a
little boy, about five years old, named Kibakola, and he was
one of the first children at Mulago Hospital to be treated
with the marvelous drug brought to Africa by the eminent
American cancer scientist.

"Three months after his treatment began, Kibakola was
still alive *and still well,*" Burkitt says. "We thought this was
colossal, because the disease usually progresses so very rapidly. Then time went on, and Kibakola *remained* well, and
his condition became more and more encouraging." He is
still well as this is written, nearly ten years later.

J76 was equally encouraging, and perhaps even more
remarkable.

"Some of the patients who did best," Burkitt explains,
"were those who ran away from the hospital during their
treatment"; and this is what occurred with J76, a little girl of
about the same age as Kibakola, whose name—an unusually
sweet and musical name—was Namusisi.

"I thought Namusisi would be a very favorable patient to
treat, that she might respond well. She was going to have
three courses of methotrexate—a full course consists of forty
pills, given at the rate of eight pills a day for five days. But
when she'd had only one course, her mother came to the hos-

pital during the night and took her home. This is something that happens frequently in Africa; they are frightened of hospitals and doctors. I was very disappointed. It seemed that we'd missed an opportunity to help the child.

"Then, about a year later, one of our African workers came across Namusisi in her home in the bush. I've seen her frequently since then: she's perfectly well, and I think we can say she's cured—on only one course of pills. She lives about twelve miles from Kampala, and anyone who's interested can drive out to visit her."

The manner in which an early jaw tumor responds to chemotherapy is remarkable beyond belief. No other childhood tumor responds with such speed, and for some scientists this tremendous response is diagnostic, a certain sign that the disease is indeed Burkitt's lymphoma. Dr. Ted Williams recalls that in January 1965 a conference on the lymphoma was held in Kampala. "People came from all over the world. At the beginning of the conference, Denis brought out a little boy suffering from the tumor who had received no treatment. Chemotherapy was started then and there, and at the end of the conference, five days later, Denis brought out the same little boy again. In those few days the tumor had gone right down.

"At this conference, too, Denis had gathered together all of his long-term survivors. When the delegates left the conference room for a tea break the children were outside, wandering around for the delegates to see: a bottle of Pepsi in one hand, and in the other hand photographs of themselves showing the tumor before chemotherapy was started."

Simple demonstrations of this kind have a stunning effect upon any audience of cancer scientists. Suddenly, the hopes and the dreams of half a century of intensive research are visible and tangible: the wild hope, the wild dream that cancer can be cured. And cured not by the mutilating knife, not by tissue-destroying radiation, but by a hundred pills or less, taken every four hours for less than a week. Burkitt's lymphoma, manifested in the jaws of a child, can be almost unbearably brutal: a huge out-thrusting mass, cruelly distorting the child's face, putting intense pressure upon an eye. But *caught at an early stage* there is a good possibility that the huge mass can be reduced, the frightened child can be saved.

It is only this disease, this particular lymphoma, that responds at present so dramatically. All the same, the implications are inescapable. If one form of cancer will respond like this to chemotherapy, it may be a portent of things to come. And in any audience of cancer scientists you can sense the thoughts going through their minds as Mr. Burkitt talks to them and shows them his color slides: *Burkitt's lymphoma is in some way related to other lymphomas. It is related also, in some way, to leukemia. Leukemia! If we could treat leukemia with a handful of pills, that would be something!*

Burkitt could not expect the Sloan-Kettering Institute for Cancer Research to provide him with an endless supply of drugs. Nor could Mulago Hospital supply them: like colored mapping pins, they were not included in his budget. In typical Burkitt fashion he went directly to the Nairobi representative of Lederle Laboratories, the manufacturers of methotrexate, and (in his own words): "I told Mr. Innes that we had a cancer that was responding to chemotherapy, and this would provide a good opportunity to test his drug *because we had no X-ray therapy.* Could we have samples to try out? If they worked successfully, there were good prospects of the government placing orders for the drug."

Mr. Innes and Lederle Laboratories listened sympathetically, and to their everlasting credit were most cooperative. "I was given the methotrexate for nothing," Mr. Burkitt says. "I acknowledge it to them. They gave me free supplies for years."

Later, at the midpoint in the long safari, Burkitt visited the huge Baragwanath Nie-Blanke Hospitaal in Johannesburg—the largest hospital in the Southern Hemisphere—and learned about another valuable drug, cyclophosphamide (also known as Cytoxan, or Endoxan). On his return to Kampala, the German manufacturer Asta-Werke gave him "liberal amounts." Cyclophosphamide is descended from the deadly war gas, nitrogen mustard, used in World War I. Its action is different from methotrexate, but it produces the same striking results.

Later still, the American pharmaceutical company Eli Lilly gave him free supplies of a very expensive drug, vincristine, which is derived from the periwinkle plant.

How, precisely, does a surgeon without research funds obtain unlimited supplies of expensive drugs? Mr. Burkitt's explanation is simple and cheerful, and should encourage others who find themselves in a similar situation: "Oh, I suppose I nagged at people a bit. When you're enthusiastic about something, you can't help driving away at it."

In fact, there was something a little more persuasive in Burkitt's approach than nagging, and it is contained in the phrase "I told Mr. Innes . . . this would provide a good opportunity to test his drug *because we had no X-ray therapy.*"

The medical significance of this remark is that X-ray therapy affects a patient's response to drugs in an unpredictable manner. Therefore, if a patient has received X-ray therapy it is impossible to obtain an accurate assessment of the precise effect of a particular drug on a particular tumor.

In Europe and America (and, of course, in other regions where the necessary equipment is available), cancer is always treated first by surgery *or X-rays*. Except in leukemia or choriocarcinoma, malignancies are never treated first by chemotherapy. Drugs are used as an adjunct to X-rays or surgery; and thus there is little opportunity to learn what a drug can really do.

What Burkitt was offering in exchange for free supplies of the drugs he needed so urgently was just this: an opportunity—"a golden opportunity," he calls it—for various companies to test their drugs on patients who had not received any radiation therapy. They had not received radiation therapy because there was no equipment available in the three thousand miles of East Africa between Cairo and Salisbury.

The situation was tragic, because patients with malignancies such as skin cancer, which is nearly always curable by radiation therapy, had to be sent away, often to a miserable death. But the situation also had another aspect, and a man with a very remarkable kind of genius happened to be on the spot and was able to exploit it. Dr. Ted Williams points out, with great insight, "Burkitt's tumor would never have been treated with chemotherapy if there had been a radiotherapy unit in East Africa, and so no one would ever have found out how effective chemotherapy is.

"In South Africa and in parts of Rhodesia they were treating the tumor with radiotherapy, and it was very ineffective.

"The breakthrough in chemotherapy had to happen in a poor country like Uganda. It could *only* happen in a country which lacked radiotherapy facilities.

"If we had radiotherapy here in Uganda, we would never

think of using chemotherapy first. Ethically, we'd feel we must first use radiotherapy. Ethically, we must do what we *know* is best, or *believe* is best for our patients. That's the basis of our patient-doctor relationship—to do the best for the patient.

"Therefore you are always hesitant to use something untried, when you have available something that is tried and proven. When you are responsible for people's lives, you know you *might* hit on something that's better than what you've been using; but you dare not try it. It might turn out to be not better but worse.

"Our circumstances were different. If radiotherapy had been available we would have had to use it. But there was none available, and we were left with chemotherapy.

"And the chemotherapy happened to work."

Mr. Burkitt's good luck? Mr. Burkitt's good fortune? After it happens again and again, one begins to wonder.

13

The Place of Cold Water

Nairobi, in January 1897, when Dr. Albert Cook and his fellow missionaries reached it on their safari from Mombasa to Kampala, consisted of a few mud and grass shacks standing on a swamp beside the Athi River. Dr. Cook and Katherine Timpson and the rest camped there that night, but they did not sleep well. A band of Masai was nearby, decked out in ostrich feathers and red capes, carrying long spears and heavy shields, and they might only too easily cause serious trouble—a year before they had attacked a safari of fifteen hundred people, killing three hundred. Throughout the night the missionaries saw fires blazing in the distance, they heard yells and shots and the beat of war drums, but in the morning they learned that many of the Masai had been slaughtered by their bitter enemies, the Wakamba, nomadic, pastoral people who obviously were not overawed by the legendary prowess of the Masai warriors. The missionaries did not linger to witness any counterattack.

The shacks by the swampy river were called Martin's Camp. With the coming of the Mombasa-Uganda railway a station was built here and the settlement became known by its Masai name, Nairobi, the place of cold water (or, as some people have it, the place of fresh water). It grew to be the capital of Kenya, and until 1961 only Europeans were permitted by law to settle in the region. It was built by the white man to serve his various purposes in East Africa; for the most part it still looks like a white man's city; and you cannot by any effort of the imagination turn it into what in fact it now is, an African city.

It is all somewhat commercial these days, with a great many new hotels that seem to have been brought over intact from Miami Beach, but as you walk the broad and sunny streets you get an occasional whiff of the past, an occasional glimpse of ghosts who in their time were strong and vigorous and very arrogant. Sit at a table outside the New Stanley, and you are inevitably reminded of Ernest Hemingway and his bold white hunters and his disagreeable heroines and their feeble husbands—they are still climbing in and out of Land Rovers, bustling in and out of the old hotel, carrying vast amounts of expensive luggage, and huge hand-chased elephant guns, and Fortnum and Mason hampers, and the red and yellow Shell Road Map of East Africa.

The great climactic confrontations between man and beast are gone forever, though. Hardly anybody is allowed to shoot Kenya's glamorous animals—they are a precious asset, and the authorities are desperately trying to preserve them. Nairobi is a trade center and a tourist center: the bold white hunters take you out to the game parks just to photograph the animals and not to encounter them on any Hemingwayesque kill-or-be-killed basis: you may not even *annoy* them. The animals are bored to death with being photographed, the lions yawn in your face; and when you yourself have become bored with their boredom you can go shopping in the best Western style. You can buy the most expensive cameras, the finest guns, gorgeous jewels, elegant clothes to wear on safari or to garden parties; and in the charming little boutiques they will murmur in madame's ear, "Signor Pucci paid us a visit yesterday afternoon. Such a nice man." Meanwhile, the poachers, despising the authorities, go on killing the game freely, in authentic African style: silently, with the spear or the club, in traps, in pits. They need the meat. They are hungry.

If you have reason to go to East Africa, not as a tourist but on Burkitt business of some kind, you might go first to Mulago Hospital in Kampala, Uganda, and then to the Kenyatta National Hospital in Nairobi, Kenya; or vice versa. The two hospitals, four hundred miles apart, are in a sense twins: both have a very deep commitment to the strange lymphoma that has aroused such widespread excitement. Mr. Burkitt, of course, was the leading figure in Kampala; his counterpart in Nairobi, also a surgeon, is Mr. Peter Clifford, who enters the narrative for two good reasons—first, as another of the remarkable human beings who give the story such a heroic quality; and second, because he brings to it something every good story should have, the element of conflict.

Kenyatta National Hospital is in process of being rebuilt. A young Swedish cancer scientist, Dr. Jan Stjernswärd,* said

* Dr. Stjernswärd is on the staff of the famous Department of Tumor Biology at the Karolinska Institutet, Stockholm. In

of the plans for the new hospital, "When it is finished it will be magnificent, the best hospital in Africa, one of the best in the world. We have nothing like it in Sweden."

The old hospital is still tremendously active, like any African hospital. In Europe or America the entrance to a hospital is usually quiet, subdued. Here there is noise, color, endless drama. A Mercedes-Benz 230 comes screaming up to the entrance, doors are flung open, two young Africans jump out and drag out a third young African in a Madison Avenue suit who is unconscious, sweating, limp as a rag doll: he seems to be dying of—what? You cannot even guess. Young girls—they can hardly be twelve years old—in gay *basutes* sit on the grass nursing their babies and giggling. Men with bandaged heads or a broken arm, a broken leg, a broken collarbone, replay for visitors the fight or the car crash that caused their disability. A beautiful Bedouin woman, swathed in black, sits on a stone step, smiling remotely: two children play near her, a lovely little girl, and a little boy, about four years old, with the swollen jaws of Burkitt's lymphoma. A brisk blond English nurse tells you, "Oh yes, the hospital is full of Burkitt's tumor. A lot of cases."

Then, if you go inside the hospital, past the patients sitting in rows in the foyer, and turn right along the corridor, and climb a flight of stairs, you will come to the Burkitt wards. They are airy; the beds are widely spaced; everything is very neat; the children—those who are not asleep—look at you with interest; a couple, with paraplegia, sit in wheelchairs on a balcony.

If it is early in the morning, Mr. Clifford may be making

1967 he was awarded an Eleanor Roosevelt International Cancer Research Fellowship (funded by the American Cancer Society) and he elected to go out to work with Mr. Clifford in Nairobi for more than a year.

his rounds; then he has a number of operations scheduled. He is a busy man, pressed for time, but he may be able to spare you a few minutes to tell you what he is doing or, better still, what he is thinking; and he takes you into his office, which is about as large as a broom closet and contains nothing much more than a battered old desk, a couple of battered old chairs, and a bookshelf.

He is a quiet, handsome, aristocratic man, the perfect image of an eminent surgeon. His voice, no matter how long he speaks, remains at the same level, rather hushed, neither rising nor falling, and always very precise. His friend, George Klein, said of him in a mysterious yet magical phrase, "He is unique: he has climbed Kilimanjaro, but he does it every day—his whole life consists of climbing Kilimanjaro. He has a profound wish, a desperate wish to do something for these children with Burkitt's lymphoma, and he's trying everything that might help them. There are few medical men who have this as their primary motivation. In his case it is really so."

Peter Clifford came to East Africa after the end of World War II. He spent two years in Tanzania before going back to London and to Newcastle, in the north of England; then, in 1954, he returned to Kenya. He is a Roman Catholic, but he did not come out to Africa with any missionary intent, nor, he says, "do I have any missionary inclinations."

It is an idea that he finds important, and he discusses it in detail: "Many of the doctors working in Africa are people who are highly motivated and who have a great interest in the performance of their duties. This relates to several things.

"First, in England—as you know—there is a growing dissatisfaction with working conditions. It is felt that the present system destroys any interest, any initiative, that the doctor has directly in his patients. If he diagnoses a condition it is then passed over to somebody else, and in the end he bears little responsibility. This feeling of *responsibility* which the doctor bears to his patient is something that every doctor values a great deal.

"Secondly, in Africa there is an enormous field for any type of work. If, for instance, you send a gynecologist to work in Kisumu (northwest of Nairobi, on Lake Victoria), he could quite easily fill the Nyanza Provincial Hospital entirely with gynecological work. There is a vast amount to be done. And the physician realizes that very often he is the only person who stands between a patient with a painful, dreadful disease, and nothing. And death.

"A third point, of course, is that most of the patients with Burkitt's lymphoma are young children. And there is always something very pathetic and sorrow-making about a child with a horrible and ugly mutilating tumor.

"The health of the people here is a growing problem. The population of Kenya alone is increasing at the rate of 6 percent annually. We now have about ten million people, and it has been estimated that at the present rate of increase we will have twenty-five million by 1981–82.

"Health is, within limits, directly related to economics; economics is related to education. So, to enable the country to train doctors, to buy doctors from the outside, to buy medicine, to find the money to build hospitals, the economic status of Kenya must be improved; and the only way this can be done is by improved education.

"It's a circle. Obviously, the first step that will enable us to break out of it must be more widespread education, and this is proceeding—within the limits proscribed by the resources available to this country. But we are short of teachers, both in primary and secondary schools; we are short of schools, both primary and secondary; and the greater part of the population of Kenya is at present completely illiterate.

"What one must remember when dealing with Africans—or, I should say, people living in the African context—is how very little hope there is in the average man's life.

"Take, for instance, a man owning a small shamba [a plot of cultivable land] in a place like Nyeri [about seventy miles north of Nairobi, not far from Mount Kenya], and imagine that he gets a disease like cancer of the esophagus, which carries a grim prognosis anywhere in the world. Where does this man go? To whom does he turn? He has very little money—if he has any at all; and the situation easily becomes totally hopeless for him. I think that the means to provide a way out, a means to provide hope that things will be better, that things can be *made* better, is what the average person in Africa requires most at the moment.

"Or, if you drive a little further, up towards Meru or Embu, you will go through the heartland of the Kikuyu country. Try to envisage what one of these smallholders feels when he is faced with a major problem in his life, something as simple (to us) as paying the school fees of his children. How can that man, completely illiterate, completely without training, find money, find employment, find the means of improving his condition so that he can make the lot of his children better?"

These are some of the problems that affect every person of sensibility working in Africa. They are at present inescapable and insoluble. Is there any hope? "Hope is something that exists in the mind," Peter Clifford says, "and I think the people have more hope now than they had a few years ago."

Soon after he arrived in Kenya, in 1955, Clifford saw his first case of the tumor. The following year he demonstrated three cases to a distinguished visitor, Professor Mackenzie of the Royal College of Surgeons.

The nature of the tumor, of course, had not yet been established. It was variously taken to be Ewing's sarcoma, a form of cancer that occurs in children and young adults, involving the bones but not the viscera (that is, the internal organs), or a neuroblastoma, which often seems to originate in one of the adrenal glands and spreads to internal organs and also to the skeleton.

Treatment was in part by surgery, and in part by nitrogen mustard. "It may not have been the best form of treatment or the correct form of treatment in the light of present knowledge," Clifford observes, "but it benefited the patient to some degree."

Then, in 1960, Dr. Joseph H. Burchenal came out to Nairobi with other scientists to set up new methods of treatment: an event of considerable importance. "The original members of the team," Clifford says, "were Bob (R. D.) Sullivan, then of Sloan-Kettering but later at the Leahy Clinic, and two girl technicians. Sullivan remained here for two years; then Dr. Herbert F. Oettgen came out for two years, and during this period he visited Kampala about once a month."

Dr. Sullivan used methotrexate, but (in technical terms) "it was given as an intra-arterial infusion"—that is to say, it was administered through a catheter, or tube, into the artery supplying blood to the tumor. "At the same time," Clifford explains, "the specific antidote to methotrexate was given to the rest of the body. In this way you retained a relatively high concentration of the drug in the tumor, which the child could not tolerate unless his body was protected by the citrovorum factor."*

When Dr. Oettgen arrived in Nairobi he began to use a

---

* This is a remarkable example of medical ingenuity. The citrovorum factor is a substance found in liver extracts. It is also

large variety of drugs for treating the tumor—Clifford estimates as many as fifteen or sixteen. And it is here that we encounter the element of conflict: a technical conflict, maintained on the highest professional level, that is as intriguing as anything else in the Burkitt story.

Mr. Burkitt, of course, had used methotrexate and other drugs with remarkable success; and as a result he developed some striking ideas about the way drugs should be employed in the treatment of Burkitt's lymphoma. On one occasion, in particular, he expressed these ideas in clear and emphatic terms.*

"The normal approach to chemotherapy is to give the patient all the drugs you can without killing him, to try to destroy all the malignant cells, but our experience in Mulago Hospital was that the patient did better if you gave him not too big a course of treatment. . . .

"I repeatedly gave patients one single injection, and saw not only total clinical regression, but total radiological recovery of diseased bone (that is, regrowth of the bone, as shown by X-ray photographs); and my policy was that when I saw total regression of the tumor on one dose I did not give a second dose.

"We have seen patients go along to what we believe to

---

known as folinic acid, and it is related to the vitamin folic acid. It counteracts the action of methotrexate, which is a form of *counterfeit* folic acid. The cells of certain kinds of cancer have an excessive need for folic acid; when they take up the counterfeit folic acid they are destroyed. Thus, by administering the methotrexate only to the tumor, and supplying the rest of the body with the antidote, citrovorum factor, the patient is protected to a large extent from the toxic effects of the methotrexate.

* The passage that follows occurred in the course of a conversation with the author of this book in Tokyo at the end of 1966.

be total cure after one dose, but this depends on seeing them early. In my experience, if you saw an early jaw tumor you could expect to get total clinical remission which would not recur at that site in the large majority of cases, after a single dose of a cytotoxic (cell-poisoning) agent.

"The very fact that we see long-term remissions (which we believe to be cures) following what would normally be considered totally inadequate therapy means, I believe, that the drug helps to stimulate the patient's own defenses. . . . If you over-treat the patient you may knock out more tumor cells initially; but because at the same time you knock out his defense mechanisms, you lose more than you gain.

"From ordinary observation, I would suggest that the minimum dose consistent with clinical elimination of the tumor is the best dose, and to go on giving more drugs does more harm than good."

In every respect this is an extraordinary statement. We are dealing with a malignant tumor of childhood that has the ability to grow very rapidly indeed; *we are dealing with a form of cancer, the most dreaded of all diseases;* and we have here an experienced and respected surgeon claiming that when the tumor is seen early *it can be cured* with a single injection of a drug or, alternatively, with what amounts to a handful of pills.

What is more, the results obtained at Mulago Hospital in Kampala fully supported Burkitt's claim. Relying chiefly on this minimal form of treatment he was obtaining long-term remissions* in 15 to 20 percent of his patients; and he was prepared to argue that these long-term remissions were in fact cures: "I know that you are hardly allowed to claim a

---

* "Remission" means that the disease is not apparent for a substantial period.

cure for chemotherapy in cancer. You aren't allowed to say a patient is cured until he's dead*; but that doesn't suit me. I am claiming cures on this ground: that if the patient is symptom-free after a year, some—but very, very few—ever get into trouble again. And therefore, nineteen times out of twenty, the patient who is symptom-free after a year will, I think, go on living and will not die of this tumor."

A similar claim, of complete cures by means of chemotherapy alone, could be made only in the case of choriocarcinoma. Here, while the cure rate was considerably higher, it was obtained by intensive treatment. But choriocarcinoma is a peculiar tumor; it is unique; and the success achieved in its treatment cannot be applied directly to the treatment of any other malignancies.

On the other hand, Burkitt's lymphoma is related to the other lymphomas, including Hodgkin's disease, and to the leukemias; and scientists all over the world reacted with sharp interest to reports of minimal drug treatment that resulted in 15 to 20 percent long-term remissions *which could be considered cures*. Dr. Burchenal, at the Sloan-Kettering Institute for Cancer Research, commented with deep feeling, "If we could get 15 to 20 percent long-term remissions in leukemia it would be wonderful"; and in a famous paper entitled "Geographic Pathology—Burkitt's Tumor as a Stalking Horse for Leukemia," he urged intensive study of Burkitt's lymphoma in the hope that an understanding of its features might be turned to use in the treatment of all those other related diseases.

In Nairobi, however, Peter Clifford was dealing with the problem in a different manner. He, too, was treating Burkitt's

* An age-old medical quip.

lymphoma by means of drugs; but, unlike Mr. Burkitt, he was using *intensive* chemotherapy.

And with intensive chemotherapy Mr. Clifford was obtaining survival rates that were exactly the same as Mr. Burkitt's: 15 to 20 percent of his patients were going into long-term remissions.

Mr. Burkitt relied, wherever possible, on a single injection, or a handful of pills. Mr. Clifford carried his treatment to toxicity—the point where the patient shows clear signs of poisoning.

Yet both men achieved the same results; and to many onlookers the situation seemed to make no sense.

Mr. Clifford's attitude was this: "A great many dogmatic statements have been made about Burkitt's lymphoma as a result of generalizing but without any real proof. Every Burkitt tumor in each individual child presents as a separate problem, and the relation of each child to his tumor is a separate and individual thing.

"In one child, with a single dose of chemotherapy you will kill off a certain proportion of the malignant cells; and then regrowth will occur.

"In the next child, with the same dose you will kill off a different proportion of the malignant cells; and then regrowth will occur.

"In a very fortunate child, with the same dose you will kill off all the malignant cells.

"But in the majority of Burkitt patients you will get this pattern: they will require successive doses of chemotherapy before the tumor cell population is completely eliminated.

"If the patients are followed up and kept under observation, you may find that this regression bears no relation to what ultimately happens. For example, you may completely eliminate all systemic tumors (that is, throughout the entire body) and yet the child may die of a tumor other than the presenting (original) tumor, or as a result of extension of the disease into the central nervous system (the brain and spinal cord).

"Again, a great number of enthusiastic and generalized statements have been made about the patient's immediate response to chemotherapy. I agree that the tumor is enormously sensitive to chemotherapy; but the aim of any form of treatment is, at the end of five or ten years, to have a live child."

Physicians often do not see eye to eye about the best form of treatment for a given malady. But here the dispute seems to go somewhat beyond the limits of a simple difference of opinion. The lives of many children are deeply and directly involved in this issue; and because of the broader implications of Burkitt's lymphoma, there could be serious effects upon the understanding and future treatment of other childhood malignancies (and, for that matter, adult malignancies).

"The point I want to get across," says Clifford, "is that the chemotherapy of Burkitt's lymphoma is not easy. And although 15 to 20 percent of patients go into long-term remissions—a most encouraging figure compared with acute leukemia—one must not forget that 80 to 85 percent are still dying of the disease. For each of those individual children who make up the 15 to 20 percent, survival really represents 100 percent survival; whereas it is no encouragement to the parents of a child who dies to tell them that 15 to 20 percent survive."

Clifford was particularly alarmed because at least two children whom he had treated in 1963, and who appeared to be completely cured, had died five years later when the disease recurred.

Yet Denis Burkitt had stated that such recurrences could be expected: "If the patient is symptom-free after a year, some—but very, very few—ever get into trouble again."

So, a problem was raised. And this problem in itself raised another problem: how could anybody possibly attempt to solve the problem? For, in the case of a child suffering from a disease that might be fatal, a physician is not permitted to experiment. In the words of Dr. Ted Williams, "Ethically, we must do what we know is best, or *believe* is best for our patients." But what is considered to be best when one expert urges minimal doses of chemotherapy, and another expert—equally committed—urges maximum dosage?

The problem and its accompanying problem-within-a-problem may eventually be solved in an ancient hospital hut in Kampala, formerly the Maternity Centre of the old Mulago Hospital and now a center for the treatment of lymphomas, principally Burkitt's. A rough wooden sign at the entrance reads:

> The Lymphoma Treatment Centre
> Is A Joint Effort Of The Makerere
> College Medical School And
> The National Cancer Institute
> Of The United States
> Public Health Service

This sign nailed on to the wall of a hut in Uganda requires a few words of explanation.

The National Cancer Institute is one of the nine Institutes and four Divisions that make up the National Institutes of Health of the United States, and it is the Federal government's principal agency for research on the cause, diagnosis, treatment, and prevention of cancer.

In recent years so-called task forces—groups of experts—have been formed to concentrate on certain particularly urgent problems; among these have been an Acute Leukemia Task Force and a Lymphoma Task Force. Inevitably there is profound interest in Burkitt's lymphoma, and a sub–task force was established in 1966 to investigate it. One group of scientists works at the National Institutes of Health in Bethesda, Maryland; another group is based at the Lymphoma Treatment Centre in Kampala; a third group is in Accra, where American and Ghanian scientists are cooperating to study the disease.

Following the precedent set by Denis Burkitt, members of the Kampala group visited district hospitals in outlying areas where the lymphoma had previously been reported and urged medical officers to keep an eye out for new cases of the disease and to send children to the treatment center as speedily as possible. Small sums of money were left wherever necessary to pay for transportation.

As a result, in a period of eighteen months the center admitted forty-eight patients who had received no previous treatment.

The physicians in charge of the center now came face to face with the question nobody could answer: Which form of treatment was best for these children—Burkitt's minimal treatment or Clifford's intensive treatment? Dr. Richard H. Morrow (who, in the cheerful words of a colleague, Dr. John L. Ziegler, "single-handedly built this unit up from a mud hut to the gleaming clinical center it now is") expressed the dilemma in a paper published in 1967: "The major problems of which drug to give, the best total dose (of a particular drug) to give, and whether this should depend on the 'extent' of the disease, remain unsolved. It is our belief that these problems will not be resolved without strictly controlled clinical trials."

But how do you go about carrying out strictly controlled clinical trials on children suffering from a highly malignant cancer that may kill them in twelve weeks?

The answer is, by employing a procedure called randomization.

The initial steps are routine. The child receives a thorough examination, his (or her) condition is fully assessed, and so on.

The physician then proceeds with his duties. But instead of deciding upon such and such a form of treatment, so many courses of such and such a drug, he reaches into a file cabinet, takes out an envelope, opens it, and draws from it a slip of paper (as if he were conducting a lottery). It is this slip of paper that determines, *at random,* the precise treatment the child will receive. In the Lymphoma Treatment Centre the slip of paper may say *Minimal*—that is, the treatment advocated by Mr. Burkitt on the basis of his experience at Mulago Hospital; or it may say *Intensive*—the treatment advocated by Mr. Clifford on the basis of his experience at Kenyatta National Hospital. From another envelope, in the same way, the physician will then draw a slip of paper instructing him which of several drugs shall be used; and once the slips of paper have been drawn, the child's treatment goes forward. Minimal. Or intensive. This drug. Or that drug.

Randomization, at first sight, seems to be utterly inhumane, substituting blind chance for the intelligence and the experience and—above all—the concern of the physician. It seems to be a total abandonment of responsibility; and it seems, furthermore, to be seriously unethical insofar as it implies experimentation upon human beings who are suffering from a grave disease.

But the fact is (as many researchers have pointed out), nobody really knows the "best" treatment for these children. Mr. Burkitt's treatment will result in long-term survivals of 15 to 20 percent. Mr. Clifford's treatment will result in long-term survivals of 15 to 20 percent. Both, in the present state of our knowledge, are "best" treatments, and thus no experimentation is involved.

The same uncertainty affects the various drugs used in chemotherapy. Nobody has established which is the "best" drug for the treatment of Burkitt's lymphoma. All have virtues, all have disadvantages.

Randomized treatment of a large series of patients will provide the answers—it is the *only* way, according to the experts, to provide the answers. And of course, in actual practice, the physician has not really abandoned the patient. He is constantly present, constantly alert; and if the patient fails to respond to treatment the physician can instantly resume his traditional posture. Meanwhile, this failure in itself adds to the store of knowledge, so that in due course there will be sufficient information to decide exactly how the greatest number of these children can be kept alive for the longest possible time.

Randomization. An ugly, contrived word. A disturbing procedure. "We shall have the answer in about eight months," says one scientist. Another says, "Eight years."

One of the men working on the problem in a hut next door to the old Maternity Ward is Malcolm Pike, a young South African medical statistician who sports a red beard that gives him the appearance of a rebellious pirate. Dr. Pike summed up the matter in a few passionate words: "Probably there has never been such striking progress in medical history as there was in the first few years after World War II, when scientists at the Medical Research Council in England concentrated on anti-TB drugs. They found *exactly* what was the right dose, *exactly* under which conditions people would respond, and so on. And they did this by randomization. This didn't stop the scientists from investigating each patient minutely, to see why his lesion collapsed and disappeared. . . . Today, if a TB patient walks into a hospital in England we know exactly what we can do with him because we've *systematically* explored everything about the disease and its treatment. And we will soon know when a child walks into the Lymphoma Treatment Centre whether we should treat him the way Mr. Burkitt thinks he should be treated, or the way Mr. Clifford thinks he should be treated. This debate, which has been going on for a long time, will soon be settled one way or the other."

14

A Rabbit in Entebbe

In March 1961, some six months before he set out on the long safari to Johannesburg, Denis Burkitt went on leave to England. Among his other activities there he addressed two meetings in London.

One of these is best described in his own words: "I was asked to speak at the Royal College of Surgeons. It was a depressing talk in a way, as talks at the Royal College tend to be. It was given in an enormous hall which could hold hundreds—no, thousands—of people; and there was a total audience of about twelve. After all, why should anybody be interested? A lymphoma in Africa. Terribly dull."

Mr. Burkitt is a lively speaker. He stands very erect, he talks rapidly, he has much to say, he is enthusiastic and often witty. One has no way of knowing the reactions of the twelve distinguished surgeons who listened to him on this occasion; but he made a definite hit with his second address, which was given to clinical students at the huge, rambling, old Middlesex Hospital in central London. Dr. M. A. Epstein, who was then in charge of a research unit in the Bland Sutton Institute (which is attached to the hospital rather as the Sloan-Kettering Institute for Cancer Research is attached to Memorial Hospital in New York), has given an interesting account of what occurred:

"Mr. Burkitt had for many years a connection with the Medical School here at the Middlesex Hospital because he knew the Director of the Department of Surgical Studies at that time; and whenever he came on leave, every three years or so, he gave a lecture for the clinical students. He described himself as a bush surgeon, and he'd give descriptions of fantastic cases—the biggest hydrocele, the largest elephantiasis, and so on—huge conditions which were seen in Africa and weren't seen here.

"Then, in 1961, he came and gave us another talk, and an announcement was put up on our notice board. I happened to see this, and afterwards I took it down and kept it. It read:

A COMBINED MEDICAL AND SURGICAL STAFF MEETING
will be held
on Wednesday, 22nd March, 1961, at 5.15 p.m.
IN THE COURTAULD LECTURE THEATRE

Mr. D. P. Burkitt from Makerere College,
Uganda will talk on "The Commonest Children's
Cancer in Tropical Africa. A Hitherto
unrecognized Syndrome."

"I had been working on tumor viruses, and I went along to the lecture out of curiosity.

"I listened to him, and after he had been talking for ten minutes it was absolutely clear that he had something tremendously important. It had immense theoretical implications. . . . After the lecture I asked him over to tea, and he came two or three days later.

"The important thing was his idea that the geographical

distribution of the disease indicated that there might be some infectious cause. This was what caught my imagination because I had been working with tumor viruses, or viruses that cause tumors in animals, for more than ten years.

"At that time, early in 1961, there was very little interest in Burkitt's work, and if I hadn't gone to the lecture I probably wouldn't have heard about it until very much later. It was just one of those accidents."

When Burkitt came to tea at the Bland Sutton Institute, Dr. Epstein discussed ways and means of getting supplies of tumor material. ("Tony Epstein was at my lecture," Burkitt said later, "and he immediately said, *This is hot stuff*. He saw implications in it which hadn't occurred to me.")

"The essential thing was to have material constantly available in our laboratory here in London," Dr. Epstein explains. "It's all very well having six patients with the tumor in the ward at Mulago Hospital, but you can't put sophisticated tools to work in Uganda." Soon afterwards, with funds supplied by the British Empire Cancer Campaign and with valuable support from Sir Charles Dodds, Chairman of the Scientific Advisory Committee of the Campaign, Dr. Epstein went out to Kampala and set up machinery for sending tumor samples overnight by air to his laboratory in the Bland Sutton Institute. "We went out to London Airport to pick up the material no matter what time of the day or night it arrived."

So Michael Anthony Epstein, M.A., M.D., D.Sc., Ph.D., F.C.Path., joined the list of characters in this extraordinary drama.

Anthony Epstein was not alone in recognizing the potentialities of Burkitt's work, even at this early stage. Other scientists were hot on the trail.

One of these was the great American virologist Gilbert Dalldorf, who was making important contributions to virology (the study of viruses) as far back as the 1930s. In 1947 he discovered the first of the Coxsackie family of viruses, which cause a variety of diseases, from a noninfectious form of poliomyelitis to "summer grippe," as well as many ill-defined aches, pains, and intestinal upsets.

Gilbert Dalldorf and Anthony Epstein were well aware of the pot of gold that might be buried at the distant end of this rainbow. Dalldorf, an unusually eloquent writer, had expressed it long ago: "The virus theory of cancer . . . remains a theory as far as human cancer goes because no one has found convincing evidence of a causal relationship between a virus and a malignant tumor of man. Proof of such a relationship for any one of our human cancers would have a tremendous impact on cancer research." And any man or woman who found and proved that a particular virus causes a particular human cancer could be sure of scientific immortality.

It is probably enough, in order to follow the drift of the story, to note a few very elementary facts about viruses: that they are microorganisms responsible for numerous afflictions in plants, animals, and man, such as (to select a few human diseases caused by viruses) measles, chicken pox, smallpox, influenza; that *animal tumor viruses* are, as the name implies, viruses that cause tumors in animals; and, similarly, that *human cancer viruses* are viruses that are presumed to cause cancer in human beings—the qualification "presumed" is necessary because no viruses of this kind have been identified.

There is some question whether viruses can be called living organisms. The argument that supersedes all others, perhaps, is that they are capable of reproducing themselves, and therefore they must be alive. Alternatively, they can be killed in many different ways so that they are totally inactive and unable to reproduce themselves, and it is reasonable to argue that a virus has to be alive before it can be killed. The name "virus" means, simply, a poison; but a great many viruses are harmless to man, and one writer on the subject even refers to "the friendly viruses," because they seem to help mankind by attacking bacteria that may be harmful to us.

In general, viruses are considered to be the smallest of organisms on this planet, but at least one is of appreciable size and can be seen fairly well through the ordinary laboratory microscope—the cowpox virus, about 1/100,000 of an inch in size. But most viruses can be seen only by means of the electron miscroscope, and at tremendous magnification—up to 300,000 times. The sheer minuteness of some of these organisms is hard to grasp. One researcher happened to cut a section through a cell that was full of tobacco mosaic viruses*; and he found, by calculation, that the cell contained about sixty million virus particles.

Viruses come in a variety of shapes, but essentially they are all constructed of two kinds of material. They have an outer coat of protein; and an inner core of nucleic acid. Here we have a slight complication: nucleic acid has two forms, chemically very similar but functionally dissimilar. One is called deoxyribonucleic acid, or DNA; the other, ribonucleic acid, or RNA. Thus, rather conveniently, viruses divide into

---

* The tobacco mosaic virus has a place in history as the first virus to be discovered. It causes a curious mottling of tobacco leaves; and it is so stable and resistant that it can be transmitted in tobacco smoke.

two broad groups, and we have the DNA viruses, responsible for certain diseases, and the RNA viruses, which are responsible for different kinds of diseases.

As far as the rest of creation is concerned, the trouble with viruses is that they are parasites and can only grow and multiply within living cells of other organisms. Once they have entered a cell that suits them they can utilize the cell's nucleic acid to manufacture nucleic acid cores similar to their own. They also requisition the cell's proteins to manufacture protein overcoats; and so great numbers of new viruses come into existence, each with the ability to colonize neighboring cells. The sum total of all these actions—breaking into the cell, robbing the cell of its nucleic acid and protein, the destruction of the cell, the colonization of other cells, together with the efforts of the invaded organism to defend itself and exterminate the viruses—results in the specific disease. That is, the disease is not simply invasion by viruses. It is the sum total of aggression and defense. In the words of Dennis Wright: "The disease isn't just what the baddies do; it's the combination of the baddies and the goodies."

In certain circumstances (nobody knows what they are or why they should occur) a virus may refrain from aggressive multiplication; instead, it will incorporate its nucleic acid somewhere in the cell's nucleic acid. The cell is thus transformed: its nucleic acid, carrying the cell's genetic information, now also carries the genetic information of the virus. Then, after the transformed cell has undergone numerous cell divisions, the virus may reappear and resume its virulent aspect, multiplying rapidly at the cell's expense and destroying it.

But something else may happen. The transformed cell, its normal functioning disturbed by the incorporation of the virus's nucleic acid, may go out of control and begin a process of wild, unrestrained growth; and this may lead to the disease we call cancer.

We know that viruses cause various forms of cancer in animals.

We know, furthermore, that certain human viruses will cause malignant tumors when they are inoculated into certain animals.

We also know that certain animal viruses will cause human cells in a test tube to become cancerous.

We have, therefore, a great deal of evidence that clearly demonstrates the responsibility of viruses in the causation of cancer—outside the human species.

But, at the present time, we have no proof that any virus causes cancer in man. The discovery of such a virus would have, as Dr. Dalldorf stated, a tremendous impact on cancer research; and once we were certain of the relationship between a particular virus and a particular cancer we might be on the way to developing new techniques for treating the disease.

There was gold under the Burkitt rainbow, sure enough. Not a pot of gold, but gold ore that would require patient refining.

Gilbert Dalldorf reported that he found a number of viruses, "some of which have not been identified (while) those that have been identified do not seem to be related to the disease." To this extent his results could be termed negative. However, he was responsible for several brilliant observations, which affected all future thinking about the lymphoma.

First, he pointed out that childhood leukemia occurs infrequently in tropical Africa, whereas it is comparatively common in Western countries. The reverse is true of Burkitt's lymphoma: it is comparatively common in tropical Africa, rare in Western countries. But, *if one combined the incidence of both diseases in a given area,* the rates would be the same. For example, the sum of the low rate of leukemia and the high rate of Burkitt's lymphoma in tropical Africa would equal the sum of the high rate of leukemia and the low rate of Burkitt's lymphoma in North America.

In scientific terms, there appeared to be an inverse, or reciprocal, relationship between Burkitt's lymphoma and childhood leukemia. From this simple base, some scientists went on to discuss the concept that the two diseases might, in a sense, be the same disease; that this might be a disease which in tropical Africa expressed itself as Burkitt's lymphoma, while in more temperate regions it expressed itself as acute childhood leukemia. The idea was exciting because Burkitt's lymphoma responded, in one case out of five, to chemotherapy, and there might be a possibility of finding similar treatment for leukemia. Other scientists disagreed emphatically with this concept, and maintained that Burkitt's lymphoma and acute childhood leukemia are separate conditions, and are not reciprocally related. The controversy persists.

In addition, Dalldorf pointed out that in areas where Burkitt's lymphoma is common, the population is susceptible virtually from birth to heavy infection by malaria parasites. Malaria has considerable effect upon an individual's immune system, and Dr. Dalldorf suggested that malarial infection might be a factor in the causation of the tumor, and that there might be, additionally, a secondary factor such as a virus carried by the Anopheles mosquito. But this virus, if it existed, eluded him.

*   *   *

Dr. Dalldorf's team had its headquarters in Nairobi. Another team, under the auspices of the Imperial Cancer Research Fund, was based at the East African Virus Research Institute in Entebbe.*

One of the scientists who organized this team explained: "We built a small laboratory with Dr. Thomas M. Bell in charge. His approach was different from Epstein's. Tom Bell used a sort of amplification technique. Side by side with cells containing small amounts of virus—perhaps only one virus particle—he put cells that are very sensitive to virus. The idea was that when the virus left the lymphoma cells it wouldn't have to struggle around to find another cell it could infect and in which it could multiply easily: it would find another cell close at hand. In other words, it would go out of the back door of the tumor cell and in through the front door of the sensitive cell without even crossing the street. Under these conditions, Dr. Bell was able to pick up a reovirus."

Reoviruses in the past have been associated with various mild disorders designated, in medical parlance, *respiratory* and *enteric* (relating to the intestine). But they have not been implicated in any particular disease, and virologists were apt to describe them in a rather sentimental fashion as

* This was originally the yellow fever research laboratory supported by the Rockefeller Foundation. It is now officially described (in its 1967 Report) as "one of the self-contained departments of the General Fund Services of the East African Community (recently the East African Common Services Organization). . . . Most of the Institute's expenditure is met by contributions from the Governments of Kenya, Uganda and Tanzania, with a generous matching grant from the British Government. The Government of Zanzibar also makes a valuable contribution." The Institute now has full control of all investigations into Burkitt's lymphoma in the West Nile District.

viruses without a home of their own, or orphans. From Respiratory and Enteric Orphans came the prefix *reo;* and in the course of time three distinct forms were found, known as type 1, type 2, and type 3. It was the latter, reovirus type 3, that Dr. Bell consistently found in Burkitt's tumor.

The precise relationship of reovirus type 3 to Burkitt's lymphoma remains to be established. Some authorities, such as the distinguished Australian virologist Professor N. F. Stanley, believe it plays an active part in causing the tumor. Other authorities have not found convincing evidence that the virus is active in causing Burkitt's lymphoma. But the story does not end there, in polite disagreement. Once more the story line breaks away and we are confronted by completely unexpected developments.

In the course of his experiments in Entebbe, Dr. Bell—an amiable young Scottish virologist who lectured at the University of Aberdeen before coming to Uganda—inoculated a rabbit with several large doses of reovirus type 3.

Eight months after the first inoculation the rabbit was found to have a large mass on its neck.

Dennis Wright has described the events that followed:

"Dr. Bell and his colleague Dr. G. M. R. Manube brought this rabbit over to me in Kampala; and Tom Bell said, 'Here's a rabbit with a big lump on the front of its neck.'

"Rabbits aren't as meek as they are made out to be. They often fight among themselves, and when they do so they tend to inoculate a bacterium which grows into a sort of lump. I thought Tom Bell's rabbit had a similar kind of lump—I'd seen examples of it frequently in the past.

"They left the rabbit with me and went off to talk to somebody else in the Medical School. I examined the rabbit, and to my amazement it turned out to have a lymphoma in the neck and lots of deposits elsewhere. I very quickly made an imprint for examination under the microscope, and then I went off posthaste to tell Dr. Bell and Dr. Manube that this was really most exciting and it looked as if they had hit the jackpot. We did a number of things: we prepared tissue for electron microscopy, we froze down some of the tissue; but the most important and the most immediate thing to do was to put some of the lymphoma into newborn rabbits so that the tissue could keep growing.

"There were no newborn rabbits in the Medical School. But as luck would have it, one of my children's pet rabbits had produced a litter the day before. So, at lunchtime I went home and bribed the children to let me have the newborn rabbits. I couldn't move them, of course—they were in a hutch in my garage—and I had to take all the materials and inject the rabbits at home. We were able to maintain the tumor, and after that we kept breeding rabbits, so there was no shortage."

The jackpot, as Dr. Wright called it, would have been the discovery that Dr. Bell's rabbit, after inoculation with reovirus type 3, had developed Burkitt's lymphoma or something very close to it. But this turned out not to be the case. The lump was eventually identified as a myeloma (which means a tumor arising from tissue in the bone marrow) or plasma cell tumor.

A few technicalities are unavoidable here. Briefly, plasma cells are cells, found in the blood plasma, which produce antibodies; and antibodies are a major component of the body's defenses against infection. Dr. Bell and Dr. Wright, and their colleagues, now had a tumor which could be made to produce any kind of antibody. Furthermore, study of the tumor might reveal how antibodies are made.

There was another aspect to the discovery. Antibodies are constructed of proteins. Study of the tumor might lead to an understanding of protein formation. ("One of the world's leading protein scientists," Dr. Bell said happily, "would sell his soul for one gram of this plasma cell tumor.")

The greatest significance of the discovery is this: antibodies are indispensable to the body's defenses against infection, but occasionally something goes wrong in the immune system and cells or antibodies may act *against* rather than in defense of the body. The result may be an *autoimmune* disease. With knowledge acquired from study of the plasma cell tumor (which may or may not have been caused by the reovirus type 3 found by Dr. Bell in Burkitt's lymphoma), scientists may learn how to treat or alleviate many of the autoimmune diseases that plague vast numbers of human beings, such as rheumatoid arthritis or asthma. "It could mean a major breakthrough," says Dennis Wright, a cautious man, "in protein chemistry and antibody studies." The benefits, the potentialities, are enormous.

In London, meanwhile, Anthony Epstein went a different way and whipped up some excitement of his own.

15

Man Meets EBV

The Bland Sutton Institute in London is not one of the showplaces of contemporary medical science. It does not gleam, it does not impress. It is reached (at least from one direction) by proceeding through a sort of elongated boiler room under the Middlesex Hospital; the Institute lies somewhere up and beyond—rather gray, rather dismal, putting the visitor in mind of an abandoned wing of Wuthering Heights. But what it lacks in chrome and stainless steel it makes up in certain rare and intangible qualities, notably brains, energy, and vision.

Bland Sutton, in the person of M. A. Epstein, made its acquaintance with Mr. Burkitt by sheer good fortune in March 1961. Thereafter Dr. Epstein went to Kampala and arranged for biopsy samples—that is, tissue taken from the tumor—to be sent to him by air.

His tactics were quite different from those of Dr. Bell at the East African Research Institute in sunny Entebbe. Bell had decided upon a sort of cell-amplification technique. Ep-

stein set about trying to grow the cells in tissue culture—
that is, in vessels containing the requisite nutrients, maintained at the correct temperature, and so on. Superficially
this sounds easy enough; it was in fact exceedingly difficult, because Epstein was attempting something that had not
hitherto been accomplished.*

"For two years we tried to get these things to grow," Dr.
Epstein says. "I tried twenty-four different samples, without
success. Obviously, we were doing the wrong things in all our
efforts. But eventually, if you go on hard enough, you see
your way through; and in 1963 we were able to get the first
of the biopsy samples to grow. It is still [in 1968] growing
in our laboratory: it recently passed its fourth birthday. The
child from whom the cells came is long since dead, but his
cells are going on, and in a way this is a form of immortality."

Once the technique of growing the cells in tissue culture
was established there was a widespread demand for samples
from scientists eager to investigate them. Dr. Epstein's records for a short period in 1963, for example, show shipments
to Canada, the United States, the USSR, Czechoslovakia,
Israel.†

* The technical explanation, in Dr. Epstein's words, is that
"up to this time nobody had ever grown members of the human
lymphocytic series of cells in continuous tissue culture, and
Burkitt's tumor is composed of malignant cells of this type."
Lymphocytes can be described as white blood cells formed in
the lymph nodes, the spleen, and other lymphoid tissue throughout the body.

† The nonscientific reader, who may be disturbed by the
thought of cancerous cells traveling all over the world, is hereby
assured that no health hazard is involved. Persuading the cells
to grow in the laboratory, as Dr. Epstein explained, requires
special technology, as well as loving tender care; outside laboratory conditions the cells die only too quickly. On flights from

Grants from the National Cancer Institute, in 1963, enabled Dr. Epstein to expand his laboratory; Dr. Yvonne Barr joined him, to work on the lymphoma; and as a result of this conjunction the first line of Burkitt tumor cells grown at the Bland Sutton Institute was given the code designation EB_1 (*E* standing for Epstein, *B* for Barr). "It was simply a piece of laboratory shorthand," Epstein explains. "We used it for purposes of identification—for labeling our bottles, among other things." Future cell lines were designated EB_2, and so on, up to EB_7.

The Bland Sutton researchers could now go to work on electron microscope studies, and very soon it became apparent that the Burkitt cells were carrying a virus. "We were able to identify the *kind* of virus," Dr. Epstein says, "but not exactly what it was. That is, we knew the family: it was one of the herpes group. But it wasn't any *known member* of the herpes group."

The herpes group of viruses resemble each other somewhat in form, but they vary considerably in their effects, particularly on human beings. The name is derived from the Greek *herpein,* to creep (thus, *herpeton,* a snake); and the herpes viruses tend to manifest themselves in creeping eruptions in one form or another. Pigs, horses, cattle, monkeys, all have their own specific herpes viruses; until recently there were only three that were known to affect man. The most familiar

---

one country to another the cells are in liquid suspension, within a metal canister; they travel in the cabin with the crew, since if they were put in the luggage compartment they would freeze and die.

In the laboratory one sees flasks partially filled with slightly brownish broth, usually rather cloudy. The cloudiness is caused by Burkitt tumor cells clinging together in clumps.

is the kind that causes chickenpox—the varicella virus; but the same virus may behave in a different way—it is then called herpes zoster—and cause shingles, an infection characterized by small eruptions that follow the course of a nerve, resulting in severe and persistent neuralgia. Herpes simplex is also well known in civilized circles: it causes "cold sores," which appear and disappear for no clear reason. The third group affecting man consists of the cytomegaloviruses, which simply means viruses that cause enlargement of cells in various organs; their chief interest seems to be the salivary glands.

But the herpes virus found in the Epstein-Barr cell lines of Burkitt's tumor did not belong to any of these three groups. Epstein termed it "a highly unusual virus which had not hitherto been discovered." It soon became known as the Epstein-Barr virus; and this, very quickly, was abbreviated to EBV.

EBV was a remarkable discovery. Yet anybody talking about it, or writing about it, had to exercise considerable restraint, because although it was invariably *found* in Burkitt's tumor there was no positive evidence that it *caused* Burkitt's tumor. It was interesting. It was exciting. But one could not point to it (or, for that matter, to any other virus) as the cause of any form of human cancer. "No herpes virus," Dr. Epstein says, "has ever been implicated in any kind of malignant disease. And, besides, they are DNA viruses, whereas the viruses that cause all the known malignancies in animals, such as the lymphomas and leukemias of mice and chickens and cats are RNA viruses."

A technicality of some importance.

Any reader who thinks he is going to be bored to death by a dissertation on viruses is advised to hang on to his seat.

Something quite startling and unexpected is on the way. *Nobody* expected it. It came clear out of the blue.

The story now crosses the Atlantic, to the Virus Laboratories of the Chlidren's Hospital of Philadelphia, the base of two of the world's most distinguished virologists, Dr. Gertrude Henle and Dr. Werner Henle.

"My husband," says Gertrude Henle, "is one-quarter Jewish—he had a Jewish grandfather—and he could not get a post when he finished his training in Heidelberg because of the Nazis. So in 1933 he came to the United States, and in 1937 I followed him." She is a woman who is blessed with both physical beauty and intellectual brilliance. Werner Henle is handsome, genial, and equally brilliant. They are an extraordinary team.

Werner Henle's Jewish grandfather happened to be the anatomist Jacob Henle, who lived from 1809 to 1885 and whose name was given to numerous anatomical features which he discovered, or first described: Henle's loop, Henle's fissures, Henle's glands, Henle's membrane, and a dozen more.*

Finding work in the United States was no problem for the grandson of this medical genius; and Werner and Gertrude

* Fielding H. Garrison in his *History of Medicine* calls Jacob Henle "one of the greatest anatomists of all time . . . his histological discoveries take rank with the anatomical discoveries of Vesalius. . . . As a lecturer, Henle was vivid and inspiring, winning love and admiration by his sincerity and charm. He was not only a skillful artist, but something of a poet, and an accomplished musician, beginning with the violin and eventually learning to play both viola and violoncello." He was a friend of Felix Mendelssohn, says Garrison, and had a very romantic first marriage. One could hardly ask for a more admirable grandfather.

Henle were soon investigating the possibility of population control by means of immunization against spermatozoa (an idea which has recently been revived); they went on to study influenza viruses, and then did extremely valuable work on a phenomenon called viral interference (in which one virus in a cell "interferes" with another invading virus). The course of their joint career was changed in 1956 by a telephone call from the National Institutes of Health, which set them off on a lengthy program of research into cancer viruses; and this was brought into focus by Dr. Everett C. Koop (whom they describe as "our surgeon"), who came to them after a visit to East Africa and said, "Henles: if you want to work on a human tumor that is likely to be virus-induced, Burkitt's tumor is it." The world of science, as we have seen and as we shall continue to see, proceeds in a curiously nonscientific way: great events spring only too often from a chance remark, some utterly unlikely event, a wild coincidence.

The following year, the Henles received a letter from Anthony Epstein asking if he could send them the EB cell line—he had then reached EB_2—for isolation and identification of any virus it carried. The Henles agreed, but their first efforts were unsuccessful. They were unable to isolate a virus by any of the conventional methods.

Now, any "foreign" organism that succeeds in invading the body is met, as a rule, by special particles designed to attack and destroy that particular invader. These particles, of course, are the antibodies, and it has been estimated that an adult human carries some ten thousand different kinds. The important fact, in this context, is that each kind of antibody is specifically tailored to attack a specific invader: if some organism invades the body, and no antibody exists to challenge it, the appropriate antibody is quickly manufactured.* We start our lives with so-called maternal antibodies, acquired from our mother; these serve to protect us for our first six months or so, and gradually disappear. Then, as we encounter our various micro-enemies we form an ever-growing collection of antibodies to deal with them. From this it follows that the presence of a certain antibody in our blood serum implies that at some time or another we have had an encounter with the foreign organism which that antibody was designed to combat.

The Henles, after their initial failure to isolate a virus from the EB$_2$ cells, argued that if there *was* a virus, and if this virus had anything to do with Burkitt's lymphoma, then a patient with the lymphoma should possess antibodies to the virus.

This very far-reaching assumption proved to be correct. Using a technique called immunofluorescence, in which antibodies receive a coating of a fluorescent dye and can thus be seen by ultraviolet rays in a special microscope, the Henles were able to select individual cells that had attracted fluorescent antibodies, and these cells were found to be "loaded" —as Werner Henle says—with viruses.

Like Dr. Epstein, the Henles were unable to make a precise identification. Almost certainly they were herpes viruses, but they did not match any known *human* herpes virus, nor did they match any known *animal* herpes virus. The safest thing to say about them was they were *herpes-like* viruses.

Investigations now showed that this virus was found, without fail, in every Burkitt patient. *Every child with Burkitt's lymphoma had the Epstein-Barr virus.*

This was a hopeful and encouraging sign. EBV, one

* Microorganisms and chemical substances that provoke the manufacture of a specific antibody are called antigens.

could say with confidence, seemed to be *associated* with Burkitt's lymphoma.

But now came the first shock.

The Henles continued to find antibodies to EB virus.

They found the antibodies, in fact, almost anywhere they looked.

And the people carrying these antibodies were generally perfectly healthy normal human beings.

Up to 85 percent of all people tested, Africans, Americans, and Europeans, had EBV antibodies, showing without any possibility of a doubt that at some time in their lives they had been infected by the Epstein-Barr virus; and no matter how far you went from civilization, the virus was still prevalent.

Men and women living on lonely farms in Iceland had antibodies to the EB virus.

The Tirio Indians, deep in the forests of Brazil, four hundred miles north of the Amazon, had antibodies to EB virus.

And about the only thing you could say about it with any measure of confidence was that it was primarily a human virus. It was not found in animals. But even this generalization was not altogether true because there is an infectious disease of chickens called Marek's disease, which seems to be caused by a virus that is, in Dr. Epstein's words, "indistinguishable from the agent we have here in Burkitt's tumor." *
Not EBV, perhaps, but very, very similar.

Virologists call a virus which has a very broad distribution *ubiquitous*. The Henles believed that a virus found so fre-

---

* This disease was first described by a scientist named Marek about sixty years ago. It involves lymphomas of the nerve trunks and various organs; it is highly infectious, and a serious economic hazard for poultry farmers.

quently in human beings must be responsible for some human disease and, in their own words, "We started to look for a disease to fit the virus." Burkitt's lymphoma was still present in their minds, but the principal locale of Burkitt's lymphoma is tropical Africa, although rare cases occur elsewhere. The Henles had a ubiquitous virus, and they were looking for a ubiquitous disease.

It was waiting for them on their own doorstep.

Working in their laboratories in Philadelphia was a technician named Elaine Hutkin. At the time of these events she was nineteen years old—an exceptionally pretty girl, with dark hair and the neat, graceful appearance of a ballerina.

In the course of normal laboratory routine her serum had been tested by the Henles, and by a stroke of luck she had proven to be EBV negative—that is, she possessed no antibodies to EBV. She belonged to the minority of Americans who had escaped infection by the Epstein-Barr virus; and because of this she had contributed blood—in minute amounts—several times for cultures to be used in the Henles' experimental work.

Then, one day, she felt too sick to go to work. "I had chills, a sore throat, swollen glands in my neck," she says. "I felt awful—I was tired all the time." She remained at home for six days. "Then I went back to work, and after a couple of days—I was still feeling awful—I developed a rash."

"She developed a rash under our very eyes," says Werner Henle with justifiable enthusiasm. "We didn't know what it was, but she was obviously not cured. So we said to her, *Let us set up another leucocyte (white cell) culture, and maybe we will find your virus.* We took some plasma from her for another EBV antibody test; and to our surprise it was positive."

The sequence, therefore, was this:

Before falling sick Elaine lacked EBV antibodies, an indication that (in all probability) she had never been infected by the Epstein-Barr herpes-like virus.

She then fell sick, with distressing but vague symptoms: chills, sore throat, excessive fatigue, and so on.

After a total of eight days of this illness she developed a rash.

Tests now showed a high level of EBV antibodies in her serum, which meant that since her last test she had been infected by EB virus.

Examination of a leucocyte culture confirmed the presence of EB virus.

The next stage was totally unexpected: after developing the rash, Elaine was seen by her physician. He diagnosed her illness. It was infectious mononucleosis.

Infectious mononucleosis!

And although the evidence was derived only from this one case, it was possible to suggest that Elaine's infectious mononucleosis was caused by Epstein-Barr virus.

The Henles must have felt as if a bomb had exploded overhead. EBV was unquestionably associated with Burkitt's lymphoma—it was found in every patient with the disease. But nobody in his wildest dreams would have thought of associating it with infectious mononucleosis, which is non-malignant.

But here, at last, was a ubiquitous disease, and the Henles had been looking for a ubiquitous disease to match the ubiquitous EBV. Their problem now was to confirm and prove the relationship.

"We sat down and asked ourselves, who in the United States is interested in infectious mononucleosis," Dr. Gertrude Henle recalls.

"And then we remembered: the Yale boys."

Infectious mononucleosis, or glandular fever, was first described by the Russian, N. F. Filatow, in 1886. It has yet another name: because it is highly infectious, and often occurs among young people in schools and colleges, it is sometimes called kissing disease.

It is known all over the world. Typically, it causes the symptoms described by Elaine Hutkin: sore throat, chills, headache, fatigue. Glands are inflamed, and there may be enlargement of the spleen or liver. Unusual, or abnormal, white cells appear in the blood: these cells give the disease its name. In general, it is a fairly mild illness; in rare cases there may be serious complications.

The disease resembles infectious hepatitis (according to one medical handbook, "it is sometimes virtually impossible to distinguish between the two"). It also resembles leukemia, lymphosarcoma, and Hodgkin's disease, although—as far as anybody knows at present—it is not related to these malignancies.

Until Elaine Hutkin developed a rash in the Virus Laboratories of the Children's Hospital in Philadelphia, the etiologic agent of infectious mononucleosis—that is, the organism causing the disease—was completely unknown.

So Elaine enters medical history and joins such immortals as the milkmaid Sarah Nelmes, who provided Edward Jenner with material for the first inoculation against smallpox, and nine-year-old Joseph Meister, who led Pasteur to the treatment for rabies.

The Yale boys came to the Henles' mind for an excellent reason. All freshmen entering Yale University, over a period of six years from 1958 on, were requested to supply samples of blood, together with their medical history, for a study of infectious mononucleosis begun by Dr. James C. Niederman. Records were kept most carefully, and selected serum samples were frozen for future reference.

Through the kindness of Dr. Niederman and Dr. Robert W. McCollum, of the Yale University School of Medicine, the Henles were able to draw upon this goldmine. Coded samples of the frozen serum were sent to the Henles; and in a crucial test they were able to identify—without a single failure—all samples taken from students who at one time or another had suffered from infectious mononucleosis.

In every case, antibodies to the Epstein-Barr virus were present in the serum.

Students who lacked these antibodies had never been ill with infectious mononucleosis.

To the satisfaction of most scientists (but not all, which is a perfectly normal state of affairs in medicine) the cause of infectious mononucleosis, or glandular fever, or kissing disease, was shown to be the Epstein-Barr virus, EBV, originally isolated from cell lines of Burkitt's lymphoma.

Where did Burkitt's lymphoma stand now?

16

Twenty Thousand Little Elaines

The Papuans of New Guinea are among the forgotten peoples of the earth. They have been isolated for centuries, civilization has passed them by, and we know little about them except that some of them still on occasion indulge in headhunting. The Tirio Indians are equally remote: they tend to hide away in their Amazonian rain forests, shunning their fellow man. The people of Uganda are more accessible; and yet, until recently, most of them spent their entire lives in the villages where they were born.

So we are surprised when we find that all these diverse human beings, as well as most Americans and Europeans, share the same lowly virus. And, as far as we can tell, *exactly* the same lowly virus: for the EBV antibodies of a Yale freshman will react to the EB virus in a cell line grown from a Ugandan child, and EB viruses from a Papuan will excite the EBV antibodies of a Londoner. One cannot help marveling at the sheer persistence of living things. How did these microscopic organisms *become* so ubiquitous? How did they reach the forest of Papua and Brazil, and the jungles of tropical Africa, and the Ivy League campuses? Apparently they are mighty travelers. They sweep in multitudes around the world. And they provoke many questions.

From the good, careful research of Gertrude and Werner Henle it is clear that vast numbers of Africans, Europeans, and Americans carry EBV antibodies, showing that at one time or another they have been infected by the EB virus. Moreover, it appears almost certain that the EB virus is the cause of infectious mononucleosis.

Why, then, do so few people, relatively, come down with infectious mononucleosis?

If EB virus is associated with Burkitt's lymphoma, why do so few children, relatively, come down with Burkitt's lymphoma?

And is there any relationship between infectious mononucleosis and Burkitt's lymphoma and, for that matter, any other disease?

The answer to the first question is fairly simple. Few people, relatively, come down with infectious mononucleosis, even in an epidemic, because most of us have already had the disease in some form.

We know that when young adults contract the disease, the effects range from headaches, nausea, swollen glands, and so on, to a severe and possibly dangerous illness affecting the liver, the spleen, the lungs, and even the heart and the brain.

In early childhood, though, infection with the EB virus rarely reaches the status of a disease: it is more often a vague chill, a cold, an upset stomach—nothing serious enough to warrant a visit to the doctor. These are the years when we suffer from a variety of infections; some may be bacterial, some may be described by the physician as "an unidentified viral infection." On the whole these episodes are not dangerous, and they provide us with antibodies that we can draw upon as long as we live. A familiar example is polio: most people encounter and acquire polio viruses very early in life, and as a consequence they are endowed with antibodies which provide valuable protection against poliomyelitis. They also *keep* some of these viruses, so that they continue to manufacture a steady supply of polio antibodies. But some people, particularly those who have lived in well-kept, sanitary homes, do not acquire any stray polio viruses, do not manufacture polio antibodies, and therefore require inoculations of polio vaccine (which contains polio viruses and thus stimulates the body into producing polio antibodies).

In all likelihood, then, about 85 percent of the populations of America, Africa, and Europe have experienced some mild childhood form of infectious mononucleosis, after acquiring EB virus. These people possess EBV antibodies, and are fairly secure from disease caused by this virus.

The remaining 15 percent—those people, like Elaine Hutkin, without EBV antibodies—are the future victims of infectious mononucleosis, and they may come down with the disease at any time up to the age of thirty-five or forty. When we arrive at early middle age, virtually all of us are immune.

Immune, at least, to this specific disease, infectious mononucleosis. But we have no positive knowledge that after we have reached the age of forty, Epstein-Barr virus ceases to affect us. We have absolutely no idea what happens to it, whether it ignores us, whether it becomes harmless, or whether it is capable of providing us with other surprises.

＊　　＊　　＊

The story is very different when we turn from infectious mononucleosis to Burkitt's lymphoma.

The most significant difference is that infectious mononucleosis is a self-limiting disease. As a rule it manifests itself for a fairly short period of time—about three weeks—and then, no matter how we treat it, it gradually disappears. On the other hand, Burkitt's lymphoma is a highly malignant disease: it is a fast-growing cancer, and without suitable treatment the patient's death is virtually certain within a few months.

Some scientists have argued that EB virus may be benign in some circumstances, malignant in other circumstances. Perhaps if we acquire the virus in an unusual manner—say, directly into the bloodstream—it might behave in an uncharacteristic way and initiate changes leading to a malignant growth.

But we have another fact to consider: the striking ubiquity of EB virus. It is found everywhere. Some 85 percent of the human race has encountered it.

Yet even in tropical Africa, Burkitt's lymphoma is by no means common. Outside tropical Africa, except for New Guinea, it is exceedingly rare.

So we have here a statistical discrepancy. With such vast numbers of children exposed to EB virus, we would expect to see many more cases of the lymphoma. *If, that is, EB virus alone caused the disease.*

However, we might come within the bounds of statistical possibility if we assume that the disease might be caused by the EB virus plus *something else.*

This *something else* (Gilbert Dalldorf suggested it years ago) could be malaria. Malaria comes under suspicion in the first place because it is widely prevalent and occurs in a very severe form (it is called holo-endemic) wherever Burkitt's lymphoma is common; and secondly, because it has many strange effects on the body, particularly upon the immune system. Thus, a child whose immune system has been altered by malaria might be infected by EB virus—perhaps by an unusual route—and in this way become susceptible to the tumor.

But this does not completely solve the difficulty, for there are many areas in the world where malaria is common, where the EB virus is common, yet Burkitt's lymphoma is uncommon.

We have to take an additional step, therefore, and postulate that Burkitt's lymphoma may be caused by EB virus, plus the effects of severe malaria, *plus something else*. And the virus discovered in the tumor by Dr. Tom Bell, reovirus type 3, might well be the third factor, boosting or completing the tumor-inducing effect of EB virus.

So, to account for Burkitt's lymphoma, a disease which occurs comparatively infrequently even in tropical Africa, we can envisage a complex (and wholly theoretical) series of events which would occur just as infrequently. The EB virus must, in some unusual manner, enter the bloodstream of a child whose immune defenses have been affected by malaria. The EB virus must then encounter another infective agent, possibly a reovirus type 3. The two viruses, complementing each other, might then work together to initiate the changes in the child's lymphoid tissues that would result in the growth of the tumor.*

* In much the same wholly theoretical way we can account for the cases of Burkitt's lymphoma that occasionally occur in England and the United States and other nontropical areas. Again, we can visualize Epstein-Barr virus and reovirus type 3 as the principal infective agents. They are both, after all, ubiquitous; they are found everywhere. But the child's immune

Normally we acquire EB virus, as scientists say, by the oral route: through the mouth. How could the Epstein-Barr virus take an unusual route directly into the bloodstream?

The answer is simple and reasonable, and it carries us right back to the beginning of the story, to Denis Burkitt and Ted Williams and Cliff Nelson setting off in their old station-wagon on a ten thousand mile safari to learn more about this mysterious tumor: the virus might enter the bloodstream as the result of the child being bitten by some arthropod.

Being bitten—for example—by a mosquito.

At the end of 1968 some forty scientists came together in one of Nairobi's less glamorous hotels for a roundtable conference on Burkitt's lymphoma. Mr. Burkitt was there, after an exhausting safari through the Congo; Mr. Clifford was there; Dr. Gertrude Henle and Dr. Werner Henle were there; so were Professor George Klein—one of the world's greatest immunologists—and Dr. Gilbert Dalldorf, and many other scientists who have appeared in this narrative: Dr. Thomas M. Bell and Dr. Malcolm Pike and Dr. Jan Stjernswärd; Dr. R. H. Morrow and Dr. John Ziegler, as well as Dr. B. de Thé of the International Agency for Research on Cancer, which functions under the umbrella of the World Health Organization. Most important, about thirty African medical scientists were present. They encounter the lymphoma more frequently than anyone else.

---

system may have been altered not by malaria (which is now fairly uncommon in Western nations) but by some other ailment, or even by a genetic defect. The chances of this happening in temperate climates are exceedingly small, compared with those areas where malaria affects the entire population; consequently the lymphoma *may* occur outside tropical Africa or New Guinea, but its incidence will be very, very low.

For several days these distinguished scientists discussed the possibility of setting up a unique experiment.

What, in a sense, they wanted to do was to recapitulate the Henles' experience with Elaine Hutkin, but on a vast scale. They wanted to enlist twenty thousand East African children in this experiment; all considerably younger than Elaine because the scientist's primary interest was not infectious mononucleosis but Burkitt's lymphoma, which reaches its peak at the age of seven.

The plan of the experiment, as it emerged from the conference, was to set up a scheme whereby the twenty thousand children would be kept under close medical supervision for several years. The immediate benefits would be great. As one scientist said, these would undoubtedly be the best-treated and healthiest children in the whole of Africa, and an immense amount of information would be acquired about anemia, malaria, and other problems of concern to the East African health authorities.

Once a year the scientists would take blood samples from each child. These samples would be coded, frozen, and stored.

No child would be exposed to danger of any kind. On the contrary, they would be safeguarded in every possible way. But since they live in the region of tropical Africa where Burkitt's lymphoma occurs most frequently, a few inevitably would come down with the disease. On the basis of statistics, perhaps ten of the twenty thousand would develop Burkitt's lymphoma in the course of two years.

These ten children would receive, of course, the best of care. Their chances of survival would be higher than average because they would be at all times under the supervision of pediatricians and medical assistants trained to recognize the early symptoms of the disease.

However, it would then be possible for the scientists to follow the procedure of the Henles, when Elaine Hutkin became ill with infectious mononucleosis. They could compare a child's blood after developing Burkitt's lymphoma with the stored blood samples taken from the same child before the disease manifested itself.*

Unfortunately, the probability is that for many reasons the experiment will never get under way. It is too ambitious; or it is too costly; or it is politically too dangerous.

Nevertheless, sooner or later, in one way or another, the scientists will discover the precise role of Epstein-Barr virus in Burkitt's lymphoma. *Can human cancer be caused by a virus?* The answer will be a landmark in medicine, for man will then be close to cracking one of his grimmest and most baffling problems.

Then, having cracked one form of this terrible disease, he could be on his way to cracking others: lymphosarcoma, Hodgkin's disease, and the mysterious leukemias. That, ultimately, is the significance of Burkitt's lymphoma. It might lead to a whole series of discoveries, of profound importance to all mankind.

It might open the door.

* It is worth repeating the scientific argument: We know that all patients with Burkitt's lymphoma have the EB virus. If the early blood samples of a child who developed Burkitt's lymphoma carried antibodies to EB virus, then the virus (probably) played no part in causing the disease. If the early blood samples were free of antibodies to EB virus, then the EB virus was recently acquired and (probably) played a part in causing the disease. With only one patient there would be an element of doubt, but the results obtained with ten patients, or more, would provide a conclusive answer.

17

Homecoming

Burkitt's lymphoma has made an extraordinary impact upon the world community of cancer scientists, so much so that it has been said (with some truth) that for some researchers Burkitt's lymphoma has become a way of life. "I think there must be an article or a new paper about the tumor published every week," Mr. Burkitt said recently. He added, "But I can't keep up with them because for the most part they are outside my competence. Immunology, viruses—they aren't my field at all."

One cannot even begin to summarize the vast amount of work being done. Most of it, as Mr. Burkitt hinted, is highly technical; but in a survey entitled *Burkitt's Lymphoma: A Study in Medical Detection,** he drew attention to certain studies which he felt were of special interest. For example, Victor Ngu, Professor of Surgery at Ibadan University in Nigeria, has demonstrated on several occasions that a patient suffering from the tumor will show a marked (though temporary) remission when he is given *blood serum* from an-

* *Abbottempo*, Book 4, Abbott Universal Ltd., 1967.

191

other patient whose tumor has disappeared after treatment. The implications, Mr. Burkitt points out, are most encouraging, for if we can learn how to make use of this kind of immunological treatment, "how much more welcome would it be than more and more radical surgery."

Another exceedingly valuable piece of research was carried out by Dr. Malcolm Pike, in collaboration with Dr. E. H. Williams of Kuluva Hospital. Dr. Pike, then working in Gower Street, London ("You climb seventy-eight rickety stairs to my office at the top of the building"), was shown Dr. Williams' lymphoma maps of the West Nile district and immediately recognized, as he says, that "something very peculiar was happening there." He went out to Uganda and worked with Dr. Williams, investigating in minute detail the incidence of Burkitt's lymphoma in West Nile over a period of five years; and he was then able to show that the disease seemed to occur in a pattern of clusters in space and time—that is, there would be several cases (a cluster) occurring fairly close together in a particular area (space) at the same time. Then, the following year, there would be a sort of drift, with several cases occurring in an area some distance away.

The significance of Pike's finding is that this is the way the well-known, common infectious diseases occur. An epidemic of measles, for example, will drift from one school to another and then, perhaps, back again. Thus, space-time clustering and an epidemic-like drift supported the idea that an infectious agent of some kind might be involved in Burkitt's lymphoma. "We investigated another area around Kampala and found no evidence of the phenomenon at all," says Dr. Pike, "but it continues to happen in West Nile. You can stand on a Land Rover and see twelve homesteads where Burkitt's lymphoma happened."

Dr. Pike is a member of the Medical Research Council's Statistical Research Unit; for this work he was seconded to Makerere Medical School. He says, "Most lymphoma patients get lost, and we don't know what happens to them. We decided to look at all cases treated at Mulago Hospital in the past five years, and we employed two medical assistants to help us, Mr. Josiah Mafigiri and Mr. Aloysius Kisuule.

"Mr. Kisuule is a Muganda, of the race of Buganda, and he speaks probably every language in Uganda. We sent him out to find all the patients who hadn't reported back to the hospital—about eighty, altogether; and we knew that this was a quite impossible task, it just couldn't be done. Well, he found seventy-seven of them. We wanted, for instance, to find a boy who'd given his address as Msambya Hill, two miles outside Kampala. Aloysius couldn't find the boy there, so he simply sat down on a convenient spot, and whenever anybody passed he'd ask if they had seen a boy with a swollen jaw. After he'd sat there for a week a passer-by remembered the boy, and Aloysius tracked him down to a place called Kimuli, ninety miles away."

This, too, is cancer research. This, too, benefits humanity at large.

In June 1963, Denis Burkitt went on leave to England, and was invited to join the staff of the Medical Research Council. He accepted the offer. Then, he says, "Thanks in many ways to Dr. Horsfall [Frank L. Horsfall, Jr., M.D., Director of the Sloan-Kettering Institute for Cancer Research], I spent six weeks in the United States and Canada. We visited Sloan-Kettering in New York and the National Institutes of Health in Bethesda; we went on to Chicago, Michigan, Ontario, San Francisco, Vancouver, Saskatoon,

Winnipeg, St. Louis; and arrived back in New York the day President Kennedy was assassinated."

Soon after his return to Kampala he officially handed over his surgical duties and transferred to the Medical Research Council, a change that was accomplished without moving his chair from the Department of Surgery. From this time on his work was concerned only with geographical pathology: the role of environmental factors in Burkitt's lymphoma and, later, in other forms of disease prevalent in Africa.

At the end of 1966 he returned with his family to England. They now live in a house in Shiplake, Oxfordshire, on a road "far worse than anything we ever saw in Uganda." Coming home meant that his three daughters could complete their education; that Mrs. Burkitt at last had a place truly her own; and that in his spare moments Denis Burkitt could dabble in carpentry. And, as he commutes to his office in London, he can answer the innumerable letters he received from his multitudes of friends all over the world.

"I feel that my role in all this lymphoma business has been in a sense beating a way through the bush," he says. "In chemotherapy, now, far more efficient and competent people have taken over. They're better equipped and backed; and they will do the kind of very detailed, very thorough studies I couldn't possibly have done. The same is true in virology: I know nothing about it, and the new virus experts who are coming in will make all sorts of breakthroughs. And that's true, also, of immunology. To some extent, most of what I am likely to contribute I *have* contributed.

"Now I am particularly interested in the role of diet in disease. I go out to Africa two or three times a year. I've limited myself largely to Africa because I know the terrain better than any other; but if one is studying any disease, what happens in the rest of the world is always of interest. I had a long talk recently with the Professor of Surgery in Shiraz, Iran: I realized his patterns are much closer to ours (in Africa) than they are to Western patterns, and I would love to go out and see what he is doing there. . . . It might be that as we did with the lymphoma we can find clues to other forms of cancer in their geographical distribution; and then we would call in the experts to test the soil, to test this, that, and the other, and work things out in detail."

As for the forces that compelled him to follow up his initial observations on the tumor, that sent him off on his safari with Ted Williams and Cliff Nelson: "I realize that unless certain things had taken place we would never have managed to get off the ground at all. I realize, too (as the text on my wall puts it), *Anything I possess is what I've been given,* and therefore I can't really take the credit for it. So many things occurred—you can call them coincidences, or divinely planned happenings, however you like to look at them—which fitted perfectly into place all along the line, that I naturally feel I have no legitimate cause for any tremendous pride in myself. In a hundred and one places the whole thing might have damped out if something exactly right hadn't come along."

If Hugh Trowell had not drawn his attention to little Africa with the swollen jaw, if George Oettlé had not said, "We don't see this tumor in South Africa," if Dr. Burchenal had not presented him with samples of methotrexate, if Dr. Epstein and Dr. Bell had not arrived to investigate viruses, if Dr. Wright had not in some mysterious way attracted lymphomas . . . the recapitulation can go on and on. Coincidences? Divinely planned happenings? Who can say?

He continues, "If somebody had described this tumor

twenty years ago I don't think it would have been noticed. But it was described just at a time when there was a revival of interest in viruses, and people were interested in Africa, and people were interested in cancer. If you put together viruses and Africa and cancer you were almost bound to attract attention.

"Twenty years ago there wouldn't have been adequate air service to get tumor material to the laboratories in England and America. We would have had great difficulty doing the geographic investigation; and so on and so on. All sorts of factors dovetailed at the right time, not only to make these studies possible but also to bring in all the people who could supply the particular and distinctive contributions that were required in the circumstances.

"But I knew nothing about all this when I first began to think about the tumor. Nobody could have suspected it."

The story of Burkitt's lymphoma is far from complete. Nobody can guess what will spring from it next, where it will lead some new group of scientists. And the same can be said of Mr. Burkitt himself: his story is still only half told, there will be more to come. "Forgive me if I reiterate two points," he wrote in a recent letter. "In any sphere of life, Fruit depends upon Root. I spring from a long line of God-fearing and praying men and women, and this I know has had a great influence on my life. . . . We have a large commentary in the house on the New Testament written well over 100 years ago by one of my Burkitt forbears. Yet I must stress, as one of my uncles said to me, 'Grace isn't hereditary,' by which he meant that each man must personally and individually face up to the claims of God on his life. What I am trying to say is that my work is in many ways but the fruit of the faith that was implanted in me. It is therefore in a sense of secondary importance. Certainly to me. . . . I may be over-stressing a point, but nothing means more to me in life than a happy home. I am blessed by being deeply in love with my wife after more than 25 years of marriage. In many respects I have been made, moulded, and fashioned by Olive. Separa-tion, even for short periods, is far harder now than 20 years ago." And so, quite certainly, his story will go on.

One can turn, finally, to another witness; and this book will end on a personal note, with the author stepping momen-tarily out of the shadows in order to provide a few words of explanation. In the course of my research I visited East Africa and spoke to many of Denis Burkitt's colleagues; but I arrived in Kampala late in December when the staff of the Medical School of Makerere University College had dis-persed for the Christmas holidays. Subsequently, Professor Sir Ian McAdam was kind enough to send me some of his recollections of Mr. Burkitt at Mulago Hospital; and with Professor McAdam's permission some extracts from his letter are printed here. They need no further comment.

> Perhaps if I give you a few facts, this may assist you in piecing together the jig-saw puzzle of the Burkitt story.
> After the war, Mr. Burkitt was recruited to the Uganda Medical Service and posted to an up-country station in the northern part of Uganda. He must have worked there for at least 18 months and during this time I met him at Mulago Hospital when he appeared from time to time to deliver a lecture to the British Medical Association. The subject matter of these talks was related to the disease pattern seen in his district. I recall that he talked upon spontaneous rupture of the

spleen and also on hydrocele, which was endemic in the area. These lectures were well illustrated with photographs.

In 1947 he joined me at Mulago Hospital and for the next 20 years he worked with me, living in the next door house with a family that matched my own and who today remain the greatest friends.

Mr. Burkitt by training was a General Surgeon and at first we shared not only the teaching of Undergraduate medical students but also the curative work that was carried out in the 350 beds available for surgery. It was evident at an early stage that he had unusual powers of observation and these observations were recorded by photography. A filing system was started and at our weekly Clinical/Surgical meetings he drew on his collection of photographs to show that the unusual case which was being presented had been seen on previous occasions.

This in fact was how the tumour that we know as Burkitt's lymphoma was eventually unearthed as a separate entity. These tumours had been previously reported by the Histopathologist as being neuroblastomas and I recall most vividly at a Saturday Clinical meeting his very convincing deduction that if these tumours that we were seeing were in fact neuroblastomas then the incidence of this tumour was about a thousand times as common here as anywhere else in the world. The challenge was taken up by the Pathologist and there followed a prolonged controversy between Clinicians and Histopathologists over the identification of the tumour.

The clinical observations made by Burkitt clearly identified the tumour as a new entity long before the Histopathologists reached the same conclusion. Whatever claim any authorities may have to originality in the study of this lymphoma must date after the time Burkitt had established its clinical identity.

The next part of the story follows the usual pattern after an original observation has been made. Pathologists added greatly to the existing knowledge and Burkitt in discussion with colleagues such as Professor Haddow of the Virus Research Institute suggested that the distribution of this tumour was sufficiently local to postulate an infective origin of the tumour. Burkitt, who had been making contact by letter with other workers in Africa, was now determined to go out into the field and collect information. His safaris will be well known to you and no doubt you have good photographs of the sort of area he covered. He is not one of the most practical people in the world and he does not always care for the creature comforts. I am sure that Dr. Williams and others who accompanied him on these safaris will add the light touch which is essential if Burkitt's character is to be portrayed.

. . . Burkitt's genius lies in his powers of observation; from a maze of apparently disconnected facts he can see the thread of relevance.

As a colleague he was the most loyal and conscientious person I have ever known. He is a practising Christian who thinks action more important than words. He left behind in Africa a store of goodwill, and I doubt whether there has ever been any doctor working in Africa who has either been better known or more loved.

Yours sincerely,

I. W. J. McAdam
Professor of Surgery

Appendix: *Three Men on a Safari*

Nearly every day on the ten thousand-mile safari to South Africa, Denis Burkitt found time to type a long letter home. It was in a sense a group letter, intended to be read by the families of all three men; and it described the progress of the expedition, the sights and the scenes and the various adventures encountered along the way. There was little mention of technical matters: scientific data was entered in separate journals. Later, when Burkitt returned to Mulago, the letters were collected and became known as the Lymphoma Safari Diary, *a document running to more than forty thousand words.*

The extracts printed here, in a very condensed form, are taken from letters which were written in the course of the first half of the safari, from Kampala to Johannesburg. It is important to stress that they were typed whenever Burkitt had a few minutes to spare—in the bare rooms of rest houses, in dismal little hotels, even by the roadside when the three men stopped for lunch. In these circumstances there was no opportunity to rewrite or to polish a phrase; and, indeed, part of the interest and charm of these letters is their spontaneity. They tell of the camaraderie that existed between the three men, and of their deep and ever-present faith; and, perhaps more than anything else, they reveal Denis Burkitt's remarkable powers of observation.

Bukoba: 7 October 1961

We have been planning this trip for over a year. The prime purpose has been the investigation of a tumour, but we are making use of the opportunity to investigate a number of other conditions. The Medical Research Council have provided the funds. Ted Williams procured the car from an ex-Congo missionary. It is a large 35 hp Ford V8 American station wagon. Just the thing for a safari like this but far too large for normal use. As well as our clothes and personal belongings we have camp kit with beds and collapsable chairs and table; drinking water, spare petrol, and two extra spare tyres and tubes. Also, chains in case of very muddy roads, and a certain amount of food plus a primus stove.

We packed up this morning. Saying good-bye is the worst part of any journey, but this is a sign of the love we know follows us. We eventually got off at 9:15 on our estimated 9,000-mile safari.

Today has been a perfect day. The first 86 miles to Masaka were on good tarmac road. The country is rather monotonous with fairly low hills all of approximately equal size with uniform flat tops. The grass is very long, and plantains with their enormous leaves are the main feature of vegetation. There are coffee and cotton, of course, and approaching Masaka the coffee is more profuse. The green is broken by the bright red of the Erythrinum trees. The houses are mostly mud and wattle; a few are of red brick with roofs of corrugated iron or red tile. Those who can afford it like to give up thatch.

The tarmac ends at Masaka. Beyond this the country becomes more open and the grass is shorter. Mango trees and euphorbia come more into the picture. Bicycles are common all over this country, but we expect there will be fewer later on. We saw many plantations of eucalyptus, planted for firewood and building poles, and passed a number of buses with the usual feature of African buses—large bicycle racks on the roof.

We had a picnic lunch some 40 miles south of Masaka. Olive had prepared a perfect meal, with everything labeled. We remarked how much better it was than a 10-course lunch at the Imperial Hotel in Kampala. We stopped miles from anywhere, and yet Ted said, "Don't let's stop in a populated area"!

We crossed the border into Tanganyika at a small place called Mutukuku. There was no road barrier, just a notice. A ferry held us up for about half an hour, but it was full of interest. A heavy wire cable crossed a fast-flowing river. The cable ran along the deck of the ferry, and the ferry was propelled across the river by a string of Africans, as it were, walking along the cable holding on to the ferry. Thus the ferry was pushed in relation to the cable. I had never seen this before. Nearly all ferries in Uganda are now motorized. A small mud and wattle building on the other side of the river was marked "Hotel Superior."

Bukoba is really very attractive, not unlike Entebbe. The little hotel at which we are staying is almost on the lake shore, with a lovely view across the lake. There are far more Arabs here than one usually sees in Uganda. We are sharing a room, with our own bathroom and electric light.

After a cup of tea we went to look for the District Medical Officer. We had been told he is an Indian. On entering his very tidy house I was confronted with the text, "Christ is the head of this house, the unseen guest at every meal, the silent listener to every conversation." I then saw several other texts on the walls. It took no time to discover that he is a keen Indian Christian and knew some of our Indian Christians in Kampala. We went through our medical questionnaire with him, and he had kindly brought the operation registers from the hospital for us to inspect. Before we left we made arrangements to meet later this evening for some Christian fellowship and he was to invite in some of his Christian friends.

Sunday, 8 October

(Sitting in the bush beside the car, about 17 miles south of Bukoba) Before breakfast we walked along the sandy shore of the lake [Lake Tanganyika]. We saw several crested cranes and returned after breakfast to photograph them.

Duties have been apportioned between us. Ted does everything about the car and is also treasurer, paying all accounts and keeping a cash book. Cliff has himself offered to be in charge of laundry.

After leaving the hotel we looked around the Bukoba hospital. Apart from Dr. Phillips, the staff seems very poor. For the benefit of any medical person reading this letter we saw heart failure treated with penicillin, and an anaemia with Dextran [a form of glucose]. This is the only Govt. hospital with doctors for a population of 600,000.

We called at an R.C.M. [Roman Catholic mission] hospital 15 miles south of Bukoba and were warmly welcomed by two German lady doctors. One was a really most experienced surgeon. I had recently operated on a Dutch sister from this hospital. The doctors gave us all the information we wanted, and insisted on showing us around the hospital and giving us lunch, although we told them that we had a picnic lunch with us. We left immediately after lunch so that we could sit under a tree and write letters. We are on our way to a Swedish mission hospital where we have been invited to stay the night.

(*Later*) Swedish Mission hospitals at Ndolage near Kamachumu, which is 10 miles off the Bukoba-Biharamulo road. This is at nearly 500 feet, with a lovely view. We had tea with the doctor and his wife; her sister and husband were there too. I had removed the tonsils from this lady only a few weeks ago, and she and her husband were in All Saints, Kampala, last Sunday morning when Dick Brown preached. Ted and I have been given a whole house to ourselves; it belongs to a doctor who is on leave. This is a magnificent site, with a view over the lake nearly 10 miles to the east. The hospital is very well built and equipped.

Monday, 9 October (7:00 a.m.)

We went to bed at ten and were up shortly after six. We had a pleasant simple supper with the Buchs and Petersons—cold meat and bread and jam or cheese on one plate, with warm tea. They told us that in Denmark (they are all Danes) it is correct to rest both wrists on the table throughout the meal. They, of course, don't do this.

It is another lovely morning. Cliff and Beth Nelson were due to leave Kola Ndoto [near Shinyanga] at 5:00 a.m., so they will be on their way now. Ted has been using his tape recorder to record bird song at different places. After breakfast we will push off to meet Cliff, and will give these letters to Beth [who was to stay with Olive Burkitt]. We propose to spend tonight at Kibondo, a little over 150 miles from here.

(Later: Kigoma.) We are in a small thatched rest house. No boy has appeared. We asked the D.C. [District Commissioner] if it was booked for us, and he said yes. Cliff lit a wood fire under a big oil drum to heat our bath water and is now doing the laundry in the bathroom. Ted is cooking the supper on our primus stove. We asked in a shop if it was possible to buy either eggs or bread in this village and the answer was no. We are therefore having baked beans, biscuits, cheese, fruit, tea, and coffee.

. . . Just finished supper. Lovely meal. The tea was made in a plastic measuring jug: it was excellent. After eating the beans and bully beef on our plastic plates, Cliff produced a new roll of toilet paper to wipe the plates before putting fruit salad on them. Ted remarked, "What would Olive say?"

Beds and mattresses are provided but not bedding. We have our own. Also we have one hurricane lamp.

To go back: we met up with Cliff and Beth at 11:30 this morning, after travelling some 80 miles. They had travelled nearly 200 miles. We had a picnic lunch together and then [*leaving Mrs. Nelson*] we pushed on south, travelling another 100 miles through rather uninteresting bush country. It is terribly dry and dusty here. No green anywhere. Not a place one would choose to live in.

Tuesday, 10 October

(*7:45 a.m.*) After bath and supper last night we had a walk in the dark. There were a lot of grass fires all around. When we got back to the rest house a boy lit a pressure lamp, so we were able to read and write before going to bed. We had biscuits, bully beef, and Nescafé for breakfast.

(*7:45 p.m.*) We have travelled nearly 200 miles today. Yesterday we passed about one car in 10 miles. Today we passed two cars in the first 98 miles and two more in the next 70 miles. In 170 miles there was one turning off to the right and three to the left. We passed some stale elephant droppings today and yesterday but saw no game. The first 90 miles today was through endless bush. It is tsetse country and when we stopped for a few minutes to inspect the car I received several bites. They are quite harmless, but annoying.

This country is extremely thinly populated, and the people are very primitive. For the first time we saw women with masses of wire bangles around their ankles.

Kasulu was our first small township. Dirty, dusty, and altogether miserable. There was one petrol pump, but no petrol. We turned off on a diversion road up the hills to visit a Seventh Day Adventist hospital, 30 miles up through magnificent hills with the most colossal views over to Rwanda. The car boiled once, but otherwise the cooling system has been good. There have been a few minor faults. The speedometer jammed near Masaka but righted itself. A queer noise developed at Kabondo but later disappeared. The petrol tank indicator has ceased to work but this is not serious—Ted will look at it when he has time. On the whole, the car has run magnificently.

We had a picnic lunch of biscuits and beans, overlooking a superb view, and then called at the S.D.A. hospital. Very nice missionaries from South Africa, Afrikaans-speaking. I received more help with the tumour there than at any place on the trip so far. They would have loved to put us up.

The road from this hospital to Kigoma was about the most

twisty I have ever been on. Ted was driving, and went very carefully. Some sections of the road were just carved out of the side of the mountain, with a sheer drop on one side. Ted commented, "A cliff on both sides of me."

Between the Seventh Day Adventist hospital and Kigoma we descended over 3,000 feet.

Ujiji [on the eastern shore of Lake Tanganyika] is a most interesting town. Entirely African: narrow dirt streets lined with mud and wattle square houses, either thatched or covered with old flattened petrol tins, some roofed with corrugated iron. It is obviously strongly Arab, and reminds one of parts of Zanzibar.

It was almost an emotional experience visiting the Livingstone memorial, standing under the mango tree under which Livingstone and Stanley met on November 10, 1871, when my father was 15 months old. There is a great stone map of Africa with a black cross on it. Nearby is a plaque saying that Burton and Speke had visited Ujiji in 1858. We took photographs from all angles.

Kigoma is about six miles from Ujiji. We met the District Medical Officer, who directed us to the hotel and told us we must have a swim in the best pool in Africa. We followed his advice and had a lovely swim in a portion of the lake with netting around it, free from hippos and bilharzia.

The hotel is not pretentious. The bathrooms are lit by light-rays which get through a three-inch gap between the door and the lintel from a bare electric light bulb in the corridor outside. This enables you just to see the bath. Water economy is ensured by such a slow stream that few have the patience to wait for the bath to fill up with more than a couple of inches of water.

(Later: 11:00 p.m.) We had an excellent dinner with the D.M.O. We started with two empty plates plus a soup plate,

and used them one after the other as the courses arrived.
We then had two very profitable hours with the D.M.O., who
was extremely knowledgeable and gave us a great deal of
information about the tumour and all sorts of other things.

Wednesday, 11 October (8:20 p.m.)

I can't remember ever before typing by the light of a hurricane lamp—the same lamp that I bought as my first purchase
on arriving in E. Africa in the army in 1943. It is the only
lamp other than torches [flashlights] we have with us, so it
has been invaluable. We are in a rest house in the most isolated township of my experience, Mpanda.

We left Kigoma at 8:45 this morning. I have never travelled through such endless, monotonous African bush as we
did today. Mile after mile, 10 mile after 10 mile, and hundred mile after hundred mile, for 250 miles on dusty earth
roads. Everywhere was dry as dust, brown and burnt. Just
occasionally we went down an escarpment or through a pass
bordered by great rocks. On the first 60 miles to a Roman
Catholic mission we passed only one car. We were warmly
welcomed at the mission by a lady doctor and had fresh
orange drinks, and then discussed all our medical problems.
For the next 170 miles we didn't pass a single moving vehicle—just three stationary ones. We saw hardly a soul. It
really was a most desolate stretch of Africa, utterly dry and
inhospitable.

Ted was a little worried because of the occasional strange
noise in the clutch, though the engine was running magnificently. Then it began to miss, and we first thought it was
dirt in the petrol. It would stop and then start again. Finally
it stopped altogether, about 70 miles from anywhere. What
an immense comfort at such times to have a two-gallon plas-

tic bottle full of drinking water. This was Olive's Christmas present, and it has been a joy. Ted is magnificent. He nipped out of the car, and instead of spending time to find the fault he just used a piece of wire he had brought specially for the purpose, and connected the battery directly to the coil. One push of the starter, and the car went beautifully. He left the wire on until we reached Mpanda, and in twenty minutes he not only had this fault located and repaired but had repaired the petrol gauge, also an electrical fault.

We weren't sorry to reach Mpanda. While we were filling up with petrol we met the African O.C. [Officer Commanding] police, a charming chap. He found the keys of the house and led us to it. There were two bedrooms, a bathroom and water flush toilet. The other two always insist that I have the single room as leader of the expedition!

I am now writing at Sumbawanga. For supper we had two tins of spaghetti in tomato sauce, and bread and jam and tinned pears, with lots of tea. We cooked it all on our primus. A boy lit a fire under the old petrol-drum used for heating bath water and we not only bathed and shaved but I washed my hair and we even did some laundry.

After a good night, and with all the car faults fixed, we started off just after 6:00 a.m. in high spirits; and if there had been any people on the road they would have heard coming from the heavily-laden Ford the strains of hymns started by Cliff, who had brought a hymn book with music. We sang, "Will your anchor hold?", "All hail to the power," and the theme song of the Africa Inland Mission (to which both Ted and Cliff belong), "Great is thy faithfulness."

We saw some game this morning. First elephant, then kingoni, and later giraffe and sable. Ted is an honorary game ranger and can identify the animals.

Before we left Kampala we had a big metal plate fitted under our rather low petrol tank and this has been an enormous comfort. We have so often hit bottom on roads consisting of two ruts with a mound between that we would have worried about damaging our tank but for this added protection. Actually, Ted has a way of carrying on even with a holed tank, and has brought the wherewithal with him. He feeds the carburettor with a pipe direct from the petrol drum. We did once today sit on the mound of dust in the middle of the road. Cliff and I got out of the car and Ted freed it by driving backwards.

The country was much more open and interesting than it was yesterday. We passed the result of one appalling smash —a lorry literally wrapped around a tree. He must have been going too fast and left the road, and both sides of the lorry were on either side of the tree. We had to photograph it; and then took a close-up of the bumper, which had a sign, "Insure With Jubilee."

The population is sparse, and obviously very poor.

Ted is under the car; Cliff has just heated the bath water to do the laundry in the bath. Ted has now discovered the cause of the noise in the clutch. What a wonderful companion to have, or wonderful pair of companions. I couldn't wish for better. Cliff has brought a washing board and two irons!

The African houses are all square, with grass roofs. No rondavels [round huts]. We have hardly seen a bicycle between Kigoma and here, and until the last ten miles hardly a cow. What the people do for water I can't think.

Entering Sumbawanga the avenues of jacaranda were a staggering sight. The main road must have been more than half a mile long with jacaranda every ten yards on each side of the road, all a mass of blue with no green. Other avenues were the same, and in such a dry barren country it was all the more striking.

Friday, 13 October (6:16 p.m.)

(In the Abercorn Arms Hotel) I have just had a most delightful bath, the first with electric light and ample room since Bukoba. I felt I must wash my hair again, having washed it by hurricane lamp at Mpanda; but one gets quite incredibly dirty in this intensely dusty country. I also did some laundry, though Cliff accepts the laundry voluntarily.

I spent about an hour last night with the D.M.O. [District Medical Officer] and P.M.O. [Provincial Medical Officer]. We had boiled eggs for supper, and having no egg cups we gave Cliff a toilet roll, which held an egg nicely, and I used the sandwich-spread bottle, while Ted used an empty jar.

We had filled thermos flasks with tea last night, so we managed to get off just before seven this morning. The country was much more interesting—very open, with considerable hills in view. One very striking difference between this country and Uganda or Kenya is the presence of definite African villages, closely-knit bunches of houses and even sort of streets. Uganda has no villages in this sense. Moreover, all the houses are square.

We have done all our cooking on a primus stove. At meals, we take it in turn to say grace. Yesterday we passed our first thousand-mile mark, and this will have been some of our hardest travelling.

The Medical Officer [in Abercorn] is a very charming South African and a definite Christian. We discussed our business with him and he offered to take us in his Land Rover to two river falls and the southern tip of Lake Tanganyika, Mpulungu.

On our drive with him we learned a lot about the country. It is very thinly populated—only two and a half million people in the vast country of Northern Rhodesia, only three million in Southern Rhodesia, and the same in Nyasaland. Yet there are 70,000 Europeans in N. Rhodesia and 350,000 in S. Rhodesia, as against 5,000 in Uganda. There are extremely few well-educated Africans, and the salaries they get are quite fantastic: over £1,000 a year for a medical assistant, not by any means equivalent to a doctor.

On the lake shore near Mpulungu we were shown the well-preserved ruin of the first mission church in this area. The London Missionary Society started work in 1883, and the church was built in 1895. This was a terrible area for trypanosomiasis [sleeping sickness], and fifteen of the first fifty missionaries died of this disease. In 1908 the whole population had to be moved 10 miles away from the lake shore.

Saturday, 14 October

(6:00 p.m. London Missionary Society Hospital, Mbereshi, near Kawambwa) We had a pleasant evening with Dr. and Mrs. van Kant yesterday. It was nice to have grace before our meal. She is a granddaughter of Dr. Robert Moffat, the well-known missionary, and has lived her life in Rhodesia. They told us many stories about the famous characters around Abercorn. One local celebrity was piloting his own plane in the London to Cairo air race in [about] 1936 and crashed at Abercorn. His companion was killed, but he married the nursing sister, who looked after him and has been there ever since.

We had breakfast at 6:30 and got away from Abercorn at seven, and then drove 250 miles through endless, interminable, identical bush, bush, BUSH, mile after mile. Most of N. Rhodesia, I believe, is like this. It had some beauty in the different shades of leaves from deep red to green, like autumn tints at home. The only view is the road ahead and the hundred yards or so that you can see between the trees. In 200 miles we passed two vehicles, a lorry and a Land Rover. Moreover, for 230 miles there was not a single petrol pump. Northern Rhodesia is three times the size of Uganda, with only one third the population.

Abercorn is the place where the remnant of the German armed forces surrendered to the British in November 1918 [at the end of World War I].

A remark I made has been frequently quoted on this safari. From a medical point of view we must be one of the safest safaris ever, as we are all doctors, all carry medical supplies, and we make a bee line from one hospital to another! At breakfast yesterday we remarked that we should go for a drive one day, just for a change!

We had a stand-up lunch of biscuits and a tin of peaches and arrived here in time for tea. The doctor in charge here, a Dr. Parry, worked for his first year in Africa with a Dr. P. K. Dixon, one of the founders of the Christian union at T.C.D. [Trinity College, Dublin].

This is a well-equipped and well-built hospital of seventy beds. The London Missionary Society work started here at the turn of the century. Education is, of course, a problem for Europeans, as it is very isolated; and Mrs. Parry is at present home with the family, leaving Dr. Parry alone for six months. The hospital is on the Mbereshi river, which is a tributary of the Luapala, discovered by Livingstone, and one of the main tributaries of the Congo, near its source.

Sunday, 15 October

We went to a service in the finest mission church I have yet been in. The segregation of the sexes is very strict, as in much

of Africa. Even the European couples sat one each side of
the church. Instead of the collection being taken up, the
congregation went and placed their contributions on the
communion table. The service was conducted by a senior
lady missionary, and she spoke to the children. The sermon
was given by an African; and, of course, we understood none
of it.

After service we had a cup of tea and then did a round of
the hospital. It was nice to be able to help with suggestions
here and there, and I am doing an operation for them at 7:15
tomorrow morning.

(*Later.*) We drove some six miles to a leper settlement
this afternoon and were shown round by a sister who is now
in Government [medical service] after thirty years in the
mission. This Government settlement is run almost entirely
by ex-missionaries and the head African is a local church
elder.

It is actually raining, the first rain we have had since we
left Uganda.

(Undated)

I last wrote on Monday morning (16 October) before leaving Mbereshi and posted the letter in Fort Rosebery. The
150-mile journey from Mbereshi was very uninteresting, just
bush, bush and more bush. One gets the impression that there
are hardly any people, but the roads tend to follow the
watersheds to avoid bridges, while the people live in the val-
leys. Even so, the country is very thinly inhabited. At the
turn of the century there were less than half a million people
in the whole of Northern Rhodesia, which has an area at least
three times that of the British Isles. There are about three
million today.

We arrived at Fort Rosebery at about one o'clock. A most unattractive place, consisting of a tarmac street and a few shops, government departments, officials' houses, and a poor hotel. It is impossible to describe the utter dryness, dust and barrenness of the country at this time of the year.

We visited the hospital and discussed our business with ——, a very immature, over-confident, and incompetent young man. Some of the surgery done there is quite appalling. One good piece of fortune was that the doctor in charge of a Roman Catholic hospital some 60 miles from Fort Rosebery came in that evening, and we could discuss our problems without travelling out to her hospital. She is a doctor and a nun, with the name Mother Scholastica. I discovered she was in Trinity College, Dublin, a year behind me and knew several of the people I knew. I didn't like to ask what her name was before she entered orders.

Tuesday, 17 October

At Kasama, 224 miles from Fort Rosebery, we met two delightful doctors, Mr. Braithwaite, the P.M.O., and Dr. Wright, an ex-missionary, the D.M.O. They have a very good hospital with excellent equipment, but Dr. Wright more or less has to run the 200-bed hospital singlehanded. Braithwaite helps, but has the whole province to look after. We gained a lot of very valuable information from them, and they had seen our tumour in other places where they had worked. They asked me to look at a European lady who was in the small European hospital with abdominal pain; as Braithwaite was leaving for Ndola next morning they were worried about leaving her. I operated on her after tea, and they were very grateful. In Rhodesia they seem to have money, good equipment and good buildings, but are very short of doctors. We have infinitely more doctors but less money, poorer buildings, and worse equipment.

The road from Kasama to Abercorn runs due north. Our next stage was 120 miles due east to Tundumu, which is little more than a name on the map but has a petrol pump. We could look down into the upper end of the great Luangwa Valley. The Luangwa runs south for some 600 miles to join the Zambesi at Zomba and only one road crosses it near its southern end. Livingstone had to return his porters to the country near Zomba, after he brought them on his journey across Africa and back to Tete. Yesterday I was reading the description of this journey, which he made with Dr. Kirk in 1858. I never before appreciated the difficulty of trekking on foot through country like this.

We passed our 2,000-mile mark between Abercorn and Tundumu. A few miles before Tundumu we turned off to a small hospital which was formerly run by the mission but is now staffed by Government [medical personnel]. The doctor in charge is a well-known personality—a very wide-awake lady of over eighty, Dr. Trant, who trained at Trinity College, Dublin. She was able to give us information about one case of the tumour we are investigating, which came from the upper part of the Luangwa Valley—very valuable information.

The road improved after Tundumu, running southeast to Nyasaland, which has been called the Switzerland of Africa. We were aiming for a rest house which we knew to be situated in a most impressive setting. We hadn't booked it, and hoped it would be available. In all we covered some 320 miles and arrived here shortly after four o'clock and, fortunately, it was empty. The view is quite superb, with magnificent mountains about four miles away.

It is incredible how much dust you pick up on a trip like

this one. Everything gets impregnated with dust. I washed shirts, vests, stockings, etc., before my bath last night, and had to change the brown water repeatedly. I then washed my hair in the bath water before bathing, and immediately the water was thick brown. One really feels a bath is worthwhile!

For supper we had two fried eggs each with nearly a pound of bacon between us, and baked beans. Then a tin of pineapple, and tea. Our butter has turned to oil floating on top of a white sediment, something I have never seen before.

Saturday, 21 October (5:45 a.m.)

I am at Livingstonia, overlooking perhaps the finest view in the Federation. This is the famous Church of Scotland mission station perched more than 2,000 feet above Lake Nyasa.

The journey from Karonga to Livingstonia yesterday was most interesting. The first 30 miles is through country with numerous palms and baobab trees (which look like trees uprooted and then planted upside down with the roots in the air). Next, some 30 miles of bush. Then we turned to the mountains and climbed the most colossal, terrific and almost terrifying mountain road I have ever been up. We thought the road from Lake Thun to Beattenburg was steep and twisty, but it was just a slightly curved road with an occasional gradient compared to this. I have never, ever, anywhere, been on such a road. It climbed over 2,000 feet in seven miles, which was only about two miles as the crow flies. There were 112 bends and 22 hairpin turns doubling back virtually 180°. Moreover, at these hairpin bends the turn was so steep that our car could only just make it in bottom gear. On six of the bends we just couldn't get round in one turn even with the wheels fully locked, and had to back on the corner. Fortunately, the corners are constructed to make this possible or one couldn't get up at all. The radiator boiled repeatedly and we had to refill it and pour water over it to help the cooling.

When we reached the top we certainly had our reward, in perhaps the finest view in the Federation. We are staying with the doctor and his wife. Dr. Maclean was in the past Deputy Director of Medical Services in Tanganyika, then Director in Trinidad. After retiring from Government he came out as a missionary with the U.M.C.S. He then retired again, but after hearing an appeal for a doctor to come out here, he returned. He is now seventy-two, and one admires him enormously. We were given an empty room and a balcony overlooking the lake. We put up our camp beds with our own bedding. Mrs. Maclean is seventy-nine, and what a remarkable character! Bubbling over with humour, and such a lady. The two of them are just like a Victorian couple from a very refined family stuck in the middle of Africa. Their manner, and all about them, is cultured and radiant with Christian sweetness. In this old rambling house, so much in need of repair, there was a silver tea-pot, and nice china, and good table linen.

Monday, 23 October

We went to morning service yesterday at Ekwendeni, in a large red brick church. We were impressed by the very poor quality of dress. A man who was leading the community singing before the service started was dressed much more shabbily than our garden boy on Sunday. As in nearly all African churches there was a strict segregation of the sexes, men on one side and women on the other.

Dr. Ken Irvine runs the hospital with no medical help.

At present he has no [nursing] sister. This means that he never really gets off, and he has all the buildings and engines and electrical fittings to look after, as well as patients. I do admire enormously the sacrifices such a man is prepared to make, not the least being the professional isolation. Another sacrifice is the primitive latrine, a tin hut in the yard with a box over a deep pit.

It's very hot, as hot as we ever get it in Kampala, but cooler at night. Ken has the same text on his wall as we had seen at the outset of our safari on the wall of the Indian D.M.O.'s house at Bukoba: "Christ is the head of this house, the unseen guest at every meal, the silent listener to every conversation."

He has a girl, instead of a boy, to help in the house, and she served our supper with a baby, fast asleep, strapped to her back!

We were up at five this morning and off at six. Cliff remarked that an unusual aspect of this safari is that we always seem to start *before* the time scheduled! We drove, first, east to Mzuzu, the Provincial Headquarters, and then south over the very lovely Vipya plateau—some 50 miles of the most delightful country. There seemed to be virtually no population, but good areas of afforestation, and large plantations of *tung* which they are growing for the useful oil.

Mzimba is some 80 miles from Ekwendeni. We met the African doctor, a Nyasa man who spent seventeen years in South Africa and was at Fort Hare and Witwatersrand in Johannesburg. Unfortunately, they no longer admit [black] Africans there. Bwanausi is his name; he had only recently come to Mzimba but had served in Port Herald, in the extreme south of the country, where he had seen five of the tumours in seven months. We must visit this hospital.

Ken Irvine had given us a letter to leave with a missionary on the outskirts of Mzimba. We met a charming couple who were obviously radiant Christians. We asked where they came from, and they replied, a place called Enniskillen in N. Ireland! We found then that we had many mutual friends, and they asked if I was a son of J. P. Burkitt! Such an unexpected and pleasant contact in the middle of Africa.

It was about 170 miles from Mzimba to Fort Jamieson, where I am writing. The country is similar to the rest of Northern Rhodesia, though I was impressed by the lovely green and brown fresh new leaves coming up in virtual desert earth. The strange thing is that all these fresh green shoots come out *before* the rain, and *in anticipation of it*. Really quite remarkable.

"What unusual methods of doing research," we remarked, "and how pleasant." One usually associated research with white coats and test tubes.

We arrived at Fort Jamieson at four and went to the hospital. I met a sister, and asked if I could ring up the P.M.O. I told him I was looking into some children's jaw tumours. The sister, overhearing this, sent to the ward and produced an absolutely typical case of the tumour we have been looking for. I have been back since to photograph it and take notes. This is very important for our work.

I have just had a bath and hair wash. One really does enjoy them on this trip. Cliff is an absolute brick, and has just been round for my laundry. Ted has been under the car, making sure all is well. I couldn't have had two more congenial colleagues. Ted has a very great knowledge of medicine and was obviously an unusually good student. Cliff, too, is obviously a very good and dedicated brain. Although I am leader of the party I feel in many ways intellectually behind them, but have had more opportunities.

Tuesday, 24 October

It is 90 miles from Fort Jamieson to Lilongwe. Uninteresting bush. For part of the way the road runs along the border between Rhodesia and Mozambique. We reached here about 2:30 and spent some time in the hospital. A sister showed us round one of the wards, and I asked where she came from. She replied that she came from a town in N. Ireland called Enniskillen! Fancy meeting two—no, three—people from Enniskillen in the heart of Africa in two days. Her name is Sherriden.

Ted is making all the entries in the cash-book. He does this most professionally and meticulously, and it saves me a lot of work. I leave all the finance to him, and just draw the money from the bank.

Friday, 27 October

(Blantyre) We had dinner last night with Mr. Laycock (the surgeon at the hospital here) and his wife. He has had a very wide experience, having served in China, Somaliland, Tanganyika, and Nyasaland. He and his wife married in Somaliland seven weeks after first meeting. At the birth of their child a doctor was to fly from Aden. At the last moment he couldn't come, and Laycock eventually had to do a Caesarean section on his own wife, assisted only by Somali orderlies. His wife was a tutor sister, and she sat up on the trolley in the [operating] theatre and checked the instruments before she was given the anaesthetic!

This morning I did a thyroidectomy on invitation, and then we went and visited the Director and his deputy. This is always a diplomatic move. They showed great interest in our work and offered every assistance.

Monday, 30 October

(Beira) We all slept well, but were up by 5:30, and spent most of the morning at the hospital trying to describe our tumour to Portuguese doctors who knew some English. Quite a strain. Eventually one who had worked in America joined us and helped with interpretation. Quite obviously the tumour is common throughout this country, as we had anticipated. They actually produced one classical case for us.

We have been asked to have drinks with some of the senior members of the staff. I hope there is some light wine that we can get down without too much difficulty. After that we propose to try a Chinese restaurant for supper.

Tuesday, 31 October

(Umtali) We are in a new world. After weeks of heat and dust and drought it has rained in a continual drizzle all day, just like the United Kingdom, and we have been cool again. Last night we went round to the house of the Beira surgeon. A beautiful house, with exquisite furniture imported from Lisbon and Macao, off the China coast. It was air-conditioned, and no money had been spared on it. The daughters, aged about twelve and fourteen, came in, and the younger kissed us all. We struggled through a glass of port wine and ate nuts and cake.

The shops are well stocked with beautiful things, all imported. There is no doubt that the Portuguese have built a magnificent modern town at Beira. The architectural styles, with bizarre colours and totally unorthodox shapes, were really exciting and often very pleasing.

We left Beira before eight this morning in the rain, and enjoyed the 186 miles of tarmac road through green country, with mists hanging over the hills as in Scotland. It was most interesting to us to find that the first hospital we visited, at 2,000 feet, was obviously above the belt where the tumours occur. This was further evidence to confirm our theory.

Umtali is a quite magnificent town. We seem to have returned to civilization completely in the past two days. There are masses of flowering shrubs, various shades of bougain-villaea, carpets of fallen blue petals under the jacaranda trees, well-kept parks and trim lawns. It is all so obviously a European town. Magnificent shops, where you are served by English men and women. It is smaller than Nairobi but much more attractive.

First impressions of the hospital are also very favourable. We are looking around tomorrow, and I am giving a lecture tomorrow evening.

We have decided to be gay tonight, and to go to the cinema to see the life of Franz Liszt.

I imagine colour segregation is pretty acute here, and the cinema is for Europeans only. We have never come across this before.

(Wednesday evening)

We had dinner at the club with Dr. Montgomery. He told us there was at least one Enniskillen man in Umtali, a name not known to me.

Friday, 3 November

(Salisbury) Yesterday's drive was by far the most beautiful of our whole trip. We LONGED to have our wives with us. We left Umtali shortly after 7:30 and drove to Salisbury via Inyanga, marvelously beautiful mountain scenery. The road, the scenery, and the weather, were all superb. Great rocky hills,

immense vistas, patterns of wattle plantations, and Paul
Henry clouds. Changing views all the time and crisp fresh
air. The hilltops were wrapped with flimsy mantles of drift-
ing cloud. I have never seen so many examples of rocks and
great smooth boulders perched precariously on top of one another. For mile after mile we were entranced by these queer
bundles of enormous stones, many apparently about to topple
over. I suppose this is due to rain and wind, over the centuries, removing the supporting earth.

We reached Salisbury at about 4:00 p.m. The approach is
very like Nairobi, with pleasant houses and well laid-out
gardens, and masses of bougainvillaea and jacaranda. As one
approaches the town it is like suddenly striking Manhattan
in the middle of Africa. Quite a remarkable sight: a skyline
of skyscrapers.

Saturday, 4 November

After breakfast yesterday Mr. Hammer, one of the local surgeons, drove us around Salisbury. A very fine city indeed. We
spent most of the morning in the hospital and met many of
the staff. A magnificent and well-equipped institution. There
is so much more money here than in E. Africa, and of course
a considerable number of private surgeons and physicians
and specialists.

We had lunch with the radiologist. The house seemed entirely furnished with delicate antique furniture, Louis XV
chairs with tapered legs and covered with tapestry. The cup-
boards were filled with Dresden and other china, and cut
glass was strewn about in profusion. I must say that I would
long for a comfortable chair or sofa I could relax in.

After lunch I had an appointment with the Director of
Medical Services. There had been an absurd farce arising

from our visit. I had written to one of his deputies months ago announcing my coming. This was just for courtesy and required no action. The deputy, however, was a stickler for red tape, and referred the matter to Rhodesia House in London. Not knowing what to do, they referred it to the Colonial Office. They, in turn, contacted the Imperial Cancer Research Fund and other bodies. Even the Prime Minister here was asked if he knew about my coming! All utter rubbish. I have now cleared up any misunderstanding. I don't know what they thought I was going to do to the Federation.

Sunday, 5 November

Ted and I very much enjoyed a very nice service in a Methodist church. It was strange to us to see a cross in a Methodist church.

After service we visited the hospital to find the doctor. He was not in, but a sister from Newry, Co. Down, gave us a cup of tea and put us on the phone to Dr. Stover. Later he came round to our hotel, and we had a long talk and derived much information from his continuous twenty-five years here. There are a number of doctors in S. Rhodesian towns who have refused promotion and who might have been Directors by now but preferred to remain in one place and make it their home. Dr. Montgomery has been twenty-five years in Umtali, and a Dr. MacGladdery (another Irishman) has been twenty-five years at Owelo. A Dr. ———, also of Irish descent, has lived for thirty-five years in a small town some distance from here.

After lunch we drove out to the famous Zimbabwe ruins, probably the most famous and mysterious archaeological remains in all Africa. A quite fantastic sight. There is one structure, called the temple, some 50 yards across, with great walls of cut stone 40 feet high and some 4 to 6 feet thick. Within this huge circular wall there are the remains of many buildings, and scattered for many acres around it are other buildings in poor preservation. Then, on a neighbouring hill covered with enormous rock boulders there are steps, and remains of buildings which make use of the boulders as walls and arches, so that the whole thing is like an uncovered rabbit warren with paths running in and out of the rocks, and often under them. These ruins have been dated back to between the eighth and twelfth centuries A.D., using methods employing measurement of radioactivity. The remarkable thing is that a civilization existed, capable of building structures of this nature; and then for a thousand years nothing more elaborate than mud huts were built. It would seem that a whole civilization disappeared, rather as happened on Easter Island in the Pacific.

Later we drove out to see Dr. ——— referred to above. We felt we must draw on his long experience of nearly thirty-five years in one station. We found his lonely house; and he was having a typical bachelor tea. He was a stout man, not looking his sixty-three years, but when we talked to him his brain was that of an older man and he had difficulty collecting his thoughts. The reason was, I think, long years of excessive whiskey and gin. He wasn't really able to help us very much, and we realized that he found memory and concentration difficult. He had been a great hunter in his time, and had actually shot over 800 buffalo. Not many men have done this. The guest room was rather unusually furnished, 49 framed pictures, nearly all of dead game, with a few African gun bearers, and one bottle of scent together with some talcum powder! He also had framed on the walls of another room some photographs of larger tumours and other medical conditions he had seen. We felt very sorry for him. Obviously a thoroughly unhappy and disillusioned man. We noticed that he was reading some religious books, and we thought we might post him something that might be helpful.

Wednesday, 8 November

(Pretorius Kop camp, at lower end of Kruger National Park) We have just returned from seven hours in the park, and had a wonderful time. We must have seen a thousand impala in all. We also saw lots of wart hogs, water buck, gnu, kadu, one elephant, one sable antelope (a very large animal). We had some remarkable experiences. I was about to photograph some vervet monkeys when one with a baby on her breast jumped up and actually sat with her baby on the ledge of the car window at my shoulder. It was too close to photograph! Later we encountered some baboons, usually shy animals. As I was getting ready to photograph them one jumped in the open window and sat on the back of the seat behind my neck! Ted had to chase it out.

Friday, 10 November

We were up at five yesterday morning and left the park at about 6:45. It was a very pleasant and easy drive to Lourenço Marques. We chose a hotel from a guide book; very comfortable, central, and not expensive.

After a light lunch we went to the hospital to make contact with a Prof. Prates, the best-known name in medicine in Mozambique. I had been in correspondence with him. He welcomed us cordially and showed us the work he has been doing. We saw his records and some lovely plaster models of patients with tumours and other lesions, made by a man who worked at the museum but who is now dead. We recognized our own particular tumour among these models. In his office we met the representative of a drug firm from Johannesburg, a Mr. Thomas, and later in the evening he very kindly gave us supper in one of the cafes.

I should mention that the sisters in the hospital are, of course, nuns, and they seem extremely good. The white bed-linen would completely shame Mulago Hospital.

The above was written after lunch. It is now 6:30, Friday evening, and it has been an extraordinarily interesting day.

We had breakfast in the hotel at 7 and then all three of us went down town and decided to have a haircut. It was a real experience. While my hair was being cut a boy gave my shoes a superb polish, making them look like new. A lady with highly painted and polished nails wanted to manicure mine, but I declined. The haircut took as long as a major operation, and included being smothered in talcum powder, drenched in sprayed scent, and drowned in hair oil. Even my eyebrows were trimmed. All this cost me more than 6/–, but the three of us walked out of the shop feeling real dandies. The whole car was fragrant with perfume. It was a particularly novel experience for Ted as his hair is usually cut by Muriel, and he hasn't been to a barber for years.

After this we went to the hospital and had the most useful morning of our whole trip. Prates has his records beautifully tabulated and we were able to get out the records of all children's cancers for the past five years. We made notes on over forty cases of the tumour we are investigating and also got their addresses so that we can plot them on a map. As Lourenço Marques is the most southerly place from which the tumour has been reported this information is of very great value. We also took photographs of the magnificent models he has collected, and these will add real spice to lectures when used as illustrations. Not only did we get this valuable information on lymphomas, but we also got valuable information on other tumours. Prates is certainly a remarkable man and his records must be almost unique.

Sunday, 12 November

(Mount Hermon Mission, Mankaiana, Swaziland South African General Mission) Supper with Prof. Prates and Mr. Thomas, the drug firm representative, on Friday night in Lourenço Marques, was another experience. Prates took us to a cafe, where he seemed to know everyone. After selecting a table he disappeared, in order to inspect the prawns prior to cooking! We had the special Mozambique dish of enormous prawns, like little lobsters, grilled and served in rather strong sauce. They were very delicious. Bread is provided in the form of long loaves which are cut in two. Each person helps himself to half a loaf, which is lovely and fresh. We three drank Coca-Cola and tried some light wine, but I found it ghastly stuff. Prates and Thomas got through quite a lot of whiskey.

Prates is really a great character. Definitely the personality of the medical world in Mozambique, and very excellent at his job. He has done quite remarkable work with very limited staff and facilities. You can understand that he doesn't like being treated as a "dago" by some young white South African, and he was telling us of occasions when he was over-exasperated and just jumped over the counter at some office or airport to smack the fellow on the face or report him to the government.

(Swaziland) We called at a large and very fine hospital run by "The Church of the Nazarene," very fine Christian people. This is at Manzini. There are three doctors at this hospital, and they have 250 beds, a great number for a mission hospital. The senior doctor insisted that we stay for lunch, and we found him and his wife very charming: his father was one of the medical pioneers out here, while she comes from London. The buildings are some of the finest we have ever seen at any mission hospital. It was a very useful contact for us from a scientific standpoint as they do not see the tumour we are hunting, and their long experience is a more valuable "negative" than a "no" from a government doctor with only a few years' experience.

Tuesday, 14 November

(Johannesburg) Morning service in the little church at Mankaiana was—as in most African churches—with all the men on one side and all the women on the other. It was characterized by a sermon lasting about 50 minutes, which tends to be tedious when in an unknown language. In contrast to Uganda, the married women all had some covering on their heads.

Cliff spoke to a boys' Bible class in the afternoon, and I spoke at a weekly prayer-meeting in the evening. We had agreed that if we were invited to speak we would take it in turn. Ted had his first turn at Mbereshi.

We left Mankaiana at 6:45 yesterday, and the 260-mile drive to Johannesburg was most interesting. Swaziland is a very attractive country: there is no dividing line between it and Eastern Transvaal—it continues as vast rolling hills covered with short green grass and patterned with wattle plantations and attractive bungalow farmsteads, like an enormous version of the Sussex Downs. This vast, open, arable country stretches for over a hundred miles.

We saw many instances of teams of oxen ploughing—the old methods persist alongside the modern. In fact, we passed one old couple with bowed heads sitting in a trap drawn by two donkeys, proceeding along the road at about one and a half miles an hour, a striking contrast to the great American cars dashing past. I suppose the old Boer trekkers covered hundreds of miles at this snail's pace.

After we got to Springs, some 30 miles east of Johannesburg, we were virtually in built-up territory for the rest of our journey. Such a contrast to what we have seen of Africa on this trip, with miles and miles of nothing and stretches of a hundred miles with hardly another vehicle on the road. We might almost have been approaching Birmingham—a succession of towns, and in every direction the great man-made mountains of soil turned up by innumerable mines. Some of these are like great pyramids, others just truncated pyramids with bases several hundred yards long, but still growing. The traffic was reminiscent of English roads, with streams of great heavy lorries. Fortunately, we had a map to help us to find our way through the maze of streets and skyscrapers to the South African Institute for Medical Research. There we met Dr. Oettlé, who is arranging our programme. We found a great and welcome mail waiting for us, and after some preliminary discussions we were directed to a hotel into which we'd been booked. A *much* more pretentious hotel than we would ever have chosen for ourselves, each in a single room with private bath.

My lecture to the Institute staff was scheduled for 5:10. It was very well attended and extremely well received, almost embarrassingly so. The discussion that followed gave me a great deal of information which was most helpful. They have now found two cases of this tumour in South Africa, where it was believed to be unknown.

We were brought out to dinner with Mr. Thomas, the drug firm representative we met in Lourenço Marques, together with his wife and an American scientist who works for the same company in a research capacity. We went to one of those restaurants which it is an experience to visit occasionally if the meal is being charged on someone else's expense account: carpeted floors, subdued lights, waiters in dress suits, and everything on the menu three times the price it would be elsewhere.

After dinner we were brought to the hotel where the American is staying (rather more pretentious than our hotel) and we got down to shop. Ted and Cliff are going to do some trials on a new drug for schistosomiasis [bilharzia], which is common in the areas where they work. I promised I would ask one of our physicians to do the same. If they can get their drug pushed it is worth spending £6 on dinner. But I must emphasize that Thomas has been most helpful, and I believe he brought us out for kindness.

Wednesday, 15 November

Our first session yesterday was with a pathologist who had seen a European child with the tumour syndrome we are investigating. This will be the first time it has been described in a European. Although the child lives here, it had been to lower altitudes for holidays, a significant fact.

We were then brought to the great Baragwanath African hospital standing near the enormous "Native locations" south of the city. This is the largest hospital in the southern hemisphere. The traffic on our way out was terrific—three and four lanes all going the same way. I believe there is one car for every three people in Johannesburg. It is a hutted type of hospital, covering therefore a very large area. Excellent work seems to be done there and the staff are really keen. We were very warmly welcomed and shown different departments and wards by various members of the staff. . . . We got the impression that a large section of the whites, including many of the staff of the Baragwanath, don't favour the [racial] policy of the present government.

We all picked up many useful tips in this hospital to bring back to our respective units. Ted is always on the lookout for what he can adopt for Kuluva, and I think it is wonderful what he manages to do there.

Thursday, 16 November

Yesterday was, if anything, an even more full and interesting day than Tuesday. We were first driven out to the Virus Research Unit, about 7 miles from here. A full programme was laid on for us so that we could meet the workers in charge of the various departments. We saw tissue cultures of living cells and the maps of distribution of various viruses. Whatever virus is responsible for our tumour, and whatever insect carries it, must of course exist in the specific areas where the tumour occurs. We were given all sorts of interesting lines of thought to follow up.

We spent the afternoon at the Institute for Medical Research with the expert on maps, distribution of insects, animals and vegetation, etc. This was relevant to our problem—to find out what factors may be responsible for the distribution of the tumour. We were able to procure a lot of useful maps to bring back to Kampala.

(Later) Oettlé brought us out to his home, four miles out in the suburbs. We went by double-decker bus, and Ted particularly enjoyed it as he hasn't done any "strap-hanging" for many years.

We found George Oettlé and his wife a delightful Christian couple. Plymouth Brethren. They have six children under the age of nine, the youngest being two weeks. We all sat around a big table, and George gave thanks. Then, after the meal, before the children went to bed, they all gathered round and each in turn read a couple of verses of the chapter of Scripture for the day. Then George led us all as we knelt in prayer. It was such a very pleasant, free, happy evening. Oettlé is a world name in cancer research, and last year he was at conferences in Tokyo, England, Kampala, etc. Next year he is due in Moscow, Philadelphia, Dakar, and other places. This travelling is, of course, most interesting, but he and his wife hate parting. As I said before, we three have found that the only cloud over this trip.

This morning we are due to meet three more authorities in different subjects, and then we have lunch with the Professor of Surgery before spending the afternoon with Prof. Murray and Oettlé. We shall feel quite exhausted when we leave here, but it has been enormously valuable. We leave Johannesburg early tomorrow for Pietersburg. We are due to spend this evening again with the Oettlés.

That evening, after supper with the children and family prayers, an elderly lady of eighty who was staying with the Oettlés played the piano "beautifully," and Mrs. Oettlé ("who," Burkitt remarks, "has a very fine trained voice") sang several solos accompanied by her friend. Ted Williams also played the piano, and so did one of the children ("a nine-year-old daughter, who plays extraordinarily well").

This marked the end of the first half of the safari. The following morning, Friday, 17 November, at 8:30, the three men left Johannesburg on the return trip to Kampala. They encountered tremendous rainstorms as they approached Uganda, the worst seen in a hundred years; again and again

*the stationwagon had to be dug out of the mud; and on one
stretch of road it took them nearly three and a half hours to
cover fifteen miles. On Sunday, 17 December, they arrived at
Mulago, and the final entry in the* Lymphoma Safari Diary
describes the homecoming.

Sunday, 17 December

(Mulago) We left Mbale at 6:30 on Thursday morning and
reached the road block beyond Tororo at about 7:30. There
was a row of lorries in front of us and a police post at either
end of a quarter of mile of road over which water was flowing pretty rapidly. It was just possible for vehicles to get
through in single-line traffic, one way at a time. The water
was up to the floor boards of the car and the road very rough,
but we got through. There was one bus upside down in the
swamp at one side of the road, with its wheels and part of
the chassis above the level of the water. There were two lorries on their sides, and one Land Rover in the swamp. Several people had been drowned here the previous day. After
getting through I took off my shoes and stockings and waded
half way back to take photographs of cars getting through
and of the vehicles in the swamp.

At Bugiri we telephoned Olive to announce our arrival at
Mulago about noon. We stopped for a little at Jinja to photograph the unusual gush of water coming through the sluice
gates at the Jinja dam. When we reached Mulago at 12:10
we found palm leaves along each side of the entrance to our
house laced with colored bunting, and a "Welcome Home"
arch. We were showered with confetti from the families, all
three wives being there to meet us, and Molly Williams,
Judy and Rachel and Geoffrey Nelson. After the greeting,

Ted took the car out again to get photographs of it coming home! And thus happily ended the safari of a lifetime.

And yesterday, Ted was backing the car just outside the house and went too near a slippery bank, and got badly stuck in the mud. We had to dig him out!

Our hearts are full of thankfulness to God for all His mercies to us.

The trip is over, the diary closes. I hope you have found it of some interest.

Our love to you all.

WHERE
MERCY
FLOWS

WHERE
MERCY
FLOWS

KAREN HARTER

**CENTER
STREET**

New York   Boston   Nashville

Center Street
Time Warner Book Group
1271 Avenue of the Americas, New York, NY 10020

The Center Street name and logo are registered trademarks of the Time Warner Book Group.
Printed in the United States of America
ISBN 978-0-7394-6668-1
ISBN/10 0-7394-6668-2

To Jeff, the father of my children,

to Daddy,

and to my Father in Heaven.

I am truly blessed.

ACKNOWLEDGMENTS

Many thanks to my hard-nosed writer friends who provided the perfect blend of critique and encouragement: Erika, Gloria, Juanita, Lani, Mary, Margo, Nancy, Peggy and Mary. I love you all.

Renee Riva Capps, you have a knack for popping in by e-mail just when I need a good belly laugh. Carrie and Grace, I loved the late-night dream sessions, and yes, I will wear tangerine.

Ryan and Michael, thanks for allowing me to be a mom who sometimes forgot to do motherly things like cooking and baking. I'm getting better at it now, so please come home. I'm grateful for my family (oh, how blessed I am to have each one of you!), whose love and belief in me means more than you may ever know. Daddy, you were a tough editor and coach; Mom, my loyal fan no matter what I wrote about you; and Maria, a great cheerleader. Jeff, I know it took a lot of faith to let me do this thing. Thanks for believing.

To my incredible agent, Deidre Knight, as well as my editor, Christina Boys, and the team at Time Warner Book Group, thanks for helping to make my dream come true.

WHERE
MERCY
FLOWS

THE JUDGE ALWAYS had the final say. Right or wrong, he was God. His truth was a hard, unbending line that never wavered. Not even for me.

When I was young I called him Daddy.

Of course, I also lay in the cool grass of summer and imagined that clouds were dinosaurs and that just as the sky had no beginning or no end, life held limitless possibilities for me.

My world was twelve acres framed by a wadable creek in a gully to the east, the Stillaguamish River to the south, a stand of poplars lining our long driveway on the west and Hartles Road to the north. Our river came like a train from far away. It slowed as it rounded the bend to pass our house on its way to somewhere—the ocean, I guessed, and I believed as children do that my life, like the river, was destined to flow as easily around each bend.

I knew little of death, except that Great-grandpa Dodd had died while plowing the back quarter of his sixty acres. The job accomplished, he promptly had a heart attack and drove the old John Deere straight down the hill into the churning river. No one seemed to mind much, because he was very old and they thought it fitting that he and his rusty tractor had gone down together. It was symbolic, they said. His job on earth was done, and then he was swallowed up by the very river that had sustained him.

There were no lamenting dirges at the graveside and only a few quiet tears. Great-grandpa was laid out in his Sunday-go-to-meetin' suit, looking to me like he was taking his after-supper nap on the sofa, but for once he didn't snore. Most of the friends and relatives gathered in the dewy grass were in full Salvation Army uniform—dark military suits with rank designations on their shoulders, the ladies in bonnets with bows on the sides as big as cauliflowers. They sang hymns and played their cornets and trombones. My father didn't sing much. He stood silently, gripping my hand firmly so I couldn't take off my shoes and socks or stare down into the hole where they put Great-grandpa. My sister held a tissue in her white gloves and sang all the songs by heart. Auntie Pearl smiled at me afterward and said Grandpa had gone home to be with Jesus.

That seemed right to me. The way it was supposed to be. My life and the lives of the ones I loved would follow a similar course, meandering yet purposeful, and ending only upon reaching our destination. Old age.

My father, the only son of the fourth generation of American Dodds, had been expected to churn and plant the rich valley soil as his fathers had before him. Instead, he enrolled in the University of Washington to study law. His father, Lee Dodd (I called him Grandpa Lee), raised his children within twenty square miles of farms and woodlands in northwest Washington, venturing as far away as Seattle only for the rare funeral or special Salvation Army meeting. I suppose the way my father turned out was largely due to this narrow and rigid upbringing.

The sound of windshield wipers squeaking across dry glass

broke my muse. I switched them off, wondering when the rain had stopped and how I had driven so far with no memory of the passing scenes. The last thing I remembered was the ghostly shape of the Space Needle standing in the fog and then crossing an overpass to see the sprawling University of Washington campus off to my right. Now, as I continued north, an expanse of bright sky burned a path from the Olympic mountain range on the west to the Cascade Range on the east.

I was going home. After seven hard years, home to my river valley, Mom—and the Judge. The thought alternately warmed and then chilled me to the bone.

"TJ?" I ran the fingers of my free hand through my son's dark hair as I steered onto the freeway off-ramp. His eyes opened and he immediately raised himself to peer out the window.

"Are we there?"

"Not yet. We're getting close. I want you to see this."

"What?"

"The scenery. Look how green it is."

He glanced at a field of black-and-white cows and craned his neck in all directions before reaching for the rumpled map on the dashboard. His pudgy fingers traced the lines leading to the X that represented his grandma and grandpa's house as they had done at least a dozen times in the past two days. "You gotta go right there, Mom. Down this road, then turn on this road . . ."

"Turn it around. It's upside down."

He righted it with clenched brows and then studied it some more. "Don't turn on this line, Mom. This is a river."

"That's the river that runs behind their backyard. And don't you ever go down there alone. You hear me?"

He nodded. I made a mental note to mention it again.

"Does my grandma make cookies?"

"Probably."

For the next twenty miles TJ asked questions and played with the spring air rushing by his open window while I became increasingly apprehensive of what was to come. The heaviness in my chest was noticeable again. I took several deep breaths and tried not to think about it.

I slowed the Jeep as we bumped over a railroad track and pulled into the parking lot of a small store with gas pumps out front. The Carter Store. The sign had big letters that lit up now and a newer roof that extended over a large porch that hadn't been there before.

"You want a pop or something?"

TJ's head bobbed enthusiastically, which it would not have done if he knew how close we were to our destination. I parked next to a shiny black pickup, pressing my hand to my chest. TJ jumped out and rushed toward the wooden porch and then turned back impatiently.

"Come on, Mom!" His brows rose imploringly above his dark eyes, and I marveled for the thousandth time at how beautiful he was and that he could possibly be mine.

"Give me a minute," I called out my window. I took another deep breath. "For Pete's sake, we just got here." I climbed out and stretched my stiff legs, smoothing the damp wrinkles behind the knees of my jeans before following him into the store.

When I was a young girl, the Carter Store was owned by a spunky old woman named Nellie. I wondered if the new proprietor was related. The store had been smaller then. Just the essentials crowded the board shelves, in no logical order. Dish soap and tinfoil were lined up next to motor oil. There were ropes and wire racks for making toast over a campfire, stale marshmallows, and hot dog buns. Best of all, and worth every mile of the bike ride in the sweltering sun, was the array of candy in a glass case by the cash register. If she wasn't too busy, Nellie let my sister, Lindsey, and me arrange our penny candies and licorice whips on the counter, offering free advice on how to get the most bang for our quarter. One lucky day we happened to arrive just after the store's old freezer had wheezed its last. We rode away with all the Popsicles we could carry, licking frantically as the juice ran down our arms.

TJ knew his way around convenience stores, even this little Ma and Pa shack way out in the country in another state. He headed straight for the glass doors of the cooler at the back and pulled out an orange soda. "You wanna soda, Mom?"

Actually, I craved something stronger. "I'll have whatever you're having." He passed me a bottle and followed me to the cash register, where a tall young man stooped with his elbows on the counter, talking to the middle-aged cashier.

"Oh, sorry." He waved me up to the counter. "I'm not buying anything. Just yackin'." He stepped aside, pulling a fly-fishing magazine from the worn wooden counter. I nodded a half smile and felt him watching as I paid the heavy-jowled man behind the cash register.

"Did that fish come out my grandpa's river?" I turned to see TJ pointing up at the cover of the guy's magazine.

"I don't know. Which river is your grandpa's?"

TJ looked to me for help. "The Stilly," I said, which was the local abbreviation for the Stillaguamish River.

"Oh, no. This fish isn't from around here." He pointed to the red print beneath the photo of a glistening brown trout. "Says here this guy came out of the Yellowstone in Montana." He passed the magazine to TJ for closer inspection. "You ever caught a fish like that?"

TJ shook his head. "I never caught a fish yet. But I'm going fishing with my grandpa. He doesn't know I'm coming. We drove a long time, 'cause we're going to surprise him."

The guy tossed me an amused glance and then resumed a serious expression. "And what is your grandpa's name?"

He giggled. "I just told you. Grandpa."

"Judge Dodd," I volunteered.

The guy shook his head. The name meant nothing to him. I surmised he was new to the area or just passing through.

"The worm man." This came from the store proprietor as he passed me my change. I squinted through strands of wavy auburn hair that had fallen across one eye. The old man was obviously confused.

"My father is Judge Blake Dodd. He lives about three miles downstream." I passed TJ his soda and turned toward the door.

"Did you say Blake?" The tall guy slapped his thigh and rolled his eyes toward the man behind the counter with a *how-could-I-be-so-stupid?* look. "I know Blake. Met him fishing under the bridge one day. There was a mayfly hatch on and I had nothing but wet flies. He gave me one of his. Tied it himself. I didn't know he was a judge, though."

"Anyway, see you around." I removed the magazine from TJ's fingers and took his hand.

"Hey, wait a minute!" The proprietor's voice sounded gruff and mildly annoyed. He turned his back and shuffled to an antique Coca-Cola cooler behind him, lifted the lid, and rummaged around inside. "Tell him I need more baby crawlers. A couple dozen cartons."

"What?" In my confusion I glanced back at TJ's new friend, who flashed an amused grin.

"So." He paused long enough to push his hands into his back pockets and lean against a display case full of reels and fishing lures. "I take it you and your father are not real close."

He had unknowingly trodden on forbidden ground. "First of all," I snapped, "my relationship with my father is none of your business! And second, you guys have him mixed up with someone else." He backed up a step and held up the palms of his hands in defense. I immediately regretted my overreaction. My voice was more controlled when I spoke again. "My father is a justice of the State Superior Court. If you've read the papers at all, you've probably heard of him."

My tone must have been condescending. The tall guy adopted a moronic expression and cocked his head toward the storekeeper, who had returned to his post. "Well, we got one o' them city newspapers out here once . . . but none of us could read the big words." The old guy thought that was pretty funny. A laugh gurgled up from his belly like a big belch, which then turned into a disgusting cough.

"Come on, TJ." I grabbed his arm and pushed through the door, while he called weakly over his shoulder, "Bye, guys." I accidentally sprayed gravel on the shiny black truck on my way out of the parking lot.

The town of Carter consisted of the store, with its gas pumps and a built-in post office, Fraser's Tavern and a Methodist church. The nearest schools were a twenty-mile bus ride down the highway in Darlington, where one could also find a single movie theater and a good slab of meatloaf at the Halfway Café.

My childhood surrounded me as we drove. TJ baaed at passing sheep through his open window and I was him, admiring the black lamb who lifted his head before stepping closer to his mother and nudging her underside. Outside the fence posts, beyond the sheep's hungry reach, swayed bouquets of wild white lilies on slender stalks. Maple trees shone like gold-green neon in the low afternoon sun, and the air smelled as sweet as it had each spring of my first seventeen years. Where the road forked I caught glimpses of my river between the trees. "There it is! There's the river, Teej." The trees parted to reveal a long stretch, wide and clear, rippling over smooth stones and rushing around a great chunk of rock. As it turned away from us, it narrowed into a deep, mysterious pool. Then, teasingly, the trees closed our window.

The Duncans' Appaloosa Ranch appeared on my right, just as I had left it, and with a pang I wondered what ever became of Donnie Duncan, my childhood friend. Another stand of woods and finally the stretch of rail fence on my left that ended at the familiar gravel drive, lined on the far side by a windbreak of poplars standing like giant soldiers. To my surprise, stuck in the ground between the entrance and a roadside ditch was a cockeyed sign with WORMS $1.00 hand-painted in red.

I nosed the Jeep into the long driveway. TJ began to chatter with delight. "We're here! This is it! Are we here, Mom? Why are you going so slow?"

I wanted a cigarette. Out of habit, my hand crawled toward the purse beside me but returned empty to the steering wheel when I remembered that I had thrown them away for good, and to seal the deal with myself I had actually told TJ, who believed in me with the unshakable faith of a child. How or why he still believed in me after all the broken promises was as much a mystery to me as the reason for life itself. But I accepted it as one receives a gift of great sacrifice—with a certain amount of awe and humility. So, to light up again—at least in his presence—was unthinkable.

Too late to turn back. I took a deep breath and massaged my chest. What had happened here in the past seven years? What could possibly have driven the Judge to selling worms? What would they do when they saw us? This is for you, TJ, I thought, but a quiet whisper blew through my mind and I knew there was more to it than I had been willing to admit, even to myself.

The left side of the driveway was fenced pasture, now overgrown and going to hay. The barn still stood beneath the ancient broadleaf maple whose gnarled branches cast weird shadows across the waving field. Directly in front of us was the house, a sprawling log rambler with a deep covered porch stretched across its front and wrapping around its west side. The garage was attached to the house by a covered walkway. If the Judge and Mom were home, their cars were concealed behind its closed doors.

I stopped the car and waited for who knows what. Maybe for my mother to come running out in her apron and slippers and hug me like I'd been gone for a long weekend and invite us in for pie. Instead, we were greeted by a silently staring house and a breeze that sent a shiver through my bones. TJ jumped out, his footsteps making loud crunching sounds in the gravel. I imagined my parents peering through the blinds, asking themselves who these strangers were who had just arrived in a dusty Jeep loaded to the tops of its back windows. Even if they hadn't heard the rumble of the long-neglected engine or the tires on the noisy gravel, our presence was certainly announced now by TJ's excited babbling. He ran toward the barn and then wheeled back to the house, charged up the front steps and knocked on the heavy door. I was still safely belted to the seat of the car.

When no one answered the door, I got brave. I stepped out and joined TJ on the long shaded porch. We peeked through the window into the spacious living room with its vaulted ceiling and log beams. I didn't recognize the leather furniture or the Oriental rug on the polished hardwood floor, and fleetingly I worried that my parents had moved. But there above the stone fireplace hung the familiar painting of a trout bursting from the water in a defiant spray, a dry fly hooked neatly in its upper lip.

TJ sighed. "You should have told them we were coming, Mom." He stomped around the corner to the side of the house. I followed. At the kitchen window I lifted him to see for himself that Grandma was not there. Everything was spotless and in its place, and it occurred to me for the first time that they might be sipping tall lemonades somewhere off the coast of Aruba. The porch turned another corner, opening to an uncovered deck complete with deck chairs and tables and big pots of spring flowers. My son was not impressed. He had heard the river and now he could see it through the young alders at the edge of the lawn. Someone with a good arm could throw a stone from the deck and hit the water. TJ jumped off the steps and headed for the river without looking back.

"Hey! Where do you think you're going?"

"I'm not going *to* the river," he said with an air of authority. "I'm going *by* the river."

"Oh." I sat on a wood step leading down to the lawn. TJ stared at me for a moment, rocking indecisively from foot to foot, and then came back and put his hands on my knees. "Do you don't feel good again, Mom?"

I kissed his forehead. "No. I don't feel very good."

"Do you want me to wait for you?"

I smiled and shook my head. "Do you see that picnic table there?" He nodded. "See how long it is? That's how far you need to stay from the river." Like a good mother, I made him pace it out and then he was gone.

I watched him hurl rocks toward the swirling water for some time before dropping my head to my knees. It had been a long, tiring day. The miles of Oregon and Washington freeway re-played swiftly in my mind, along with numerous pop and potty stops and the incessant mind-tangling questions of a five-year-old. I wanted to be home. I longed to take a nap in my own bed, which I no longer had, and even if I did I didn't have the money to get back there. When I lifted my head, seemingly only seconds later, TJ was not in sight. My heart fluttered un-comfortably and I pushed myself up from the step.

Low shrubs and alder saplings obstructed my view of the river. I strode quickly across the yard to the scrubby strip be-tween the lawn and the surging stream. My son's dark hair ap-peared momentarily behind a salmonberry bush about twenty yards upstream. I called to him, but the rushing river drowned my voice. A dirt trail, muddy enough in spots to capture the geometric design from the bottoms of his shoes, followed the course of the river, in some places veering dangerously close to the edge of the bank. I knew I was a fool and a poor excuse for a mother and flogged myself as I stumbled along the bumpy ter-rain. How could a five-year-old with a two-inch attention span be expected to carry around the mental measurement of a pic-nic table?

The trees that gathered by the river now were taller and thicker. I came around a cedar stump and saw TJ on a spit of sand and smooth rocks and a fly fisherman just beyond him standing knee-deep in a quiet stretch of water. TJ seemed planted where he was, watching for the first time with obvious wonder the graceful flight of a dry fly on the end of a tapered line. The sun had dropped below the treetops, leaving that whole stretch of river in evening shadow. I hugged myself against the chill and leaned on a ragged cedar as my eyes adjusted. The fisherman had not noticed TJ. He cast into an upstream eddy, poised and ready as his fly drifted across its intended path. No takers. The feathered bug took off again, swooping like a tiny remote-controlled plane above his head. My heart suddenly burst into flight like a startled bird.

It was that perfect stance, arm moving just so. That slight tip of his head. Despite the unfamiliar cap, I knew. TJ stepped closer. Upon hearing the crunch of the boy's shoes in the river rocks, the Judge turned to face him. I gasped and ducked behind the stump.

2

M Y FIRST IMPULSE was to retreat up the trail. Then I remembered that I was a grown-up now. I dug my fingernails into the ragged cedar and watched. The Judge glanced upstream and down. His voice was deep and rumbly like the river, so I could only guess that he was questioning the little stranger as to the whereabouts of his parents.

A shrill childish voice pierced the air. "Up there!" I heard the slosh of my father wading to shore and then the rocks displaced by heavy hip boots. I peered around the stump. The Judge placed his hand on TJ's shoulder and pointed his rod tip up toward the trail. They hiked toward my asylum in silence. What was it about this man, I wondered, that caused even TJ to fall dumb and obey without question?

When they were almost upon me, I stepped onto the trail.

The Judge stopped short, incredulous. TJ ran to me. "Mom!"

I pulled him in front of me like a shield. "Hi." I tried to make my voice sound strong. "Remember me?"

"Samantha." He breathed my name as if I had been dead and buried for seven years.

Thank God for TJ. Oblivious to the chasm between my father and me, he became a sort of bridge. "This is my son, TJ."

The Judge's eyes stayed fixed on mine for several long seconds before he dropped to one knee before my son. "Hello, TJ." He laid down the rod and held out his massive hand. "I'm . . . your grandpa."

TJ returned the handshake but seemed puzzled. He cocked his head. "You don't look very old like a grandpa." It was true. I felt like I had aged a decade beyond my actual twenty-four years, but my father looked the same. TJ stretched his small hand to the Judge's face and traced a shallow line at the corner of one eye. "But there's a wrinkle."

"I'll get more." A hint of a smile washed across the Judge's face. "I promise."

Suddenly TJ had a revelation. He really did have a grandpa and here he was in the flesh. His awe turned to unbridled excitement. "Grandpa"—one pudgy hand patted the Judge's thigh—"I came to see you! I came to go fishing with you!"

At that the Judge melted. TJ could do that to anybody. He scooped my son up and waltzed around that muddy trail like TJ was his long-lost lamb. The two of them laughed and chattered, weaving some almost visible cord between them, while I grabbed the fly rod from the grassy edge of the trail and led them back to the house. Their banter relieved the tension. My son did the talking and I only had to fill in the technical details, like *Wednesday* and *Reno*. Still, I felt the Judge's eyes on me and his unspoken questions circling like vultures in the air.

My mother saw us from the porch. She looked tentative at first, as if she couldn't trust her eyes. I took bigger strides across the yard, and Mom swooped down the steps, a dove in her gray silk skirt. I felt her cool damp cheek against mine, and when she eventually pulled away there were tears in her eyes.

"Samantha Jean. Where have you been?" She pushed the

bangs off my face and studied me. I knew I was being read like the morning news.

"Reno."

Mom's forehead drew together and her face took on a concerned frown. I expected her to point out how sallow I looked. "Red hair is nice on you," she finally said. "You look real nice."

"It's auburn." In my mind, apples and fire engines were red and the box with the shimmering model on its front had clearly said *auburn*.

Her gaze turned to TJ as the Judge slid him gently to the ground. "Sam"—she looked from his round face to mine as if searching for some resemblance—"is this my grandson?" I had never mentioned in my sparse letters that TJ had the smooth pecan-colored skin and black eyes of his Mexican sire. Mom gently cupped his face between her hands as if it was the last papaya on a desert island.

For that moment I was happy. If my parents were shocked at the color of TJ's skin, they hid it well. In fact, they seemed to embrace him and their role as grandparents instantly.

I had not craved my mother's presence during nine hours of grueling labor in a Nevada hospital. I hadn't needed pep talks or hand-holding. But when I first held my son, touched his tiny feet—when he nuzzled and found my breast, his fingers gently kneading as he sucked—it was then that I wanted my mother desperately. He was the most beautiful thing I had ever seen. He was the best thing I had ever done. Now my mother knew—I saw it in her eyes—that something good could come from me.

No one asked why we had come, or how long we would stay. I guess it was evident by the amount of stuff that we all unloaded from the Jeep (which included my bedside table, two favorite lamps, TJ's Donald Duck bank, and a stack of mismatched towels) that it might be more than an overnight visit. Mom seemed to sense my fatigue. She warmed some chowder while the Judge foraged in the garage for a cot for TJ. I watched her flit from stove to counter to table like she had in one of a thousand childhood scenes, comfortable and familiar. It felt good to be mothered again.

That night I slept in my old bedroom. My Ferrari posters had at some time been replaced by a couple of tastefully framed floral prints, and the bedspread was new. But when the light was off and the window opened just a crack, the sweet scent of the cottonwoods that thrived along the river floated in to me like it had on hundreds of childhood nights. Their green buds were new and fragrant. I could hear the water rushing past. The sound of it used to stir longings in me that I couldn't understand, just as the distant whistles of the midnight trains that ambled across Carter trestle had. Wordless, invisible beckonings that caused my mind to wander.

Maybe it was the river's fault that I had wandered so far, for so long. Maybe it had wooed me away subliminally while I slept. Then again, it was possibly the very thing that called me back. Tomorrow I will explore it again, I told myself, and in my dreams I was twelve again, running as fast as the river.

THE JUDGE AND TJ tromped past my bedroom window at some ungodly hour of the morning. After that I couldn't sleep. I followed the scent of coffee down the hall, still wearing the long T-shirt I had slept in. The kitchen was empty so I poured myself a cup, draining the pot dry, and took it back to my room.

My hand smoothed the bright new quilt at the foot of the bed. I had been seventeen the last time I slept here. I wondered what ever happened to the collection of animal skulls that had graced my shelf. There were deer, coyote, rabbit, possum and my favorite, a beaver whose curved yellow teeth slid up an inch into its skull. That one still had flesh and fur attached when I found it on the creek bank. I buried it next to Mom's daisies and dug it up a few weeks later to bake in the sun. It had turned out real nice.

My son's voice snapped me back to adulthood. I opened the window and called to him.

"Mom!" He bounded toward me through field grass half his height. "Me and Grandpa went to the river!" He was a beautiful sight and the morning air smelled sweet.

The Judge waved to me. "Come out here! I want to show you something!"

What could it hurt? I stuffed my nightshirt into my jeans and slid out the window until the dewy grass surprised my toes.

"Hey!" The Judge sounded stern. "What have I told you about using the door?"

"Sorry," I called back, "just habit."

"Bring the garbage bucket by the back porch!" he called, and he and TJ headed off toward the barn.

By the time I caught up, there were coffee grounds and something orange on my leg. "What are you doing? Raising pigs?"

The Judge just smiled proudly and guided us through the open barn door. It was dark inside and smelled of damp earth. My pupils adjusted to the dim light as he led us between two long wood-framed troughs filled with dirt. "Look here." At that he pushed up his sleeve, thrust his arm into the soil and pulled up a writhing fistful of purplish-red worms.

"Worms!" TJ was impressed. "Can I hold them?"

My father placed them tenderly on his little palm and then looked at me like a boy himself. "What do you think, Sam? Do you want to hold some too?"

"I'll pass."

Then he went into a long, boring scenario about how to build a worm bed and how you use a mixture of peat moss and manure, at which point I made TJ dump his handful back in the box.

"You don't have any animals. Where do you get the manure?"

"From the Duncans' Appaloosa Ranch. Chester gives me all I need. Of course, it has to be aged beyond the heating stage and the urine's got to be leached out. Then you just have pure manure."

"Pure manure," I said. "Uh-huh." I thought to ask about Chester's son, Donnie, but something caused me to hold my tongue.

"What do they eat, Grandpa?"

The Judge reached for the bucket at my feet. "See that oatmeal you didn't finish?" TJ peered into the mess of scraps until he recognized his breakfast and then nodded. "That's their favorite. Now, I'm going to need your help, son." He set TJ on a turned-over washtub and passed him the pail. "Okay, dump it on in there."

They dug and dumped and smoothed out the soil, while I sat on a stool observing the man I used to know as my father.

Actually, I can't say that I ever knew him. The Judge's mind had always been a mysterious universe to me. There seemed to be no question he could not answer, which was good if you were too lazy to look something up in the encyclopedia but bad if you wanted to blast through your homework and get on to more worthwhile things. A simple question about the length of the Panama Canal would inevitably turn into a dissertation on the history and politics of its construction. Worse yet, after the unwelcome barrage of information, my father had a habit of asking questions back. "So, what do you think? Should the U.S. have agreed to return ownership and control to the Panamanians?" I never had a clue.

My sister didn't freeze up like I did. She would screw up her face thoughtfully and then blurt out an opinion with no sign of fear that her answer might be idiotic. Of course, it never was. Probably because she actually paid attention to what he had said.

The Judge's opinions were as solid as boulders and God help the man or child who stood in their path when they rolled. As a teenager I was crushed by them. Flattened out like Wile E. Coyote, only I didn't spring back so fast. My policy now, and believe me I had given the subject much thought, was to avoid any subjects deeper than the weather. So far we were doing just fine.

I watched him touch my son and wondered if the Judge might have softened up a bit over the years. I could only hope.

In the courtroom the Judge's words had been known to bring hardened attorneys to the brink of tears. He didn't put up with any high-sounding verbosity, and anyone who spent time in his presence left either loving him or hating him. There was no in-between.

When I was old enough, I became aware that my classmates, most of whom had never met the Judge, had an opinion of him, which they had inherited from their parents. Regina Wiggins said my father was a "mean, horrible man" and told some kids on the playground that he beat me and that was why I always had bruises on my legs. I didn't know about that rumor until about a year later. The day I found out, I ambushed her on her way home from the bus stop. I ran ahead to where she always took a shortcut through the woods and hid in the salal bushes with a stick. She never knew what hit her. She ran home screaming and babbling and the next day told everyone that a crazy man had attacked her, but I set them straight. I told them that her father kicked her because she didn't say, "Yes, sir," fast enough when he told her to take out the garbage.

I defended my father blindly for a few years, not understanding my schoolmates' accusations any more than they did. What went on in court was never discussed at our dinner table. Any conversations between my parents about my father's cases were held in private, and I rarely thought about his identity outside of our home unless someone brought it up at school. My classmates had an unfair advantage over me, as their parents rarely made the news.

My ninth-grade social studies teacher, Mr. Murchy, had us dissect the *State of Washington v. Ronald Enrich* case because it was a current event, and one that raised quite a buzz around the beehive since both the accused and the judge (who happened to be my father) made their abode right here in Carter. Ronald Enrich was only seventeen when, in a fit of rage, he smashed his mother's head repeatedly on the stone fireplace mantel in their home.

Once the wave of horror at the actual crime spread through town, people began probing for a reason. Ron was such a handsome boy. He had big brown eyes and a disarming grin. Sure, he was involved in a few angry scuffles with players on opposing football teams, but that aggressive tenacity also got Darlington High into the state play-offs. (The team's ensuing loss, while Ron was in jail awaiting his trial, was an outright embarrassment to the community.)

Thelma Romack, a waitress at the Halfway Café, said Carol Enrich never left a tip and of course it was no reason to murder a person, but didn't she have the most annoying laugh? Alice Forsythe said now that Carol was dead she held no grudge, but she would always remember how Carol took the credit for the success of last year's homecoming weekend when Alice was the one who did most of the work.

It turned out Mrs. Enrich had been reading Ronald's mail. The public defender apparently had no qualms initially about the judge and the defendant being from the same small town, obviously thinking it would work in his client's favor. He was wrong about that. The Judge had Ronald tried as an adult and he was sentenced to life in the state penitentiary. The public outcry was heard beyond Carter and our river valley. The case was discussed on a local radio talk show and followed by the Seattle network news stations. I saw my father's picture on the second page of *The Seattle Times*, and the headline above it that read, THE JUDGMENT OF ALMIGHTY DODD.

The class chewed and swallowed the facts as presented by *The Herald, The Seattle Times* and the *Darlington Weekly*, and then barfed up the verdict. Seventy percent thought Ronald ought to have been given leniency. Most of my classmates thought my father was a merciless tyrant, and the rest were undecided. I was in the seventy percent.

As a child, I remember the Judge going to the courthouse every morning, returning as faithfully as the tide every night.

Sometime after dinner he would retire to his study, which was sort of like the Holy of Holies because you had better have a good reason for going in there—or have a rope on your leg so someone could pull you out. The Judge was pretty intense when he was deciding a case. If Lindsey and I weren't noisy, he might keep his door open just a crack. I rarely watched him read his boring old books, but once in a while his strange murmurings drew us to the bright wedge of light in the hall to spy. He would lean way back in his chair and talk to the ceiling and then he might be quiet for a long time, running those powerful hands through his dark hair. Finally, he would lurch forward, his open hand smacking the desk, and proclaim, "That's it!" tumbling his startled spies backward in the hall.

That's the way I remember him. And now the powerful hand that raised the gavel was elbow-deep in a trough of horse dung.

"So what's the plan? Are you going to retire from the bench and sell worms?"

The Judge looked up, obviously amused. "No. I don't think so."

"That old guy at Carter Store said he needs a couple dozen more cartons."

The Judge's face brightened. "Did he now?" He turned and reached for a stack of white foam cartons on a plank table. "How high can you count, TJ?"

"Fifty hundred."

"Good. Here we go." He proceeded to scoop a pile of dirt from the bed onto a wire mesh screen and shake it like a miner panning for gold. The black earth mixture and the smallest of worms fell through the holes. The rest wriggled frantically, as if suddenly caught naked in public. "There's a nice one," the Judge said as he dropped it into his cup. "Two, three . . ."

"Four!" TJ chimed in.

"Then why are you doing this?" I asked.

"Well, I enjoy it." He raised one eyebrow halfway up his forehead. "I didn't mean to have so many when I started out. I just wanted a few worms handy for guests who didn't fly-fish. Matt used to bring his boys over here to toss a line every once in a while, you know. Then your mother started using them in her planters to improve the soil. She says her geraniums are heartier and bloom longer. When I got too many, I stuck a sign in the yard. At first I gave them away free, but that makes people uncomfortable. They don't come back. Then I painted '$1.00' on the sign. You'd be surprised how many people stop now."

"You want people stopping here at all hours so you can walk all the way out to the barn and dig worms for them? For a dollar?"

He smiled like he had a secret I couldn't possibly understand. "It's no bother. When I'm not here the locals know to just dish up their own. Sometimes I find bills on the workbench or nailed to the wall. Don comes by every once in a while." I must have looked confused. "Donnie Duncan. He asks about you."

"He's still here?" I was shocked. Donnie was the one who couldn't wait to get out of this nowhere town that didn't even show up on some maps. The Judge paused and looked at me then, his eyebrows curving down like lazy question marks. He was always frugal with his words, careful to assemble them just right before they touched his lips. I knew that somehow a connection had been made to the past simply by the mention of my old friend's name. Not yet. I wasn't ready for questions. I turned back toward the open barn door. "I think I'll go see what Mom is doing."

Over my shoulder I saw him staring after me. He forced his eyes back to my son and dropped the last worm into the cup. "Thirteen. Always give 'em more than they expect. Right, TJ?"

TJ looked up at the worm man like he was God. "Right!"

$\sim$ 3

I HAD NO VALID reason for parking my Jeep against the curb beneath the spreading branches of a Japanese cherry. The house across the street was painted green now. Someone had done a sloppy job on the trim, splotching white onto the green siding. The tiny laurel hedge had grown thick and tall. There was no tire swing hanging from the maple tree, no red Chevy truck with a lanky young man reaching beneath its hood.

Sometimes revisiting the past is a mistake. Some things are better left in your mind the way they were, or the way they seemed, anyway.

Every time a breeze blew, pale pink blossoms wafted across my windshield and onto the seats of the Jeep. They stuck in my tangled hair. I had pulled off the road between Carter and Darlington to roll back the canvas top. It was a warm day and the air was saturated with the sweet scents of new green grass and flowers. Like the spring when I fell in love with Tim. But he didn't live here anymore. He and I had left town in his shiny red Chevy seven years ago. I thought maybe his mother had moved on also. The house was just too different. She would never have let the gardens go to weeds or leave that hedge untrimmed. There was no sign of life in the house, no vehicles in the drive. It was a hauntingly lonely sight.

I don't know what I would have done if Mrs. Weatherbee had poked her head out the door and waved. Not that she would. If she recognized me sitting out there like a stalker staring at her house, she would be more likely to turn away and close the drapes. But then, she would have heard only Tim's side of the story. I would have liked the chance to explain.

I drove around Darlington for a while, past the Dairy Barn Drive-In and my alma mater, Darlington High. A cluster of students sprawled on the lawn with books open. They looked so young. Was I really that young when I left? I had felt so much older. I thought I was ready to run my own life. I thought I understood everything there was to know about life and death, but on both concepts I was wrong.

My stubbornness had been my downfall more than once. It was one of the things I got from my father. But in our final contest my bulldog tenacity had won over his, or lost, depending on how you looked at it. I packed what I could carry in a duffel bag and my backpack and walked right past the Judge. He didn't stop me. In fact, he opened the front door. My mother followed, trying to reason with me, but he reached out his hand and held her. Before I was all the way off the steps and onto the walk, the porch light went off. My father would no longer be a lamp unto my feet and a light unto my path. He made that clear. I could find my own way through the dark.

It wasn't until after TJ was born that I started admitting how much I missed them. Mom especially. I always wondered what she would do about this and that. How do you soothe a colicky baby? Is this diaper rash or the plague? I reached for the phone sometimes but always stopped myself. My life was way too complicated to explain. What if the Judge answered the phone? I was sure he was finished with me and I certainly had nothing to say to him. I did send short notes with selective information on occasion, but I feared that once I heard my mother's voice, I might spill my carefully guarded secrets like dirty motor oil and never be able to clean up the mess.

Coming home to the river had been TJ's idea originally. All those nights as we cuddled in our big chair back in that dreary Reno apartment, I told him stories. Sometimes I made up bizarre creatures that lived in stumps or distant lands, but more often than not the characters were my sister, or our friend Donnie from down the road, and me in any one of our true adventures by the river. In TJ's mind the river valley of my childhood was more magical than any elfin kingdom, more glorious than victorious knights on stately white horses. "Tell me about the bad boys that killed the big salmon, Mom," he would say, and I would tell it as if he had never heard the tale before.

I described the moods of the river, the sounds and the smells, the great blue heron poised like a statue in the shallows, waiting for fry. I told of the small creek that cut through the ravine beyond the barn. Every summer salmonberries hung faithfully over its banks—orange, yellow and red, like the bright jars of salmon eggs lined up on the shelves at Carter Store. Where the creek swept wide around a meadow of wild grasses with hitch-hikers that stuck to my socks, blue forget-me-nots flocked at the water's edge. Crawdads hid in the silt beneath the creek banks. Periwinkles in homemade shells clung to the rocks and sticks in the shallows until I pulled their hideous bodies out to use as fish bait, their spidery legs flailing in protest. TJ listened wide-eyed to the recounting of the dams Donnie and I built on the little creek and forts made with woven boughs and bracken ferns, where we hid undetected during pinecone wars.

And then there was fishing. Fishing was the thing that intrigued TJ the most. Maybe because I could not speak of it without a wistful longing, nor could I separate the Judge, his grandfather, from this inherited passion for the pursuit of fish. I couldn't pinpoint the nucleus of our common fever if I had to. Was it the challenge of developing the perfect cast or of landing a fly exactly where I meant it to go? Was it the thrill of the hit, or of playing the fish, or of finally seeing it roll exhausted onto its side as I pulled it ashore? I don't know. I only know that a glistening trout is a thing of beauty to me, as moving as standing before an original Renoir might be to some. But the trout itself is nothing without the river; nothing but seafood destined for a pan. The river—that rushing, gurgling ribbon of light that swirled at my ankles, its sweet breath in my nostrils—was essential. And as strange as this may seem, the river was nothing without my father. The two had been to me somehow one and the same.

My son often interrupted our story time with questions, which as he grew older became harder to answer. Once he had asked only things like *Do fish have mothers?* and *What do frogs eat?* But after he deduced that my having parents meant that he had grandparents, I sometimes felt that he was a prosecuting attorney and I was a reluctant witness on the stand. "Why don't we ever go there?" he would ask.

"Because it's too far."

"We could take a airplane."

"Plane tickets cost money."

"Or we could drive our Jeep. How long will it take if we drive our Jeep?"

I explained that driving costs money too. I said I couldn't get off work for that long and changed the subject as skillfully as I could, but he would always bring it up again.

The truth was a horse pill, too big for a five-year-old to swallow. He had never known shames that caused him to avoid mirrors. TJ had scraped his arm and bumped his head, but so far he didn't know the kind of pain that Band-Aids and ice packs couldn't cure. And I certainly didn't want to tell him of such things. There really was no one to tell. I had estranged my family and my husband, and I had no real friends. My pain was the closest thing I had to a friend. It was constant and dependable, by my side all day and lying on my chest like a Saint Bernard until I finally slept at night.

It was physical pain that eventually caused me to consider TJ's plan. Both TJ and I had caught a flu bug that winter. I took time off from my job to care for him, and in a few days he was back to normal, flying around the apartment making jet engine noises. My initial symptoms (including a fever of 104 degrees) lingered a few days longer than his. After that I had a cough for weeks and very little energy. I did go back to work at the Starlight Room, bartending and waiting tables, but found it increasingly hard to work a full eight-hour shift. There was this heaviness in my chest that just wouldn't go away, and I'm not talking about sadness now. That, I had learned to live with. But this—well, some days I just couldn't cope. I would be exhausted before I got TJ dressed and fed and off to day care. I have to say my boss was patient for a long time. But one day, when I had to ask if I could leave early, he just said to go home and don't bother coming back.

I didn't have medical insurance. After paying the rent that

month, I had exactly $172.58. My roommate was in about the same financial condition, only she still had her job.

Hard times were not new to me. When things got tough, I just had to get tougher. But this time I didn't have the strength. I worried myself into a dither. What was wrong with me? I couldn't get any answers from my doctor until I paid my overdue bill. If I paid the bill, I would have nothing left. How would I feed my son? When would I be well enough to work again?

TJ found me crying in my room one night. I had thought he was asleep until I felt his soft hand rubbing my cheek. "What happened, Mommy? Did you get hurt?" I immediately swiped at my tears and sat up on the edge of the bed. The lamp was still on and he could see the red blotches on my face that always resulted from a good cry. TJ had never seen me in this condition before.

"No, I'm not hurt, baby." I managed a sheepish smile. "I just felt like crying tonight. I feel better now."

"But why?"

"I don't know. I guess grown-ups cry sometimes for the same reasons kids cry. Remember the first time I left you at the new day care?" He nodded. "That was a brand-new situation for you. You weren't comfortable with it and it made you cry."

"I wanted you to come back." He climbed onto the bed. I put my arms around him and we fell back against the pillows. I sighed and stared at the ceiling while his finger idly explored the paths of my outer ear. "Maybe you want *your* mommy."

I rolled my head to look at him, astonished. One whack and he had driven the nail home. His beautiful dark eyes blinked. He was so right. I needed someone to take care of me. I desperately wanted to find healing. I certainly hadn't found it anywhere else.

"Let's go home, Teej," I finally said. "You've got a grandma and grandpa to meet."

Eight days later and here we were, back in the familiar home of my childhood. I didn't mention my illness to Mom or the Judge. It might have seemed presumptuous after a seven-year absence to show up out of the blue just because I had no other conceivable plan to take care of my son, nor, for that matter, myself. I was as helpless and dependent as a toddler again, only not so naive. I could never crawl up on my father's lap again as I once did, believing that he was my daddy and I was his own flesh and blood and that his love was as constant and binding as the law of gravity. I wished I could have remained a child forever, living and playing along the river's edge in innocent bliss without knowing what I knew now. Love, it seemed, had its limits. And I had a knack for charging beyond them.

My shames were stacked stone on stone now, a wall between the Judge and me. A monument to the lines I had crossed.

Oh, he tolerated me. What else could he do? Cast me from his back porch into the pit of hell? Besides, I had brought my angel-faced son, his grandson, an offering that seemed to please him, and we were a package deal. If nothing else, TJ had bought me some time.

Just after lunch that first day back at the river, the Judge and TJ had headed for the creek with a can of worms and spinning rods. TJ had to half run with a little skip in his step to keep up with his grandpa's huge stride. I had declined their invitation to come along, stating that I hoped to run into Darlington to look up some old friends. That was true, though my primary reason was that I was not sure I could make it down the steep ravine and back in my weakened state. The creek was actually high on the list of old friends that I wanted to see.

The old friends were gone, of course. Married and moved away. I wished I could have warned them that there are no greener pastures than those in the Stillaguamish Valley. Trudy (according to her mother, whose bread-loaf breasts almost smothered me when she hugged me on her front porch) had married a stockbroker and lived in New York, along with two kids and three Persian cats who had all won awards at cat shows. Mrs. Simpson wrote Trudy's new name and address on a recipe card and tucked it in my pocket. I apologized for not keeping in touch. How could I have been so thoughtless? I had left town without saying good-bye to my best friend.

The friend I missed the most was Donnie. I had assumed he was a big-city lawyer by now, married to some svelte lady, frequenting operas and live theater. That was until the Judge told me otherwise. Donnie was once my best friend—I have to say even better than Trudy, though I would never have admitted that to either one of them. It would have hurt Trudy, and Donnie—well, he didn't need his ego puffed up, that was for sure. I drove past the Duncan ranch for the third time on my way home that day; it was only a quarter mile down the road from our driveway, on the opposite side of the road. But for some reason I was not ready to go down that gravel lane yet. He was a boy when I left. I did not know the man, Don Duncan. If he had changed as much as I over the years, we were nothing but strangers now. I guess you can't leave your treasures scattered along the roadside and expect them to still be there when you come back.

It was late afternoon when I pushed through the back door and into the kitchen, where I saw TJ standing on a chair pulled up to the counter, watching the Judge gut a trout in the sink. Déjà vu. It used to be me watching wide-eyed as the tip of the knife was poked into the hole in the fish's belly and the sharp blade slit the white flesh up to the gills.

"Mom, look! We caught two fish!"

They were small cutthroats, barely legal keepers. The big trout were mostly in the river, but TJ was not old enough to fish beyond the creek yet. "Wow! They're beautiful."

"We're cooking them for dinner!"

The Judge looked over his shoulder at me. "Want to see what they're eating?"

I nodded. I was still curious even after all those years. He separated the stomach sac and ran the dull side of the blade down its length. "Periwinkles."

The phone rang. The Judge held up his bloody hands helplessly, and I reached for the portable phone on the end of the counter. "Hello; Dodd residence."

The caller didn't speak, but I sensed that someone was there. I shrugged my shoulders and held the phone away from my ear.

Immediately, the Judge snatched the receiver away, bloody hands and all. "Hello?"

I heard a voice then, a male voice, and my father spun away. He strode out of the kitchen and down the hall toward his study. Curious, I followed, pausing just outside the door, but heard nothing else until the receiver slammed down on his desk. He let out a long sigh.

"Who was that?" I asked.

He looked up, startled to see me there. "Nothing; nobody. Just a prank call."

We returned to the kitchen in time to see TJ *cleaning* his fish with soap and a sponge. I laughed, but the humor seemed to be lost on the Judge. He took the sponge from TJ to clean off his phone, rinsed his hands and left the room without speaking.

4 ✐

MY SON FOLLOWED Mom from the open oven to the counter with his mouth and eyes agape. "Grandma, that's a giant chicken!" She had prepared a Thanksgiving feast, though it was not quite May.

Mom laughed. "TJ, don't tell me you've never seen a turkey before."

"Yes, I have. I colored one at day care." He eyed the golden-brown bird with a hint of a frown. "He was the Pilgrims' pet."

I picked up a bowl of green beans and headed for the dining room. "We ate in a restaurant last Thanksgiving. TJ had a hamburger."

The family congregated in the dining room, along with Matthew, my father's comrade since they had roomed together in college. Matthew was a medical doctor with a family practice in Seattle. I sat facing the window where the river winked at me through the trees.

My sister, Lindsey, scooted next to her new husband, who looked like she had cut him out of an Eddie Bauer catalog. His dark wavy hair seemed to be polished with something and a supposedly wayward strand was carefully positioned on his forehead. I wondered if he ironed the crease in his khaki pants himself.

The last time I saw Lindsey, we were both seventeen and she wore a ponytail. Now her hair was bobbed and she had graduated from cheerleader skirts to a sophisticated silk dress and pearls. She tossed a blond wisp behind her ear with a perfectly manicured hand. "So, Samantha." She smiled too hard, like someone you run into in the grocery store who can't remember your name. "We have so much catching up to do."

"You first," I said. I still had not formulated an appropriate account of the last seven years.

Mom placed the turkey platter at the head of the table near the Judge and everyone grew quiet, all eyes on him, until he bowed his head. "Father, we are grateful for all You provide. . . ." I peeked and saw TJ staring at his grandpa's face. When I caught his eyes, I closed mine demonstratively and bowed my head. My father's voice was soft and low like distant thunder. "And for bringing Samantha and TJ home . . . Lord, we are truly thankful. Amen."

"Amen," we repeated in unison.

Lindsey remembered where we had left off. "Okay"—she tipped her head adoringly toward her husband—"where do I begin? Well, as you know, David and I were married about two years ago. Oh, Sam, I wish you could have been there! It was a fabulous wedding! David's parents' home is right on Lake Washington. We had the ceremony and reception out on the lawn and then we left for our honeymoon from their dock, waving good-bye from the deck of their cabin cruiser."

The Judge arched one dark eyebrow and smiled only with his eyes. "She couldn't see who she was waving at, with that veil blowing across her face."

"Oh, I saw enough to know that you were crying!" Lindsey teased. "I expected Mom to be the gushy one, but it was you, Daddy."

"That was the wind in my eyes." He winked at her.

A familiar pain bored into me, long and slow. I looked away from them. "TJ, eat your potatoes."

"I don't like potatoes."

"You like French fries."

"I know. But I don't like potatoes."

"Anyway," Lindsey continued, "David passed his bar exam last June and had a position waiting for him at Wiley and Murdock. They're already talking about making him a partner."

"That's good," I said as sincerely as I could. "Where do you work, Lindsey?"

"Oh." The question seemed to catch her off guard. "Well, I don't really." She fiddled with her watch and I noticed it was the kind some of the rich women wore where I had tended bar in Reno.

"You work, honey," my mother pitched in. "You just don't get paid for it." Then she turned to me. "Your sister does a lot of volunteer work at the hospital in Darlington. She uses puppets to entertain children in extended care, runs errands, and even decorates the wards. Sometimes the nurses call her in to sit with a worried mom."

Lindsey smiled humbly. "I've made a lot of friends."

I tried to concentrate on cutting my son's turkey. Lindsey was still perfect. The Judge's eyes ignited at her smile. She had married the perfect man, the son that our father never had, educated and respectable and a law enthusiast to boot.

Matthew spoke next. "Samantha, one of my favorite memories is of watching you on your hands and knees in the creek,

groping under logs for crawdads. You must have been about fifteen." Matt's wiry hair had crept away from his dark forehead
and had gone prematurely gray. I had loved to pat his head
when I was young. Back then Matthew and his family were the
only black people I knew.

Lindsey giggled. "She was always like that! She would stay
down at the creek all by herself until after dark." She turned to
me. "Remember when you were on that wildlife photography
kick? You made a blind out of branches and sat in there for
hours on end!"

"I was going to sell my pictures to *National Geographic*," I
said. As I recall, no animals wandered remotely near my hide-
out, except for a batch of birds that twittered and picked at the
roof above my head.

"But you ended up in Nevada." Matthew shook his head.
"Quite a contrast. Any decent fishing there?"

I shrugged. "I don't know. Seems like I was working all the
time."

"What kind of work did you do?"

"I waited tables mostly. Before that I worked on a ranch outside of Reno."

"And she was a dancer," TJ volunteered proudly.

My head jerked toward him but too late to shut him up.
"Who told you that?" My face was instantly hot.

"Mindy." We had shared an apartment with Mindy and her
son for the last two years. She worked a different shift and
watched out for TJ sometimes. "She said you were a dancer just
like her."

I couldn't think of a thing to say, so I told the little tattle-
tale to eat his vegetables. It's not like I ever took tap or ballet
lessons. Mom mercifully began to offer second helpings and

fussed over David for not getting any homemade jam for his rolls. When I raised my eyes, they met Lindsey's, but hers flitted nervously away.

I wasn't imagining things. My father became broodingly silent. His eyes took on a distant glare and the flames of hell began licking at my toes. I studied the green hill beyond the river, wishing for my own private tree house with a view of the bend.

David and my mother started comparing their stocks and mutual funds. David advised her to pick up more of some company I had never heard of, because they were about to merge with so-and-so, but I could tell she didn't think it was a good idea. She said Microsoft stock was down now due to their recent legal battles and she was going to pick up a few more shares tomorrow.

"What does she mean by a few?" Matthew looked to my father with amusement in an obvious attempt to lighten him up. Matt was one of a handful of men who were not intimidated by the Judge. He had been like a beloved uncle to us as far back as I could remember. "Are you checking in here, bud? Don't forget the alpaca caper." He threw the next comment my way. "Did you know your mother had eight alpacas grazing out here before she realized you gotta get your shoes dirty to take care of them?"

Mom shook her head. "Nasty animals."

Lindsey said they had sweet little faces.

"What's an alpaca?" TJ asked.

"A cross between a giraffe and a goat," Matthew said seriously.

The Judge leaned back in his chair for a moment and sighed deeply before letting his eyes sparkle at Mom, with just a hint of a smile. "She knows what she's doing. If she can just cut down a little on new shoes, I can retire soon."

"Are you serious?" I blurted. "About retiring, I mean."

"Why not?"

"How old are you, anyway?" I remembered our mother reading a clipping from the local paper to Lindsey and me once. The article said that our father was the youngest man ever elected to the bench in our state.

"Forty-nine."

I studied him for a moment. "You look pretty good, for an old guy."

"Old!" He acted insulted. "I'm in my prime . . . right, Doc?" Matthew nodded. "I challenge you to a game of tennis, young lady. Then we'll see who's old."

Matthew had succeeded. The smoke had cleared and everyone seemed more comfortable. "You play tennis now?"

"I had to take it up. Your mother made me."

"We play poker, don't we, Mom?" Good old TJ. "You wanna know how much money I have now, Grandma?" He held up six fingers. "I have seven dollars." He apparently hadn't noticed that I borrowed it from his Donald Duck bank to put gas in the Jeep. He giggled along with everyone else at the table. "One time my mom won all my quarters and then I had to give her my shoes." He was as delighted with the telling of it as he had been during the game.

"That's terrible!" Lindsey feigned shock. "Then what did she do with them?"

He shrugged. "I don't know. Probably gave them to the poor people after I went to bed." He could be so dramatic. Little did he know that *we* were the poor people and that most of his shoes had been broken in before I found them at yard sales.

"Well, I'm going back to cash-only with you," I said, shaking my head. "Those shoes of yours pinched my toes. And they light up in the dark when I'm trying to sneak around."

When the hill beyond the river turned to blue-green, the Judge pushed back his chair. "It'll be dark soon."

Matthew nodded and stood, removing the napkin from his lap. "Can you still handle a fly rod, Sam?"

"I've done it in my sleep."

"Come on," my father said. "I'll rig you up."

Lindsey helped Mom clear the table and David followed us out to the garage. We equipped ourselves with rods and reels, but David didn't come to the river, as he didn't have the proper shoes. TJ begged to come, but his grandma bribed him back into the house with a piece of pie.

The Judge's rod tip pointed the way through the trees along the riverbank, a route he could surely navigate blind. He paused to pinch a new bud from a cottonwood sapling and then trudged onward, rolling the sticky, aromatic gum between his thumb and forefinger beneath his nose. My father had always loved the perfume of the cottonwoods.

Before we spread out on the river, he offered me his open fly box like a box of cigars. I chose a parachute Adams and waded into the shocking coolness until I was wet to the thighs. I probably should have asked for advice on the fly. The river showed no signs of a recent insect hatch. The Judge and Matthew had positioned themselves downstream and were already casting as I planted my canvas shoes among the rocks and fumbled with rod and line. My casts were a little awkward at first but got worse as I imagined my father's watchful eye.

It was on my twelfth birthday that my father gave me my first fly rod. Until then it had been enough for me to wade the creek that cut through the ravine behind the barn until I found a deep hole and to let the current bounce into it a worm weighted with split-shot. Back then I preferred to fish alone. Few of my friends had the attention span I did for fishing, and it was annoying to get a half mile upstream only to turn around because someone thought their mother might be calling. My mom and I had an understanding. I would eventually come home.

But the fly rod changed everything. It was like going from wooden-crate go-carts to driving a real car. It meant learning a new set of techniques and equipment, as well as graduating from the little creek to the river it fed. My father had coached me on the front lawn. "Forward, pause, back, pause." His hand was wrapped around mine on the cork handle of the bamboo rod. "Watch the path of your line. Now let it load behind you."

I knew he was an expert. From my perch in my favorite old cottonwood tree I had observed him many times, hypnotized by the graceful dance of arm and rod and line. I had seen his fly light on the water at the perfect spot to ride the current behind a rock and the ensuing flash of fish and taut line. He always talked his fish in. "Okay, run," he would say as a trout stripped the whining line from his reel. "Now come on back. That's right," he would say, reeling it in. But he was delighted when a fish refused to cooperate and burst through its ceiling in a defiant spray, violently attempting to shake the hook, running upstream and down. My father had great respect for a fish like that and he always told it so as he deftly removed the hook from its lip and let it slip from his hand back into the cold stream.

I always liked my father best when he was knee-deep in the river. He wore soft flannel shirts instead of the stiff white ones that he wore to the courthouse. And he rarely frowned. That first day of lessons, though, when we moved from the lawn to the river, I had tried his patience. My awkward casts scrambled the air above me and not once had my fly landed anywhere near target. I snapped off three hand-tied nymphs in rapid succession. He gestured to a spot about ten yards upstream. "See that white rock? Plop your fly right down on the middle of it."

It was too far away. I made a sloppy attempt just to humor him. "I can't!" I called to him over the sound of rushing water. "It's too far!"

"Do it anyway!" he said.

I tried again twice and failed. "I can't do it!"

"Samantha Dodd!" His tone was sharp. "Don't say that. Don't ever say *I can't!*" He waded out to me and wrapped his big hand around mine on the rod handle. His other hand reached around me to the loose line hanging from the reel. Together we flung the rod tip forward and then back. "Ten o'clock . . . one o'clock," he said, holding my wrist tight. The loose line slid silently up through the eyes of the rod with each cast until a long arc of line almost touched the white stone and then flowed behind us in the same graceful motion, only to return and this time drop the dry fly on the exact middle of the rock. "Anything you believe, you can achieve," he had said. "If you want to be successful at anything in this life, see what you want, not what you don't want. Then speak it. Speak it until you believe it. That's called faith." I reeled the line in and watched the fly drag along the top of the water. "And faith has the power to move mountains."

Standing in the river, I wondered what my father thought of me now. Everything he had taught me about life and success and fly-fishing had stagnated through seven Nevada years. Long, dry years. TJ was all I had to show for them. I had expected questions, but there had been none from him and no reference to what had happened between us. I cast again, this time feeling the grace come back, feeling in control until what should have been the last smooth arc of line before delivery snagged a vine maple behind me. I glanced downstream and saw the Judge release a small trout. Maybe he didn't even notice me flogging the sky or catching trees. He quipped with Matthew but I couldn't hear their words because of the river. My line pulled free without the fly, which seconds later fell from the tree and was snatched by an impatient fish that could not wait all night for me to deliver his supper.

I shuddered. My bones were cold and I found myself too exhausted to wade downstream for another fly. It was almost dark. I found a rock at the river's edge and sat hugging my knees for what seemed like a long time until the two men finally joined me and started up the path toward home. My father said the bite just wasn't on tonight. (I didn't mention the greedy retrieval of my snapped-off fly.) They took long, quick strides in their heavy hip boots and I couldn't keep up. My chest hurt, worse than ever before. I had to slow down and concentrate on breathing. My whole body shivered like a vibrating chair.

I followed them up the trail all the way to the edge of the backyard before stopping by a tree, suddenly becoming desperate for breath. My chest heaved in motions beyond my control. I couldn't get enough air.

The Judge and Matthew were talking. They couldn't hear the strange sounds that grated past my throat as I clung to the scabby bark of the tree trunk. My knees buckled and I dropped to the moist grass.

5 ✦

I HEARD MATTHEW'S alarmed cry and the hollow thuds of hip boots on the lawn as the two men ran back to me. I was on my hands and knees now, fighting for air, desperate for relief from the pressure in my chest. It had never been this bad before.

"Samantha, what is it?" My father's hand was on my back.

"Get her inside and get her warm!" Matt barked as he ran off.

I couldn't answer. I just shook my head. The Judge scooped me up and bolted for the house. I was aware of his strong arms, muscles clenched in his chest, the closeness of my face to his as his breath grazed my cheek. His boots had taken on water and sloshed noisily.

"TJ," I finally managed to whisper. "Don't let TJ see me."

But it was too late. Matthew's 911 call had alarmed the whole household. They hovered anxiously above me as my father laid me on the leather sofa, muddy feet and all. Mom stripped me of wet socks, shoes and jeans and tucked a blue satin comforter around me. The pain soon subsided and I found myself breathing normally again. "I'm okay now," I said, but no one would call off the emergency aid car. The closest town with a fire department was Dixon, a fifteen-mile drive on the state highway that twisted along the course of the north fork of the river.

Matthew the fisherman metamorphosed back into a doctor. He sat calmly on the edge of the sofa, taking my pulse and gently asking questions, while TJ hugged my feet.

"Yes," I said. "It's happened a few times, but never like this. Mostly when I overexert myself. At first I thought it was some lingering symptom from a flu I had."

"Did you see a doctor?"

"No." Actually, I had tried to make an appointment at the clinic where I took TJ whenever he had an ear infection or a bean stuck up his nose. Like my own doctor, they had a problem with my unpaid bill and sent me to the bulldog lady in their collections department, whose nasal, condescending tone made me want to push her fat face into the doughnut by her keyboard. Instead, I deliberately answered her humiliating questions, glaring at the nosy young woman waiting next to me at the counter until she self-consciously sat down in the waiting area. After enduring the whole interrogation, I was informed that I would have to pay off the entire outstanding balance on my delinquent account before a doctor would see me. I was a bad financial risk.

Matthew listened to my chest and then without comment nodded reassuringly at my parents. I felt relieved. Finally, I was not alone. Whatever it was that had been plaguing me would be discovered now. Matt would probably prescribe some antibiotics or something and soon I would be my wild old self again. A siren wailed from somewhere in the darkness.

I swore and slunk into the couch. "Do they have to do that?" TJ shook his head at me and I apologized for the bad word.

Within minutes a pickup truck with a strobing cherry on top stormed down the long driveway. A huge man barged through the door, dropped a metal supply case on the floor and began hooking me up to things and asking questions. Matt and my father did much of the talking. I just watched his hands— tough, hairy hands—as he repeated some of the same tests Matthew had done. His jeans were attached to wide red suspenders, and I knew by the boots (and the fact that he was from Dixon) that he must be a logger. There were no full-time firemen in this part of the county—just volunteers. The woman who followed him repeated my vital signs into a radio transmitter. She must have been painting her kitchen when she got the call. Yellow paint highlighted the tips of her dark hair and her chin.

They were there a long time. Mom served coffee while the men exchanged top-secret fishing-hole locations. Poor David. He obviously didn't know the difference between a graphite rod and bamboo and probably had wanted to go home long ago but felt it might be considered rude with one's newly discovered sister-in-law dying on the sofa. Lindsey had forgotten him. She was busy mothering me and asking the woman with yellow paint what we should do next. The general consensus was that I should rest at home through the night but see a specialist first thing in the morning.

Which I did. Matthew said not to worry, but he heard something irregular when he listened to my heart. He sent me to a Dr. Talbot in Darlington, who took blood, urine and half my day. My mother came in to wait with me between tests. I read her the quiz from *Glamour* magazine, "How Daring Is Your Sex Life?" but she was pretty uncooperative. Finally, Dr. Talbot came back in. "Okay, Samantha. One more test. Did you ever have an ultrasound when you were pregnant?" I said I had. I obediently opened the front of my gown again and lay on my side while he slid a short, fat wand between my breasts. The room was quiet as we studied the image that appeared on a nearby monitor. My mother rose slowly to her feet, clutching a twisted tissue to her chest.

I found myself staring at a gray, sluggish shape. Some wounded animal in a cage of ribs. The revelation came to me slowly. It started as a dull, heavy sensation in my chest and then spread, pulsing into my arms and finally to my brain. I was looking at the very organ that I felt, almost heard, laboring even now and on which my life depended. Biology was not my best subject but I knew the basic shape and structure of a heart. Something was wrong.

Dr. Talbot called it viral myocarditis. He pointed to the swollen mass and said that the muscle had become inflamed and was not working as it should. "That's why you've been having chest pains and shortness of breath. Your heart has to work harder, especially when you exert yourself, to pump the blood your body needs." He sighed and ran his hands down the thighs of his pants. "Tell me more about this flu you had. Did your symptoms begin immediately after that?"

I thought they had.

He asked more questions and scribbled more notes.

"What caused this?" I asked.

He shook his head. "My guess is it's the work of that virus."

Mom lifted her chin and acted confident and collected now, for my sake. "How do we fix it, Doctor?"

"I'm going to refer Samantha to another specialist." He passed her a card. "Dr. Sovold is a cardiologist at the University Medical Center in Seattle. Let him take a look and we'll go from there. In the meantime, Samantha, I'm going to put you on a drug known as an ACE inhibitor." He began writing out the prescription. Mom reached out and gently rubbed my back.

He passed me the little slip of paper. "I'm not going to lie to you, Samantha. Your heart has already suffered severe damage. We're going to do everything we can to relieve your symptoms and hopefully this drug treatment will succeed. If not, sometimes surgical treatment of the problem is possible."

I asked him what I could and couldn't do, and he basically ruled out anything fun. No exertion, no overeating, no drinking, no smoking. "Listen to your body," he said, "and call me immediately if you notice any of your symptoms becoming more severe."

Mom and I walked down the cracked steps of the doctor's office into a light rain. Dr. Talbot's office was one of several Victorian homes on the block that had been remodeled into professional buildings. Tulips and daffodils bloomed in every neatly landscaped yard, and the sidewalk beneath our feet was bulged and cracked from the roots of trees planted eighty years ago. We didn't say much. Mom was always good about giving me my space.

We ate lunch in a house-turned-restaurant with window boxes that burgeoned with geraniums and blue lobelia. Mom was still being very brave and in control. It was one of the things I loved about her. She never panicked. She never screamed. If I brought home a snake, she would flinch almost imperceptibly and then smile and ask if it had a name. She glanced at the menu and recommended I try the chicken Caesar. "They make a good one here."

I could have eaten dog food. I didn't taste a thing.

"Is this why you came home, Sam?" she finally asked.

I nodded, rearranging the food on my plate idly with my fork. Yes, it was the heart thing. But it was more. There was a time when my soul did not ache like this. A time when I skipped and laughed and wondered at the way delicate dandelion seeds drifted like Mary Poppins and her umbrella above the fields. Back then I had no past clamped to my ankle like a ball and chain. When I looked up at her, my eyes were watery. "I knew something was wrong. I just didn't know what. I didn't know what to do." She reached for my hand, but I withdrew it self-consciously and scratched the back of my neck. There was so much more to say. "Mom . . . I haven't been able to work lately. I was waitressing, but I just couldn't keep up anymore. Then I started calling in sick. Anyway, they said sayonara and there I sat. Me and TJ. No money. No medical insurance. I owe his day care about three hundred bucks; I owe Mindy, my roommate—"

"Shhhh. It's okay, Sammy. You did the right thing. You came home. We'll work out all the details. You need to work on getting better, that's all."

Good old Mom. Here we were, sitting across the table from each other like two grown women taking a break from an afternoon shopping spree, but I was snuggled on her lap with my thumb in my mouth, believing again that everything was going to be all right. It *was* the right thing. I felt it in my gut. "I like how you are with TJ," I said. "He's been needing a grandma."

Mom laughed. "I didn't know how much I missed him, Samantha, until I saw him face-to-face. I guess I couldn't let myself think about him too much. I knew so little about him. I wish you had written more. You could have at least sent me a picture!"

"Then you would have seen that he's a Mexiwegian and I'd have had to explain, and I didn't want to explain."

She smiled imploringly.

I stared at the mess of food on my plate. *That's my life.* I pushed it aside and the waitress appeared from nowhere to whisk it away. "Mom . . ."

"Sammy"—she put her hand on my arm, and this time I didn't move it away—"you tell me all about it when you're ready, okay?"

I didn't look up and a tear fell on the table. "Okay."

M Y FATHER TOOK the news of my diagnosis as calmly as if the doctor had said it was only indigestion that had caused me to crumple to the ground on the river path. As Mom and I related the details of my heart condition, his fingers drummed the arm of his big chair—the way I remembered from my childhood his fingers rhythmically rising and tapping when his mind was in a courtroom miles away from us. He nodded from time to time, his forehead slightly pinched.

"Well," he finally said, "we'll know more after you see the other cardiologist. Hopefully they can correct this without surgery. Do you have medical insurance, Samantha?"

For some reason I felt like I had regressed to teenaged status, sitting there across from him in that living room as I had so many times, guilty somehow and dependent on him to bail me out of trouble again, knowing I would probably be required to do penance in one way or another. I shook my head.

"I told her we would take care of the finances," Mom said. They exchanged a glance that I couldn't read. I had never heard my parents fight, but I wondered if there might be heated words exchanged behind closed doors that night. In my mind I could still hear his tirades over lights left on when we had left a room or phone bills with long-distance calls. I had seen the Judge pick up a penny from a parking lot and drop it into his pocket. I wondered what open-heart surgery might cost.

"Yes. Good," he said without expression.

"I'm sorry. I wasn't eligible yet for insurance on my last job." My heart was so heavy just then, not just physically but with the newfound knowledge that I was *really* sick and helpless, with a son to raise. We had barged into my parents' empty nest with all of our possessions. Where there had been order and tranquillity, there were doors slamming, a child's sometimes loud and whiny voice, a row of books lined up in the middle of the hallway as a road for toy cars. TJ wandered into the room. He crawled up to my lap, tucking his head under my chin, his bare feet sticking out of pajama bottoms that had become too short for him. I held him close like a soft, comforting blanket. "I want to get a job; I just don't know right now. . . ."

"Don't worry about it," my father said. "Let's just do what it takes to get you well."

TJ patted my upper chest. "Does it hurt, Mom?"

"No. It just makes me tired sometimes."

"You better take a vitamin."

I kissed him and squeezed his toes. "We're talking grown-up talk here. It's way past your bedtime too. Say good night to Grandma and Grandpa and get to bed."

He oozed off of my lap onto the floor. "Is that really my bedroom now, Grandma?"

She smiled. "For as long as you need it, sweet pea. You and your mama can stay here as long as you want."

He looked pleased. "I never had a room all by myself."

I glanced at the Judge. He didn't flinch. I imagined he must be thinking how convenient it was for me to just show up when

I happened to need a roof over our heads, food to eat—oh, and someone to pay a pending heap of medical expenses besides. Good old Samantha. Independent as one of those aloof cats until it's hungry enough to come rubbing against your leg as if it really liked you all along.

I did like my father once.

Back then he smelled of damp earth and the spicy cottonwood. If I had been stricken blind as a child, I could still have picked my father from a lineup just by the lingering scent of cottonwood buds on his hands or the bruised leaves tucked into the pockets of his shirts. His eyes sometimes glimmered like sun-dappled ripples, though they could quickly take on the hard gray of angry winter water. Like how I felt about the river, I loved and feared him. It was a healthy fear, I suppose; maybe *respect* is a better word, knowing that though he might appear placid on the surface, there was a powerful current pushing just below.

His course was steady and predictable—a daily routine that rarely changed. Breakfast was wheat toast with marmalade and coffee—black as tar. His brown leather briefcase, swollen with briefs and opinions and an occasional law book, secured under one arm, a sack lunch and a thermos of coffee for the long road to the city in the other, he would kiss our mother in the kitchen doorway. The kisses were not like in the movies where in the next scene they've got the sheets pulled up to their armpits, but they weren't Ward and June Cleaver pecks either. Our parents lingered there, sometimes whispering and smiling, sometimes quiet with their foreheads touching before he winked at us and walked out the door.

The calm and quiet would probably not return to our household again until we saw his headlights in the driveway that night. Then all banging, stomping, hollering and chasing one another around the ottoman came to an instant halt. It was unspoken. Our father was the king of our house and we knew it. Our mother must have taught us that, though I don't remember. I just remember the peace that came through the door with him and the way our world revolved around his presence. When our father sat in his big chair, we huddled near him, telling amazing stories about the adventures of our day. He would put the daily paper aside, cross one leg over the other while one foot went slowly up and down. He smiled and touched our hair thoughtfully as we chattered.

One time he scared me. Right in the middle of my story about the owls in Donnie's barn, he grabbed Lindsey and me and held us too tight, and when he let us go he was crying. Mom told us later that a bad man hurt a little girl and our daddy had to hear all about it in court.

On Sundays we went to church. Rain or shine, hell or high water. Literally. Even when the road was covered with a sheet of water and wild mallards and snow geese paddled happily around in the fields. We never discussed it. At least until I was in my teens, at which time I felt strongly that Sunday mornings would be better spent beneath my warm quilt. I could not reason with my father. He said one day out of the week was not too much to give back to the Lord after all He'd given us. I couldn't understand what pleasure God could take in the whole thing. Didn't He hear the same boring hymns coming up from churches all over the world? English, Spanish, Swahili, Portuguese—they all must sound the same to Him. And what difference would my absence make? I could hardly carry a tune anyway.

Lindsey, who seemed perfect in every way, somehow understood that even she was a sinner. She liked to go confess her sins and take communion. I stopped taking communion when I was fourteen. The pastor read from the Bible where it says: "Whosoever shall eat this bread and drink this cup of the Lord unworthily shall be guilty of the body and blood of the Lord." I didn't need that. At the time I didn't know what made one person worthy and another unworthy, but it was safe to say I was in category two. My guilt was sufficient without adding to it the crucifixion of God's son.

After church, our parents mingled with the other locals, mostly farmers and blue-collar workers. Some of them still called my father *sir* or *Your Honor*, though we had been living in the valley for years. Lindsey would lean against the Judge and wrap her little arm around his leg while he rested one hand on her shoulder, the other on mine. But grown-up conversations bored me. I tended to ease away as quickly as possible until a rock-throwing incident in the parking lot one Sunday. His grip on my shoulder grew firmer after that. Then, for a time, I succumbed to fidgeting by his side where his deep, liquid voice filled my ears and eddied safely at my feet.

Like the river, he was a boundary around my small world. The problems came when I grew older and realized that there was more to know than what my father taught me; there was a realm to be explored beyond his rigid control. But the raging current of his will was a dangerous thing to cross.

Maybe that was why I did the things I did. Any prisoner longs for freedom. I found mine by crawling out my bedroom window for clandestine meetings with stupid boys, boys whose names I could barely remember now. I took up drinking. I was the life of every party, the one who could be counted on to do the unexpected or downright crazy thing that we could all laugh about back at school. Wayne Bly hung me by my feet from a three-story window so I could spy on the tenant below who played concert-style piano but never came out of his apartment. Trudy and I *borrowed* my parents' car one night when I was fifteen and without a driver's license, planning to return it before they awoke. That was a plot gone bad. We made it as far as Dixon, where I nearly crashed into a truck when I made an illegal left turn. We were helping the old driver gather the boxload of potatoes that had spilled onto the road when a green patrol car pulled up. The Judge actually called the sheriff on me—his own daughter! After that I was sentenced to cleaning out the garage and doing yard work for an eternity of Saturdays, and when I was finally allowed to go out into the real world again, my curfew was ten p.m.—not a minute later.

But these were not the things that caused the Judge to send me packing when I was only seventeen. I finally committed that unforgivable sin—the one that still lurked behind me like a menacing shadow. I resented him for that. It was his standard—not mine—that sent me away. But he was the Judge. Guilty! The angry smack of his gavel still echoed in my mind. Worst of all, his verdict clung to my back like a clawed thing that I had not been able to shake even after all those years.

TJ straddled the Judge's lap, facing him and patting his hands on his grandpa's cheeks as if he had known him from birth instead of for just a few days. "Do you wanna go feed the worms when we wake up, Grandpa?"

"Tell you what, son. Let's do it when I get home tomorrow night. You'll probably still be asleep when I go to work. I have to drive a long way." He tousled TJ's hair. "What I need you to do is catch some bugs—as many as you can. Grandma will give you something to put them in."

TJ nodded in earnest. "Okay."

Mom and I exchanged amused glances. My son—my treasure, my trophy—then went over to kiss his grandma, and when he eventually wandered off toward his new bedroom we were all smiling.

"So, what are the bugs for?" I asked.

The Judge shrugged. "To keep him busy. A man needs a mission. Besides, you need a lot of rest." He looked at his watch. "In fact, it's after ten. Why don't you go on to bed now too? Your mom and I have some things to talk about."

I nodded, gathering up my empty water glass and the shoes I had kicked off, though I had not considered retiring that early. Just like old times. I had been dismissed. I was back in his household, willingly, helplessly subjecting myself again to his reign. I paused by my mother's chair, thinking of bending down to kiss her as I used to do, but it would be awkward. "Good night," I said from the doorway.

"Good night."

"Sleep well."

But I tossed and turned until dawn.

7 🪶

I FOUND MYSELF at home in the semidarkness at a table in the rear, like a coyote finally back in her den. Not that I'd ever been inside this particular establishment, though I had pedaled my bike across the gravel parking lot of Fraser's Tavern at least a hundred times. Lindsey and I witnessed a fight there once between a local farmer and a logger who smashed each other up against the parked trucks. They spewed words that were foreign to us and broke someone's side mirror off and there was blood. After that Lindsey swung wide whenever we crossed the lot, keeping a wary eye on the big wood door of the tavern.

I hadn't planned to end up there. I just knew I needed to get out of the house for a while. I needed to think, to adjust to the recent flood of changes in my life. The image of my enlarged heart seemed to appear on my eyelids every time I blinked, and with it came an overwhelming sadness. I was grateful for the fact that my parents had taken us in. Without their generosity, TJ and I would be homeless—and the thought of what might become of my son if my heart should fail me was enough to send the sluggish organ into gyrations. It was good to be home, good to be in a secure place with family where I could get away like this sometimes, knowing that TJ was with people who loved him. On the other hand, there was this thing between the Judge and me. I could almost feel the vibrations of negative electrons between us, pushing us apart, causing me to revert emotionally to the confused and defiant teenager who once lived in his house. Honestly, even being there in Fraser's Tavern felt like an outright act of rebellion, though I had frequented similar establishments back in Reno without finding it necessary to park my Jeep on the dark side of the building, away from the street.

I leaned back, propping my boots on a vacant chair. The night was young and many tables were empty. A few men straddled stools at the old bar, loudly offering advice to the baseball players on an overhead TV screen. Two women played darts in the corner nearest me. The skinny one with bad teeth lunged and thrust. The projectile wobbled and bounced off the wall about three feet from target. Her friend snorted a laugh, grabbed the darts and shot three missiles—a bull's-eye, a triple twenty and a bouncer. The faded red T-shirt stretched over her ample belly said *I'm from Dixon—What's Your Excuse?*

"You lied." The voice startled me. "You said you'd never grow up."

I turned to gaze into the strangely familiar face of a young man carrying two brown bottles and a glass mug. I squinted up at him, suppressing any sign of recognition. "Are you the waiter? It's about time."

He grinned and pulled the chair out from under my feet. "How ya doin', Sam? I heard you were back." He sat down, ceremoniously poured cold beer into the schooner and pushed it toward me. "You're lookin' good."

"Hello, Donnie."

"It's Don now. Just plain Don, if you don't mind."

I smiled mischievously. "You'll always be little Donnie Duncan to me." My eyes fell on the crop of hair protruding from his open shirt and the bronze forearms resting on the table like two legs of mutton, and I was well aware that Donnie Duncan had grown up.

"And I'll always remember you as the weird little kid who hung by her knees from cottonwood branches with her shirt falling over her head."

I laughed. "Those were the days, weren't they? Remember the rope swing by the river?"

He took a swig and pounded his bottle on the table. "How about the night we swung out double and you fell off? Your sister and I heard the splash, but it was so stinkin' dark we couldn't see a thing. We called and called, but you didn't answer. Then Lindsey went blatso on me. Why did you always do things like that?"

"I lived to freak out Lindsey. It was my major life purpose."

He shook his head. "You were a strange child."

"What do you mean by that?"

"Anyone who would traipse through the pouring rain to bury a brand-new doll in the mud . . ."

"She was dead."

He threw his hands up and tipped back his head. "Oh! Well, that explains it. But just out of curiosity, what killed her?"

I twisted my face thoughtfully. "Natural causes, as I recall. I never played with dolls after that."

He nodded in mock sincerity. "Too much heartache?"

"Yup." The doll was a Spanish dancer with real eyelashes, sleek black hair and a red dress. Lindsey got one for Christmas too. Hers was a blond Southern belle in a frock of blue lace, who lived a long and healthy life.

For a moment we just surveyed each other. Donnie's coarse blond hair was cropped short like mowed hay, his brows a little wild and his eyes bluer than I remembered. "Last time I saw you," I said, "you had hair down to here and you were singing 'Stairway to Heaven' at the school prom." I emptied my mug and Donnie signaled the waitress to bring us a pitcher.

"And *you* danced with Tim Weatherbee all night. At least when you two weren't off in some corner arguing about something. Next thing anybody knew you dropped out of school and ran off with him."

"But I'm back."

He raised his brows. "No Tim?"

I shook my head. "No Tim."

Don seemed to be waiting for an explanation. I paused before changing the subject. "Looks like you're still bucking hay." I nodded toward his burly shoulders.

He shrugged. "That's right. You didn't believe me when I said I was going to be an attorney, did you?"

I studied his face. He was acting too casual. "Yes, I believed it. And so did you. What happened? You know you're smart enough. I heard you one time when you were on the debate team."

"You did?"

I nodded. "I was just walking by the door of the classroom and I heard your voice. I stopped and listened for a long time. You were good."

"Tell me more."

"You were arguing the case for capital punishment—which I am totally against, just for the record—but you were convincing. All those facts. I tried to make you laugh. Don't you re-member that? You just looked right through me like I wasn't there. You kind of reminded me of the Judge."

"Thank you."

I cocked my head. "What makes you think that was a com-pliment?"

He sighed. "You still have that burr in your boot? I like your dad. I buy worms from him. We hang out in the barn for an hour or more sometimes, talking about the way things are, the way they should be. Then I go home and toss out the worms."

"Good for you," I said. "Tell me, has he measured you up yet? Has he taken out his invisible tape and run it from your toes to the top of your head and left you feeling like a midget? Has he given you the map of your life—the only acceptable route—and informed you that any other road will lead to de-struction?" My words tasted bitter and I knew they were mak-ing my eyes get squinty and mean-looking. I deliberately swallowed and raised my brows, which helped pull the corners of my mouth up. "So. Come here often?"

He shook his head. "I saw a pretty girl speed by the ranch in a dirty old Jeep. Followed her here."

"I was thinking about calling you. I've only been here for a little over a week."

"I heard you've been in Nevada. What brought you back?"

I brightened. "Donnie, I didn't tell you. I have a son." I reached for my wallet and placed a small snapshot on the table. "His name is TJ. He's five now. This was taken last year."

"Good-lookin' kid. Your dad told me you had a son. I've al-ways asked about you, you know. Not that he ever seemed to know much." He studied the picture some more. "So. Does Tim have some Indian blood in him?"

"Subtle," I said. "Hey, if you want to know who I've been sleeping with, just ask. I've never kept secrets from you."

"Yeah, right." He frowned.

I poured him a glass from the full pitcher. "Here. Drink this. You're getting moody."

His mouth spread slowly into a grin and his blue eyes danced. "Dang, I've missed you. I didn't know how much until just now. You're still just the same. And you haven't answered my question. Why did you come home? The truth."

I wanted to tell him everything. Who knew me better than my childhood playmate? We had fought side by side in countless wars. He saved my hide from the James Gang, a ruthless batch of brothers from the other side of the creek who launched cow pies from a catapult instead of throwing pinecone grenades like the rest of us. And when it came to building dams, Donnie was an engineering genius. He made a swimming hole on the creek that lasted for two years before a spring flood washed it out. I always admired him for that.

We had been best friends up until puberty. Then things got confusing. Donnie started playing basketball and hanging out with some guys from school. He didn't want to fish much anymore. When he did come over it was usually with a friend or two and they just draped their lanky bodies over the porch rails while Lindsey served them iced tea. Once, when I went over to the Appaloosa Ranch to help him with his chores, he pressed me up against a stall door and kissed me. I kicked like a branded mare and wiped the kiss from my mouth in disgust. He never tried that again.

After that I avoided him for a while, and he didn't seem to have much interest in me. Sometimes he helped me get my homework done on the morning school bus, though. Donnie was smart for a rancher.

I couldn't tell him I came home because I was sick or that I couldn't keep a job. Tim was long gone. I had been feeding my son Top Ramen three nights a week. "The truth is," I finally said, "I needed to smell the cottonwoods again." That was not a lie. "Also for TJ. A kid needs a family. He needed to meet his grandma and grandpa and know he has roots. He's so happy now, Donnie. You should see him run and play in the big field, just like you and I used to. He's a wonderful person. I want you to meet him."

"Are you going to tell me about his daddy?"

I drained my beer. "TJ has no daddy." Donnie refilled my glass. I made a mental note that this would be my last one. I had planned to have just one beer when I came in. Then I would get on the wagon and do everything the doctor said. "I'll tell you the gory details after you tell me why you're still here in Carter and not fighting for justice in the courtrooms of America."

He held up his glass and stared into the golden liquid. "I don't know. Seems like there's just never a good time to get away. There's always a barn to rebuild or a lame tractor or a fence down. My dad pretty much takes care of the horses but there are a lot of things he just can't do anymore."

"Is he sick?"

He glared. "You really have been out of touch. Four years ago August, a hay fork came out of the loft and nearly nailed him to the barn floor."

My jaw dropped. "A hay fork *came* out of the loft? How? How did that happen?"

"I threw it."

I stared at him and waited. He swirled his beer like it was a fine merlot before taking a sip and setting the glass down. "I didn't mean to hit him. We were up in the hayloft, rigging up a pulley. You know how he can be. A first-class jackass. He expects everything, appreciates nothing. I put off law school for two years because he needed me at the ranch. I was all set to go to the U Dub that fall, and he starts in on me again. Tells me it's a waste of money and a lost cause. 'Sixty percent of all law students drop out in the first year,' he says. He reminded me for the thousandth time that I was just a country hick and I could never hold my own against those slick city boys. 'Your place is here, boy,' he says, and he goes down the ladder. I thought he had left the barn. I started kicking things. I grabbed the pitchfork and hurled it into space like a javelin. Then I heard him scream." He paused. "It got his right thigh and severed a tendon in his knee. He walks with a limp now. Has to use a cane on bad days."

I whispered a curse. "I'm sorry. Sorry for you mostly."

"Why?"

"Because he's got you now. He's got you right where he wants you."

Don pushed away from the table. "Let's get out of here." He threw some bills on the table and took my arm.

"Let me go to the bathroom first." I stopped at the restroom and when I came out there was the cigarette machine looking right at me. What the heck, I thought. I'll be good starting tomorrow. Donnie was already outside on the porch with his back to me. I popped my money in and a pack of Kool filters slid out. As I tapped the first one out of the package, someone shoved a lighter in my face and flicked it to flame. It startled me and I recoiled. The man's face was too close to mine, lit up by an orange glow, with deep grooves running from the outer corners of his eyes down to his jaw. He lit my cigarette. "Those things'll kill ya, you know."

"Yeah," I mumbled. "Thanks." When I stepped toward the door, he blocked my path. He just stood there staring at me like the Big Bad Wolf with an evil smile that made me feel sick. I pushed him aside with a few choice expletives and stormed out the door.

"You okay?" Donnie asked. He glanced at my cigarette and frowned.

I held up my hand. "Don't say it." I gestured toward the man who was still watching me through the tavern window. "Who is that guy?"

"Him? That's Dwight Enrich. Was he giving you a hard time?" I nodded. "He's just a bitter old drunk. Remember Ron Enrich? The kid who bashed his mother's head in? That's his dad. Fraser's is his home away from home. Ignore him." We hopped in his shiny Ford truck, leaving my Jeep behind in the parking lot in a cloud of dust.

The moon was a half disk of white neon in a glittered sky. Scents of green alfalfa and honeysuckle rode the wind through the open windows, and Ray Charles sang "Georgia on My Mind" on the radio. We sang along until I couldn't stand it anymore.

"Okay. That's it," I said. "You sing the blues like a cowboy." I pulled a pencil out of his console and tapped demonstratively on the dashboard. "From now on you're rhythm; I'm blues."

The next song was peppier. He drummed on the dashboard, the window, the steering wheel and my head. I sang my heart out, making up words wherever necessary, and we laughed all the way to Dixon, where we stopped for a bag of chips, huge navel oranges and some beer. After that we pulled off at a rest stop by the river.

"How do things turn out the way they do, Sam?" Donnie leaned against his door with his feet on the dash, while I sat cross-legged, ravenously attacking the bag of chips. "You're the one who said you'd always live within earshot of this river. You said you'd build a cabin on the other side and live off the land and never get a real job. Remember that? And I said I'd hit the road the day I turned eighteen and never look back."

I bit off all three corners of my tortilla chip methodically before popping the rest of it in my mouth. Was I supposed to have an answer to that question? Was life actually supposed to make some kind of sense? It was not like I left the valley on purpose; I was more or less shot out of my father's cannon and landed in Reno with powder burns that still hadn't healed.

"And what about you and me?" he continued. "Why didn't we ever date or anything?"

I looked at him like he was nuts. "Correct me if I'm wrong, but as I recall you never asked me out."

He laughed. "I kissed you once. What do ya want?"

"A little warning would have been nice, for starters. You scared the snot out of me. You never acted like that before."

"You never looked like that before. At least it was the first time I really noticed. After that I figured I'd keep my distance until you were mature enough to handle a real man." His chest swelled and his voice deepened at the end of his sentence. "Guess I should have checked in a little sooner. Tim slid in there ahead of me. So, whatever happened between you two?"

"We're still married."

"Oh. I didn't know. You're not wearing a ring or anything."

"Well, after I didn't see or hear from him for a few years, I just took it off."

"That jerk! He walked out on you? Takes you away from your family and friends to some godforsaken desert and then dumps you there? Sam. I wish I had known. I would have come and kicked his butt up around his ears. I wish you had kept in touch." He twisted the cap off a beer and passed it to me.

I took a long swig and let my head fall back on the seat. "It wasn't like that exactly." It wasn't fair to let the blame fall on Tim. Tim loved me. I never doubted that one minute of one day. Not even when we were fighting. I was such a shrew that summer of my third trimester, my belly protruding halfway to Texas, ankles swollen from the heat, still trying to earn my keep on the ranch. The pregnancy was a terrible inconvenience, totally unplanned, but after what happened the first time— well, I couldn't consider that alternative again. So I suffered through it, along with Tim. He rubbed my back at night while we lay on our sides naked, an electric fan propped in the open window stirring the air like in a convection oven. He told me if it was a girl we'd get her a pony as soon as she was big enough to ride. But I knew what he really wanted was a boy. "My son's gonna know how to rebuild his own truck, from headlight to tailpipe," he would say. "I'm going to teach him to spit and scratch and pee his name in the dirt."

Donnie was respectfully silent. Finally, I raised my head. "Tim was not the bad guy. It was me."

"You left him?"

"No. The last time I saw Tim was in the hospital after TJ was born. He was there the whole time I was in labor. He made me focus and do all those breathing techniques we learned; he brought me ice and put cold washcloths on my forehead. He held my hand while I was pushing and I thought I was going to die, but he just stayed calm. He was a very patient person." Suddenly, I felt embarrassed. I hadn't talked about this to anyone. Why was I spilling my guts to a guy I hadn't seen in seven years? "I think I've had too much to drink," I said.

Donnie shook his head. "No, you haven't. Talk to me. I'm listening."

I took another swallow. "Well, I finally just reared up and pushed until I thought my guts were going to come out. It was like I wasn't in control of my own body anymore—it just took over. And out popped TJ. He just slid into the doctor's hands and I lay back on the bed exhausted. I didn't even ask if it was a boy or a girl at first, I was so worn out. But I saw the doctor's face and then Tim's and I got worried. I asked if everything was okay and the nurse smiled and said I had a beautiful baby boy. Tim looked like the whole experience had been too much for him. He went and sat down in a chair like he had the wind knocked out of him. Then they laid the baby on my belly and I knew. I knew the minute I laid eyes on him that he wasn't Tim's. He was as brown as milk chocolate with a head full of coal-black hair."

"Seems like there's a big chunk of this story you've left out."

"Tijuana."

"What?"

"Tijuana. That's what everyone called the guy who gave me TJ. That's how I came up with his name."

"So where's this Tijuana now?"

I shrugged. "Siberia for all I care." I felt myself relaxing into the truck's upholstery. "Maybe we should take a little nap."

Donnie had other ideas. He slid an orange into each of my jacket pockets and stashed the brown bag containing the six-pack under his arm. "Come on." He opened his door and pulled me out on his side.

"Where are we going?" It was unlike me to ask. Usually, I was up for any adventure, but it felt late. I could have crawled into the back of the pickup with a blanket and called it a night. We walked down a dirt trail through some alder trees to where the railroad track paralleled the river. The cool night air and the fresh scent of the river revived me, but I took the tracks in slow double steps. Even in my slightly inebriated state, I remembered that I had to be careful.

The moon had slipped some, but its light still touched the edges of the metal rails. The tracks veered off to our left up ahead and then spanned the river on a huge suspension trestle whose framework was hazily silhouetted on the sky. I knew then where we were headed.

"Hey, Donnie! Slow down."

He stopped and waited for me to catch up. "What's the matter? You haven't gone wimpy on me, have you?"

"I can still kick your butt."

"At what? Scrabble?"

His backside happened to be a good target at the moment, so I kicked it. He grabbed my leg in midair, I lost my balance and almost went down, but he caught me. He had me by my jacket sleeves and was laughing, until he pulled me up closer to his face. "You okay?"

I smiled my cocky smile and brushed his hands off my arms. "Of course I'm okay." I pointed out to the trestle. "Onward!"

Donnie took the tracks in long strides while I walked the rail like a balance beam, but with one hand on his shoulder. The river swirled below us in the moonlight. The span of the railroad bridge seemed longer than it was when we were kids. We finally reached the middle and without discussion sat on the edge, our legs dangling high above the current. Long, unbroken spirals of orange peel dropped into the darkness and disappeared without a sound.

"So . . ." I felt compelled to break the silence. "You never got married?"

"Nope."

"What's the holdup?"

"Pretty slim pickin's around here. Did you see those women playing darts at Fraser's?" I nodded. "Those are Carter's most eligible bachelorettes."

"Not good," I said. "Well, you're not getting any younger. You might want to consider shopping out of town."

He looked at me funny for a moment. "Yeah. Good idea."

We drank beer in silence for a while. My light jacket ruffled in the breeze and I shivered. Donnie reached out and pulled me close to him. "Don't kick me or anything," he said, pulling off his jacket and wrapping it around my shoulders. "I promise I won't kiss you."

I settled comfortably into his side like I'd been there before. In the distance we heard the first muted thunder of the train. "Here she comes." We listened to the low rumble fade in and out as it rounded hilly bends. Orange juice dripped through my fingers as I pushed the last whole section into my mouth. I licked my hands clean and wiped them on my jeans. Ten minutes later, the whistle blew pure and clear, heralding the train's slow clatter through Dixon, and then the thunder mounted as the engine picked up speed outside the little town. By the time it neared the trestle, I was trembling from the vibration, the loud clamor and a rush of adrenaline.

Donnie stashed the remains of our picnic in the paper bag

and helped me to my feet. "Okay, it's showtime!" He pulled himself onto part of the metal gridwork above the bridge and held an arm down to me. "You coming?"

I shook my head. "No. I want to be right next to it!" The train erupted onto the bridge, a roaring, billowing volcano now, racing straight for us. Engine lights blazed on the tracks in its path. My whole body was sliced by the warning scream of the whistle. Feet planted on a railroad tie, I leaned against a girder for support. Donnie became a part of the superstructure above my head. In seconds the train was upon us. Donnie hollered something, but his voice was strangled by the explosion of diesel power and the crashing and clanking of each passing freight car. Sparks flew at my feet. I knew if I stretched out my arm, I'd draw back a bloody stump.

This was the part where we used to hoot and howl with laughter, defying the monster and leaning as close as we dared. The strange thing was that I was not having any fun. Rhythmic sound blasts beat violently against my chest, pounded inside my head, shook me like a rat in the jaws of a terrier. My heart ached. I felt it trying too hard. My eyes closed and I tottered dizzily before grabbing the girder. I wanted the train to pass, but boxcar after boxcar after gondola after flatcar, it torpedoed on. It was the train from hell. The never-ending train from hell. I backed away. My mind swirled in the darkness like the river below. When I looked down everything became a blur. I felt myself falling.

The next few seconds were recorded in slow motion in my mind. The clanking of the passing train, the thud and sharp pain in my shoulder, my body slamming hard against something, the top of my torso hanging precariously over a sharp edge. My arms flailed for something to hang on to. The train began to sound farther away and then it was the river that roared in my ears. I threw up.

"Sam! Don't move!"

My body stopped vibrating as the last freight car left the bridge. I heard Donnie drop to the railroad ties. He pulled me from the low metal railing, laying my body alongside the warm track. "Sam, are you okay?"

"I think so."

"What happened?"

The railroad tie was a little rough but it felt cool against my face. "Lie down here and listen to the river with me. Let's just rest for a while."

Donnie hoisted me to my feet. "Come on, you little lush." He wrapped my arm around his shoulders and started walking down the railroad tracks. My legs were surprisingly weak.

"I'm not drunk."

"Yeah. And you just puked your guts out for the fun of it. Dang it, Sam! If I had known, I never would have left you alone down there. You could have fallen off the bridge—or worse yet, onto the track. You'd be raw hamburger right now."

"I think it was the orange." I tried to walk without Donnie's support but found myself leaning back into him. The labored pulsing in my chest had calmed, but I felt achy and tired. Donnie got me back to the truck and we drove in silence. Long, peaceful silence. I think I dozed off. The crunch of gravel under the truck tires roused me and I knew I was home.

"Stop here, Donnie." We were only halfway down the long driveway. "I'm just going to get out here, okay?"

"Why?"

"I'm not in the mood to talk to anybody." He shook his head and started to put the truck back into gear. "I *am* a little drunk," I finally admitted, "and I don't want TJ to see me like this. If you let me off here, I can just sneak in the back door without anyone hearing me come home." Warm light glowed from most of the windows, but I knew my mother would never have let TJ stay up past nine o'clock.

He studied me suspiciously for a moment before succumbing. "Okay. You're a grown woman. I guess I don't have to check you back in like a library book."

I slid out on my side and crossed over to his open window. Neither of us knew our next lines. We just stared at each other for a moment. "Thanks, Donnie."

His face broke into a grin; he winked and shoved the truck into reverse. I watched him back all the way to the street before I climbed between the fence rails and headed across the field toward the barn.

8

THE GRASS in my parents' field was long and cool, but not long enough to cut. No one in the valley ever mowed their hay until after the Fourth of July. I saw my mother's shape cross the living room to turn off a lamp. Hopefully they would turn in soon and so could I. Mom had been fine with watching TJ when I told her I needed to get out for a while, but it had not occurred to me when I slipped into Fraser's Tavern that I would be gone so long. I felt a twinge of guilt for not phoning. My foot sank into a rat hole, sending me sprawling on the dew-laden grass. The earth smelled of the summers of about a hundred years ago when my biggest worry was whether my creamed peas would be discovered in the spider plant. I rolled onto my back and relaxed, almost oblivious to the grass clump poking my kidneys, which was one of the advantages of being plastered. A dark blanket of sky with starry lint fell over me and there was silence except for the lazy sounds of the river and an owl hooting in the cottonwood grove.

The nausea had passed with the freight train, but the ever-present laboring in my chest still nagged ominously like snapping branches in the darkness beyond a campfire. I had tried to ignore it all day. Lindsey had come by that morning with frozen raspberries from last year's garden. She made a happy face with them on TJ's cereal and then she and I took our coffee onto the deck. Mom had gone into town with the Judge and wouldn't be back until afternoon. Maybe that was why Lindsey was there. I felt watched ever since the night of the 911 call. Mom or Lindsey was always taking TJ off my hands, or asking if I didn't want a sweater or something. I hated that.

Personally, I found most sick people very unattractive. No one knows what to say to them except, "How are you feeling today?" which of course is a big mistake, especially if it's Aunt Lilse you're asking. She used to go on about things you really didn't want to hear, like how she had diarrhea all last week and now she can't eat anything but Cream of Wheat. The worst part was when she pulled up her pant leg and made you look at how swollen her legs were. Her blue veins had as many tributaries as the Amazon and her legs just looked fat to me. Other sick people, who are not in it for the pure pleasure of depressing their loved ones, you just feel sorry for and you hope nothing scary or disgusting happens while you're visiting them.

I certainly didn't want it getting out that I had a slushy heart. It didn't suit my image. What if Donnie had known tonight? He probably would have driven me home and delivered me to my mother by eight p.m. Out of pity or guilt he might stop off later with flowers or send a card and that would be the end of that.

I remembered the cigarettes in my pocket. A fresh crisp pack, missing only the one I had savored before Donnie informed me that his truck was a "no smoking establishment" and I crushed it into the gravel at Fraser's Tavern. Just one smoke before bed. Tomorrow I'll throw them away. I got up and wandered to the barn, where I heard the flapping of wings in the rafters—a barn owl, no doubt. I hooted into the dark interior of the barn and waited for a reply. The back screen door slammed on the house, probably Mom setting out a bucket of kitchen scraps for the worms. Just inside the barn door on one side was a pile of loose hay surrounded by bales. It was TJ's new fort. I made myself comfortable on one of the ramparts and hooted again. Still no reply.

Suddenly, I heard a sound to my right and at the same instant the barn was shocked with light. Like a guilty twelve-year-old, I whipped the cigarette behind my back.

The Judge didn't see me at first. He started off toward the worm troughs with his pail of scraps.

"Hey," I said.

He spun around. "Samantha! What are you doing in here? Why are you sitting in the dark?"

I shrugged. "I was getting ready to come in. I've been talking to the owls. What are you doing out here so late? Giving your wormies a midnight snack?"

He scrutinized me for a moment. "We didn't know where you were. Your mother and I have been waiting for you to get home."

"Wow, I'm having déjà vu. I'm twenty-four years old now in case you didn't notice. I'm a grown-up. A mom even. You don't need to wait up for me anymore. I've been on my own for seven years, you know. Don't you think I can take care of myself?"

"Well, I would," he said as he casually picked up the bucket of scraps he had dropped, "but you have a serious heart condition, you're drunk and you're on fire."

He was halfway to the worm troughs before I noticed the smoke. A curse leaped from my throat. I jumped up and started stomping on the little blaze I had kindled behind me. Stumbling, my foot scattered a smoldering patch of hay, fanning it into flame. Dry stubble ignited instantly all around it.

My father calmly dumped his pail of goodies into the worm beds and raked the soil.

"Hello!" I shouted. "Are you going to help me here? Your barn is about to burn down!"

He glanced at me over his shoulder. "It's just a barn."

This was not funny. While he played his little game, TJ's fort was becoming an inferno and burned dangerously close to the bone-dry planks of the barn. "Water! Do you have any water in here?"

He set his bucket down and gestured with his head. "Right over there. There's a hose. Do you want me to get it?" He finally sauntered over toward the wall around the corner and returned with the hose. First he sprayed the vulnerable wall of the barn, and then the loose hay. He kicked the burning bales toward the center of the barn floor and sprayed them until they were sopping sponges.

"What the . . . ?" I felt a wounded bird flailing in my chest. "What was that all about?" I demanded when I caught my breath. "If you'd waited a few seconds longer, this whole place would have been the Towering Inferno! Your hose wouldn't have done any better than spitting on it!"

Suddenly the Judge yanked an antique lantern off its nail and swung it like a bat against the wall. Glass shattered and metal crumpled. The fire blazed now in his eyes.

I took a step backward and stared at him in shock. That lantern had been there forever.

"Does that bother you?" he shouted. "Does it seem a little destructive? You know, you can destroy things different ways, Samantha. You can do it deliberately, or you can do it by just not doing the right things in time. When are you going to start taking care of yourself? You're playing some kind of denial game that's going to kill you. What were you thinking tonight? Drinking, smoking, staying out late. If your doctor hasn't made it clear to you, I will. Your condition is serious. Life or death serious! And this is not just about you. You have a son to think of. For God's sake, Sam. Do the right thing this time!"

"Or what? Are you going to kick me out again?"

"I never kicked you out."

"I was barely seventeen years old and you kicked me out on my fanny!" I was furious now and hot tears stung my eyes. "It's always been 'my way or the highway' with you!"

"I didn't want you to go. I wanted you to make the right choice."

"Yeah. *Your* choice. *Your* way. There never was any other way but yours! Never another side. Did you ever think about me? About how I felt? Do you have any idea what it's like to face raising a kid for the rest of your life when you haven't even lived yet? When all your friends are playing baseball and going to proms?"

"We weren't dealing with a disagreement over summer school, or whether or not you got braces. You wanted to kill your own baby, Sam. That's the truth. You can ignore it, white-wash it and call it your *choice*, your *right*. You can march with a hundred women, or two hundred thousand, or millions who all agree a woman has a right to do what she wants with her own body, but it doesn't change the fact. The fact is you can't have an abortion without killing a baby. A person. An eternal soul whom God knew before it was conceived. This is not my opinion, Sam. It's straight out of the Word of God."

I didn't need to hear this from him. Not again.

"You could have at least let someone else raise the child. It was wrong. You wouldn't murder TJ, would you? No matter how inconvenient he may be sometimes."

"Shut up!" I put my hands to my ears and staggered toward the door. "That's enough!"

I tripped. He reached to help me to my feet. "Look, Sam, that's all over now. There's nothing that can be done about it. Let's put it behind us."

I pushed him away and headed for the house.

What he didn't know was that it was always behind me. Like a wolf lurking just out of sight.

IT WAS NOVEMBER the night I awoke to squeals of laughter. I remember because I had just turned eight. My mother and her old friend Minnie from Redwood City were having midnight cups of coffee. I crept from my bed and peered into the living room, where they sat cross-legged by the fire, looking more like teenagers than moms. The streamers and wilted balloons from my party still hung from the dining room chandelier. I had been about to head on to the kitchen for a drink of water when I heard their voices hush and take on a serious tone. My mother shook her head sadly. "If Blake hadn't done something—well, I can't even think about that."

"Tell me from the beginning, Lucy." Minnie's satin pajamas shimmered in the firelight. "I remember you and Blake tried for so long to have a baby and the next thing I know, you've got two. We sure got sloppy about writing to each other after our babies came along." Minnie was not as pretty as my mother, and I thought with a name like Mini she ought not be so tall.

She had long pearly fingernails and chunky rings and twice I had seen her leaning on the porch rail smoking a cigarette. I took Mom aside and told her, but she just smiled and said not to worry about it.

Mom stretched her feet toward the fire and wiggled her toes. "This woman was an attorney at the firm where Blake started out. Kathleen Mayes," she said with a frown. "What a loud, obnoxious . . ." She caught herself and smiled sheepishly. "Well, I guess you've got to have some voltage to be as dramatic and, I must say, effective in the courtroom as she was. She had such wild hair; it was red at the time, but in reality probably closer to plain brown like Samantha's. I know Sam inherited the wildness. It takes forever to get a comb through her hair in the morning."

I lay silently on the hardwood floor of the hallway. What were they talking about? What did this wild-haired woman have to do with me?

"The first time I saw her was at a Christmas party at the home of one of the partners." She sipped her coffee and put it down on the hearth. "Elegant home. Everyone was dressed for the Emmys—tuxedos and floor-length gowns. Anyway, Kathleen shows up in tight red satin pants and cowboy boots with some weird spangly halter top contraption." Minnie laughed with delight at my mother's contortions as she described the top. "Of course, everyone was shocked, and Kathleen loved every minute of it. She sat with her legs apart and her elbows on her thighs, and no matter where you were in that huge room, you could hear Kathleen.

"A few months later, Kathleen is standing by the coffeepot at the office and announces to anyone and everyone that she is pregnant. Blake didn't even mention it to me at first. He's not one to pass on that sort of thing. Besides, here we were trying so hard to get pregnant with nothing happening and this single woman who doesn't even want a baby . . ."

"Who was the father?"

"Supposedly a former client. A married man. He denied his paternity, of course. Not that she really pursued it. She had no intention of having the baby. When Blake found out she had scheduled an abortion, he tried to talk her out of it. He said it was wrong. My husband has always been passionate about his beliefs. And when the law, to which he has devoted his life, so blatantly conflicts with what he believes to be right . . . well, needless to say, Blake was furious. Imagine that debate—two skilled attorneys, one equipped with *Roe v. Wade*, the other the Bible. He came home that night still brooding and told me all about it. That's when I thought of it. If she didn't want the baby, why couldn't she just give it to us? That would solve the problem for all of us."

Minnie leaned forward. "Go on."

"So we drew up a proposal. We pay all her expenses; she gives us the baby. Of course, it was more elaborate than that. Attorneys are like engineers, you know. Take a simple thing, complicate it to the max, put it on paper and then let everybody argue about it. What we ended up paying her was probably about a hundred dollars an hour with overtime on weekends and a stiff fine for every time the baby kicked.

"Poor Blake. He tried to avoid her at work. She would pat her belly and make embarrassing innuendos about 'their' baby when she was in a good mood. The rest of the time, which was most of the time, she complained bitterly about every ache and pain and tried to make him miserable." She shrugged impishly. "But I was happy. I painted a mural on the nursery wall, refinished an antique crib, shopped. I was so busy and so happy that I hardly noticed my own symptoms. I honestly thought there was some mental-spiritual-physical connection going on between my baby and me. I mean the one Kathleen was carrying."

"You always were naive." Minnie stretched her body onto the floor and began doing leg lifts, her painted toes pointed toward my hiding place behind the hall door. "So when you found out you were pregnant, didn't you try to get out of your contract with Kathleen?"

It got quiet. I held my breath.

"Yes. I did."

"And?"

"Well, the idea never got past Blake. I'm glad now, of course," she inserted almost guiltily. "At the time I was overwhelmed with the thought of having two infants at once. When I realized that I myself was carrying a child, flesh of my flesh—of our flesh, Blake's and mine—well, it changed everything. I suddenly wanted all of our attention on the little miracle happening in my body. I no longer had any desire to live vicariously through some brash woman with big orange lips."

"Of course you didn't." Minnie touched my mother's arm reassuringly. "That's perfectly normal."

I couldn't see my mother's face. She poked the fire and a flurry of embers raced up the flue. "Blake said it wasn't the written contract that bound us to our agreement. It was his word."

"But, honey, sometimes circumstances change. Everybody has to go back on their word sometimes."

Mother shook her head. "Not Blake." She looked Minnie square in the eyes. "Not ever."

I crept back to my bed. People always seemed confused when Lindsey and I were introduced as sisters. They would inevitably ask our ages, which eight months out of the year were the same. "One is natural, the other chosen," my father would say, just like that. Matter-of-fact. No explanation. Immediately he would turn the conversation to something else, which I realized now was his way of saying none of your business. If anyone dared to ask the details, they never asked in front of me. I knew that I was adopted but until that night I had no concept of what that really meant. It had never seemed important somehow.

In the morning I poured cereal in a yellow-rimmed bowl and sat by the kitchen window. My mother stumbled in with her short blond hair sticking up in the back and began making a pot of coffee while Minnie used the shower. Lindsey popped cinnamon bread in the toaster, humming a tune from the Mary Poppins movie we had seen the night before. My father's newspaper and empty coffee mug were abandoned in their usual place, and I knew without asking that he had left for the courthouse.

Everything seemed the same. Everyone seemed normal, except for me.

9

MOMMY, WHEN'S GRANDPA COMING home from work?" TJ was draped over the ottoman by my chair, pulling and twisting my shoelaces.

"Hmm? I don't know, baby." I kept trying to read my book.

"Is Aunt Lindsey coming today? *She* might take me to the creek. She likes to run and play even though she's a grown-up."

I sighed. "I like to run and play too. I just can't right now. Why don't you go out and catch some more bugs?"

"Ohhh, they keep getting away," he breathed dejectedly. "We should have brought Mikey with us when we came here."

"Don't you think Mikey would miss his family?"

TJ climbed onto my lap, pushing my book aside. "Mommy, tell me a story. About when you were a little girl and you lived here with Grandpa and Grandma and Aunt Lindsey."

I placed my novel on the table beside me and smoothed his hair while I thought. Being home had breathed fresh life into so many memories. "Okay. I think I have one you've never heard." He sprawled across my lap with his head on one arm-rest, his feet on the other, gazing up at my face.

ONE FINE SATURDAY, the first bright morning after five consecutive days of torrential rain, I awoke to the elated calls of robins fluttering in the trees beyond the barn. I must have been about nine at the time. I pushed my window open and hung my torso over the sill. The river roared louder than usual, like someone had turned the volume up on the radio noise between stations. All that rain had funneled into it, along with snows melting off the Cascade mountains. My heart skipped with excitement. Maybe the river was over its banks! Rather than risk waking my parents by opening a squeaky drawer to find clothes, I hoisted my long cotton nightgown, crawled over the windowsill and dropped to the ground.

The grass was long and wet, and soon the hem of my nightie became a wick. I had no specific agenda beyond obeying the call of the morning and the robins, who repeated the same sweet melody over and over in an entrancing chant. The river gushed muddy and high. So high that the sandy spit where I often played was completely covered and some of the alder trees waded tentatively at the river's edge. I threw a branch into the powerful current and watched it disappear into the boiling gravy. I turned away from the river and loped across the field toward the barn. Beyond the barn and pasture my beloved woods dropped into a ravine carved by Haller Creek, which meandered down to the north fork of the river, forming the southeast corner of our twelve acres. This was my haven. The trees were my older brothers and cousins—surrounding, comforting and watching over me. They held the ropes for tire swings. Their branches formed the thatched roofs of forts. They hid me, high in their boughs, when I needed to cry.

This particular morning, I paused at the top of the hill, straining my eyes to see the swollen creek through the trees. The trail that traversed the side of the ravine and zigzagged to the meadow below oozed between my bare toes. But I was shocked when I reached the place where the trail was supposed to zag. The trail was gone! To my amazement, a large chunk of the hill had simply broken off and slid into a huge brown heap below me on the floor of the ravine. I stared in disbelief for some time before deciding that the phenomenon must be observed from another angle. Grabbing the protruding end of a cedar root, I stepped gingerly onto the slope.

It seemed like a good idea at the time. What happened next was disastrous, or absolutely wonderful, depending on how you looked at it. My feet shot straight out from under me. The root slipped through my fist and my backside slapped onto the slick clay-mud hillside. I was off. At first I fought it. I grasped wildly for newly exposed roots to no avail. I flipped onto my belly and then spun, shot headfirst down the slide like an otter, skimming over the right edge of the pile of loose mud at the bottom and landing abruptly on terra firma.

I raised my chin from the mud and gazed up at the disfigured hillside. "Holy macaroni," I whispered in awe. This was too amazing to keep to myself. Taking an alternate route, I scrambled up the hill. My muddy nightgown felt as heavy as chain mail, slapping and chafing my legs, but I didn't care. I pulled myself up with roots and branches, sometimes crawling, until I reached the top. I took the pasture in a minute flat, arriving breathless beneath Lindsey's bedroom window.

My sister slept with her window shut. I jumped with the

grace of a leaping sea cow to tap the pane. When that failed, a branch from my mother's hydrangea became my window scratcher. "Lins!" I whispered loudly, tapping and scratching until she opened the window and stuck out her sleepy head.

When she saw me, her eyes bugged out. "Samantha Jean! Oh, my, what have you done now?"

"Shhh. Come on, Lins! I'll show you. It's absolutely fantabulous!"

She just stared at me, shaking her head. "You're really going to catch it this time, Sam."

"It's not my fault. It was a mud slide. Now come on!"

"It's Saturday, you know. We have chores." She began to unbutton her nightgown.

"There's no time for that if you want to be back before they wake up." I nodded toward our parents' window at the other end of the house.

She sighed. "Okay." She hoisted herself onto the sill. "But I'm not getting dirty."

That gave me an idea. Lindsey's bare legs dangled from the window momentarily before she dropped to the ground. I led the way across the field, stopping behind the barn for my snow saucer. She followed me, the hem of her nightgown pinched together in her fists, stepping cautiously as she watched for the slugs that cruised through the dewy grass, leaving slime trails behind them. At the edge of the hill, she paused. "The trail is all muddy." I kept going and she eventually followed. Her jaw dropped when she saw the gaping hole where our hillside had been. "Oh, my! Oh, Samantha. It looks like someone took a gigantic bite out of it! How did this happen? What if it had happened while we were here on the trail? We would be dead right now. Buried in mud. And no one would ever know where we went."

I leaned the saucer against a stump for Lindsey, who still surveyed the damage in shock, and then poised myself like a proud circus performer about to execute a dangerous stunt.

"Aren't you going to use the saucer?"

"Bombs away!" I hurled my body past her. The slick clay slid me off its back in a wild ride as I whooped with glee. I picked myself up at the bottom and spat mud. "Your turn!"

"No way." Lindsey's arms were crossed and her feet firmly planted on solid ground, but I saw the look of envy in her eyes.

"Get in the saucer and hold on. You won't even get dirty!"

"Yeah, right."

"I'm serious," I called up to her. "Think about it. Pretend it's snow. You can just sail right over the top of it!"

Her head cocked slightly to one side. I was getting through.

I crawled up the hill, my nightie too heavy for me to stand erect without great effort. My next run was feetfirst, which was a mistake. The heavy gown dragged behind me and my panties scooped mud like a shovel. I peeled them off and dumped them. Even so, walking became extremely uncomfortable. I didn't let on to Lindsey. "Are you coming or not?" I shouted. "You're going to be sorry if you miss out. This is a once-in-a-lifetime opportunity, you know!"

Finally, she picked up the saucer, setting it tentatively just above the edge of the slide. "Will you catch me at the bottom?" She placed her feet daintily in the saucer and sat down slowly like an Indian princess. "Okay, here I come!"

Where she went wrong was her takeoff. The saucer sort of dragged over the lip of the slide. I yelled to her to give it a good push, but she refused to get her hands in the mud. There was a good slick spot in the middle and she started to get some momentum. The saucer spun and tipped to one side and she screamed bloody murder. I couldn't see why. She was still just crawling down the hill compared to my speed runs. I positioned myself strategically at the edge of the mud pile, but stopping her proved unnecessary. The saucer came to a rest in a little dip right smack in the middle of the mushy earth deposited by the slide.

Of course, Lindsey blamed me for this. I explained to her that she should have made a running jump onto the saucer and now that she hadn't, she was just going to have to get a little muddy and wade out of that pile. She started crying about her new nightie getting ruined, which Grandma Dodd had made with her own two hands.

"Take it off and throw it to me," I suggested.

"Don't even think about touching me or my nightie! You look like a swamp monster." The Indian princess sat there and pouted. "Why don't you come up here and push me out?"

The idea had occurred to me, but the mud and clay at the bottom of the slide were too deep and loose. Even at the edges my feet sank deeply before meeting the bottom. Another good idea overtook me. I was full of them that morning. "Wait here," I said.

All I needed was a rope. The journey up the hillside was laborious until I got smart and shed the two-ton mud nightgown. Then I was a gazelle, bounding up the hill and across the field to the barn. Sunshine warmed my shoulders and baked a crackly clay crust onto my skin. Inside the barn, my pupils adjusted slowly to the deep shadows. Hay scattered on the dirt floor smelled sweet and prickled the bottoms of my feet.

The barn was our huge playhouse. Our family did not keep

animals. Well, we had chickens once—five banty hens and an obnoxious rooster that pecked noisily on the metal garbage can by the side of the house and had a sickly crow like someone trying to scream while being strangled. I hated him. He always chased me and I threw rocks and cherries at him. Lindsey could walk right up and pet him, though. It was the weirdest thing. The chickens roamed free during the day, laying eggs wherever they pleased. Our daily egg hunts turned up speckled brown eggs from beneath bushes and in the garden. They were so petite it took four of them to bake a cake.

I found the rope where I had left it, up in the hayloft. My father had made me undo the rope swing I tied to a rafter. He said only a monkey could have climbed up there, and if a monkey tied the knot, it might not hold. It would have, though. I'd been tying knots since I was a little kid. I coiled the rope and wore it like a bandolier, climbed down the ladder and was about to make the dash back to the woods to rescue my sister when I turned and saw a large figure looming in the doorway.

My father. I suddenly felt small and very naked.

"Samantha Jean!" The thunder of his voice rolled and echoed from every recess of the barn. I stepped behind the ladder, which proved to be poor cover. "Where are your clothes? Where is your sister?"

I pointed.

"What is that all over you?" I looked down and saw the mud-smeared body of an Aborigine right off the pages of *National Geographic*. Thick clods hung from my head like strings of beads.

"There's a mud slide, Dad, and Lindsey's in it. I was just going to save her."

"Where?" He sounded overly alarmed. "Show me where she

is!" I hesitated. In a corner of the barn, Lindsey had set up housekeeping with a table and chairs, a plank counter full of dishes and empty cereal and cracker boxes in a neat row. My father strode to the window in quick, determined steps, yanked a cherry-patterned curtain off its nails and tossed it to me. He clapped his hands. Smack! It resounded like a gunshot. "Let's go! Move! Move!"

"Okay!" In one motion I wrapped the musty cloth around my bare body and bolted for the barn door. He grabbed the rope I had dropped and we headed for the woods, my father barking at my heels if I slowed down, until we heard a distant intermittent cry like that of a baby crow in distress wafting up from the ravine.

"Sa-man-tha!" Lindsey's pathetic pleas sounded hollow and hopeless. She seemed surprised when she saw us working our way down the steep trail. "Daddy! Help! I'm stuck here and the mud is too deep and squishy!"

He quickly surveyed the damaged hillside and Lindsey's dilemma. "Stay put, baby." He circled the mud slide, gingerly descending the slope using branches of undergrowth for anchors. Finally, he positioned himself adjacent to her. She was about five yards beyond his reach. He poked a long stick into the mud to test its depth. The stick disappeared up to his fist. I caught a swift sideways glance from him like a slap. Like all this was my fault. Like I had caused the days of incessant rain and had somehow sabotaged the hill, dumping tons of earth onto our valley floor.

"Lindsey," he said, "I'm going to toss you this rope. I want you to tie it around you and make a real good knot. Can you do that?" She did it, still sniveling, a tear dammed up on each lower lid. "Good job. Now stay low and hang on tight to the saucer. That's right. I'm going to give you a little pull now." He crept downhill a bit. "Don't let go, baby. Okay." He tugged gently at first and then a little harder until the snow saucer broke free of the pothole. It was an easy, uneventful glide to the bottom.

Lindsey hardly got in any trouble at all. She just had to weed a garden in addition to her usual chores. My father switched my behind with an alder branch, but I didn't cry. On the inside I was screaming, but I didn't let on. It wasn't fair. Then I had to endure his science lecture about what happens to a human body that gets swallowed up by mud. He sent me back for the wad of mud that was once the nightie Grandma Dodd made for me. It had been identical to Lindsey's except the ribbon on her bodice was pink and mine was blue. Grandma insisted on calling us "the twins" even though I was a full four months older than my sister and we had nothing in common but that we were the same sex.

I hosed my nightgown off and Mom washed it three times before it came out an acceptable shade of gray. Lindsey's, of course, survived pure white with perfect little pink rosebuds that are probably unfaded to this day.

10

MY TROUBLES were temporarily forgotten on the Fourth of July. They burst into tiny manageable fragments like the brilliant chrysanthemums of colored sparks that would soon fill the night sky over the field. I basked in the smell of the sweet corn boiling and the hickory smoke from the barbecue, the hot sun on my hair and shoulders, the laughter of the river as it winked between the wild huckleberries at the edge of the yard, and TJ's squeals of delight at catching a young cutthroat in the creek. The fish was too small but ended up on the barbecue anyway because it had swallowed the hook so deep—and because TJ was not much for the silly rule that said a keeper trout had to be at least six inches.

Dr. Matt brought his sons. They used to play with Lindsey and me sometimes, though they were younger. We didn't see them often because they lived with their mother in Tacoma. Sweet little Kevin turned out to be a bruiser, a Big Mac away from two sixty and none of that was fat. He played linebacker for the Huskies. His older brother, Jess, arrived wearing slacks and a pressed shirt, looking ridiculously out of place among the rest of us in our shorts and T-shirts until Lindsey's husband, David, showed up.

Donnie brought his parents and a load of horse manure from the Appaloosa Ranch. Old Chester had insisted that as long as they were coming over, they might as well make the trip count, though they lived less than a half mile down the road. Donnie backed the truck to a spot behind the barn, and while the Judge passed out shovels, David ducked into the kitchen.

I followed him in from the deck. "Hey, David. Dad wants you."

"He does?"

"Yeah. He wondered if you could help get that pile of poo off the truck out there," I lied.

"He did?"

I snuck a spoonful of potato salad from the serving bowl and glanced over my shoulder. "That's what he said."

David walked tentatively onto the deck and peered around the corner of the house, where he could see Chester and Donnie leaning against the tail of the pickup, talking to the Judge, who had a shovel in his hand. I watched David saunter across the field slowly, as if hoping the other men might heave to and get the whole stinking pile of recycled hay unloaded before his arrival. I was laughing when Lindsey came up behind me.

"What's so funny?"

"Oh, just your husband. He's about to suck up to the father-in-law. Shouldn't he be over that stage by now?"

She shaded her eyes and peered toward the barn. "Is he . . . ? He's not going to get in that . . ."

"Yup. There he goes. Dockers and all. What a trooper. What a great guy." I couldn't stop grinning.

Lindsey shook her head in disbelief. "That's so unlike him."

"I think it's a male bonding thing."

As it turned out that's exactly what it was. After unloading the truck and hosing out its bed, the men attempted to spray the gourmet worm food off each other's feet. The hose got away from someone and it turned into a water fight. By the time they joined the rest of us on the deck, laughing and punching and tossing insults, we were all wishing we had shoveled manure. Even David seemed undaunted by his dripping clothes and scrambled hair. He carefully placed his socks and leather loafers on the edge of the deck to dry in the sun, not with remorse but as proudly as if they were trophies, and then stretched out on a canvas deck chair, wiggling his bare toes. I had done my good deed. Not intentionally perhaps, but just the same I felt good inside. One less stuffy person in the world—at least for today.

Chester limped up and nodded to me. A bee buzzed around his weathered face and lit on his bare arm, but he didn't seem to mind so I didn't mention it. "Hello, Mr. Duncan. It's nice to see you again."

He nodded again. "Samantha. You kinda grew up on us, didn't ya?" The bee crawled around on his wrinkled and mottled skin. Maybe he couldn't feel it. "Don tells me you worked on a ranch down there in Arizona. And here I always thought you didn't like horses."

"Nevada. I was in Nevada, and it wasn't so much that I didn't like horses. Your horses didn't like me."

He chuckled. "Maybe they never forgave ya for startin' that stampede. Horses have great memories. They never forget smart-aleck kids with firecrackers."

"I've been meaning to tell you, I'm sorry about that." The bee crawled up his short sleeve.

"Um . . . Mr. Duncan . . ." I pointed toward his arm and at that instant he flinched. He reached up, pinched the bee hard and flung it to the ground.

Donnie pulled up a chair. "Did he get ya?"

"Dang yellow jackets. They don't usually get ornery till August." Chester surveyed the yard, where TJ spun in circles making bubbles until he got dizzy, falling and spilling his bottle of soap on the grass. "Where's your boy?" he asked.

"That's him," I said.

"That little Indian kid?" Chester recoiled almost imperceptibly. Like when he got stung.

"He's Norwegian and Mexican." I called to him and he came running, holding the empty soap bottle out to me. "It's okay, Teej. I know how to make more." I pulled him onto my lap. "TJ, this is Donnie's dad, Mr. Duncan." Donnie had dropped by on several occasions, so he and TJ were already friends.

Chester asked what TJ stands for, at which TJ said, "It stands for my name. Mommy, why do people always ask me that?"

I played with his hair. "Maybe they think your name should be longer or something. Maybe we should change it. You wanna be Thaddeus Bigglewiggle?"

He considered it. "No."

Donnie suggested Alexander Wimbledon Waddlesworth, but TJ didn't warm up to that either. He lay back against me and fiddled with his shoelace. Suddenly, he brightened. "How 'bout Blake?"

I kissed his head and put him down. "That one's taken. How 'bout we stick with TJ?"

The Judge and Matthew manned the barbecues, producing platters mounded with juicy steaks and chicken. A table was set up on the lawn, and we piled our plates with everything but the lime gelatin with peaches I had made, which didn't set up. Donnie called it pond water and said all the goldfish had died and sunk to the bottom. Some of David and Lindsey's friends arrived carrying a bare-legged baby, with a little boy about TJ's age in tow. TJ ran to him. Minutes later the two new best friends scampered off to the barn to see the worms.

The only adults who didn't join the rowdy volleyball game were Donnie's mother, Gladys (who I swear wore a bib apron every day of her life and would rather putter in the kitchen than take a trip to Tahiti), the nursing mother and me. Even Chester, bad leg and all, got in there and fought for a while. I hated sitting there watching like an old lady. When I told Donnie I had a bad knee, my mother gave me a sideways look. I shot a look back that said *I'll tell him when I'm ready—which isn't now.* Mom rarely touched the ball at first because Kevin the linebacker was on her team, playing every position. I yelled at him but he ignored me. Finally, he and David collided in midair and went down in a heap of hairy legs and elbows. Mom sprang with all her pent-up energy and spiked the ball over. It bounced on the ground between Matt's legs. The Judge, her opponent, high-fived her through the net.

When the sky turned to steel, we loaded every available chair onto pickup trucks and set up theater seating in the big field by the barn. A cool breeze came off the river. Mom sent out blankets and quilts to bundle in while we sat around the bonfire, waiting for the sky to become the perfect backdrop of black felt. Donnie pulled his chair up next to mine. I had hoped he would, but when he reached for my hand I pulled it away, pretending I hadn't noticed his attempt. Better not start something I couldn't finish. "Where are the sticks for marshmallows?" I asked. Someone passed me a whittled alder branch. I smiled at Donnie. "I'm going to make you the best s'more you ever had." I put a marshmallow on the end of the stick and turned it slowly over glowing coals until it was golden brown on the outside and hot and gooey inside. "Chocolate!" I held out my hand.

"Chocolate!" Lindsey repeated like a surgical nurse as she slapped a small square into my palm. I pressed it carefully into the hot marshmallow and returned it to the oven.

"Uh-oh, Mom. It's on fire!" shouted TJ, who had settled on the foot of Donnie's lounge chair.

"Yup." I removed it from the fire, still blazing. "Cracker!"

"Cracker." Lindsey closed two halves of graham cracker around the ball of flames and slid the sandwich off the stick. "Voilà." She held it out to Donnie.

"Am I supposed to eat this? It's burned."

"It's perfect. Taste it."

He bit into it suspiciously at first and then popped the rest of it into his mouth. "Not bad."

"That's the way we make 'em," Lindsey said proudly. "It's the only way to get the chocolate to melt." We exchanged wry smiles. She remembered.

My sister passed crackers and sticks around the campfire and poured coffee from a big insulated bottle. She wouldn't let Mom get up from the old love seat that had been hauled out from the garage, where she sat with her feet up, hugging her knees and chatting with Mrs. Duncan. When Lindsey asked if anyone needed a jacket or anything, I made her sit down and quit fussing over everyone. "This is not the Hilton," I announced. "If anyone needs anything, they can get it themselves."

Matt and my father laid a sheet of plywood out in the field as a launching pad. Fireworks were unloaded from several car trunks, including a huge box of goodies from the local tribal reservation, which we knew would be saved for the grand finale. At this point, every grown man regressed to adolescence. It was too dark to see whether they had sprouted acne, but their voices intermittently shot into higher octaves as they discussed which rocket to fire and how. Eventually the boys tired of conventional methods. A mass missile attack was staged by arranging bottle rockets all along one edge of the platform. Matthew was the self-appointed general. Five brave missile launchers were poised and ready. "Five, four, three, two, one, blastoff!" At his command ten fuses were lit simultaneously and the launchers dashed to safety, laughing and squealing like pigs. The darkness was instantly pierced with screaming projectiles that burst into fountains of colored light punctuated with loud bangs. The crowd clapped and cheered.

This was all new to TJ. He didn't even ask to light a sparkler. He snuggled with me inside a quilt cocoon, his dark eyes wide with wonder, reflecting brilliant showers of light. His hair smelled of smoke and sweat. Before the grand finale, he was gone. He slept through the oohs and aahhs and loud cheering and hardly stirred when Donnie carried him across the field and into the house, where we tucked him into his bed. I think it aroused some kind of paternal instinct in Donnie. He touched TJ's hair and smiled down at him and then looked up at me like we were in some Norman Rockwell painting. What was I supposed to do? Clasp my hands at my chest and smile lovingly back?

After Donnie and the other guests had gone, Lindsey popped her head in my bedroom doorway. "Got room for one more in that big bed?"

"That depends on who it is."

"Me. I sent David home. I'm staying over so I can help with cleanup in the morning."

"Oh. Are you a thrasher?"

"No. I lie perfectly still, flat on my back like a princess. See?" She plopped onto the bed to demonstrate. "And I don't snore."

"That's what they all say."

Mom peeked in. "Lindsey, do you need a nightgown?"

"No, thanks. I sleep naked."

I passed her a long flannel shirt. "No, you don't." We dressed for bed and shared the hall bathroom.

The Judge came by on his way to bed. "Okay, girls." He tried to sound stern. "I want lights out in fifteen minutes and no giggling."

Lindsey tossed a pillow at him when he turned to leave. She sprawled across the foot of the bed on her belly with her toes pointed to the ceiling. "Donnie turned out nice, didn't he? I've hardly seen him in the past few years. I thought he would have gone off to law school by now."

I told her about how old Chester caught a pitchfork in the leg and had been using it to his advantage ever since. "It's too bad," I said. "Donnie has a brilliant mind. He could be a great trial lawyer and he knows it. If I were him, I'd just take off. Chester would survive. He could hire someone to do what Donnie does."

"So, what's going on between you two?"

I shrugged. "Same as usual. We're friends."

"Well, you better tell him that. He wants more. You do see the signals, don't you?"

I sighed.

"He's a babe, Sam. You could do a lot worse. He's funny and—"

"Lindsey," I interrupted, "do you know I'm married?"

She seemed taken aback. "Well, I knew you and Tim . . . You mean to tell me you and Tim never got a divorce? I just assumed . . ."

"Nope. We're not even legally separated. He's just gone."

"Have you tried to find him?"

I fell back on my pillow in exasperation.

"Sam. Talk to me. It's me, Lindsey, your almost-twin. I'm on your side. Whatever it is, you need to talk about it. You can't keep holding all these secrets inside of you. It's not healthy." She had that pouty look. "I always tell you everything about me."

I pondered for a moment and then sat up with a sigh. "Okay. You want it from the top?"

She nodded. "From the top."

"Tim is not TJ's daddy."

She rolled her eyes. "I figured that part out all by myself."

"Well, you know the part about Tim and me working at the ranch. I wrote to Mom about that, right?"

"Sam, you've got to tell me everything. We've had less than a dozen notes from you in seven years and four of those were Mother's Day cards."

"Sorry. I lumped you in with the Judge for a while there. I figured you and Mom were on his side. I also pictured him reading anything I wrote. I couldn't get too personal."

She shook her head with a disapproving frown. "Why do you call him that?"

"Anyway, when I ran away from home, I went to a clinic in Seattle for the . . . well, you know, abortion. We stayed with a friend of Tim's down there for a few days until I was feeling better, and then we drove straight down to Elko because Tim's uncle Rich told him if he ever needed a job, just show up and he'd put him to work as a mechanic. We found Uncle Rich drunk on his butt barbecuing hot dogs outside a ratty single-wide trailer. He didn't even own a garage. We slept on his hide-a-bed couch for two weeks before we found work at the Wilders' ranch. Tim was put in charge of maintaining all the vehicles, and he did odd jobs like fixing fences and building cabins for the tourists to stay in. It was a functioning horse ranch with a dude ranch on the side."

"What did you do?"

"Housekeeping for Mrs. Wilder. Babysitting. In the summer I was like a maid for the dude cabins. Tim and I both helped with the horses sometimes, but we were no good at it. Anyway, they gave us our own little cabin to live in. The Wilders were good people."

"What happened between you and Tim?"

I fiddled with my toes and took a deep breath. "Well, we had a fight. It was no big deal, really. We were both tired from working all day and I guess we both wanted someone to dote on us. I loved that little cabin, but sometimes it was too small. No place to get away and think, you know? Anyway, I got mad and stormed out; took one of the horses and rode off into the sunset. Not for good. I didn't even take a toothbrush."

When I got to that part I had to think for a minute. Despite my bent for shocking my sister, I felt uncomfortable. Was there a version of this story that was suitable for Pollyanna? "It was dry out there, so barren. Just a lot of scrubby grass and bushes. After a while I got cold and hungry and wanted to go home, but it was too soon. My exit had been so dramatic; I couldn't just stroll in an hour later and stick my head in the fridge. So I

rode around singing the blues to my horse, until I saw a campfire down in this dry creek bed."

I remembered the first time I saw Tijuana out in the corral,
breaking a chestnut stallion. He was shirtless and as brown and
sinewy as the horse. The stack of clean bedding I was delivering
to a cabin ended up on the rusty tailgate of a pickup truck
while I observed from the rail fence. The horse was beautiful,
wild and defiant, his ears flicking back and then forward, every
muscle tensed. But it was the man who captured my attention.
It wasn't just that he was tall, or that every muscle seemed
sculpted in smooth clay, or even the way his powerful back and
shoulders glistened with sweat. It was the way he moved—his
dark head held high as he wielded the rope to direct the dance
of the stallion, each move calm and confident. Sometimes only
the brawn of his chest and arms and back would flinch ever so
slightly while he and the horse calculated each other's next
move, and then he would flash a grin like the white light of an
opened door on a moonless night and say, "Okay, *caballo. Venga.
Venga.*"

I was mesmerized. No one at the ranch knew much about
him. He had walked out of the desert one day with a bedroll on
his back and approached Mr. Wilder for a job. Hank Wilder
didn't speak Spanish and became frustrated when he couldn't
get answers to his questions. He finally shook his head, said,
"No. No job here," and walked away. When he glanced back
over his shoulder, Tijuana (which was the nickname the ranch
hands gave him) stood silently in the corral, staring down a
wild horse that had been brought in just that morning. The
horse's head was down, nostrils flared. In an instant he wheeled.
His powerful flank swept within inches of the man. When the
dust cleared, Tijuana stood in the same position, as cool as an

ice statue. Hank and a couple of hands sauntered over to the rail. After an hour-long performance, the men watched in awe as the Mexican walked up to the rather subdued stallion, ran his hand along the sweat-streaked neck and slid a rope over its head.

No one ever heard Hank ask to see a green card. He showed the stranger the bunkhouse and that was that.

When the Wilder family, their employees and guests gathered in the large informal dining room off the kitchen of the main house, the lone Mexican spoke little. I usually sat by Tim, the first and only love of my life, the only man I would follow to a remote Nevada ranch without a cottonwood tree within a hundred miles. So it was unsettling to feel myself blush when the dark-eyed caballero looked my way. A rim of white showed beneath his black irises and full lashes shaded his eyes like awnings. His nose had a slight crook in its bridge like that of a regal Indian chief I had seen in a picture. When his meal was done, he often leaned back in his chair, arms folded across his chest, and surveyed the room. Once, when our eyes met they lingered too long. The corners of his lips spread into a smile and I looked away.

He invaded my fantasies. I should not have been thinking what I was thinking in the cabin after twilight while Tim rubbed my back. I should not have pretended as I kissed Tim's blond hair in the dark that it was the color of a crow's wing or that his skin was as smooth and brown as a chestnut. But I did. I meant nothing by it. It was like my own personal movie of which I was the director and the star, Tijuana the handsome and mysterious leading man.

The Mexican never stayed in the bunkhouse. He wrangled, broke and trained horses—some for sale, others to serve as riders for the weekend cowboys. In the evenings after supper he could be seen walking out on the range, a bedroll and pack on his back, until he disappeared beyond the low hills.

I have wondered since that fateful night when I stumbled upon him in a dry gully a mile outside the ranch if it was really in the back of my mind all along. Hadn't I thought I might run into him somewhere out there? The moment he saw me, he dropped his blanket and stood forebodingly as my horse and I descended the sandy slope. When my face came into the fire's glow, he nodded and flashed that grin, almost like I was expected. As if I was as predictable as one of his wild horses. All it took was time and patience and dark entrancing eyes that could tame the wild—or in my case, corrupt the tame.

He helped me down and tied the horse to the branch of a lone tree. I drank my first tequila from a red plastic cup, which we shared. He told me he grew up in a small town in Michoacán and his papa was a *carnicero,* which I didn't comprehend until he explained, "Ju know, he keel cows and porks," which made me laugh. He was the oldest of eight, and when I asked why he had left, he shook his head slowly and stirred the embers of the fire. Maybe he didn't understand the question.

"My father is a judge," I said. "You know, he says, 'You're right; you're wrong.'" I pointed my finger back and forth authoritatively. "'You live; you die. You're good; you're a worthless pile of dung.'" Now he laughed. I was glad he had beef jerky because I was hungry and the tequila was going to my head. When I shivered, he opened his blanket and drew me in as if I was a wild mare hypnotically yielding to the first rope around her neck.

What happened next was a wildfire—a blaze of passion that swept over us like flames on a dry plain. Hard, almost painful kisses led to groping and clothes frantically discarded. His skin was hot and smelled of soap. I like to think now that I had no choice. The fire was beyond my control and even a river could not quench it. But it did eventually burn out, leaving a charred wake of stubble and bones that would haunt me for years to come.

I later realized that he never spoke my name. I lay awake staring at the stars until his breath was shallow, and then crept around, gathering clothes by waning firelight. Tim. Kind, strong, tender Tim. I suddenly yearned for him and yet dreaded looking into his clear blue eyes. I pulled the sleeve of my sweater from the embers. It was burned to the elbow.

The squeak of the saddle and the horse's hooves on loose gravel woke Tijuana, and when I looked down he was up on one elbow. "I was not here," I said. *"Entiendes?"*

He grinned. *"Sí.* Ju was not here."

I couldn't tell Lindsey everything. I couldn't tell her about the lust or that I didn't even know his real name. I told her it was a terrible accident, which it was. She asked me why I never told Tim. "When you were pregnant, didn't you ever wonder if the baby might be from this . . . Tijuana?"

"Of course I wondered. But it seemed to me the odds were in Tim's favor." I shook my head. "Got that one wrong." Lindsey smiled sympathetically. "Anyway," I continued, "when we found out I was pregnant, Tim was so happy. The first time, you know, he sort of wanted me to keep the baby but the timing was all off. We didn't have jobs; we weren't married. I'm the one who insisted on the abortion. But this time he was sure about being a dad. He danced me around and talked about the baby more than I did. He told everybody at the ranch, and I guess he got me believing. . . ." I felt like an idiot. "Well, I just got caught up in it, that's all."

Lindsey nodded as if she understood. "So, when TJ was born . . . ?"

"He came out looking like a little Milk Dud. Hair black as shoe polish. Tim knew right away, but I think it took a while to sink in. At first he went along with everything—cutting the umbilical cord and holding the baby—but he looked like he was in shock. He went out for a while and I held TJ for the first time. The nurse showed me how to breast-feed, which TJ already knew. He just went for it like he'd been doing that forever. It was pretty amazing to me that he came preprogrammed. Anyway, Tim came back about forty-five minutes later and just stood in the doorway of my room."

At this part I felt myself choking up. I had to take a deep breath before continuing. "He said, 'That's not my son, is it?' I couldn't look at him. I just looked down at the little brown baby at my pale breast, and when I looked back up, Tim was gone. Just like that. I never saw him again."

Lindsey was respectfully silent. She brought me a tissue and I blew my nose.

"Mrs. Wilder had to come pick me up from the hospital the next day. She said Tim had packed up his things and left that morning and asked her to bring me and TJ home. He never said where he was going or anything. I thought he might have gone to his uncle Rich's place, but the phone number there was disconnected and when I finally drove out there someone else was living in the trailer. They didn't know where Uncle Rich went, but they heard he got evicted for not paying his rent."

"What about Tijuana? Does he know about TJ?"

"He was long gone before I was even showing. Maybe he

heard that I was pregnant; I don't know. One payday he got his check and wandered into the desert, never to return. And that was fine with me." Actually, it was a great relief. He had been an unwelcome reminder of my shame every time our paths crossed.

"Sam." Lindsey hesitated. "You were very young when you left home. You made some mistakes. My biggest decisions back then were what outfit to wear with which shoes and fortunately, those weren't life-changing choices."

I was tired. We crawled under the yellow quilt and turned out the lamp. My sister prayed out loud, thanking God for the wonderful day we just had. When she got to the part about forgiving us for our sins she added, "And help Samantha forgive herself."

I didn't say a word.

"Good night, Sam."

"Good night."

IN MY DREAM I was back in my first apartment in Reno. The one I got soon after the Wilders informed me that they didn't need my help on the ranch anymore.

The baby was crying. I was busy getting ready to go to my senior prom. Someone was there with me, the girl who sat behind me in freshman English, who was suddenly like my best friend because there she was pinning up my hair and sewing a doily to my dress. We tried to ignore it, but the baby just cried louder and louder like it wanted something, but we didn't know what. Finally, I picked it up, blanket and all, and wandered around the apartment like I was looking for something.

My friend said to quit wasting time. Get back there so she could sew a hanky to my sleeve.

There was a garbage can just outside the back door. I put the baby on top of whatever was in there and put the lid on. The baby was fine now. It was real quiet.

Then I went to the prom. It wasn't really a prom. It was dinner at the Wilders' ranch. I just happened to be wearing a long blue dress with doilies all over it.

I was back in my apartment. Someone knocked, and when I opened the door, there was my father, smiling and carrying a big pink teddy bear with a bow. "Where is she?" he asked. Suddenly, I remembered the baby. I ran to the back door, but it was too late. The lid was on the ground and the garbage can was empty.

I awoke with a start, my eyes wide open in the dark. Lindsey's breathing was slow and steady. I tried to calm myself by concentrating on inhaling deeply, blowing out slowly. My heart squeezed painfully. At least I knew now that the pain in my chest was physical and not some heartache for which there was no cure.

The dream was not entirely new to me. It had come many times, in many versions. But this time was different. This time my father said her name. "Where's our little Annie?" he had asked.

Annie. The nice people with no faces vacuumed her out of me and then I got up and went away. Like nothing was changed. Like I had a bad toothache but now it was gone. I went to Reno with Tim and got married in front of a justice of the peace with a bouquet of marigolds from under the sign at the Mobile Haven trailer court and Uncle Rich as a witness, and then we went to the Pancake House for breakfast. I got a husband and a job and a little cabin with checkered curtains. Life was busy. Life was good. We never spoke of the abortion again. I never told Tim what I suspected—that the vacuum machine had gone too far. That part of my soul was gone and ir-replaceable, sucked out by a shapeless machine that I can't re-member because my eyes were closed. It left a void. An aching, echoing void that even Tim could not fill.

Lindsey didn't stir when I slid out of bed. I tiptoed down the dark hall to where TJ slept, his frog night-light illuminating his face in an eerie green. It was only a twin bed, but I crawled in and held his little hand on my face. He didn't know I was there, or that I was crying for our Annie and wishing she was with us.

11

THE MORNING'S SERIES of tests had left me tired. More mining for blood from my tiny, almost invisible veins. Another echocardiogram. That's where some guy I've never seen before runs an instrument around my upper body like a little boy with a toy car while we discuss last night's Mariners game—as though neither of us have noticed my bare breasts staring blindly at the wall.

I slipped into my jeans and tossed the faded blue hospital gown over a chair. Dr. Sovold's family, complete with a well-groomed collie dog, smiled at me from a gold-framed photo on his desk. The last time I was here, Dr. Sovold, my cardiologist, mentioned surgery. Open-heart surgery. I'd been having nightmares about them sawing through the bones in my chest and opening me like some gory book.

Derek Klett gave a report on that in tenth grade and showed a documentary movie of open-heart surgery being performed on a cow by a university medical research team. The boys in class loved it, especially the part where blood squirted all over one of the interns while he fumbled with a clamp. I felt sick. I stood to leave but made the mistake of looking back at the bigger-than-life cow with her guts exposed, her heart pumping madly—and then the cow turned her head and blinked. I dropped to my knees and tottered like an indecisive nine pin before toppling to the floor. Mrs. Phelps sent someone for the nurse and someone must have run to Lindsey's algebra class too, because when I came to, it was my sister who helped me back into my seat and wouldn't leave my side.

Finally, there was a light knock and Dr. Sovold entered. He was tall and had a turtle's neck with deep wrinkles that stretched like limp rubber bands when he lifted his chin. Long strands of hair were carefully plastered across his bald spot. They didn't move when he bent to adjust his swivel chair. He straightened and looked directly at me without even attempting a smile. "I've been reviewing your test results, Samantha." His eyes dropped to the papers in his hand.

"I want my mother," I said. "She's out in the waiting room."

"Yes. Good idea."

After Mom slipped into the chair next to mine with a reassuring smile, the doctor continued. "Well, Samantha, as you know, your heart is the most important muscle in your body. It pumps oxygen and nutrient-rich blood to every cell and organ. When you work or play hard, your body's need for oxygen increases and your heart pumps harder and faster. Your heart has been struggling just to keep you supplied with adequate oxygen while you're at rest." He pulled out a picture of my floppy heart and pointed out the deformities once again. As if the image was not already burned into my mind. "Unfortunately, I understand that your family has lost contact with your birth mother. Having access to her family history, as well as your natural father's, would have been helpful. Still, we are convinced that this damage was caused by a virus."

I had heard all this before. "Do I have to have surgery?"

He took a deep breath and nodded. My stomach rolled.

"Since reviewing your previous test results, I've consulted with the other cardiologists on staff here at the hospital as to whether your heart walls can be repaired surgically. The consensus at that time and again after seeing today's test results is that the damage is too widespread. In fact, there are signs of decreased pulmonary function since those first tests. We don't feel that this can be corrected surgically. What I would like to do, Samantha, is get you lined up for a heart transplant."

He paused to let that sink in. My mother gasped. I just stared at him.

"This is not something I recommend lightly. It is really our last resort. It can be a long, drawn-out process and will require a commitment from you, Samantha"—then he looked at Mom—"and your family and friends. You are going to need a strong network of support."

"What other options do I have?"

He shook his head. "None that I can see."

"So, what are you saying? If I don't get a heart transplant . . . I die?"

"Well . . . we can't really predict an exact timeline on these things." He leaned toward Mom. "What we do know is that current treatments available to us have not proven successful and the quality of life for someone—"

"Dr. Sovold," I interrupted. "Cut the canned doctor talk." I stood and found myself glaring down at the twelve hairs on top of his bald head. "And please, talk to me, not her."

"Samantha!" Mom was obviously mortified.

"If you don't get a hair transplant, Doctor, you'll still be here next year and the one after that, a little balder maybe, but you won't miss your son's graduation or your daughter's wedding because of it. I want to know the facts. I need to know. If I don't get this heart transplant, will I see my son enter first grade?"

Dr. Sovold paused. "No. No, Samantha, you probably won't."

I held my stomach as if I'd been punched. He sat me back down in the chair and placed his fingers gently on my wrist for a pulse. "Put your head between your knees if you need to." I did. He spoke, but I barely heard. I was glad my mother was there to process all the details, because I was watching movies in my mind. Past. Present. Future. TJ with infant colic. I couldn't assuage his pain. We walked the floor of that first apartment and cried our lonely hearts out. I saw TJ bounding through the tall grass, heard his musical laugh, pictured him standing confused and forlorn by my grave. I sat up straight and watched the doctor's lips move. Concentrate.

". . . and once you're registered with this network, you'll be placed on the waiting list for a donor organ. When a donor heart becomes available, the organ procurement organization enters all vital information in their computer. That information is used to match up a donated organ with a recipient. Now, it's not necessarily going to go to the person who has been waiting the longest." He passed me a stack of pamphlets and a reading list. "There are a number of determining factors, including blood type, body size, geography . . . and the severity of a potential recipient's condition. A seriously ill patient may be given priority for an organ at a nearby transplant center. On the other hand, if a patient becomes too ill to withstand major surgery, they could be ruled out. Now, I'm glad that Samantha has given me permission to speak freely. The truth is that the number of patients on the waiting list outweighs the number of acceptable donors. There are an estimated sixteen thousand people a year in the United States who could benefit from a heart transplant. Unfortunately, at this time only about twenty-three hundred operations actually occur annually."

The avalanche of information came too fast. I couldn't outrun it. There was no place to go.

I had always considered myself an athletic person. In Reno, I had a group of friends who hiked in the summer and cross-country skied the white terrain of Lake Tahoe in winter. I took pride in at least keeping up, if not leaving my buff guy friends in the dust, or the powder, as the case may be.

I was the one who had climbed a steep rock face in Red Rock Canyon without the aid of pitons and ropes, which was stupid because halfway up I got stuck. I still remember the warm metallic smell of the rock my nose was plastered to as my fingers desperately sought a crevice, my boot toe feeling for any protrusion, paralyzed with the horror that there was no way up and no way down. I don't know how long I clung there wishing for a rescue chopper, but the sun dropped behind the western ridge, and as the sky turned purple behind me and the cold seeped through my clothes like ice water, something kicked in. I thought of TJ, who was still in diapers at that time, and I made a decision to survive. I even prayed. "God, help me," I said. That's all I remember. I don't think God made a ladder in the stone. I think the rock face probably stayed the same. But I moved, inch by inch, until finally I stood victorious—queen of the mountain—gazing down on the moonlit valley below.

Of course, I never let on to my buddies, who revered me for my raw guts and courage, that I had almost died. The thing about amazing daredevil feats is that you're a hero only if you succeed. If I had splattered at their feet, they would be shaking their heads now, saying things like "What a waste. What a careless way to die. That Samantha never had a brain in her head."

Anyway, here I was again, with my nose to a rock, suspended in a cold, lonely place between life and death, with a decision to make.

"God, help me," I said.

12

It WAS NOT UNTIL late afternoon that Lindsey mentioned it. We had been together all morning, cutting and stringing garlands of construction-paper leaves to adorn the bulletin board and cafeteria at the Darlington Hospital, where she volunteered. Then, just as casually as if she were commenting on the hint of autumn in the air, she lit the fuse. The news traveled in a spray of sparks and exploded inside me. Paper leaves fell in a flurry to the kitchen floor.

"What? How do you know Tim is in town? Why are you just getting around to telling me this now?"

"Well . . . I didn't know if I should. I mean, I didn't know if you were up to hearing this right now. You shouldn't get upset or excited. . . ."

"This is what gets me upset!" I stood and my hand involuntarily reached for my chest. "You're treating me like . . ." I sat back down, trying to breathe normally without looking like I had to try. "Just don't treat me like that. I'm not that bad off."

"Okay. I'm sorry. I really am. I wanted to tell you; I ran into Tim's sister Sarah at the hospital. Their mom is in chemo. Breast cancer." Lindsey shook her head sympathetically. "Anyway, Sarah was there waiting for her mom. We were in line together in the cafeteria and she called out my name. I didn't recognize her at first. She's lost a lot of weight since high school. So we got our coffee and sat at one of the tables until her mom came back down."

"What did you say? Did you say anything about me?"

"I said you were home."

"What else?"

Lindsey fidgeted with the scissors. "I told her about TJ. I hope that was okay."

I nodded. Surely Tim's family must know the suitable-for-soap-opera account of TJ's birth. The grandson/nephew they almost had.

"Sarah's getting married. I guess Tim has been living in Oregon, driving a log truck. He's here for her wedding and he might stay on for a while if he can get a job up here. He wants to be there for his mom, you know. Since their dad died, he's the only man in the family."

Tim's father had taken two years to die. All through Tim's sophomore and junior years in high school, his dad suffered from some rare liver disease. It broke Tim's heart. He wept openly in front of me once, an incident that endeared him to me immediately. I watched manhood overtake him while other guys in his class still begged for the car keys so they could hang out at the Mill Road Cemetery, drinking beer until they puked. Tim worked as a mechanic at the garage next to the Shell station in town. He drove his younger sisters to piano lessons. He repaired the roof, changed the oil in his mother's car and, finally, bore a corner of a sleek mahogany casket and laid his father in the ground.

Tim said I was the light at the end of his tunnel. I made him laugh. Sometimes he complained that I was unpredictable. He said I flirted with danger and that I shouldn't be so quick to make decisions, but he didn't try to change me. "At least we'll never be like that old couple that eats breakfast every Tuesday at the Halfway Café," he quipped. They always ate their oatmeal and raisins in silence as if there was nothing left to say. "We'll never be bored."

Lindsey was not volunteering much information. "Come on," I said. "There's more, isn't there?"

She punched holes in a stack of orange and yellow leaves and began threading yarn through. "Well, she invited me to her wedding."

I pondered for a moment. "Is Tim in it?"

She glanced up from her work. "Yes. He's one of the groomsmen."

"So. Are you going?"

She shook her head. "I don't really know them very well. I know you and Tim have a history, but I only knew Sarah from PE class. As I recall, when she was choosing players for the basketball team, she picked me last."

"Don't take it personally. She probably thought you throw like a girl. Which you do. And then you make that noise."

She raised an eyebrow and didn't smile. "What noise?"

"You know. That *oh, I-hope-I-don't-break-a-fingernail* helpless squeak."

"Oh, hush!"

"I'll go with you."

"What?"

"To the wedding."

"Oh, no, Sam. I don't think—"

"You got an invitation, didn't you? Did it by any chance say 'To Lindsey Matthews and Guest'?"

"Yes, but . . ." She studied me for a moment. "If you want to see Tim, why don't you call his mom's house? He's probably staying there. At least she would know how to get in touch with him. You two need to get together and talk. I just don't think the wedding is going to be the right atmosphere."

I got up and poured a cup of coffee while I considered what she said. "Maybe I don't want to talk to him. I just want to see him from afar. Maybe he's bald now and missing teeth. What if he lost both his arms in a logging accident or something?"

Lindsey gave me that long motherly look, and when she spoke her voice was soft. "I think it wouldn't make any difference to you. I think you still love him."

I swirled the coffee around in my mug, watching my distorted image spin. I would love him until the day I died, arms or no arms. But the truth was that if he wanted to, he could have found me. I had left a trail more obvious than a slug's. For five years I had looked behind me, hoping. I thought I glimpsed him driving by, or sitting in the shadows at the Starlight Room where I waited tables, or with his back to me slipping through a crowd. But it was never him. He was in my head when I brushed my teeth, when I made up the bed, when I poured myself a glass of wine at night. I had needed him when TJ fell on his Tonka dump truck and ran to me peering through streams of blood. I had wished for a daddy for TJ when I worked nights and my roommate with the big hair whom I didn't really like was the one tucking my son into bed. I guess I had always thought Tim would eventually show up at my door. He would forgive me and slide back in and embrace TJ as his own. It was a comforting delusion.

"I don't know him anymore, and he doesn't know me," I

said. I pushed my chair from the table and began cleaning up our paper debris.

Car doors slammed and a minute later Mom backed through the kitchen door with an armload of packages. TJ burst in behind her. "But why, Grandma?"

"Because it will spoil your dinner. We'll have our treats after we eat our pork roast and Brussels sprouts."

I pulled TJ into my arms protectively. "Ooh. Not Brussels sprouts. Is your mean grandma making you eat Brussels sprouts? What did you do? Shoplift or something?"

"I didn't do anything bad."

Lindsey reached for him. "Give Auntie some sugar." He obliged her with a kiss, but his mind was obviously on other things. He pushed away as politely as he knew how.

"Me and Grandma went to story time. I got some books. You wanna see?" He spread his colorful library books on the table. "I got a new one about George the monkey." He reached for another, almost toppling Lindsey's coffee. "Look, Mom!" He giggled, pointing with a pudgy finger. "This bug has a light-bulb in his bottom!"

I pushed the mug to safety in the nick of time. "Gus the Firefly. We had that when we were kids, remember, Lindsey?" I flipped through the familiar pages. "Do you think the library has ever considered buying something published in this millennium?"

"We're talking Darlington here," Lindsey said. "I'm not sure anyone knows the old one passed."

"Mom, can you take me to see Mikey?"

I knew TJ was referring to the new Appaloosa foal at the Duncans' place, which he had named after the buddy he left behind in our Reno apartment. Donnie had charged down the driveway a few weeks prior, spraying gravel behind his tires and rounding us both into the cab of his truck. We sped back to the ranch in time to witness the uncomplicated birth. Donnie had stroked the mare's quivering white neck, both of them sweating in the late August heat, while she seemed to be seriously regretting her fling with a certain stallion. I had seen the foaling process before, but that time was different. I held TJ where we sat against a stall wall in a pile of fresh hay, more moved by the wonderment passing across my son's sweet face than the miracle that the poor mare could survive passing the gangly colt from her body. I couldn't help but think it was like giving birth to a long-legged teenager, skateboard and all.

"Not today, baby. Mommy's going to take a nap."

TJ wilted dramatically, like a cartoon flower deprived of water. "You always take naps," he whined. Suddenly, he sprang back to life, his eyes bright. "Donnie could come get me."

I ran my fingertips through his dark hair, letting them linger at his temple. TJ adored Donnie. Maybe too much. "No. It will be dinnertime soon. You want to be here when your grandpa comes home, don't you? Take your books to your room and pick out one to read at bedtime, okay?" He finally obliged.

Lindsey packed up her project. "I suppose I should get home before David and do the Suzy Homemaker thing. Mom, do you have anything in those grocery sacks that you can dump out of a bag and make it look like you've been cooking all day?"

I helped carry my sister's things to her car. She patted my face before slipping onto the leather seat. "Get some rest." I didn't argue.

She had backed her SUV partway down the drive when she rolled her window down and called to me. "Hey, Sammy!"

I stopped and looked back.

"About that wedding. Let's do it! It might be fun!"

LINDSEY'S HOUSE was like her. Elegant. Tasteful. Perfect. It could have been on a postcard, the way it stood up there on a knoll with the manicured lawn, a huge maple hovering protectively over it. With some financial help from David's parents, they had purchased the five-acre parcel just outside of Darlington—about a fifteen-minute drive from the Judge and Mom's place on the river—and had built the home that some people in their forties were still just dreaming of. The general contractor told them the maple tree would have to come out—they couldn't possibly maneuver heavy equipment around it—but Lindsey had insisted it stay. The tree spread its arms victoriously into the sky, rewarding them with shade in the summer and piles of brown leaves to rake and burn in the fall. White columns stood as sentinels on the wide porch. I liked to lean on them and watch the horses beyond the fence in the neighbor's field.

"Samantha, are you coming?" I followed my sister through the living room and into the master suite and sprawled across the bed. Something like gauze was draped from corner to corner over the framework of the four posters. A bronze cherub dangled its chubby legs over the edge of an ornately carved table, sweetly tending the entrance to the bathroom. The walls were papered in a fancy print that was either flowers or lions, depending on how you squinted your eyes. An awful lot of fufu if you asked me.

Wedding photos lined the top of the cherry dresser. David and Lindsey looked like magazine people, as did the setting,

stemmed glasses. The late afternoon sun streamed through the window and the cider seemed to glow. He held his glass up to ours. "To two gorgeous ladies. I'm crazy for letting you out of my sight."

We clicked glasses. The last time I was there David offered me a soda, but I had had to get it out of the fridge myself.

"Honey, you know you can come with us," Lindsey said.

He scoffed. "If there's one thing more boring than a wedding, it's one where you don't know anybody." He leaned against the counter and watched me like I was a big-screen TV. "Sam, you look great. I had no idea. . . ."

I looked down at myself. "Yeah. I clean up pretty good, don't I?" Lindsey stood back and smiled like she was da Vinci and I was the *Mona Lisa*.

Suddenly her brows drew together. "Sam, you look a little pale. Are you sure you want to do this? We'll be out late."

"It won't hurt me. And stop mothering me. Just for tonight, okay?"

It seemed like a good idea to rest for a while. I settled into a big leather chair. Outside the window, the vine maples were already turning orange, yellow and red. Lindsey and David crammed themselves into one corner of the long burgundy leather sofa. His arm rested around her shoulders as they talked, and I remembered the comfort, the sheer joy, of being with the one person in the world who could make me feel complete. I was happy for my sister. David was boringly predictable, but he was a good guy. Lindsey deserved a good man.

I stared at the TV, trying to quiet the voice that kept saying, *This is a bad idea; call the whole thing off.* My skirt was too tight. It was a good thing, though, because I didn't have to remember to keep my legs together. Crossing them took extreme skill. I practiced crossing and uncrossing and pointing my toes. What would Tim do when he saw me? What would I do? What would I say? I sipped from my glass casually while football players scrambled across the screen, piling up into tangles of butts and elbows.

My insides were on their third down with nine yards to go.

13

THE PORT SUSAN Country Club parking lot was full. I was surprised at the number of motorcycles lined up against the front of the building—almost exclusively Harley-Davidsons. We parked along the street and I tried to walk the curb like it was a balance beam. Not a good idea in those shoes. I slipped but Lindsey caught my arm. She carried our gift, a pretty pewter platter, which we had tried to say ten times fast on the long drive from the country. I had coached her on what to say and what not to say. Bottom line, under no circumstances was anyone to know I was sick. I held my head high, took a long slow breath and walked in the door like the queen of the country club. The tapered skirt and pointy heels forced me to take dainty little steps, and I suddenly felt embarrassed, as in a dream when you find yourself walking down the hall at school in your pajamas or, worse yet, naked as a newborn hamster. Only in this case I felt overdressed. Out of character. Like when Donnie caught me playing dress-up with my sister when we were twelve. Here I was again, upswept hair, jewelry, lipstick and all. I hoped I got the lipstick inside the lines this time.

A few minglers chatted in the lobby. For the millionth time I thought I saw the back of Tim. He stood like a Marine, dressed in a black tuxedo with his arm on the bare back of a woman in a long blue dress. Only this time it really was him! My heart squished violently and all my blood seemed to drain into a vacuum like the black hole. Lindsey saw him too. We watched him take the woman's arm and guide her through the doors at the far end of the lobby. Lindsey got me to the double doors nearest us, where an usher smiled, placed my arm on his and led us to the second row from the back on the right-hand side. I fought for control. Something told me this was not a good time to stick my head between my knees.

When I dared look toward the left side of the auditorium, I saw him again. This time he showed an elderly couple to their seat. I chided myself for embracing my first impression. Of course, stupid. He's an usher. That's what groomsmen do.

I felt safely disguised and hidden among what I assumed to be the groom's friends and family, as I didn't recognize a single one. All the bikers were on our side. They stood out from the traditionally dressed wedding-goers because of the leather vests and jackets with bold Harley-Davidson logos on the backs. The man in front of me stood to wave someone over. He wore a crisp blue cotton shirt under his Harley vest. His salt-and-pepper gray hair hung in a neat braid down his back, and his thirty-eight-inch-waist blue jeans with a thirty-two-inch inseam were stiff and new. I knew that because he had forgotten to take the size sticker off the back of his thigh. He sat down, fidgeting and wiping his brow, probably dreaming of the moment he could tie a red bandana on his head and ride away from there on the night wind.

Tim went away and I didn't see him again until a girl with a guitar started singing and he appeared at the front with two other tuxedoed men whom I didn't recognize. He whispered

something to the guy next to him. They grinned and then simultaneously lifted their chins, standing tall like two boys trying to be good in church. His hair was shorter and a little
darker. Of course, he would have had it cut before the wedding
and his summer-blond locks had fallen to the barber's floor. I
couldn't tell if it was just the tuxedo, or if he had filled out
some. Anyway, he looked better than ever. Lindsey thought so
too. I could feel her watching me. Probably hoping it wasn't a
huge mistake bringing me there. I smiled and nodded reassuringly. Everything is fine. I'm not going to cry or faint or throw
up or anything. See? I smoothed my skirt and let my eyes wander to the bride's side of the room. I recognized Tim's mother,
Lila, and their aunt Lacey. Tim's mom was a nice lady. I was
glad the chemotherapy had not made her hair fall out. At least
not yet. She had cut figures of Santa and his reindeer out of plywood to decorate their front lawn and I had helped her paint
them one November day seven years ago out in their garage. I
was just Tim's little girlfriend then. We didn't know that I was
pregnant, or that my father would find out, or that within
weeks we would be fleeing to Reno in Tim's red Chevy pickup.
I didn't know then that my childhood was officially over.

I regretted that Mrs. Weatherbee and I had never had much
chance to bond. Maybe there was still a chance. I would be
proud to be introduced as her daughter-in-law. Would she even
recognize me after all these years? I wondered how Tim had explained my disappearance from his life. Would I get a chance to
talk to him? Could he forgive me for what I did to him?

The couple sitting on the opposite side of the aisle from Mrs.
Weatherbee must have been the groom's parents. She was a
large woman with long blond hair, wearing a peasant-style
skirt and blouse. The man's tux was a poor disguise. I figured

him to be the king of the bikers. He had a face as pocked as the grille of a semitruck after a cross-country run, like he had weathered some long hard rides. His hair was long and his mustache hung Yosemite Sam–style below his chin.

The music changed and the young groom showed up at the front, along with his best man. From the safe camouflage of the crowd, my eyes fixed on Tim, even as the bridesmaids stepped their way down the carpeted aisle. They all wore the same powder-blue dress, tightly fitted at the bodice and spraying out from the waist like upside-down sprinklers. The last one to park her fluffy little tail on the platform steps cast a flirtatious glance directly at Tim. She looked like Glinda, the Good Witch of the North. He returned her smile, and for the rest of the ceremony I summoned any telepathic powers I might have, hoping to knock her flat on her rosy face.

Lindsey was right. Sarah had lost her baby fat. We all stood when she strolled down the pathway to marital bliss, all of us probably wondering the same thing. Will this one last? She shone with joy; you could see it even through her veil. Her husband-to-be looked at her the way Tim used to look at me. When the pastor said the part about "as long as you both shall live," their eyes locked on each other and they spoke their vows with the same confidence TJ had when he assured me that he would never grow up and leave me.

The reception was held upstairs in a huge hall with a fireplace and a balcony overlooking Port Susan Bay. The back rows in the chapel were the last to file out and make their way upstairs, so by the time Lindsey and I arrived, the room buzzed with activity. Along one wall the wedding party had lined up to greet the long chain of guests waiting to express their congratulations. We skipped the lineup and found seats at a round table scattered with blue glitter stars, an arrangement of white candles flickering in its center. I purposely sat with my back to the reception line. Lindsey knew quite a few people, both from high school and just from living and volunteering in the area for so long. They stopped by to greet her, and when she introduced me some seemed surprised that she had a sister. I could see their eyes going back and forth, trying to find some resemblance. Her hair was blond and sleek; mine thick and dark. When they asked which one was older, we just said I was and left it at that. There was one guy who knew me from Darlington High, but I couldn't remember him. He said he had to look back at me several times before he could be sure it was really Samantha Dodd. "You were such a tomboy. Who would have thought you'd turn out so . . . well, you look just great!" He practically drooled on me until I mentioned that my husband was there somewhere. Then he cooled off and headed for the prawns and prime rib.

When we were somewhat alone, Lindsey leaned toward me and whispered, "So, what's the plan? Are you ever going to go talk to him?"

"What's he doing now?"

She glanced casually in his direction. "The line is broken up. Some people are talking to him. Uh-oh. Some girl is dragging him to the dance floor."

I stole a look. "It's Glinda, Good Witch of the North."

Lindsey giggled. "You're right! She looks just like her. All she needs is a magic wand."

"And some ruby slippers." I refused to ogle. "Is he liking it?"

She observed for a while. "I don't know. He's looking around a lot."

"Maybe someone told him I'm here."

"Probably."

"Would you get me a glass of champagne? Please?"

"No. You don't drink alcohol anymore, remember? Why don't you go get yourself some punch?"

"Because I don't want to walk by the dance floor. Not yet. Can you get me some punch?"

She decided to oblige me. She left the table, and I gathered up handfuls of glitter stars just to pass the time and dumped them into the contents of her purse. I knew she would find them stuck to things for months. After a few songs, the best man took the microphone from the band and summoned all the single ladies up front. The bride was about to throw her bouquet. What was taking Lindsey so long? I finally spied her off in a corner laughing with a bunch of friends, two forgotten and empty glasses resting in her hands.

I scanned the room. Tim was nowhere to be seen. With the current distraction on the dance floor, I decided this was as good a time as any to nose out of the harbor. I held in my stomach (although Lindsey's boa constrictor of a skirt did the job quite well), stuck out my chest and meandered my way around tables until I reached the beverage bar. A black-vested waiter made small talk as he poured the bubbly pink liquid. I was nice and got a glass for Lindsey too.

A crowd had gathered to watch the bouquet toss, blocking the way to my seat. I detoured across a corner of the dance floor. Suddenly, my right heel caught the strap of my left shoe. I felt myself lurch forward. In a split second of horror the glasses shot from my hands. I dove, half running toward the bevy of wanna-be brides. The bouquet slapped me in the chest and I was down! Flat on my face. Derriere in the air. Skirt split from north to south like a dinner bun.

When I lifted my head, I saw shoes. Lots of pointy shoes pointing right at me. Someone had the decency to throw a jacket over my exposed behind. The crowd was impressed. They whistled and cheered. "Nice catch!" "Hey, we need her on our team!" More laughter and applause. A biker helped me to my feet and perfect strangers patted my back and called me things like "Tiger" and "Champ."

I was too stunned to speak. My heart flapped like a bird against a window. Lindsey hadn't even noticed. She was still in the far corner chattering with her friends. A couple of caterers mopped up the dance floor and the band began to play. The biker still supported my arm. He had a tattoo of Jesus on his biceps and underneath it were the words "Forgiven and Free." He asked if I was okay. "I just need some air," I said, tying the jacket around my waist. "Thank you." I headed for the balcony door, almost running into Glinda. She tossed her frizzy blond hair over her shoulder and sneered.

"Well, I guess you wanted it worse than I did." She looked down at the mangled bunch of roses and gardenias that I was surprised to see still in my hand.

"Oh, go to Kansas." I pushed her aside and stepped out into the salty air.

Invisible seabirds called intermittently from the water below, occasionally flapping their wings and scooting across its black surface. A spotlight mounted under a corner eave of the country club's roof was the only moon reflected on the rippled bay. I slouched in a wooden deck chair with my shoeless feet propped up on the rail, trying to calm my breathing. With a shiver I pulled the tuxedo jacket up over my shoulders. It smelled of men's cologne.

My heart hurt. I wanted Lindsey to come find me. I wanted

to go home. The band played rock songs from another decade and even through the closed doors I heard the happy voices of wedding guests. I wondered if they were still talking about the crazy woman who tackled the bouquet. I was crazy. No doubt about it. Why did I come? What in God's green acres was I thinking? My life was a series of blunders as long as a freight train passing noisily before my eyes. One mistake after another after another. At the time I had not discerned whether I was the engineer or the one standing passively on the back porch of the caboose.

A door opened. I slid lower in the big deck chair and feigned an intense interest in something off to my right. A breeze brought a whiff of seaweed and other residue discarded by high tide. Someone wandered out. I could feel the person standing near me, probably looking out over the rail.

"I thought you hated weddings."

My head snapped in the direction of the voice.

"You always said they were boring." Tim's arms rested casually on the railing. He glanced over his right shoulder. "This one was until a little while ago." He was almost close enough to reach out and touch.

I swore under my breath. He saw me! He must have seen the whole humiliating thing. "Somebody had to liven things up. I did what I could."

His eyes still crinkled at the corners when he almost smiled. His shirtsleeves were rolled up and part of his bow tie peeked from his trouser pocket. "What's new, Sam?"

I sat up and breathed deeply to still the trembling. "What's new since when? Since last time I saw you?"

He shrugged and squinted out over the bay. I wished I hadn't said that. The last time I saw Tim, he was standing in the doorway of my hospital room, his eyes burning with pain and anger, and then the fire went cold. I held another man's son in my arms and watched my destiny walk away. He still had his back to me. After all the conversations I had imagined over the past five years, not one remnant came to mind. I stood and leaned on the rail within five feet of him. "I'm staying at my parents' place for a while. TJ and I. That's my son. He's five now." His lack of response made me nervous. "Sarah looks happy. Where did she meet this guy?"

Tim pulled a shelled peanut from his pocket and pitched it. There was a faint plop about ten feet offshore, which caused the invisible seabirds to complain and scatter. "At her church. It's kind of a biker church. The pastor is an ex-Bandido, born-again comedian. Ross is the PK."

"The what?"

"Preacher's kid. Pretty cool guy. He plays the drums on Sunday mornings. Sarah plays bass guitar."

"Oh." There was a long awkward pause. "My sister said you've been in Oregon."

He nodded. "I have a place at Grants Pass. Just a cabin, really. But I've got it fixed up the way I like it, and it has a big shop. I drove a log truck for the past few years. Also did a stint as a river guide on the Deschutes."

"Really? That sounds fun."

"It was. Never a dull day. The scenery was beautiful, always changing. I saw deer and bear and other wildlife all the time." He got quiet on me and flicked at some peeling paint on the rail. "Yeah, it was lots of fun—until a lady popped out of my raft in white water and we found her body three hours later wrapped around a submerged tree. The river never looked the same to me after that." He turned to glare at me. "Funny how one little incident can change your whole perspective on things."

I returned his gaze. "Tim. I've wanted to tell you . . . I know I screwed up big time, and I want you to know I'm sorry. I never meant to——"

With a scowl he hurled another peanut over the rail. "Save it, Sam. I don't want to hear it."

"You've got to hear it! Just let me get it off my chest, okay?" I took advantage of his silence. "I've waited more than five years for a chance to explain. I should have told you what happened with Tijuana." His jaw clenched. "It happened one time. *One time.* You've got to believe that. And I regretted it from that moment on. I thought the baby was yours. In fact, I still think of him as yours. I always have."

"Well, you have twisted thinking. You always have."

A door opened and the band grew instantly louder. Glinda, of all people, stepped out. "Oh, there you are." She smiled sweetly, swished her powder-blue taffeta fanny up to the rail next to Tim and took his arm possessively. "I thought you went out to hang cans off the car." She pretended to just notice me. "Oh, hello."

"Luanne, this is Samantha." Tim was at least civil.

She held out her hand. "Nice to meet you. Samantha . . . ?"

"Weatherbee."

She seemed relieved. "Weatherbee! Oh, you're related! And where are you from, Samantha?"

"Nevada."

"Oh, you came a long way! That was quite a catch you made in there. You didn't get hurt, did you?"

Her game was getting old. "I twisted my ankle, bruised both knees and scraped my wrist." I held up the mutilated bouquet triumphantly and a clump of rosebuds fell out. "But it was worth it. I really needed one of these."

She must have detected some cynicism in my voice. Her lips spread into one of those straight smiles you give someone just before you insult them. "Looks like your skirt was too tight, too."

"Not anymore." I bent over and flashed my leopard panties her way. "See?" I straightened and smiled a smile just as syrupy as hers.

She gasped and cast a horrified look toward Tim. I wasn't sure, but I thought I detected an amused smirk on his face before he turned away.

"See ya later, Sam."

She escorted him back to the door and then stopped. "Isn't that your tux jacket, Tim?"

"Oh, yeah." His eyes met mine. "That's okay. Just leave it on a chair or something when you go."

14 ✐

ALL THAT NEXT WEEK the clouds hung low. Raindrops
fell consistently by my window like someone had turned
the sprinkler on and left for vacation. Except for Wednesday.
Then the rain shot straight down as if God had His thumb on
the hose.

The rain suited my mood.

I had made a fool of myself in front of Tim, not to mention
his mother and everyone else close to him. Oh, the things they
must be saying about me—Tim's estranged wife, making her
first appearance in over seven years! It occurred to me that my
dramatic dive into the bevy of bouquet-grabbing bachelorettes
had been captured on video camera. I imagined the delighted
guffaws and squeals of laughter that my performance would
bring to the Weatherbee family and friends for years to come as
they played the scene forward and back in slow motion and
possibly freeze-frame at the moment my body and the coveted
bouquet made contact with the hardwood floor. Hopefully
there was not a close-up of the gaping split in Lindsey's tight
black skirt.

But I had seen Tim. Face-to-face. He was no longer the elu-
sive ghost I had glimpsed in every crowd. He was real, and he

was right here in Darlington, only fifteen minutes up the road. There was a glimmer of hope now. If only he could forgive me. If he could love me again, surely I could learn to love myself. The gnawing void inside me would be filled. Then, of course, my only little challenge would be to survive my physical heart condition.

I awoke from a nap to find the house quiet except for subdued male voices behind the door of my father's study. I was happy to see Matt's car in the driveway. He hadn't been up to the river for over a month.

Matt had always been an uncle to me, though we weren't related in any way. The thing I liked best about him was that he seemed to favor me over Lindsey, which was rare. Matt never expected me to make empty small talk. We used to sit on the porch and whittle (he brought me a pocketknife with three blades and an ivory handle) with long minutes going by without one of us saying a word. He's the one I confided in after I found out I was unnecessarily adopted. I told him that by the time my parents found out they didn't need me, it was too late. They already had me and then along came Lindsey. Their own flesh and blood and cute as a blue-eyed kitten. Matt used to laugh at me a lot, but it was not a mean laugh. He told me I was special in my own way, which I didn't take as a compliment at first because I thought he meant special like the retarded class at school. After a while, though, I understood what he meant.

I thought I heard Matt and the Judge arguing. That was unusual. I rose from my bed and listened from my bedroom door. Their voices hushed and were drowned by the sounds of rain pelting the roof and windows.

Mom and TJ must have gone to do some shopping. I walked

barefoot to the kitchen and opened a can of tomato soup. As I stood by the stove, stirring, watching the walls of water beyond each window, I had the sensation of being trapped in a submarine, pressed below the surface by a fleet of enemy warships. Claustrophobic. My Jeep hadn't been out of the garage for weeks. Everyone else came and went while I sat here like part of the furniture, hoping for the phone to ring. Waiting for someone to die. Waiting to live.

Somewhere, some healthy person was going about her day without giving a thought to the fact that she marked the *yes* box on her driver's license application where it asks if you want to be an organ donor. I pictured a woman about my age jumping in her car just to run to the store. Maybe for something she doesn't really need, like the Sunday paper or a double tall latte. Something she could have lived without.

What if her husband is still sleeping, so she doesn't bother to say good-bye? What if they argued last night and now she regrets everything she said? She will bring him the paper and a latte of his own and they will sit on the couch with their toes touching and then she plans to tell him she is sorry. Then she will tell him that he is the earth beneath her and the stars above and everything in between. And then, just as the light turns green and she starts across the intersection, a truck hurtles itself out of nowhere. There is no time to react. Crash! The horrible sound of crumpling metal and shattered glass. Silence. And she doesn't even know what happens after that. She never knows another thing, because just that fast she is gone. She is pronounced dead at the scene—or at least brain-dead.

Then what? Does a police officer go through her wallet to see if she marked that little box? Maybe the attending medic does that. Next thing you know the doctors are waking up her husband. He rubs his eyes and reaches across her pillow for the phone. "Hello, Mr. Sims? Your wife is dead, and we were just wondering, is it okay if we cut out her heart and lungs and kidneys before you put her in the ground?"

I shuddered. Somebody was going to die. There would be pain and grief and it would ripple outward in ever-increasing circles. Would the death be mine? I thought of TJ and my family and my heart seemed to droop lower in my chest. Any way you looked at it, it was not a happy thought.

The voices from the study grew louder. I edged closer to the kitchen door to listen. Matt and my father were the best of friends. I had never heard them argue, not even about politics. Now I heard only a hushed murmur. My curiosity drew me toward the study door. Matt's voice elevated again, both in volume and pitch. "Because it's asinine, that's why! Not to mention illegal. You could never pull it off. And even if you could, there are no guarantees that all the pieces would line up. You're a judge, for God's sake! Judge yourself!"

My soup began boiling loudly in the kitchen but I couldn't move. There was a long silence. My father—a criminal? I couldn't comprehend it. Why did Matt come all the way up here in the middle of the week? What kind of trouble could my father possibly be in? I remembered the strange phone call— the one he answered with bloody hands. He had snatched the receiver from me so suddenly, as if he knew who it was. As if he had something to hide. By now my ear was plastered to the study door. "Matt, I'm sorry to put you in this position, but I need your help. Believe me, if there was any other way—"

"There *is* another way! Don't you get it?"

"I've got to have a plan B. Just think about it. Please. That's all I ask."

A chair screeched against the floor. I scurried quietly back to the kitchen, working to steady my breath. The study door opened and then slammed. Matt stormed into the kitchen and stopped short upon seeing me standing there by the stove. "Sammy! Where did you come from?"

"Hi, Matthew." I yawned. "I was just taking a nap. Do you want some soup?"

He glanced into the boiling pot. Black stuff came to the surface as I stirred, but I don't think he even saw it. He shook his head and walked by me like someone who just found out his best friend wasn't who he thought he was. He grabbed his hooded raincoat from the back of a kitchen chair, stomped out the back door and headed for the river. The rain distorted his image as he disappeared among the trees.

15

TJ SAT BETWEEN DONNIE and me on the seat of Donnie's truck, straining at his seat belt to see out the side windows. Our valley in October was paradise, with maples fluttering in shades of red, orange and yellow against a backdrop of cool evergreens. The cottonwoods turned to shimmering gold. I was as happy as TJ to be getting out on such a beautiful afternoon.

Donnie wore faded jeans and a gray sweatshirt with cutoff sleeves. His burly arms were no longer as brown as they had been during summer, his short hair blondest on the ends from the sun. He whistled "Zip-A-Dee-Doo-Dah" as he drove.

TJ's lips puckered too, but no sound came out. "How do you do that?"

"What? Whistle? It's easy." Donnie demonstrated, but TJ could only blow air.

"Make a tiny hole for the air to get out. Purse your lips so tight all you could get in there is a blade of grass." TJ tried again unsuccessfully. Donnie reached his right arm around my son and patted his chest. "You're blowing too hard. Don't let the air come from here. Take a deep breath and let it out real easy, just like you're breathing." He was managing to do all this while steering with his left hand and keeping his eyes on the road. "Nope. I could feel that coming from your stomach. I shouldn't be able to feel any movement down here." This went on for several miles until we finally heard a peep as small as a baby bird's.

TJ's eyes widened and he peeped again. Peep. Peep. Peeeeeep. And then he was off, whistling like a teakettle.

Of course I later regretted this new talent, but at the time I was so proud. Not just of TJ for persevering, but of Donnie. He was patient with my son. I found myself gazing at him in awe sometimes and not just because he was a handsome man to behold. There was a strength about him. I don't mean the fact that he could probably snap a broom handle in two like it was kindling; it was more than that. He had this quiet confidence, like he knew exactly who he was and he was okay with that. In fact, I think he rather liked himself. I knew Donnie was not living his dream. His dream had been to become a trial attorney. A successful lawyer in a big city. But a careless toss of a pitchfork had changed all that. And yet he was not a bitter man; I never heard him complain.

A woman could get real comfortable with having a man like Donnie around. Don't think I never thought about that, because I did. Sometimes when I saw his truck coming down the drive for an unexpected visit, my heart felt like it just went over a bump. And when he got too close to me, a powerful force field drew me to him. I found myself wanting to touch. Wanting to explore the skin beneath his shirt. But I had gotten myself into trouble that way before.

I had a husband to think about. For five years I had regretted the mistake I made with the wrong man on the right night. I was fertile the night I stumbled upon Tijuana in that dry gulch outside of Reno. I should have been with Tim. Tim should have been TJ's daddy. And now he was so close. At least I knew within a few miles where he was, for the first time in years. I still hoped for the chance to make things right with him somehow.

"Hey!" TJ pointed excitedly. "Punkins!" Sure enough, the field on our left was strewn with row after row of bright orange orbs.

Donnie took a quick glance at his watch and turned on his left-turn signal. "We'd better get some."

"Woo-hoo!" I exclaimed. "Pumpkins!"

Donnie pulled into the lot where a weathered wood produce stand sported a big sign that said PUMPKINS 9¢ LB. As soon as I unbuckled TJ he was out the door and running directly toward the pumpkin field. I glanced up at Donnie. "We're not going to be late for your football game, are we?"

Donnie shook his head. "Not if we eat our picnic in the car."

I smiled at him. "Thanks for being spontaneous."

He just winked. "Come on. This is a big decision. I don't want any pumpkin with a flat side." The ground of the parking lot was covered with straw, but when we hit the rich damp soil, our feet began to sink.

"Wait up, TJ!" He obviously couldn't care less about the earth being scooped into his shoes with every step.

"Look at this one, Mom! I like this one."

"Ooh, that's nice. Nice and round."

Donnie shouted from about five rows over. "I've got the granddaddy of all pumpkins here! The pumpkin king!"

We ended up with three—"a daddy punkin, a mommy punkin and a baby punkin," as TJ put it—rolling around in the bed of the truck. We brought the picnic basket into the cab, where I distributed sandwiches as Donnie drove. Since both his hands were occupied, I popped grapes into his mouth on command.

The truck turned down a dirt lane between two cornfields. Donnie drove slowly to keep the dust to a low cloud. The locals had always called the riverside park Stilly Field, though there were no identifying signs. You just had to know it was tucked back there—a dirt parking lot, public access to the river via a broad spit covered in smooth rocks and a sports field. As the parking lot came into view, TJ exclaimed, "Wow, look at all the motorcycles!"

There were as many Harleys as cars and trucks combined. I looked at Donnie. "Who did you say is playing who?"

"I don't think I did. Van's Tavern against the Set Free Church. They're bikers mostly. I mean the church team. I'm on the tavern team, sort of. Actually, a temporary recruit. These guys ended the baseball season with a tie game. This is kind of an unofficial tiebreaker, only it's flag football instead of baseball."

"Oh." I knew they were the same crowd as the guests at Sarah's wedding. How many biker churches could there be?

"It's kind of a long walk over to the field," Donnie said. "Want a piggyback ride?" Since hearing about the severity of my heart condition, Donnie had never fussed over me. In fact, he rarely mentioned it. It wasn't that he didn't care. I was sure that he did. So I figured he was either in denial or simply confident that everything was going to turn out fine. Either way, it worked for me. Sometimes when I was with him, I almost forgot that I might not live to see TJ wobble down the road on a two-wheel bike.

"No. I'm fine. You go on ahead; it's time for the game to

start. I'll just take my time. TJ, you wait for me at the bleachers, okay?"

He skipped off with Donnie as I pulled out a bottle of water and locked the truck. I knew it was silly to get an adrenaline rush just because some people who were connected with Tim's sister happened to be there at the same time as me. I sauntered toward the field, a skill I had mastered, gazing around at the trees and sky as if I was just in a daydream. Yes, I told myself, to look at me one would think I was as healthy as anyone, just a bit distracted—or at the worst, lazy. I joined TJ at the weathered wood bleachers that were scattered with onlookers but definitely not crowded like they would be at an official game. I quickly scanned the crowd, not immediately recognizing anyone. We sat on the bottom row with our feet on the ground. I should say, *I* sat. TJ came and went, climbing the bleachers and exploring the area beneath them.

The players organizing themselves on the worn grassy field were in high spirits. They threw insults and grabbed and punched at one another, a strange barbaric form of communication common among the males of Stilly Valley. I knew the faces of some players from both teams, either from high school or due to small-town crossing of paths. I even saw my husky biker friend with the Jesus tattoo—the one who helped me back to my feet at the wedding. Sarah and her new husband were not there. Neither was Tim. But why should he be?

The tavern team stripped off their shirts and players began to line up for the kickoff. Donnie spat and bent forward at the waist, his hands on his thighs. His broad shoulders and back glowed in the afternoon sun. Once again I felt the pull. I knew that stance. I knew the way he stretched his neck this way and that and the intense squint of his eyes as he mentally prepared for battle. I was probably the only one there who knew how he held his tongue between his teeth and upper lip right now, which made me strangely proud and pleased, as if I had an ownership interest in him. Donnie had forgotten about me by now. He wasn't thinking about Appaloosas or ranch chores or the new tranny in his truck. He was all about the game. I remembered that from high school. Whatever he did, he threw himself into it one hundred percent. Basketball, football, the debate team. His intensity sometimes reminded me of my father's.

"There he is!" someone yelled. Someone else shouted, "Weatherbee! Get over here!" I followed their gaze and there was my husband, running toward the crowd.

"Sorry!" Tim tossed his sweatshirt onto the end of the bench not ten feet away from me as he ran past the bleachers and onto the field. Adrenaline surged through my body. He hadn't noticed me, but I saw his face up close. My eyes followed the familiar slope of his shoulders and his peculiar gait. There was my missing part. My only hope for wholeness. He slapped some guy's back and took his position in the line across from Donnie. And then, to my surprise, Donnie turned his head and glanced at me.

A whistle blew, the ball was kicked and bodies scattered. TJ appeared and climbed onto my lap. I took a deep breath to calm myself and wrapped my arms around him, resting my chin in his hair. "Where's Donnie?" he asked.

"Right there. See, he's running backward. Yes! He caught it!" We watched as Donnie let out a whoop in midair and lit on the ground like a spring, immediately dodging an opposing player trying to capture his flag. He found a hole and charged through it as the fans behind us went wild. "Go!" I shouted.

The other spectators offered their advice just as freely as Donnie ran full throttle toward the goal line like a speedboat with a wake of bodies at his heels.

In the excitement I had momentarily forgotten about Tim—that is, until I saw him press ahead of the throng. Donnie was only a few feet from the goal. Suddenly Tim hurled his body forward. He grabbed the bandana from Donnie's back pocket just as Donnie crossed the line.

Donnie threw his arms up in triumph and at the same instant the whistle blew. Tim was on the ground. "Touchdown!" someone shouted. "No good!" shouted someone else. Everyone both on the field and off had an opinion, which they voiced without restraint.

"What's happening, Mom? Why is everybody yelling?"

I was standing now. "They don't know if it was a touchdown or not."

"Did Donnie do something bad?"

"No, baby. Donnie did good."

"I'm not a baby."

The coaches and players continued to argue as if it was the Super Bowl and these were real live football players instead of a bunch of farmers and bikers playing for a crowd of about fifty between two cornfields. Finally, a decision was made. The ruling was made in favor of the church team; Tim had thwarted Donnie's touchdown. Play resumed on the one-yard line.

I explained the game as well as I could to TJ, who seemed satisfied with my limited knowledge of football. It took two more plays before Donnie successfully made his touchdown.

"Samantha Dodd?" I looked in the direction of the voice as a young woman stepped carefully down several rows of bleachers. "It *is* you. How are you?"

"Kirsten." She had gained some weight since high school but looked great. "Wow. I thought everyone I knew had moved away!"

"I thought *you* moved away." She sat down next to me on the bench. "Who's this?" She leaned forward to get a better look at TJ. "Is this your son?" TJ stared at her blankly.

"Yup. Hey, Teej. This is an old friend of mine. Her name is Kirsten."

"I have a boy about your age. What are you, about four?" TJ held up five fingers. She motioned to someone behind her. "Alex! Come on down here!" A chubby blond boy obediently scrambled down the bleachers. The boys eyed each other cautiously at first while Kirsten and I made the initial small talk. When Alex rolled a tiny truck toward TJ on the row behind us and my son rolled it back, a transaction was made. The friendship duly consummated, the two went to play on the vacant seats above.

"So who'd you come with? Is your husband playing?"

It was at moments like these that I was reminded how raveled my life really was. I had come with that virile quarterback on the tavern team. Yes, my husband was playing. He was that strapping tight end (the loose end in my life) playing for the church team. And my son's coloring didn't match either of them. "Yes, he's out there somewhere," I answered. "Hasn't this been a beautiful fall? I can't believe it's late October and we're out here without jackets. So what have you been up to, Kirsten? Are you working?"

"Yes, part-time at the library. Andy—that's him right there"—she pointed at a jovial-looking guy near the sideline—"he manages the meat department at Safeway." I could tell he was on Tim's team because he wore a shirt.

"So you must go to the Set Free Church. Do you have a Harley?"

Kirsten laughed. "No. We're not all bikers. But the pastor is. We love him, as weird as he is."

"Do you know Sarah . . ." I realized I had already forgotten her new name. "She just got married. Used to be Sarah Weatherbee?"

Kirsten nodded. "Of course. She married the pastor's son. That's her brother right there." She pointed at Tim as he wiped sweat off his face with his bandana flag and then stuffed it back into his rear pocket, poised for the next play. "Tim Weatherbee. He got recruited to fill in for Ross, since he and Sarah are still on their honeymoon. He was one year ahead of us—" She stopped herself. "Wait a minute. Didn't you go out with him?"

I nodded. "Yeah. Sort of."

"So which one is your husband out there?"

I caught myself biting a nail. "Um, well, it's Tim."

This seemed to concern Kirsten. She raised her eyebrows and got real quiet on me. "Oh" was all she said.

Just then the crowd became noisy again. We both diverted our eyes to the play in progress. She had to have known that Tim was in town alone. Maybe he was going to their church. Why had she reacted like that? Did she know something about Tim that I didn't know? The Set Free quarterback scored a touchdown. More cheers rang out from the stands. Frankly, I didn't know who to cheer for. My heart was split at the fifty-yard line.

Kirsten and I chatted off and on as the game progressed. To her credit, she didn't pry. In fact, she seemed to sense my discomfort with the whole topic of Tim and avoided it altogether. She told me about Alex's preschool program and caught me up on the lives of some of our mutual friends and acquaintances. The Set Free team won with a final score of twenty-four to eighteen. Kirsten and I exchanged phone numbers and promised to keep in touch. It would be fun to get together sometime, especially since our sons had hit it off so well.

The men on the field dispersed slowly, still chiding and challenging one another. TJ ran onto the field toward Donnie, who was caught up in a conversation with one of the players. Tim's sweatshirt remained where he had tossed it. I sat and waited on the bench. I could see him joking with some guy. Finally, Tim sauntered my way, still grinning—until he saw me. He almost stopped dead in his tracks but then recovered. He strolled up to the bleachers, plucked his sweatshirt from the bench and used it to wipe his face. "Hello, Sam." The front of his T-shirt was soaked with sweat.

"Hi." I smiled. "Good game. You looked really good out there."

"Thanks." He glanced around. "You here alone?"

"No. I came with a friend." I didn't mention TJ. Things were awkward enough as it was. He stepped toward me then, tentatively.

I stood. "I can't tell you how good it is to see you again. I've missed you."

His eyes grew soft and familiar. "Yeah." His head dropped momentarily. "Me too." A silence fell between us. I wanted to touch him, but I couldn't move. "You were quite a hit at the wedding," he said eventually. "They're still talking about it."

I smiled impishly. "I think your friend really wanted that bouquet," I said. "She didn't like me one bit."

"Luanne? No, she liked you even less when she found out you were my ex-wife."

"Ex?"

"Well, you know what I mean." There was a lot going on in the space between us—a flurry of positive and negative ions, it seemed, that made it hard to talk except with our eyes. One thing was certain. He still cared for me. "So, what are you doing now?" he asked. "Working somewhere?"

I shook my head. "I haven't found anything yet. Actually, it feels pretty good to have a break from working. I get to spend more time with TJ." I immediately saw the glimmer in his eyes disconnect. "That's my son."

"Yeah." He nodded. "I know."

As if on cue, TJ appeared at my side. "Let's go, Mom."

Tim began to back up. "Well, see you around, Sam." He turned just as Donnie approached. "Hey, Don. Good game."

Donnie still had his shirt off and used it like a towel to dry his chest. He grabbed the water bottle from my hand, tipped his head back and squirted the remaining liquid down his throat. "Yeah, it was. It felt good." They didn't shake hands or pat each other's backs. Instead, Donnie placed his arm around my shoulder and began to guide me away as if he was a dog marking his territory. "We should do it again sometime."

I was so angry with Donnie I hardly spoke on the way home. I resented him showing up when he did and even more so that he drank from my water bottle—like we were intimate enough to be sharing each other's saliva. He had made a blatant and intentional statement. My mind replayed the conversation with Tim, his every expression and mannerism, trying to translate them into what he really felt. He had missed me. That much he had said. Did he still love me? Could he forgive me for what I did?

When we pulled up in front of my parents' log house, TJ

scrambled over me and jumped out, but Donnie reached for my arm and pulled me back onto the seat. "Shut the door. We need to talk."

"What is there to talk about?"

"You know very well. Quit avoiding the issue. You're mad at me; that's as plain as stripes on a skunk."

"You deliberately ran him off."

"What did you want me to do? Invite him home for dinner?"

"How about just letting us finish our conversation in private?"

"TJ was there. How private could that be? I figured you were done. It was time to go."

"Oh, and you have some big appointment you have to get to at four o'clock on a Sunday afternoon?"

He opened his mouth to say something but must have thought better of it. His jaw went tight and he gripped the steering wheel, staring straight ahead. I looked out my side window at the poplar trees along the drive until he spoke again. "So, what did he say?"

"Nothing really. There wasn't enough time."

"Are you two going to patch this thing up? Does he want to get back together?"

"I don't know."

"Is that what *you* want?"

Something in his voice made me turn to look at him. His eyes were still fixed straight ahead at the trees beyond the house.

Tears came to my eyes and my voice softened. "Donnie, it's all I've thought about for five years. And now it seems like maybe it's meant to happen. We're both back here in the valley. I keep thinking maybe we could start over if he can forgive me for what I did. I need him to forgive me. Do you understand that? It's like I've been walking around with an open wound all this time."

"What if he can't forgive you?"

I shook my head. "I don't know." I couldn't bear to think about that. All I knew was that for one brief moment I had seen a familiar softness in my husband's eyes. Then he blinked and it was gone.

16

WITH EACH DAY that went by my hopes of Tim showing up at the front door diminished. We had both felt
the pull as we stood there by the bleachers at the football game;
I was sure of it. I busied myself with the things I could do—
reading, peeling potatoes for dinner, even working the cross-
word puzzle from the daily newspaper—but my restless soul
was not easily stilled.

My mind had too much free time, and it kept replaying the
desperation I had heard in my father's voice the previous week
when he argued with Matt. My father always seemed sinless to
me, as naive as that may sound, so I was shocked at the bits and
pieces of conversation I had overheard. Whatever he proposed
had infuriated his friend. I wondered if he was in financial trouble of some sort; something Mom didn't know about—at least
when she committed them to paying my medical bills. Maybe
he had made a bold investment that was supposed to be a sure
windfall—and lost everything. Maybe he borrowed money that
he couldn't pay back. From racketeers? Whatever it was,
Matthew seemed shocked and disappointed at the Judge's plea
to help him do something illegal, and I must admit, I was as

well. But I was left in the dark with my imagination still racing in circles, bumping into walls.

I asked my mother about it one day as she was painting. The walls of her studio out in the detached garage were adorned with her completed works of art. She liked to do cows, which were flat, lifeless shapes on muddy backgrounds. The landscapes were a little better, but not much. Her forehead drew together and she pondered for a moment. "No, honey. I can't think of any trouble your father could possibly be in. He would tell me if there was something wrong." She was dabbing green leaves onto a canvas with a fine-pointed brush. "Are you sure you heard them clearly?"

"I heard the parts with yelling. Matt said it was illegal to do whatever the Judge was talking about. Then Matt stormed off and went down to the river. It was a couple of hours later, when you were home, that he came back. You made him change into some dry pants and sit down to dinner. Remember how quiet both Matt and the Judge were at dinner that night?"

Mom frowned. "When are you going to stop calling him that, Samantha? He's your father, for heaven's sake."

She put her paintbrush down, wiped green paint from her hands, and went to the window on the rear wall of her garage studio, where she stood silently looking out at the fine, almost invisible rain and the river. Frosted-blond strands had escaped from her French roll, dangling at her cheeks. Her blue bib apron had pockets for brushes and palette knives, and the khaki painting pants she wore had permanent smudges of yellow ocher. She turned to look at me. "Whatever the problem is, your father will make the right decision," she said. Her smile seemed sort of sad, but her eyes were like the smooth gray pebbles washed with light at the edge of the stream. I couldn't read them clearly. I thought I saw faith there. She trusted my father. And yet another ripple passed and there was fear, or maybe sorrow. Did she know something about this or not?

That evening the Judge popped his head into my room and announced that he and Mom were going for a little drive. He acted jovial, but I felt it was just that. An act. He put his fishing cap on TJ and told him to "man the fort" while Mom stood by the doorway, quietly pulling on her leather gloves. "Got your pager on, Sam?" Usually it was Mom who asked that.

I tipped my head toward the bedside table. "It's right there."

"Please clip it on. If you go out to the kitchen, you won't be able to hear it. I'll have my cell phone on if you need us for anything." He winked at me and saluted TJ and within minutes the Mercedes crunched down the gravel drive and out of sight. TJ went back to watching his cartoon video on the TV in my room. I had seen that immigrant mouse get shipwrecked a hundred times, and when he started singing "There Are No Cats in America," I went out to the living room to read.

I turned on a lamp and settled into my usual reclining chair. My paperback novel was buried under a pile of magazines, which was just happenstance and had nothing to do with the fact that the Judge disapproved of "that sort of smut." I pulled it open and immersed myself in the ever-thickening plot. The wind had been picking up all evening. I heard it thrashing the bushes at the side of the house while I read. Right at the part where the heroine crawled stealthily into the dark old house through the cellar door, something crashed on our front porch. The book dropped to my knees. I always felt things first in the chest. A little startle was a boxer's jab with ensuing ripples that ran down my arms like rivulets of water. I stood and strained to see the old maple tree through a side window. Its ghostly limbs flailed wildly against the night sky. A branch must have been torn loose and hurled against the house. I opened the front door just a crack as the wind picked up some leafy debris, scudding it across the porch. Just a branch, I assured myself, and then locked and dead-bolted the door. I went in to check on TJ. The TV screen was fuzzy and he was sound asleep. This was not good. In my condition I couldn't carry him to his room, which meant we would be sharing the double bed, and TJ slept as wildly as he played. I tried to remember when he last went to the bathroom. Waking him to pee was useless, like dragging a life-size rag doll with lead shoes to the toilet. I pulled him up and under the covers and hoped for a dry bed in the morning.

I tried to read again. Mom and the Judge had been gone for almost two hours. I figured they were talking about something important and private. Too private to discuss in the Judge's study. What was going on? I found myself reading the same page over again because my mind had not been connected as my eyes traveled across the print. Why did this bother me as much as it did? I plopped the book down and rested my head on the back of the chair. Because, I finally reasoned, if my father was crooked in any way, if he did not live by his own creed, then he was a liar. Maybe there was no absolute truth. Maybe I had measured my life by a standard that was not real. Since I had always failed to measure up, this revelation should have been a great relief. Instead, I found myself grieving. There used to be a fence around the edge of my world, but it was gone. I felt myself falling, spinning like a brown leaf into the emptiness beyond.

THE RING of the phone startled me awake. Darkness covered my eyes like a strange hand that I couldn't pull away. In my confusion I felt the objects around me—the soft upholstered arms of the big chair, the table full of papers and magazines—and realized I was still in the living room. The telephone rang loudly again from across the room. Who had turned off all the lights? And who would call at this hour? Suddenly I knew. My heart. They have found me a heart! I scrambled across the black room, half crawling by the time I reached the table next to my father's leather chair. I picked up on the fourth ring. "Hello?"

There was only silence.

"Hello," I repeated. Someone was there. I could hear them breathing.

"Who is this?" It was a male voice, hoarse like an older man's or a heavy smoker's.

"This is Samantha Weatherbee—but this is the Dodd residence."

"Samantha." There was a long pause. "Samantha. Formerly Samantha Dodd, by any chance?"

"Yes, I'm . . . visiting. Who is calling, please?"

"Well, now, that's interesting." He drifted off on me like he was taking a drag on a cigarette and I was sitting across the table from him. "Hey, Samantha. Is it dark there?"

My heart did a sluggish flip-flop. For the first time I noticed that the darkness was total, inside and out. The floodlight on the garage turned on automatically every night. The lawn should have been bathed in its light.

"Who is this? What do you want?"

A chuckle rose up from his raspy throat. "What do I want? I want your daddy, girl. I want to see him squirm. Just like those worms he's got out in that barn there." There was another long pause. "He ought not have done what he done. I'm going to see him pay. You tell him that for me. You tell him I'm going to see him hang." There was another long pause. "I'm going to watch him shake until his toes curl up. Then just let him dangle in the wind."

I dropped the receiver to its cradle as if it had turned into a snake, then stared wide-eyed into the darkness. Terror radiated from my chest. I felt my way into the bedroom and touched TJ's body beneath the quilt. His breath was slow and steady. The light switches were worthless. I called into my parents' room but it was empty. The Judge's cell phone. His number would be on the list by the kitchen wall phone. I fumbled through a kitchen drawer until I felt a book of matches and lit a candle. The light danced elusively on the page of emergency numbers. Dr. Sovold, the hospital, Dad's office, Dad's cell. My fingers shook as I punched in the number. A spicy pumpkin scent rose from the candle. Two rings, and then a canned voice. "I'm sorry; the cellular customer you have dialed is not available at this time. . . ."

I swore. The wind grew wilder. Rain pelted the window in a violent spray. I held my watch up to the candlelight. Almost midnight. I checked the doors and windows. My bedroom window was unlocked. I slid the lock into place and backed away. How did the caller know that our power was out? Did he disconnect it somehow? Was he close by? I pulled the afghan from the sofa and wrapped it around me as a security blanket, staring into the darkness beyond the windows as I picked up the receiver again. Donnie's phone rang and rang. It was Saturday night. Wherever he went, he hadn't invited me. I wasn't much fun anymore. I thought of calling Lindsey and David but remembered they had gone to Seattle for a Seahawks game and were spending the night in a hotel. Weakness overwhelmed me. I huddled in the big living room chair and felt the familiar painful heaviness of my heart. My father really was in trouble. What had he done? Why had they been gone so long?

"Oh, God," I finally whispered, rocking forward and then back, hugging my knees. "God . . ." He didn't answer. The wind whipped through the trees outside and rattled the windows, but inside the house was too quiet. My own whispers were shocking. "I'm afraid." I knew I sounded like a little girl; there was a pathetic whine in my voice. "Please keep us safe. Please be real." I rocked some more and pondered what I had just said. "If You are . . . I need to know it. I need to know if You care about me. . . ." My head fell onto my knees and tears squeezed from the corners of my eyes. The wind grew momentarily silent and I imagined that God was really listening. "I know I don't deserve anything good from You. But TJ, he hasn't done anything wrong. Please don't take me away from him. And what about my father? If he made a mistake . . . Whatever he did, I think he's in pretty deep. I think he needs Your help."

A peaceful feeling settled over me then. When the wind began to howl again, it was not so scary. I pretended that the arms of the big chair were the strong and tender arms of God. I snuggled into them and eventually drifted off on a gentle cloud of sleep.

THE NEXT MORNING Sheriff Byron leaned against the kitchen counter, sipping a cup of coffee, a revolver hanging against his right hip. (That seemed strange to me—a gun in my mother's kitchen.) I used to think Sheriff Byron was a hunk. He was younger then and his belly didn't bulge at the belt. He said they didn't ordinarily respond to prank phone calls, but this was an outright threat—and against a judge. The sheriff took my statement while sitting across from me at the breakfast table, carefully writing and then looking up at me without moving his chin. He was still handsome but in an older-man way, with long black eyelashes and the rough shadow of a beard.

I never noticed his nose hairs before, though. Of course, my only close encounters with him had been at night, and both times I had been under the influence.

The first incident was at the rest stop off the highway just outside of Dixon, where you could park your car under the trees and listen to the river wander around the bend to the Fillmores' farm. Jerry Mattson was at the wheel. We had been in love for about a month before I realized that he was boring and lacked a spirit of adventure. Upon discovering his well-concealed secret, I had no choice but to drop the let's-just-be-friends line, only by then I really didn't care whether I ever saw him again. He kept telling me we were meant for each other, and that I stimulated him, which I knew to be true but he said he didn't mean it that way. He sounded like an attorney pleading a case, as if love was a verdict I should make based on the facts as he saw them. I just kept drinking his beer and trying not to be too honest because he was a nice guy and I didn't want to destroy his fragile male ego. By the time Sheriff Byron shone his flashlight through the window of Jerry's black Camaro, we had been discussing our relationship for what seemed like hours.

"Young lady, are you here of your own free will?" he asked.

I leaned toward him and let my sweater drop over the six-pack of empty bottles on the floor of the car. "Well, actually, sir, I asked him to take me home a long time ago." He suggested that Jerry drive me home. Jerry was furious, especially when the sheriff followed us all the way back to my driveway. Sheriff Byron probably hadn't placed me as the Judge's daughter until then.

Our next confrontation was not so innocent. My best friend, Trudy, had dated an older man who was nineteen and already had an apartment of his own. He told the guys at the gas station where he worked that she had gone all the way with him, which was an absolute lie. She had been forced to sit real close to him in his old Chevy sedan since he had the passenger door tied shut, with ropes crisscrossing every which way because the door was supposedly broken. He kept putting the moves on her even though it was only their first date and she had nowhere to go because of the web of ropes. She wouldn't even kiss him good night because he smelled like a pile of greasy rags. Trudy was a virgin and intended to be one until her wedding night. I knew that because I was her best friend. So when I heard what Gene had told Randy from Tim, who overheard them bragging where they smoked cigarettes out behind the Darlington Automotive Service, I was indignant. Trudy was enraged.

Our plan was not firm. We usually just went with spontaneous inspiration when things like this came up. That particular Friday night, we had been discussing the Gene thing while sampling a variety of liqueurs from her mother's pantry. We decided the best thing to do was confront him. But when Trudy pulled onto Gene's street in the Mustang her father had given her to assuage his guilt over leaving them for another family, the ground-floor apartment was dark. We tried the door. It was bolted tight. Luckily, the third window we tried gave way. We crawled into the dark living room and let our creativity flow. We had been in there redecorating the apartment by candlelight for about an hour when headlights suddenly illuminated the room. There was no back door. In a panic, Trudy climbed up on the toilet, squeezed out through the tiny bathroom window and dove into the laurel hedge that fenced the backyard. I was only halfway through the window when I got stuck.

It was Sheriff Byron who came around to the back of the house with his long black flashlight and lit me up like a vaudeville queen. "What are you doing in there? Is Gene back from Frisco already?" I acted like I was glad to see the sheriff. He went around the building and apparently crawled through the same living room window we had used. Soon I felt his strong hands guiding my feet back to the plastic toilet seat. I jumped down and turned to stare directly at his silver badge. I thanked him for rescuing me again. He nodded and led me out of the bathroom. The lights were on now. He just folded his arms across his chest and surveyed the main living area. It was an absolute mess. The pictures on the walls hung cockeyed. Half-full ketchup and mustard bottles bobbed in the aquarium. That was Trudy's idea. She had taken all the food out of the fridge and arranged it strategically throughout the apartment. While she hid open tuna cans in the back of the bedroom closet, I froze the underwear. Luckily, most of our sabotage was not visible to the naked eye. It would probably be discovered for days and weeks to come. "Would you like to tell me about it?" he had asked.

That was a long time ago but I still felt sheepish now with him standing right here in our kitchen, talking with my parents. It turned out that the lights had been off for miles around last night, not just at our house. The wind had thrown a tree onto a major power line serving greater Darlington, Carter and Dixon. That's why the sheriff asked the Judge so many questions about his relationships with neighbors and local folks. The caller had known that the power was out. But the Judge just shook his head. "The oldest James boy from over there across the ravine—Cameron—he's been through my courtroom a time or two. I sent him up to the state pen for a couple of years on his third felony charge. He's made no secret about how he feels about me, but he just doesn't fit. The voice doesn't match, for one thing. I can't think of anyone else around here who would have reason to threaten me."

I hadn't known that about Cameron, though it didn't surprise me. Of all the James Gang, he was our most treacherous opponent in the pinecone battles Donnie and I and our friends fought in the woods.

Mom's forehead was pinched and she stood with an elbow resting on her crossed arm, one hand covering her mouth. She had been quiet all morning and her eyes had the look of crying, like she had been—or was on the verge of it. She had reason to be afraid, but I couldn't help but suspect that she knew something else, maybe a reason that someone was threatening her husband. Before the sheriff came I had asked her what she and the Judge talked about last night. She shook her head and said, "Oh, lots of things. Nothing in particular." But I didn't believe her. Secrets buzzed like hornets around us and I was the only one acknowledging their presence.

My father tried to brush the phone threat off. "It was probably just someone's idea of a joke."

For some reason he didn't mention the call he had received the day that he and TJ were cleaning the fish. He had said it was nothing—just a prank call. I almost brought it up but thought better of it, remembering Matt's fiery words. *You're a judge, for God's sake! Judge yourself!* If my father was involved in something illegal, I would not be the one to implicate him. "It was a grown man," I said in a subdued voice, "and he wasn't joking."

The sheriff strode to the window. "This person might have been calling from a cell phone." He surveyed the property. "Did you hear any interference? Any scratchy sounds in the background?" I didn't think so. He turned to the Judge. "You still have people coming by here to help themselves to worms?"

"Not too much this time of year."

Sheriff Byron folded the written statement and pushed it into his shirt pocket. "I'm just going to look around outside before I go."

The Judge stood tall at the kitchen window and watched the sheriff stride through the wet field toward the barn, carrying a pair of green barn boots that were kept on the back porch. Branches and leaves torn loose by the storm littered the yard. I sat at the table with my coffee and a bran muffin as Mom rinsed dishes and placed them in the dishwasher.

My father's face was as hard to read as a map held upside down. His jaw did not flinch; his countenance was expressionless. Who was he? What was happening behind those piercing eyes in the intricate places of his soul? He was the Judge, the one with the power and authority to decide a person's fate. He had judged me, and beyond reason I felt as if the woes of my life were my punishment for failing to keep his law. For failing to measure up. But what about him? What had he done to make someone want to kill him? What had he said that shocked and infuriated Matthew? Would the Judge take the law into his own hands to get rid of this stalker? If so, he must have something terrible to hide. He seemed deep in thought, as if he had forgotten that Mom and I were there. If he had broken his own law, then more than the law would be broken. That was for sure. There would be a shattering of hearts all around him.

I realized then that I loved him. I needed him to be the towering rock we all thought he was. And worse than anything, like a child, I still needed him to love *me.*

The sheriff eventually stomped up the back steps and poked his head through the kitchen doorway. "There are a lot of prints out there, but it's a mess with all the debris from the storm. The only clear ones I could find seem to match up with your boots. Keep an eye out, though, when you go out there. If you see any prints you don't recognize, give me a call."

"So, where did you two go last night?" I asked after the sheriff had gone.

"All the way to Bellingham." The Judge was overly cheerful for a man whose life was being threatened by a crazy guy. "We had a nice long dinner. The kind your mother likes. Four courses with plenty of time to linger in between." He winked at her.

Mom only forced a weak smile and dropped her eyes before turning to leave the room.

17

NOVEMBER CRAWLED BY like a garden slug. I watched the leaves go from gold to orange to brown. They swirled in the wind and stuck to the wet ground. The old maple tree finally stood naked out by the barn, its arthritic bones reaching plaintively into the sky.

Donnie took me down to the spit on the river a few times. At first we walked slowly, and on the way back up the trail I leaned heavily on his arm. When I could no longer make the whole trek, he carried me part of the way, but only after I had tried very hard to make it by myself.

The last time we made the trip was in mid-November, when the trail was slick with brown leaves. I wore the Judge's plaid wool jacket and my hiking boots. Donnie came around the side of the house with a rusty old wheelbarrow from the barn. "Taxi, ma'am?" he said. Halfway to the river I leaned too far to my right to see chanterelle mushrooms as orange as pumpkins clustered beneath a hemlock. The wheelbarrow tipped and I spilled into a prickly Oregon grape bush. Since Donnie thought it was so funny I pulled him in to see how it felt. We rolled, laughing, to where the ground was a soft carpet of needles. He pulled a leaf from my hair and brushed something from my face. For a moment I thought he was going to kiss me. Instead, he rolled onto his back and stared pensively up through the evergreen boughs. One big hand went behind his head, his jaw went taut and some mysterious wave passed behind his eyes. He used to get like that sometimes when we were kids. We would be playing and having a good old time and the next thing I knew he didn't want to play anymore. He would just get real quiet and mopey, and I'd poke him with a stick or something and he would say, "Get out of here, Samantha! Why don't you just leave me alone?"

I didn't say anything this time. I didn't think I had done anything to make him angry. Maybe it suddenly occurred to him as we wrestled in the leaves that he was trapped on a weary old ranch out in the middle of nowhere with nothing better to do than push a dying friend around in a wheelbarrow. Or could it be that he still wanted more than this wonderful friendship between us? But how could he? He knew how I felt about Tim. Tim was my husband, after all. And besides, in my current condition I was no good to either one of them.

Donnie didn't come by for a week or more after that. I drank herb teas with my stocking feet propped on the living room windowsill. The doctor said I did not have a cold. This annoying cough was some kind of reflex in response to my huge heart putting pressure on my lungs. Mornings were especially long and quiet because TJ was gone. I had signed him up for the preschool that my friend Kirsten's son, Alex, attended. We had gotten together twice since meeting at the football game, and the boys were already great pals. The Judge usually dropped TJ off at preschool on his way in to the courthouse, and Mom (or Lindsey, if Mom was playing tennis) picked him up about noon. Sometimes he forgot to show me what he made because he had already been through all that with Mom. She told him he was definitely artist material and turned the refrigerator into his private gallery. I displayed his pinecone turkey and egg-carton bugs on my bedroom windowsill.

Lately I had visions of this busy household buzzing along without me. There wouldn't be much difference. Just that shape over there in the gold reclining chair would be gone. TJ would miss me for a while, but I knew he would be okay. He was loved. He would always have a home. Lindsey and David had agreed to raise him if I died, which was somewhat of a re-lief but I worried that TJ would turn out predictable and bor-ing like a Ken doll with black plastic hair. At least they had plenty of money. TJ could have braces and skis and a college ed-ucation if he was their son. I tried not to think about Tim any-more. Living beyond the new year was about all I could hope for.

Thanksgiving came and so did David's parents. They thought our house was quaint and Mom's elegant dream dining room was "just darling." Like this was just the summer house. Dick (that was David's dad) tried to talk fishing with the Judge but their communications missed each other like wild arrows. Dick's idea of fishing was to sit on the deck of a charter boat off the coast of Cabo with a martini and of course a camera in case a marlin actually came along. Mrs. Matthews wore an angora sweaterdress the color of buttermilk with high-heeled shoes to match. She looked constipated, standing there with her stom-ach sucked in and chest out, a pained look on her face even when she smiled. The fat she had accumulated on her last cruise swelled over her belt anyway. You'd think she would wear something a little more forgiving for Thanksgiving dinner. TJ asked her why she wore "too many rings." He invited her into his room to see his worms, but the way she looked down at him and made some lame excuse about maybe after dinner, I could tell she didn't really see him. She brushed him off like he was one of those poor Panamanian waifs who rowed out to meet their cruise ship, begging for money. They told about that during dinner. TJ asked if they threw money down to them, at which Mrs. Matthews huffed, "Oh, no, dear. You shouldn't encourage that kind of behavior." TJ said if he was on that big boat he would throw them his dinner because they were probably hungry. I know I made her uncomfortable too. She froze up every time I coughed but wouldn't look at me. I couldn't really blame her. I couldn't stand to have dying people around me either—especially at the dinner table.

Lindsey seemed to like her in-laws, but my sister saw something good in everybody. Personally, I wished I could choose TJ's potential grandparents myself. I saw maybe the skipper of a charter boat, someone who could teach TJ to carve whales out of driftwood, and his tough old wife—a rosy-cheeked adventuress who laughed right into the face of a good storm. Or forest rangers. Either of those would be good.

The following day was the holiday known as the Biggest Shopping Day of the Year. Mom and Lindsey left just after dawn and planned to stay overnight in a Seattle waterfront hotel. I could tell they felt guilty about leaving me home, but at this point there was no discussing it. Lindsey asked me to write down some Christmas gift ideas for TJ and me. For TJ it was easy. Anything to do with bugs, worms, fish or frogs. Anything *I* wanted was either too expensive to mention or not for sale in any store.

TJ and I watched cartoons in our pajamas until almost eleven a.m. The Judge never liked having the TV on in the daytime. He used to say watching TV was for people who didn't have a life of their own. I noticed he never said a word about me sitting in front of *Oprah* in the middle of the afternoon, so I must have qualified. Anyway, I finally told TJ to turn it off and get dressed. He pulled on his jeans and boots and skipped out to the barn to join his grandpa.

I stood in the shower until the water turned cold. The full-length mirror on the bathroom door was steamed up, but I wiped it off and turned to see how big my behind was getting from waiting for my pager to go off. I shook it to see if it jiggled more than usual. My breasts hadn't changed, but they would. There would be a scar. A highway through the mountain pass. I traced the line where they would saw through my breastbone and shuddered.

The phone rang. This could be the one. I called from the bathroom door. "Is anybody out there?" No answer. I swore under my breath, pinching a towel around me and walking as fast as I could down the hall. "Hello."

"Samantha?"

I froze. "Yes. This is Samantha."

"This is Tim."

"I know."

There was a slight pause. "Um . . . are you going to be there for a while? I need to talk to you—in private."

"I'm not going anywhere."

"Okay." He cleared his throat. "Well, I'll see you soon then."

I held back my cough until the receiver was down. I stared at the phone, massaging my heart for several long seconds. "Well, it's about time," I said out loud, running my fingers through my wet hair. My hair! I dropped the hair-dryer twice in my hurry to get the job done and once the brush flew out of my hands. I knew it. I had seen a spark in his eyes that night at the country club. A sign of life among the embers. And again after the football game. He said he had missed me too. It was not my imagination after all. Luckily, Mom had washed my best blue jeans—the ones that fit just right. I pulled on a white scoop-neck T-shirt. A blue velvet box on the dresser held a delicate chain with a sterling silver charm. My nervous fingers struggled with the clasp. A little lipstick, a little blush. I had just slipped on my shoes when he drove down the drive.

At that moment the back door burst open. "Mom!" TJ ran from the kitchen, almost knocking me down. "It's Christmas! We got all the decorations. Lots of 'em! We're going to surprise Grandma."

The Judge trudged in carrying a cardboard box. I could tell by his raised eyebrow and half smile that he was just getting warmed up to the idea. He put the box on the floor. "You're looking well today, Samantha."

I grabbed his arm. "Tim is here." He stared at me blankly and then glanced around the room. "He just drove up." I raised my eyebrows and smiled. "He wants to talk to me. Alone."

There was a knock on the door. TJ ran to open it. My father touched my hand. I looked up at him and I swear a sadness fell across his face and then just as quickly washed away. He winked. "Come here, boy," he said, but TJ had already flung the door open.

Tim stood there awkwardly for a moment. I came up behind my son, placing my hands on his shoulders. "Hi. Tim, I don't think you two have officially been introduced." I remembered Tim staring down at the little brown baby. His stooped shoulders just before he walked out the hospital room door. "This is TJ. TJ, this is Tim Weatherbee."

"Hey." TJ looked up at me. "He has the same name as us."

Tim nodded politely, glanced down at the porch, up to me and then nervously over his shoulder toward his truck. My father called to his grandson. When TJ didn't come, the Judge came to the door and greeted Tim with a handshake. "Nice to see you again, Tim. It's been a long time. I wouldn't have recognized you."

Tim stood a little taller. "It's nice to see you too, sir."

"Come on in and make yourself at home. TJ and I are just on our way out to find the Christmas lights." He ushered TJ toward the back door.

"Grandpa, he has the same last name as me and Mom," I heard him say before the door slammed.

Tim sat on the leather sofa across from me, elbows on spread knees, his hands massaging each other. He looked good. "So, how does your sister like married life?" I asked. What a lame question.

He nodded. "She's happy. He's a good guy. I like him."

"That's good. And how's your mom?"

"She's all done with the chemo. You know she has cancer, right?" I nodded. "I think she's going to be okay."

"Are you going back to your place at Grants Pass then?"

He shook his head. "I've got it rented out to a friend of mine. I decided to stay here for a while. This whole thing with Mom . . . well, I didn't know how that was going to turn out. There are still no guarantees." He stared out the window at the dark clouds. "They say it might snow."

I coughed. My hand went habitually to my chest.

"Are you okay?" Tim studied my face. "You don't look so good. You got that flu that's going around?"

I shook my head. "Just getting over it. I'm fine." I pulled my feet up and crossed my legs.

"You're still wearing that necklace I got you," Tim said.

My hand went to the silver mizpah, half of a heart with jagged edges. "Do you still have yours?"

He laughed. "No, I don't think so. What did it say when both pieces were together?"

" 'The Lord watch between me and thee while we are absent from one another.' "

"Oh, yeah." He looked out the window again. Finally, he sat back and sighed. "Hey, I'm getting married."

My chest constricted. The cough overtook me again, this time bringing tears to my eyes. When I could, I straightened and took a deep breath. "You're already married."

"Yeah. Well, that's why I'm here. Our marriage was over a long time ago." He reached inside his jacket and pulled out some folded papers. "You and I both know that, Sam. It's time to get on with life. We just need to take care of the paperwork."

18

A T FIRST IT SNOWED wads of cotton that disappeared as soon as they hit the wet ground. By nightfall the flakes poured like bath crystals from the windless sky, until the grass and sidewalk and driveway were uniformly white, sparkling in the light from the garage. It covered the tracks left by Tim's truck when he turned around.

I didn't sign his papers. He left them on the coffee table, still folded, saying something about it all being pretty self-explanatory but if I had any questions just give him a call. He got the forms from the stationery store in town. We didn't need an attorney, he said, because there were no custody or property issues involved.

I watched the snow all day with a grief so heavy that I could not cry. TJ came in from time to time, rosy-cheeked and wide-eyed with excitement. "Mom, I made a snowman! Can I have a carrot for his nose?" I hadn't thought to buy him a snow hat so he wore a knit cap of Mom's that drooped down his forehead and almost over his eyes. His mittens were rolled-up wool socks, which he traded for dry ones every time he came in. I made a late lunch of tomato soup and grilled cheese sand-wiches. The Judge came in from hanging Christmas lights and sat at the kitchen table with us. I guess I wasn't saying much. TJ stopped chattering for a moment and patted my hand thoughtfully. "Too bad you can't come out and play in the snow, Mommy."

I pushed the hair off his forehead like mothers do. There was so much I wanted to do with him, for him, but I had nothing to give. "I wish I could, baby." He gave me the look. I was not supposed to call him that. "Maybe we could call Alex to come over and play tomorrow. Would you like that?"

"Okay," he said as he pushed back his chair. He went straight to the back door and reached for his boots.

The Judge snapped his fingers and TJ looked up. He sighed, dropped his wet boot to the kitchen floor and came back to the table. After his plate and bowl were deposited by the sink, he returned with a sponge and wiped soup and crumbs from the table. "Now can I go, Grandpa?"

"You forgot one more thing."

TJ stretched his arms around my neck and planted a hurried kiss. "Thanks for the lunch, Mom." He glanced at the Judge for his nod of approval and a moment later he was bundled up and gone.

I started to clear the table, but my father reached out and touched my arm. "Sit down. I can do that."

"So can I. It doesn't bother me. I've got to do something."

"Talk to me."

I hesitated and then sat back down. "Okay."

"Tim wasn't here very long, was he?"

I shook my head. There was just enough soup in my bowl to smear around with the spoon and make designs. "He just came to bring divorce papers."

The Judge was respectfully silent for a moment. "Where are they?"

"Out there on the coffee table."

He rose from the table and returned with the documents, which he shook open and skimmed through briefly like an attorney. "Irreconcilable differences. Humph. There's no such thing." He removed his reading glasses. "Just people who aren't willing to work things out. What ever happened between you two, Samantha?"

I didn't know what to say. There was too much that couldn't be told. My spoon rocked back and forth in my bowl. Where was TJ when I needed his incessant chatter?

"Do you still love Tim?"

I looked my father straight in his eyes. "Yes. Yes, I do."

"Well, I can only imagine that there was some sort of love triangle. TJ tells me he doesn't have a daddy. But you and Tim and I know differently. Somewhere out there is a dark-eyed ghost that's going to haunt all three of you for the rest of your lives if you don't deal with him. Am I getting warm, Samantha?"

I nodded. "But I don't know where he is and I don't care. I haven't seen him or talked to him in almost six years."

"So he doesn't know about TJ?"

"Right. And TJ doesn't know about him. I told TJ some families have two people, some have four, some have seven. Every family is different. He seemed okay with that. But he sure was happy to find out he had a grandma and grandpa. Once I told him that, he just couldn't get it out of his head."

"Is that why you came home?"

I nodded. "That was a big part of it. Oh. And I was sick and jobless and broke."

He laughed. "Well, you came to the right place. I wish you had come home a long time ago. We've missed a lot." I knew he meant TJ. He glanced out the kitchen window. Darkness was already falling. Snow swirled in the light of the porch lamp. We heard TJ laugh out loud and both rose to watch him. He hadn't noticed the dimming light or didn't care. He was throwing snowballs at his snowman, who must have come to life and retaliated because we saw TJ recoil from the hit and roll in the snow, clutching his chest. The Judge chuckled. "He reminds me of you. There's never a dull moment in his life."

"I've had a few lately."

"This will pass, Samantha."

"Or I will." He raised his eyebrows disapprovingly. "Well, let's face it. I'm not getting any better. I feel weaker every day, and now this cough. It makes me just want to sleep. I've been waiting for months and not even one possible heart donor has surfaced." I was so sorry for myself I almost cried.

"You are going to be fine," he said with his usual annoying optimism.

"Yeah." How did he know? How did anybody know how this would all turn out?

The phone rang and as usual I lurched. My father grabbed the receiver off the wall. "Hello." A smile spread across his face. "There you are. Are you still in Nordstrom? Oh. What's the matter, did they run out of shoes?" He glanced toward me. "She's fine. We just had lunch. I know. Who says you have to eat lunch at noon? Yes, it's been snowing all day. He's playing with his snowman. Well, I can just drive Samantha's Jeep if necessary. The tires are good. Don't worry. Do you think your old dad hasn't thought of all this?"

His eyes always lit up when he talked to Lindsey. I couldn't blame him. Here she was on a shopping spree, the thing that Lindsey loved best next to David, and she was calling to check on us. My own mother mothered me less than Lindsey. I heard her excited chatter coming through the phone. My father laughed. "I love you too, baby. Let me talk to your mom."

He told her they should stay down there a few days if they wanted to. "We'll be fine," he said. "I can cook. Samantha made lunch; we won't starve. I want you to hire a horse and buggy tonight. Make the driver take you all over downtown until you have your Christmas shopping done. This is the perfect time for you to get away. I don't have to be back in court until Tuesday."

I knew what he meant by that. Someone had to be here at all times to babysit me. To be ready to drive me to the hospital at a moment's notice. Mom and Lindsey needed the break.

Having a sister like Lindsey was a blessing and a curse. She would do anything for me. She called me almost every day or just happened to drop by with a little something to cheer me up. Never a bottle of Jack Daniel's, but it's the thought that counts. She had agreed to raise my son for me after I was gone. What more could I ask—other than an occasional failure or shortcoming? Nothing Lindsey touched ever went bad. Her husband adored her. The polished cherry tables in her house never saw dust. She never had a bad hair day, her Lexus didn't break down, and if she lost a tennis match it was to avoid pulverizing the ego of her opponent. Next to her I was one of my father's worms. A pathetic squiggle peeking out of the manure of my life.

I hoped that I would live, and that someday I would make something good of my life. Maybe someday I could make my father proud of me.

Getting TJ to bed that night was easy. He crawled under the covers without being asked and fell asleep before we had a chance to read another adventure in the lives of Curious George and the man with the yellow hat. I went to my own room and read until my eyes burned and then turned out the light. The phone rang. The red numbers on my clock read ten thirty. I sat up and heard the Judge answer from his study.

"Hello." I couldn't hear much, but something made me slip out of bed and into the hallway. "Who is this?" A sudden chill raced through me and I clutched my flannel pajamas tight. From the study doorway I saw my father sink slowly into his chair. "Why are you threatening me? Do I know you?" He listened intently, his hand massaging his temples, and then placed the phone back in its cradle with a sigh. He leaned back in his chair.

"Was it him?" I asked.

He nodded, still shaken. "I know that voice."

"Who is it?"

"I wish I knew. It will come to me. I know I've heard that voice before."

"You should call the sheriff. Maybe he can trace it somehow."

"Yes. He asked me to call if it happened again." He punched in the numbers and got Sheriff Byron on the phone. "Yes, I'm sure it was the same one who spoke to Samantha. Coarse voice. No, nothing about hanging this time. He seems to be on a new tangent. Specifically? Well, let's see. The first thing he said was something about watching my blood melt the snow." He looked over at me uncomfortably. I didn't budge. He turned his back to me and lowered his voice, but I still heard him clearly.

"He said he would nail me up, they'd put me in the ground and if I was really God I would rise again. That's what he said."

He and the sheriff discussed the Judge's recent cases. Nobody seemed to fit. The sheriff said he would check out some possibilities. When my father hung up, he turned to me. "This is nothing to concern yourself about. Just some crackpot looking for attention. If the guy was really going to kill me, he'd be on my back porch. Not the telephone."

The thought of him lurking on the back porch made me shudder. I locked all the doors. It was not my parents' habit to lock up. I asked my mother about it once. She said someone might need to get in when we weren't home. Like the UPS lady. She came in to use the bathroom once in a while. It was a long way out to Carter. Donnie's mother didn't drive, so she was always running out of something. Mom told her if we weren't home to just come on in and help herself. But my father seemed okay with me bolting everything up tight that night.

Once the adrenaline drained from my system, I realized I was exhausted. I crawled into bed and pulled the covers up to my chin. My father tapped his knuckles on the door and poked his head in. "We didn't finish our talk about you and Tim." His silhouette filled the doorway.

"There's nothing you can do. It's over." My words shocked me. It had never been over. Not when he walked away from me at the hospital, not three years later when I pulled the wedding ring from my finger and placed it in a drawer. Even after making a fool of myself at his sister's wedding. Up until this moment I had hoped. I had imagined the broken edges of the mizpah medallion would fit together again. "He's going to marry someone else." The words that came from my throat seemed to release the tears that I had kept back all day. I rolled over to face the wall before my father could see them.

"Oh, Sam. I'm sorry." I felt him touch my shoulder.

"I'm very tired." I knew I couldn't hold back the sobs much longer.

"Good night, Sammy." I wanted to cry like his little girl again. I needed him to rock me in his arms, to make this hurt go away. But something held me back.

"Good night," I said.

19

THE SNOW FELL for days. From my bedroom, I heard the
back door open and close, TJ's joyful exclamations, the crin-
kle of grocery bags, my parents' voices, footsteps in the hall.
The divorce papers lay under my bed like a dead cat; sooner or
later I would have to deal with them. From time to time the
phone rang but no one came to say it was for me. The drone of
the vacuum cleaner grew louder as it approached my room and
then Mom pushed the door open and cleaned around my bed.
She brought in trays of fruit or sandwiches, a pitcher of juice,
an afternoon cup of tea. TJ rarely visited. After preschool on
Monday he came in to show me to his buddy Leon, whom
Grandma invited to stay overnight. Pudgy little Leon hugged
the doorjamb, surveying me with wide eyes. He seemed relieved when TJ said, "Let's go feed the worms."

Once I got up and grabbed the divorce papers, meaning to
sign them just to silence the voices in my head. But when no
ink flowed from my pen, I took it as a sign. Maybe I was giving
up too easily. I wrestled with the idea of calling Tim. In fact,
the thought consumed me. Could he really love that frizzy-
haired Glinda woman? She was not his type. Definitely not his

type. Besides, I clearly remembered the day he promised to love me forever, for better or worse, till death do us part.

Finally, I brought the phone into my room and closed the door. I dialed his mother's number and held my breath. "Hello, Mrs. Weatherbee. This is Samantha. Do you know where I can reach Tim?" There was a short stunned silence before she said he was right there and she would get him. I started to feel sick and faint while I waited and would have hung up if I had not committed myself by volunteering my name.

"Hello."

"Hey. It's me. Got a minute?"

"Sure."

I held my chest to keep it from exploding. "I have a problem with these papers," I said. "I don't want to sign them." There was only silence on the other end. "Um, I was hoping we could talk about this."

"I don't know what there could be to talk about."

"Tim . . . what happened back there in Reno. I'm sorry. I'm so sorry." I felt myself trembling and took a deep, calming breath. "I never had a chance to explain. You just disappeared. I tried to find you—for five years I tried to find you. I've been miserable. The least you can do is hear me out."

"*You've* been miserable? You poor little thing. And you think I owe you something for all your suffering?"

"Tim, I screwed up. Don't you think I know that? I'm asking you to forgive me. Can you . . . will you forgive me?"

I heard a sigh and then silence. I pictured him with his head dropped, fingers pinching his forehead like he used to do sometimes. "Samantha," he finally breathed, "I've spent the past five years trying—for my own sake. When I saw you again, well, I thought maybe I could. You don't know how many times I thought of calling you, of maybe giving it a try. But then I realized it could never work."

"But why?"

"Because I could never love that boy of yours."

I felt like he spat on me. I couldn't speak.

"I've finally found someone I think I can trust. I think I can love again. Don't screw this up for me, Sam. Just sign the papers. Please."

I hung up the phone and sobbed into my pillow, thankful that the television was on in the living room to drown the sounds. I cried until there was nothing left. The hope that had trickled through me all those years dried up like a creek bed in a drought. Later that night I scribbled on a newspaper until ink flowed freely from the pen and I signed his loathsome papers.

Lindsey and David came for dinner the next night. She brought a wedge of Brie, which she served as an appetizer with mugs of hot spiced cider. The sweet aroma filled my room. "Room service," she announced, pushing through my bedroom door and passing me a china plate of crackers and cheese. "Samantha, you've been in here for days. Why don't you come out and join us? I'll make a bed for you on the sofa."

"No, thanks." I slunk down on my bed, but it made me cough violently. I sat up, leaning against a bank of pillows, which relieved the pressure in my chest. "Nobody wants to hear that over and over. I haven't even showered today."

"We don't care. Come on. It's just family. Or hop in the shower if it will make you feel better. You know I'll be taking you to the doctor in the morning, and we should get an early start because of the snow on the roads."

"I'm not going to the doctor. I'm too tired. I'm just flat out too tired to live." She cocked her head and gave me one of her motherly looks. "I'm getting worse by the day. I don't need to drive all the way into Seattle to have Dr. Sovold tell me that. Not that he would. He'll just give me another pep talk. *Hang in there, trooper.*" I mimicked his Arkansas accent. "*Any day now.* Do you know how many times I've heard that?"

"Samantha, this is about Tim and those divorce papers, isn't it? You're just depressed, that's all."

"I'm not going. I've made up my mind. I need to talk to you about something else. We need to talk about TJ." I pushed myself higher against the pillows behind me. "I don't want him to be overprotected. I mean, I want him safe, of course, but a kid needs to explore his world. He should be able to run free in the woods and fish until dark or even later if he wants. Not now, of course. I'm talking about later. And if he doesn't want to go to college, that's okay. He should be encouraged to follow his own dreams, whatever they are. I can't see him sitting behind a computer all day, or fixing cars or anything like that." Lindsey wasn't taking notes, but she was listening. "It's good that you take him to church. I'm okay with all that."

Lindsey smiled sadly, patiently. "Is there anything else?"

I sighed. This was not coming out right. What was I really trying to say? "You know how TJ is? Happy, innocent. So full of life. He never wonders what people think of him. He just assumes that everybody likes him because he likes them. He marches down the aisles at Carter Store singing a song he just made up without a sideways thought. There isn't a worry in his head. No fear. Growing up should make you better." I shook my head thoughtfully. "Personally, I think I was wiser as a child." I searched my sister's eyes. If anyone had the answer to this, it was Lindsey. She was the happiest person I knew. "Can you help TJ to not lose himself in the process of growing up?"

Lindsey rose and walked to my bedroom window. The snow had stopped. "I know what you're saying, Sam." She seemed to ponder. "Jesus said, 'He who comes to me should come like a little child.' I think what he meant is to come with absolute trust." She was silent for some time before she turned to me. "No, Sam. I can't promise that TJ won't lose that sweet naïveté of his. I wish I could. But he's going to find out about life and death, good and evil, pain and suffering. If you die, well, that will be his first slap of reality. He's already meeting kids who won't share. It's just a matter of time before some redneck local points out to him that the only Mexicans around here are seasonal farmworkers. The fact of the matter is people can't be trusted. Even the people who love TJ are going to let him down. We're not perfect."

She walked to my bedside table. "Where's that Bible I gave you?" Finding it on the lower tier, she wiped the dust off the cover with her sleeve and sat next to me on the bed. "God is the only one who can be trusted like a child trusts a loving father. I'll teach him that. Whether you live or die, Sammy, that's the most important thing for him to understand." I don't think she realized that her hand was caressing the blue hardcover Bible on her lap like it was her beloved calico cat. "You need to understand that too. Good *does* win over evil. There is one truth, just like Daddy says." She held the book toward me, and when I didn't take it she placed it between us on the bed. "It's all in here. TJ will lose his innocence—we all lose ours every day. But when we ask God to forgive us, it's like our screwups never happened. He doesn't even remember them anymore."

I found myself wanting to believe her. God loomed threateningly in my subconscious mind, the great Judge glaring down with displeasure from His mighty throne. I didn't dare enter

His presence covered with my foul-smelling rebellion like Jonah after he got spit up by the big fish.

That's the way I still felt with my father, even though he had shown nothing but kindness to me and TJ. There was always this thing between us that I didn't know how to fix. A stink all over me that wouldn't wash away. And when you know you stink, you keep your distance.

Tim couldn't get past it either.

Innocence. If only I could start all over as a little child.

20

"COME ON, LAZY. Get up."

I rolled over and pulled the blanket off my face. When my eyes focused, I saw Donnie leaning over me. "Who let you in here?"

"It's not exactly the White House. You don't even have a mean dog."

"Where is everybody?"

He shrugged and walked to my closet. "What are you wearing today?"

I pulled the covers off, exposing my T-shirt and flannel drawstring pants. "What you see is what you get."

He frowned. Hangers scraped back and forth on the rod until he pulled out a long black skirt Lindsey had bought me on one of our trips to Seattle for my doctor's appointment. He tossed it onto the bed.

"I'm not wearing that." I stretched and sprawled across the crumpled sheets.

"Come on, Samantha. Get ready. Let's go."

"I'm sorry Lindsey wasted your time. I'm *not* going to the doctor. It's too far. It takes all day to go to Seattle and then go through all the usual doctor bull, and he never tells me anything I don't already know. I know my heart is failing. I'm dying and there's not a thing anybody can do about it."

"Doctor? I'm not taking you to the doctor." He slapped the side of my thigh. "Come on. I haven't got all day. Go brush your teeth and do whatever you gotta do in the bathroom."

"How dare you come in here and—" A cough interrupted me. "Leave me alone, Donnie." I coughed again. "I can't go anywhere!"

For an instant I thought he would go. He looked me over like maybe I wasn't worth the effort after all. Instead, he went out to the bathroom, returning with my hairbrush. He sat me up and began brushing my hair. "Ouch!" I yanked the brush from his hand and gave my thick waves a few swipes. "Just where is it you think we are going?"

"To a funeral. A close friend of mine. I'd really like it if you could be there."

"Believe me, Donnie. You do not want to take me out in public. I cough all the time and I can't walk from here to the bathroom without taking a break."

"It's okay. Trust me. I'll carry you if you want me to."

"Oh, yeah. That would be good. That would be real good."

THE OUTSIDE AIR surprised my face. I inhaled deeply, which caused me to hack, which almost ruined the moment. Still, I smelled winter. It was the pure scent of the river, devoid of earth smells and cottonwood leaves and salmonberries, which were gone now or covered with snow. Donnie let me stand on the porch for a minute and then he helped me into the truck. I settled against the seat and pulled my jacket tight around me. The black skirt draped just above my ankles and I wore a nice sweater but rebelliously insisted on my brown logger boots instead of the daintier black shoes that had caused my downfall at Sarah's wedding. I asked Donnie, if men thought high-heeled shoes were so great, why didn't they wear them? Time had worn the tanned leather of my boots soft and supple. I hiked my skirt up so that I could admire them and because Donnie seemed to hate them so.

"So why won't you tell me who died?"

"I don't think you're ready yet."

I gasped. "It *is* someone I know. It's Mason White." He didn't answer. "Am I right?"

"What makes you think of Mason?"

"I don't know. He was just one of those guys who seemed destined to die young. I'm surprised he made it through high school. He was into scuba diving and rock climbing and skydiving and drugs—not necessarily in that order."

"I don't know what ever happened to him. He's been gone for years. Anyway, it's not him."

I quit asking. One thing I hated about Donnie was that he could be just as stubborn as I could. It was already early afternoon. I wasn't sure what day it was. Probably a weekday, because TJ was gone. Mom must have gone to pick him up from preschool. When we got to the Carter Store, Donnie turned the truck toward Dixon. "I should have left a note," I muttered.

"I did. I left them my cell phone number on the kitchen counter." He reached into his pocket and tossed something into my lap. I stared down at my pager. He must have grabbed it from my lamp table. That was the first time I'd ever forgotten it. In a flash I remembered every time I had tested it to be sure it worked. The times I had run to it, thinking I heard the signal. It was time to go. Time to get my life back. My hand closed around the small black device and I found myself squeezing, crushing it with all the strength I had, trying to make it vibrate, scream, anything but lie there mutely taunting me. I rolled down the window and hurled it into a pile of dirty snow.

Donnie whipped the wheel to the right and skidded to a stop on the slushy shoulder. "What did you do that for?"

"It doesn't work." His glare made me recoil. "Well, it doesn't. I might as well be carrying a potato everywhere I go."

I thought he would go look for it. He should have found it and clipped it to my jacket and made me promise not to do it again. Instead, he checked his side mirror and pulled back onto the road with a shrug. "Yeah. I don't blame you, Sam. It's been a long haul. I want you to know I admire you. I don't know if I could have held on this long."

I felt good for about a minute. What did he mean by that? What choice did I have?

We drove in silence until we reached the rest stop by the river, where we had parked that summer night to climb on the train trestle. Now the lot was pocked with puddles of melting snow and streaked with tire tracks. I was surprised when Donnie pulled in. "What's going on?"

"We're here."

"You liar. This is not a funeral." Donnie came around and opened my door. "I can't walk out on those tracks, if that's what you're thinking. I'm not supposed to overexert myself."

He pulled a knapsack from under the seat. "You can do it. We'll go slow."

"It's too far."

"Get on my back." Curiosity momentarily empowered me. I stood on the running board, hiked up the skirt and wrapped my arms and legs around him. He linked his arms around my legs and strolled down the path through the trees that led to the trestle. I heard the river and closed my eyes. Donnie's hair was soft on my face. I held on tight. One hand inadvertently slipped inside his jacket and the open collar of his shirt, but I didn't move it. His skin was warm and smelled faintly spicy.

"Am I too heavy?" We were on the tracks now and his strides were long.

"No more than a bale of wet hay." He didn't say much. We finally reached the middle of the bridge, where the metal grid-work arched above us like a cathedral. He put me down gently next to a vertical support. I linked my forearm inside its criss-crossing metal and looked down.

It was not the carefree river of summer. The water was high on its banks, swollen with the melting snow; a loose flowing braid of light and shadows, more shadows it seemed than light, undulating, writhing, moaning. Patches of snow above its banks were spotted with bare brown earth and tufts of bent brown grass. Heavy clouds dragged slowly across the foothills, leaving cottony combings among the treetops.

Donnie respected my reverie. I had not been this close to the river for a while. We sat and dangled our feet like that night in June. He opened his knapsack and passed me an orange and then took it back and peeled it for me. "I can peel an orange," I said.

"But can you do it like this?" He stripped the peel off in one long spiral, pulled the orange into halves and passed me one. He reached into the bag again, this time pulling out a bottle of Irish whiskey. "I would like to propose a toast."

I laughed and slapped his shoulder with the back of my sticky hand. "You know I can't drink that!"

"Why not? You're dying anyway."

I was shocked and offended. "You jerk! I can't believe you said that. What kind of a friend—"

"The kind who calls it as he sees it. You've got lots of people telling you to hang in there. Just one more day. Tomorrow, tomorrow. And how long has that been going on? You've told me yourself, Sam, your blood type is the hardest to match. What are your chances of getting a heart in time? Look at you. Your face has about as much color as that sky. You're skinny; you cough all the time. I remember when you could climb to the top of this trestle and hang by your hands." He threw a piece of orange into the river. "A person knows when they're dying. When I heard that you refused to go to the doctor, I knew that you know. After all, they drop you from the transplant program for stuff like that. Not being totally committed to the program. But I'm not telling you anything you haven't already given a lot of thought."

"So this is *my* funeral."

He nodded. "Like a wake, only instead of propping you up in a corner and toasting a corpse, I thought you might like to really be here for it. It's a shame to give a person all that attention only after they're dead."

"Then what? Are you going to push me in front of the train?"

He shook his head. "Nah. I'd have too much explaining to do."

"Okay." I reached for the glass in his hand. "Pour."

He obliged and then raised his glass. "Here's to the only girl I ever knew who would feel around in the mud for crawdads with her bare hands." We clinked glasses. "Remember when we boiled a coffee can full of 'em over the fire?"

"How old were we then?"

"I don't know. Maybe about sixth grade. You were starting to get little boobs."

"You remember that? You little perv. I remember you making the crawdads hold up their arms and scream before you put them in the pot. What else? You're supposed to say a bunch of nice things about me."

"Oh, yeah." He pulled a tightly folded piece of paper from his pocket but didn't open it. "You were always a good guy to have on my side during a war. A good strategist. And you could throw a pinecone grenade almost as far as I could." He swirled the liquor in his glass. "Then we went to junior high and got too cool to crawl on our bellies in the dirt. We gave up climbing trees and building dams and took up sports and dances and whatever it is that girls do. Giggling and painting toenails."

"I never did that."

"We were still neighbors, rode the same school bus, but I didn't really see you anymore. You didn't see me. We just took each other for granted. Then one day I saw you again. You were holding hands with Tim Weatherbee. You laughed like you used to laugh with me. It was strange how I felt. It really caught me off guard."

"You were jealous?"

He grinned. "Yeah. I snoozed, I losed. Anyway, that doesn't matter anymore. The important thing is that we got a chance to be friends again before—" He took a swig. "As adults, I mean." He unfolded the lined yellow paper he had pulled from his pocket. "Okay. I wrote this little eulogy. Is that the right word? It might sound dumb today. I tipped the bottle a little last night. That's when I got this idea, for the funeral and all."

He cleared his throat. "Samantha Dodd Weatherbee will be

missed by all who knew her. She died at the tender age of twenty-five in the home of her youth and is survived by her son, TJ; her father, Judge Blake Dodd; her mother, Lucy Dodd; and her sister, Lindsey Matthews. She was a skilled fly-fisher and could exactly mimic the call of a loon. Her dream was to live in a house with a wraparound porch overlooking the Stillaguamish River. The river was her life. Samantha could tell by listening where the stream was on its banks and knew precisely where the fish lay in any given hole. She knew the instant that the first cottonwood buds broke through in spring and the difference between a robin's morning call and the song for after the rain.

"Those of us who knew her will not miss her frank observation of our faults or her stubborn pride. We *will* miss her passion for the people and things she loved. She loved to hear the wind in the cottonwoods. Sometimes she made anyone near stop to listen."

These were things about myself I had forgotten. I watched Donnie's jaw muscle flinch as he read. He had shaved closely but missed a spot just under his chin. His blue-green eyes were shaded beneath his wiry brow and hard to read, like a current sliding under an overhanging bank.

"She was devoted to her son, TJ, who will miss her most of all. He will miss the way she let his tree frogs crawl on her face. He'll remember the way she pushed the hair off his forehead, tucked him into bed at night and taught him how to cheat at cards. As he grows she will not be there to make pencil marks on the wall. Every birthday, every Christmas, she will be the one gift he wanted but didn't get. When he dunks the winning shot at his high school game, he will miss her face in the crowd."

I didn't usually cry at funerals and I wasn't about to start. "I want to go home now." I listened intently for distant rumblings or the woeful whistle of a train. "You know, if a train comes, I can't—"

"I'm almost done." Donnie turned the paper over and smoothed out the wrinkles. "We will grieve for a while, but life must go on. Eventually the space that Samantha took up on this earth and in our hearts will make room for someone or something else. We tend to get in a rage over the devastation of a newly logged hillside, but in a year or two the grasses and wildflowers wave in the sun and we forget. We pick sweet wild blueberries among the stumps. TJ will be loved by those who remain. Samantha's parents will pause by her photo from time to time with sad smiles and then go on about their day. I will probably move away from here. I'll marry a tall thin beauty who looks great on my arm and she'll always say the right thing. But sometimes I will long for a friend who knows me, who will call bull on my self-deception, who is never boring or predictable, and I will think of Sam. I'll close my eyes and see the mischief in her green eyes, her wry smile, and I'll reach for the phone and ·then remember that she is no longer in my world."

Donnie poured us each another shot. "And so, I tell you now"—his hand reached out and brushed my face—"while I can still touch you. I have loved you, Samantha. I'll miss you more than you know."

He held his glass to mine and I returned his gaze before we tipped them back. The liquid ran like lava down my throat.

WHEN DONNIE BROUGHT ME home from my funeral, the sky was already the dark color of the clay banks down by Carter

Bridge, though it was not yet five o'clock. Multicolored Christmas lights outlined the log rails and eaves of our covered porch. Mom invited Donnie to stay for dinner, which annoyed me because I was exhausted and wanted to be alone. He stuck his head in the oven and smelled lasagna and the next thing I knew he was cutting garlic bread and arranging the slices in a basket for the table. The lasagna was not homemade, like his mother's. Mom had discovered frozen entrées, salad in a bag, veggies that were already washed and cut, and frozen bread dough that you could slap in a pan, thaw and bake without all the mess. She was in homemaker heaven. Now there was that much more time for painting muddy cows, lunching with tennis friends and taking TJ to the zoo.

For some reason, neither Donnie nor I mentioned my funeral. He just said we drove down to Dixon and sat by the river for a while. The Judge nodded approvingly. Mom wanted to know if I had kept warm enough. TJ was indignant that we didn't bring him along, but Donnie promised to take him next time. "Just us guys," he said. "We'll launch driftwood boats and then go up on the bridge and bomb them." Donnie crinkled his nose and shook his head. "No girls, though. They might make us eat the crust on our sandwiches and be quiet." He leaned into TJ and whispered loudly, "And if you gotta take a pee, you don't have to go all the way to the bathroom."

TJ liked that idea. His eyes stayed fixed on Donnie all through the meal. When Donnie laughed, TJ laughed. He even ate his green beans after Donnie piled a second helping on his own plate, proclaiming that he grew green beans in his garden every summer. TJ said he was going to grow some too. "Green beans and apples and popcorn, cuz those are my favorite vegetables."

After dinner I crawled into TJ's bed and read about Curious George and the man with the yellow hat while the Judge and Donnie played chess on the teak-inlaid board that Matthew gave my father when he was first appointed to the State Superior Court. This was the first time I had seen the Judge play chess with anyone but his old friend Matt. I figured that by now he would have Donnie's queen running for her life but also knew that winning was not nearly as important to Donnie as the privilege of being in His Honor's presence. He still addressed my father as *sir*, and whether they discussed the pros and cons of a global economy or a man's purpose in life, I imagined Donnie greedily following the trail of my father's words, gathering each golden nugget of wisdom that fell from the sage's lips.

Later, Donnie tapped on and then pushed open my bedroom door. "Hey, I saw your light on." My father walked past him down the hall and Donnie looked over his shoulder. "Good night, sir."

"Good night, Don. I'm open to a rematch anytime. Good night, Sam."

"Good night."

Donnie waited until the Judge closed his bedroom door before coming in and sitting on the edge of my bed. "How do you feel? I hope I didn't get you too tired today."

I put my book down and shook my head. Tired? What else was there? I was tired of life going on without me. "It was good to get my funeral out of the way." Why did I always say things I didn't mean?

"Yeah. Well, they'll probably have another one. They'll have it down at the Community Church, I guess." Donnie's eyes wandered around my room until they settled on the framed photo on my bedside table of TJ and me eating wedges of watermelon on the Fourth of July. We beamed at each other, our cheeks bulging like chipmunks'. That was before I even considered death an option. Now it was just a question of when. Donnie picked up the photo almost absently. "Then all the local women will go into a cooking frenzy. Mom will bring over shepherd's pie and crescent rolls. Lots of spaghetti. I remember that from when Uncle Les died. We ate pasta for weeks."

I pictured everyone I knew gathering to grieve over Hungarian goulash and green bean casserole. They wiped their mouths, leaned back with a collective belch, pushed back their chairs and returned to their daily routines. "Ask your mother to bring lobster and caviar instead. Somebody could bring steamed clams and garlic bread. I might even come back from the grave for that. And macaroni and cheese for TJ, of course." I made light of it, though it now seemed to loom as an inevitable event. I felt the weight of the earth on my chest, pushing me into the bed, pressing me down, down into the rich river valley soil. As if trapped in a satin-lined box under a sealed lid, I screamed inside like a claustrophobic, beating and clawing, begging to be let out. But to Donnie I must have looked as calm as a lake on a windless morning. I yawned. "Are you coming over tomorrow?"

"No." He stood deliberately and walked toward the door. He must have removed his denim overshirt while playing chess out by the blazing fireplace. His muscular chest and shoulders showed through his white T-shirt. "I'm not coming by tomorrow or the next day or the day after that. I'm not going to watch you die, Sam. Today was my good-bye."

There was this long look between us and I thought he would come back to my bed and touch my face. I wanted him to hold me in his strong arms, to be close enough to smell the cotton-wood of his skin. I think I wanted to cry against his chest and then feel him tenderly kiss the tears from the corners of my eyes. But he didn't move. "Thank you," I finally said.

"For what?"

"For being my friend."

He nodded. "Good-bye, Sammy."

The door closed behind him. It latched quietly, like I imagined the lid would close on a coffin. Quietly, reverently, permanently.

21 ✦

I'M EMBARRASSED TO SAY that I was not one of those people who die graciously, like that sweet Southern belle Melanie in *Gone with the Wind.*

The reality of my pending death was just more than I could bear. I found my soul too heavy to budge, so I wallowed in sorrow in a darkened room. When TJ came to see me, I clung to him as if each visit might be our last, breaking down and weeping twice in his presence, which I had vowed I would not do. Upsetting my son was the last thing I wanted; it's just that to me it was like TJ was dying. He would be lost to me forever whether it was him or me. I would no longer see him stepping with stealth through the tall grass, head down, searching for frogs. I would no longer hear his sweet voice singing made-up songs or feel the smoothness of his perfect brown skin. I would not witness the journey to manhood and beyond. I was mourning the loss of my son.

I suppose I was thinking a lot about myself too. About how I would be leaving this world without having accomplished anything important (except, of course, for TJ) and, worse yet, not having become someone. Here I was still floundering, just getting my game piece on the board, and someone's shouting, "Sorry!" Game over.

I took some comfort in thinking that Tim would deeply regret what he'd said. Refusing to forgive someone and then having them die on you is a horrible burden to bear. I tried to picture him standing alone at my graveside and imagined what he might say. But in the end, it really didn't matter. If he couldn't love TJ, he couldn't love me. When he said that, something had clicked off inside me. I finally knew that we were done—and in some strange way it was a relief. I had done what I could to restore us, but he would not—could not—forgive.

Donnie had not been kidding when he said good-bye. He didn't visit; he didn't call. I tried to phone him a few times but he wasn't home, and after that I talked myself out of it. He had obviously meant what he said and really, I didn't want him to see me in this morose state. I was still coughing, even when I sat upright in the bed. I didn't do a thing with my hair or face. I just sat there most of each day staring at the TV the Judge had moved into my room. It was better that Donnie remember me with at least some signs of life and dignity. Let him remember me laughing, fishing with him and TJ, singing the oldies while he worked on his truck.

But I missed him. He was the one person I felt knew me to the core—and mysteriously he liked me anyway. And I knew *him,* I was sure, better than anyone—despite the seven-year interruption in our relationship.

My mother bought me a new mint-green chenille robe. Sometimes she played cheery music and insisted on opening my curtains. Lindsey offered pep talks and manicures and once got me to play a game of hearts. But it all seemed so pointless. What did anything matter anymore?

The Judge finally couldn't stand it another day. He stormed into my room one morning, tossed me the robe and insisted that I get out of that bed.

"Why? What's going on?" I asked.

"Life. Life is going on." He gestured for me to follow him and headed for the bedroom door. "Come on now, or you're going to miss it."

Curiosity got the better of me. I stepped tentatively from the bed, wrapped the robe around me and followed my father out of the room. Weak and slightly dizzy at first, I skimmed my hand along the wall of the hallway for support. Mom was in her bathrobe too, propping TJ where he stood on the sill of the big picture window in the dining room. The shirt of his pajamas had ridden up, exposing his bare tummy. He was giggling.

"I wanna play with them, Grandma."

The Judge guided me up to the window with his hand on my back. "Mama Bear wouldn't like that, son. Besides, those guys have sharp claws."

They were black bears. Two big cubs rolling, chasing and tumbling together at the edge of the back lawn. "Where's the mother?" I asked.

My father pointed. "Over there by the tree. Do you see her?"

All the snow from prior weeks was gone. The sow was rolling a rotted log with her powerful paw. "How do you know that's the mother? She's not much bigger than they are."

"I saw her with these guys last spring, when they were the size of a twenty-pound bag of flour. She has a lighter patch under her chin. Can you see it? She'll keep them with her at least through next summer, until they're old enough to go out on their own."

"They're brothers," TJ volunteered. "They're not fighting,

Mom. That's just the way they play. I *really* want to go play with them."

Mom moved aside and I leaned into him. "Sorry, baby, they play pretty rough."

The big cubs suddenly turned and scrambled toward the sow bear as if by some grunted command. Their rich brown fur flowed loosely in waves along their bodies as they ran. "Shouldn't they be hibernating now?" I asked.

The Judge shook his head. "Bears don't shut down completely like squirrels or skunks. They can actually wake up from time to time during the winter. It looks like Mama Bear got hungry." The cubs were now snacking along with their mother on something they had found inside the log. Probably grubs.

TJ turned and patted me with his hand. "Why don't *I* have a brother, Mom?"

My father shot me an amused glance with one raised eyebrow.

"Well, I never had another baby after you, Teej."

"Why not?"

Now my mother was smirking. Everyone looking at me. "Well . . . It's just that I would have to . . . These things don't just happen. You have to plan, but even then you never know . . . and in my case . . ." I stopped myself. "Help me out here anytime, somebody."

We all laughed. All except TJ, who still wanted an intelligent answer to his question. I told him that I would get back to him later on that. The bear family headed downstream with Mama Bear in the lead, and Mom announced that she was going back to making waffles.

"Eat out here with us, Sam," my father said.

"Oh, I don't think so. I feel gross."

"Go take a shower. We'll wait." He wasn't asking.

I didn't feel like showering. I wanted to hibernate like a skunk, in a sleep so deep that nothing could hurt me. But I obeyed my father.

The water washed over my body, running in rivulets down my arms, between my breasts. I realized my skin was still beautiful, my body almost as sleek as it was at seventeen. I should have been in my prime. I would have liked to present TJ with a little brother. My eyes closed and I pretended I was a child again, letting the little waterfall on the creek wash over me. Remembering my river. How as a child I thought it flowed forever; it had no beginning and no end. The water spiraled at my feet and disappeared down the drain.

At breakfast I was quiet, not on purpose but because I felt my very soul had washed down that drain. It had gone on before me, awaiting my physical body in some dark place from which there could be no escape. TJ covered my silence with questions about bears, which my father—the talking encyclopedia—answered in vivid detail. Mom said she had never seen bears so close to the house before, but the Judge said not to worry; they would disappear into the woods the minute they caught wind of us. After taking a few bites and poking at my food for some time, I excused myself and returned to my room.

Later, the Judge knocked on my door. "Samantha?"

I pulled the front of my robe together. "Yes. Come in."

He immediately walked to my window and pulled the yellow curtains aside. "It's gloomy in here. Why don't you let the light in?"

I shrugged. "I don't know. It glares on the TV sometimes."

"While you sit here in the dark, you're missing things that

go on in the light. Like the bears. That was a nice surprise, wasn't it?"

I nodded. "Life is full of surprises." The irony of what I'd just said hit me. I looked up at him sheepishly.

"You need to get back to the doctor, Samantha." He pulled a chair close to the bed and sat down. "I know you think it's pointless, but it *is* necessary. If for no other reason, just to show you're still in the program. If you're not willing to do whatever it takes, you'll get passed up. Donor hearts are too scarce to chance on someone who's not willing to fight."

I sighed deeply and coughed. My heavy heart felt like it had sunk into my stomach. "I can't." As soon as I said it, I knew I had made a mistake.

The Judge shot to his feet and his chair fell backward with a crash. "That's a lie! It's a lie from the pit of hell! *I can't.* Yes, you can! You *can* fight, Samantha! I know you're tired, but forget your body for a minute. This battle is in your mind." He was pacing now, running his hand through his hair, his eyes ablaze. "You give up in your mind and your body's naturally going to follow. But if you have faith—the essence of things hoped for, the assurance of things not seen—you can do anything." His eyes fell on the picture of TJ and me eating watermelon on the Fourth of July. He picked it up and passed it to me. "This can happen again."

In my weakness, I didn't argue. I took the photo and saw the pure joy in our eyes, our smiles as wide as the melon rinds. I let my hand with the framed photo fall to my side and stared at the window. My eyes filled with tears.

The Judge's anger ebbed. He pulled the chair upright and sat down, remaining quiet for some time. When he spoke again, his voice was soft. "If you really want to die, Samantha, then dwell on how sick you are. Think about it day and night. Imagine never seeing TJ again, never again standing in the river or smelling the cottonwoods. Think about life going on without you. But if you want to live, do the opposite. Pray for a new heart. Believe that it's on its way and speak accordingly. Speak of the future. Choose life, Samantha. *Decide* to live."

WHEN WE WERE KIDS, Donnie and I built our first dam together. A dam we were sure would put the Army Corps of Engineers to shame, that would cause them to crawl to us begging for our plans. But the plans were all in our heads. We spent several days carrying heavy rocks from the river to the little creek that fed it, placing them stone on stone, carefully fitting, chinking the gaps with smaller chunks of rock, until we had built a wall. A mighty barricade that blocked the stream, all but a wash of trickles, causing it to spread into a placid pond. Our own private swimming pool.

After our celebration swim we lay on the creek bank among the bracken ferns, admiring our work. The water level continued to rise, slowly spreading, reaching beyond the low sandy banks into the grasses, stretching out like a sleepy child.

But just at one edge a tiny rivulet made its way around the rocks. The rivulet pushed and prodded until it became a small stream. An escape route. The pent-up waters began to throw themselves at the newly discovered opening. They shoved forward, stampeding through the narrow pass. They undermined the foundation. We stood and watched in horror and delight as our seemingly benign pond rammed against the dam, tumbling its heavy stones and exploding through, rushing, gushing in a powerful rage that could no longer be contained.

That's the way it was with me.

To my father I must have looked as placid as that dammed-up pond when he left my room that day. Surely there was no outward sign of what was happening inside of me. But his words pushed and prodded. Something about what he said rang true and I found myself repeating the words over and over. *Choose life. Decide to live.*

I actually got up and dressed myself that afternoon. My hair had air-dried in its natural wavy state. I pulled it up into a high ponytail and sat by the dining room window with a cup of tea, hoping the bear family might return. TJ played with his cars and trucks at my feet and between the mahogany chair legs. I practiced what my father said. I thought of taking my son to kindergarten next fall. Not Lindsey but *me* packing his lunchbox and walking him to the door of his classroom. Once I even said, "Hey, Teej. Maybe we'll see those bears when we're fishing next summer." The words came out hollow, but at least they came out.

That night I dreamed. I don't remember the players. I don't know where the sea could be as clear and green as lime Jell-O or the sky could be so blue. Certainly not in Washington State, midwinter. We were laughing. I dove into the warm sea and swam right to the bottom with the strength of a porpoise and stayed there for a long time with my eyes wide open and never craving air. Though unaware of it at the time, now I'm sure I was absolutely naked. No tight swimsuit creeping up, no tank or regulator, no flippers. I burst up through the surface into the tepid sky, soaring and swooping like a swallow until I found myself lying on a dock panting, laughing, beads of water drying inward on my tight brown skin. A breeze as gentle as a mother's touch ruffled my hair. I was not ashamed of my nakedness but aware only of infinite freedom, dazzling light and energy that radiated from some invisible source.

I awoke the next morning to the smell of coffee and the sound of cupboard doors slamming in the kitchen. I had slept propped upright, as usual, because it relieved the pressure on my chest, allowing me to breathe more freely. I closed my eyes and tried to soar like a swallow again. If only I could retrieve the dream. I had never known the absolute joy that my soul had conjured up while I slept. Where did my mind conceive it? I gradually understood. Love. That's what it was. I was surrounded by it, swimming in it, flying through it. Fear did not exist.

I know now that the dream was a gift. I felt the love I had been so starved for—but didn't believe in. It was the love I always wished my father could have for me.

It would take a lot of love for me to break down the dam that was stopping up my life. A tiny rivulet of hope rose up in me and with it a surge of strength. I could do it. I would love my son enough to fight for my life. And Donnie. I knew now that he was the man I wanted. I would be strong for him and for my parents. I would make them all proud.

Choose life. Little by little, the dam was coming down.

22

FOR WEEKS THE MOVIES in my head had starred a
motherless boy and his blond, vivacious auntie—perfect in
every way, with her plastic-haired husband and a supporting
cast of two doting grandparents. My only lines were chiseled
into a gravestone. That was about to change.

Since I had *misplaced* my pager, the Judge stopped by Radio-
Shack on his way back from the city for a replacement.

I called my social worker, Irma Krueger, from the privacy of
my room. She had been out to the house back in late July after
my cardiologist determined that conventional treatments were
not working on my damaged heart. I knew that Irma had come
to evaluate my worthiness for acceptance into the heart transplant program and that I was being psychoanalyzed to deter-
mine whether I had the grit to stay committed to it. She also
came to discuss financial issues, which my father insisted be between the two of them. What could he do? I had somehow become his responsibility again, not by law of course, but by his
own code of honor. The same self-woven cable had caused him
to take responsibility for me twenty-five years ago because of a
promise he made to an obnoxious coworker.

Irma answered her phone on the second ring. "Hello."

"Hi, Irma. This is Samantha."

"Well, well. I thought you didn't want to talk to me any-more." Her middle-aged voice was tinged with a German accent and a smile.

"Sorry. I was having a bad day last time you called." I closed my eyes and remembered the dream. I pictured myself soaring like a barn swallow with the sun on my back, full of joy, and I drew on that strength. "Irma. I don't want to die. I want to live."

"That's good. That's good, Samantha. Now we can get back on track. Christopher said you missed your last appointment. Do you want me to reschedule?" I said yes. She gave me a pep talk and said she would speak to the doctor about giving me some kind of antidepressant. "You have to be willing to fight, Samantha. You have to do everything in your power. We will depend on God for the rest. Are you ready to fight?"

I didn't give it a moment of thought. "Yes. I'm ready."

CHRISTOPHER WAS THE NURSE assigned to me by the hospital. His dark hair was woven into a single braid that fell just short of the small of his back. A few wiry gray strands sprang rebelliously from the smooth ones at the top of his head and from his sideburns. I'd say he was about thirty, going on thirteen. He always made irreverent jokes about the hospital staff, including my transplant surgeon, Dr. Wilhelm. One day he told me not to get beeped between five and seven p.m. because that's when Dr. Wilhelm went to happy hour. "He just can't pass up a bargain. Half-price drinks and hors d'oeuvres. Come to think of it, don't get beeped after seven at night either."

"I don't want to know this," I said, still chuckling. "Anyway, he's got to be rich. He has a yacht, you know. He told me he cruises up to the San Juans every chance he gets."

"Yeah. And the whole thing is furnished with yard sale treasures."

"No way."

"Way. Trust me. I've been on it. He invited the transplant team out for a dinner cruise last summer. He poured cheap wine and took us on the tour. Chairs, wall hangings, dishes— you name it. All from garage sales. You'd think he was displaying trophies from his last safari. I came out of the bathroom and he wanted to know how many squares I used."

Christopher grew quiet momentarily as he checked my pulse. He scrawled something on the page attached to his clipboard and then motioned for me to lie back on the padded table. I had already disrobed and slipped into a cotton gown spotted with faded green alligators. I knew the drill. Christopher began preparing for the echocardiogram and I automatically untied the front. I had been chilled all morning. A fresh crop of goose bumps emerged from the flesh of my arms. We spoke lightly of this world within a world that we shared, while we both pretended that I was not a half-naked woman and that he was only a nurse and not a man.

"The doctor will be right in." He winked as he left the room.

I STARED at the faces from *People* magazine smiling their dazzling white smiles. Actors and actresses promenaded across the pages in tuxedos and glittering gowns with plunging necklines and seams split to the upper thighs. They bored me. I strained to listen to the hushed voices outside the door to no avail.

The trip to Seattle had tired me. I lay back on the tissue-covered examination table and closed my eyes. As usual my palm rested on my heart. Squish. Squish. Squish-squish. I tried to remember how it used to sound—that bold thumping in my chest when I had run up the hill from the creek all the way to the barn to hide from the James Gang after I pushed Jared James's face in the mud. How it had pounded like a bass drum when a sow bear ambled toward me as I fished. Even after she grunted to her cubs and detoured across the stream on a mossy deadfall, the healthy throbbing of my heart reverberated in my ears. Now the muscle that controlled my destiny was a weak, lethargic jellyfish. I hated it. I had trusted it to beat as faithfully as the spinning of the earth, the rising and setting of the sun. It had betrayed me.

And yet I felt I had this coming. It was God's judgment on me for all the rotten things I had done. I betrayed my husband. I was an adulteress and a liar and, worst of all, I murdered my own baby. She was unplanned and inconvenient. Her timing was off, so I killed her. I delivered her up to the butchers in the plush clinic with a smiling receptionist and mauve upholstery and sanitary white walls. I paid them three hundred and twenty dollars to do the deed and dispose of her mutilated body. I often argued with myself. The abortion was the only reasonable thing I could have done at the time. Plenty of other women had committed the same act and didn't seem to be tormented by it. Yet I felt somehow more accountable for my sins. It was the curse of being the Judge's daughter. Of having his words rise up into my head no matter how far from him I wandered, and knowing that if he was right, and that every word in the Bible was inspired by God and absolutely true, I was in a whole heap of trouble for eons to come.

I don't know when I first realized that I could never measure up to the Judge's standard. I had tried to be good like Lindsey. My sister brought home schoolwork with smiley faces and gold stars. My papers said things like: *Messy. Incomplete. Didn't follow instructions.* At parent–teacher conferences Lindsey got rave reviews. Her homework was always finished and turned in on crisp unwrinkled paper with no mud streaks or jam stains. She never talked out of turn or had dirt under her fingernails. Not once did she get into a fight on the playground. Mrs. McCrite just couldn't see how we could be sisters. She said we were as different as night and day. I knew which one she meant was night because Lindsey was everyone's Little Miss Sunshine.

Of course, once I found out the truth about my origins, it all began to make sense. I was the offspring of some brash, wild-haired woman who sold me to the Dodd family because she didn't want me. That's why I was so different. My mother and my sister both had soft shiny hair the color of a hay field in July. Mine was as brown as a cedar trunk.

Even now, I had to admit, it hurt. TJ, like Lindsey, did not bump into a wall when he approached the Judge. In his innocence, my son would rush into those consecrated arms with no thought as to whether they would open to receive him. In the evenings he often climbed onto his grandpa's lap. The Judge would rest his chin on TJ's tousled head and read aloud, sometimes petting him, massaging his neck as if he were a Lab puppy. But between the Judge and me there was a Plexiglas wall. I could see him but never touch him. And strangely, even now as an adult, I longed to feel worthy of my father's love.

Dr. Sovold's entrance startled me. He swung into the room, plopping onto a wheeled stool and sliding toward me in one motion. His lanky legs straddled the stool awkwardly. He wore a plaid shirt today instead of the traditional white coat.

"Good morning, Samantha. I hope I didn't wake you. You looked like Sleeping Beauty lying there."

I raised myself up on one elbow and studied him. "You look like a long tall Texan on a Shetland pony."

"I always wanted to be a cowboy." He grinned. "But I found out I was allergic to horses and became a cardiologist instead."

He stood and began to slide the cold wand over my chest and beneath my armpits, taking longer than usual, studying the pulsing image on the screen in silence and finally wiping the slippery gel from my skin. "Okay." He sighed. "Wrap yourself up."

I sat up, relieved that it was over. "I'm starved. My sister and I are going to this great little Thai place on the way back."

"Well, Samantha—" He shook his head. "I don't think so. Not today." He hesitated.

"Why don't you just aim your six-gun and shoot?"

He smiled apologetically like he had been caught on the carpet with manure on his boots. "Okay." He pushed back his stool and crossed his gangly arms. They were white and freckled. The skin of his face was the color of an uncooked chicken, slightly dimpled, a few stray whiskers protruding like unplucked feathers. His brows drew together slightly. "Your tests show no improvement. In fact, we're seeing increased weakness in the walls of the left ventricle. You've probably been feeling it." I nodded. "Your heart's cavity has enlarged and stretched and it's really working overtime trying to pump blood around your body. It's tired. You're tired."

I couldn't argue with that. I stared back at him, waiting.

He raised his chin with authority. "I want to check you into the hospital. You need the rest. You need to be waited on hand and foot at the Hard Knocks Hotel. Let someone else do your

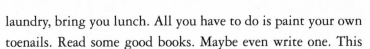

laundry, bring you lunch. All you have to do is paint your own toenails. Read some good books. Maybe even write one. This would be a good time for that."

"But it's Christmastime."

His eyes softened. "I know. But I think this is necessary, Samantha. It's time."

I had planned to call Donnie that night when I got home. I missed him so badly, and now that I had decided to live he might change his mind about not seeing me anymore. "I can rest at home. I have my mother and my sister—"

"I need to have you close to me right now. Once every few weeks is not enough anymore. I need to check on you every day. You can't make the three-hour drive into the city every day. That's no way to rest. If "—he corrected himself—"*when* a compatible donor heart becomes available to you, you've got to be strong enough to go through surgery."

"I have to go home first. My son . . . and all my things . . ."

"Your parents will bring them. They'll bring your boy too. I've already talked to them."

So it had been decided. The river that was my life had veered off course again.

My father had promised that everything would be all right. He often spoke of the future and I was always in it. He said I should check into Cub Scouts for TJ when he reaches second grade. He brought books home for me on career choices and pamphlets from Northwest Community College in Darlington. When he saw me writing in my journal, he would nod approvingly. "Working on that bestseller?" my father would ask. "I can't wait to read it." And I found myself wanting to write it. Imagining my father proudly pulling my book from the rack in the grocery store checkout line and flashing the boldly printed name on the cover. "My daughter wrote this."

I remembered Irma's lilting German voice when it hardened. "You've got to be willing to fight, Samantha." I closed my eyes and saw myself in the dream. Strong. Alive. Fearless. I would fight this battle. But apparently I would fight it lying down.

That evening, alone in my hospital room, I dialed Donnie's number. He would be glad to hear that I was fighting for my life now. I was not the pathetic weakling he had toasted at my premature funeral. How had I been so blind? I had given up on life because of Tim. Because the man I betrayed would not forgive me, though in reality it had been over between us five years ago. That truth had finally sunk to the bottom of my soul, landing with a thud. I still had my son to live for. And what about Donnie? I was free to love him now. He had said he loved me. What kind of love did he mean?

"Hey." A breathless Donnie finally answered the phone. "Sorry, I know I'm late, but I just got in from the barn. I have to get cleaned up, and I'll be there in about a half hour. You're probably wearing one of your great dresses, right?"

I was confused and didn't speak.

"Rachel?"

My hand clenched the receiver like it was a climber's last lifeline and then slowly lowered it back to its cradle.

23

FOR THE FIRST COUPLE of days I had no roommate. My mother sprawled across the vacant hospital bed with *The Seattle Times* spread out in front of her, her ankles crossing and uncrossing in the air. When TJ came he snuggled into bed with me, but only for a few minutes at a time. There was so much to see and do. My nurse, Christopher, brought empty syringes, teaching him how to suck water from my drinking glass and then depress the plunger, squirting streams across my toes and on innocent pedestrians on the sidewalk below my window. He took TJ on a wheelchair ride. It seemed they were gone a long time. When they returned TJ colored pictures of the doe and two fawns that crossed our field every morning going to the river, leaving a trail of wandering dotted lines across the snow. "This is for my friend," he said. "He doesn't have no hair." My son seemed saddened by this. When Christopher wheeled him away again later that afternoon to deliver his pictures, I was glad to see him go. I had no right to keep all that healing sunshine to myself.

On day three I got Lulu. She moved into the empty bed next to mine with much ado. Two potted geraniums tottered precariously on her lap as the nurse wheeled her in, because, she said, she couldn't trust anyone but herself to keep them alive. "My neighbor Clara, God bless her, is the Charles Manson of horticulture. She'd have this drowned to death by Tuesday." Her real name, she said, was Luella, but all her friends just called her Lulu, which was exactly what she was. A real one. She wore a pink satin bed jacket like Doris Day, open in the front, revealing three-fourths of two weathered and weary breasts. She looked down at them and sighed. "The old gray mare just ain't what she used to be." Then she brightened. "But I still have my own teeth." She looked exactly like an old horse when she drew up her lips to show me. "The originals. Not bad for an old broad, eh?"

"Hey, if you've got them, flaunt them. That's what I always say." That was a lie. I never said that before in my life. I did think it before, though. That was when I was talking myself into doing the topless-dancing thing because my roommate Mindy promised it would be so lucrative. It was not a good career move for me. Not that I wasn't built for it. That was the one thing I had over my sister, Lindsey. She would have paid big money to be able to bounce when she jogged. So I got one asset from the woman who gave birth to me. I lasted in that job for about a week before coldcocking a trucker passing through Reno with a trailer full of pork sides.

"So what are you in for?" Lulu promptly removed her swirly strawberry blond hair, placing it on a white foam head on her bedside table and giving it a little fluff before turning back to me. "Don't tell me it's the C word."

I was still a little distracted by the hair thing. Her own thin gray down was cut close to the head, causing her to resemble a seagull hatchling. "Huh? Oh, you mean cancer? No, it's not that. My heart. I have dilated cardiomyopathy."

Lulu's lips formed a pout. Actually, she had no lips to speak of, but lipstick outlined the opening where she put her food. "Oh." She shook her head sympathetically. "You poor little thing. And you're so young. I thought maybe it was lung cancer, the way you been coughing and all. I've got the heart thing going on too. Come to think of it, I guess we all do in this ward. I'm here to get a heart transplant." I watched her profile as she gazed at the black TV screen. Then she turned to me with a smile. "I've done a lot of livin'. Had two good husbands. A one-legged one that could dance till sunup and a two-legged one that wouldn't dance if he stepped in a nest of fire ants. He was a shy one." She let her head fall back on her pillow. "Old Elmer didn't know how good-lookin' he was. How 'bout you? You got a husband?"

Lulu made me smile. "I used to. He was a good one. Had two legs."

She nodded. "Never should have let that one get away."

It had been a long boring day. Lindsey had called during breakfast while I pushed canned peaches around in a bowl. No one would be able to come today. I said I understood. It was almost a three-hour drive from the river, after all. By lunchtime I was bored out of my gourd. Still, I had felt invaded when Lulu was wheeled in and hauled into the bed next to mine. I could stand the suspense for only so long. "So how did he dance? The one with one leg."

"A prosthetic. You know. One of them plastic fake legs. He pushed his stump into it and strapped it on. It's amazing what they can do nowadays."

Christopher sauntered in wearing his blue cotton scrubs and checked my heart monitor. Lulu reached for her glasses, holding them to her eyes like opera glasses. Christopher must have felt her intense scrutiny. He looked up from his clipboard and grinned disarmingly.

"Well, if I'd a known we were having a gentleman caller, I would have put on my hairdo." She ran her painted fingernails through her silver fuzz. Her gnarled fingers reminded me of the knotted limbs on our old pear tree. "Aren't you special?" she exclaimed to me. "I get Nurse Marshmallow Butt and you get Fabio. What does a girl gotta do around here to get such special attention?"

Christopher leaned toward her and whispered, "She's flying first class."

"Well, sign me up, honey. I don't care what it costs. Insurance company's paying for it anyway."

"This is first class?" I held out a plate of half-eaten meatloaf that had stiffened as it cooled. "Then how do you explain this?"

Christopher raised one eyebrow. "You should see what they got back there in the tail section." As he scribbled my vital signs onto my chart, we heard a commotion out in the hall by the elevators. Someone tuned a guitar and soon we heard the first strains of "Joy to the World."

Lulu reached for her hair and plopped it on her head. "Carolers. I love it. Isn't this wonderful? Come in here!" She yelled it before I could stop her. A face peered tentatively into the room and she motioned the young man in.

"Lulu!" I sank into my bed and pulled the sheet over my chest.

"Oh, lighten up, honey. It's Christmas."

They filed in, still singing. About a dozen strangers stood at the foot of my bed staring at us like we were primates in the zoo. *"Let every heart . . . prepare Him room . . . and Heaven and Nature sing. . . ."* Lulu clapped along, sort of. Her hands were too bent to slap together so they bounced to the rhythm, the loose skin under her arms swinging merrily along. She mouthed the words, occasionally barking one out, terribly off-key. This, of course, just encouraged the carolers, who immediately went into an encore of "God Rest Ye Merry Gentlemen." Christopher sat on the edge of my bed and grinned. When they finished Lulu apologized for having no cocoa and cookies to offer. Several of them went over and squeezed her hand and one woman actually hugged her. I gave the woman *the look* when she turned toward me. I was not a hugger. She smiled politely and they filed out to spread their cheer down in 404.

I was asleep that evening when the Judge came. When my eyes opened, his were closed. He was slouched in a small overstuffed chair by my bed, his head bobbing like a buoy in a storm. Watching him made my own neck uncomfortable. "Hey," I said.

His eyes opened and he smiled. "How ya doin' in here?"

"Okay, I guess." I glanced over at Lulu, who was also napping. "I got a roommate."

"I saw that."

"I didn't think anyone was coming today. Didn't you have court?"

He nodded. "I adjourned early. The defense attorney did more to get his client convicted during cross-examination than the prosecutor has during his whole case." He ran his thick fingers through his hair. His eyes were bloodshot. "I had to send everyone home and give this kid a private tutorial in my chambers. Last thing we need is a mistrial." He reached out and touched the tape on my arm that held my IV in place. "Does it hurt?"

"No. It's just annoying. They make me walk around the hall

and I have to drag this thing with me." I motioned toward the IV pole on wheels, which also supported my heart monitor.

He glanced at the equipment and then his eyes roamed the room. "We got the Christmas tree. TJ picked it out. He found it down by the creek." He chuckled. "I think he felt sorry for it. We'll have to put the naked side against the wall."

"I wish I could be there." I didn't realize how much until I almost choked on the end of my sentence. It had been seven years since I'd had Christmas at home.

"Donnie asks about you."

Donnie. At the mere mention of his name, my throat tightened. I had not heard from him since he said good-bye. I thought he would always be there for me, but apparently I was wrong. It didn't take him long to find Rachel, whoever that was. It was a good bet that she didn't wear clunky logger boots like me, though. I cried quietly sometimes after the lights were out, just thinking about him. Remembering his rough and tender ways with TJ and the times he looked longingly into my eyes, but I had turned away. "Tell him I'll be home soon. I hope."

He grinned. "That's the spirit." He tousled my hair. "That's my girl talking."

His comment surprised me. I always thought of Lindsey as *his girl.* I noticed I got more respect lying there in a bed that bends in the middle with a hose stuck in my arm. The same mother who used to vacuum around me at home brought flowers and designer chocolates to the hospital. And she drove three hours to do it. I must say it felt good. I had been without a foundation for too long. No one to hold me accountable. No one to care. I had been a fool to stay away from my family.

It was dark outside my window. Lulu snored softly. We

watched a documentary on penguins. My father laughed at their antics as they dove down icy banks on their barrel chests into the frigid water. He said I used to look like that when I dove onto our Slip'n Slide. I remembered spreading the plastic runway on a steep hillside and pretending to be an otter. It was the next best thing to a mud slide.

When we turned off the TV we heard Christmas melodies playing softly from somewhere out in the hall. I knew most of them by heart. Lulu stirred. Her breathing grew more labored and her mouth opened and closed as if silently calling for help, but she did not wake up. My father rose and went to her bed-side. He watched the not-so-rhythmic lines on her monitor until he was sure she was all right. I wondered what he was thinking as he stood there looking down at her. I knew what I was thinking and I wasn't proud of it, but thoughts just popped into my head uninvited and there they were. I knew that Lindsey somehow had a guard posted at the entry to her mind and that no bad thought ever made it past the pearly gate. But here was the thought in my head: Lulu is too old. She even said herself she had led a full life. I, on the other hand, had a son who would be in kindergarten next year. Lulu's kids were grown and gone. She had seen them board the big yellow school bus hundreds of times. She watched their bodies grow, their faces change and their baby teeth fall out, replaced by teeth too big for their freckled faces. She had been the tooth fairy, the Easter bunny, den mother, chaperone. She baked them hundreds of brownies and blackberry pies. She danced at their weddings.

I hoped Lulu didn't get a heart before me. Even though I liked her. Even though she had waited longer. She told me she had been on the transplant recipient list for well over a year.

She had been in the hospital before, but was allowed to go home to wait it out when she seemed strong enough. That was a month ago, but now she was back. When we padded through the halls, our IV poles lending awkward support, we passed other *pole people*, as we called ourselves. Lulu knew most of them. She had asked about Roy. A thin man in a plaid robe shook his head sadly. "Roy didn't make it, Lu." They exchanged a long gaze before Lulu reached out and touched the man's arm.

"And Curtis?"

"Oh, didn't you hear? He got a heart three weeks ago. He's out among the living now. Went to his kid's soccer game already." The man nodded and shuffled his way slowly down the hall.

Lulu watched him turn the corner toward his room. "Hank's been here longer than the rest of us. At least the ones that are still walking. He's been passed up four times. The last time a possible match came in, they got him all prepped for surgery, but the heart was too small for him. Right blood type, wrong size." She shook her head. "He was a football coach. Weighed in at about two-twenty when he came in. Look at him now. It just ain't fair."

"Why do they make us walk around like this?"

Lulu chuckled. "Because we're vultures and that's what we do. We circle and wait for someone to die."

"That's sick," I had said.

"Oh, lighten up, honey. You gotta have a sense of humor in here or you won't survive."

I now watched her tired old face twitch while she slept. With or without a sense of humor, some of us wouldn't make it.

The buzzard in me swayed grotesquely from an invisible overhead branch.

The Judge finally yawned and stretched. "I'd better hit the road."

"Tuck in TJ for me. Tell him I'll call him in the morning."

"Oh, I forgot to tell you. He's staying at Lindsey's for a few days."

"Since when?"

"She picked him up last night. They've got all kinds of plans. Shopping and Santa—"

"She never told me that!" I jerked forward. "I talked to her this morning. Why wouldn't she tell me TJ was there?" My chest grew instantly heavy. I sank back against my pillows. "I'm being replaced. I'm not even dead yet and I'm being replaced."

The Judge threw his coat onto the chair and leaned over me. "Don't ever say that again! Not unless that's what you want. Is that what you want, Samantha?"

"Of course not!" Lulu was awake now. "But what am I supposed to think? Last time I checked, I was still TJ's mother. I think I have a right to have some say in where he goes and what he does. I have a right to know where he *is* at least. Why wouldn't she tell me that?"

The Judge scooted the chair up and sat with his elbows on the edge of my bed. "I'm sorry, Sammy." He sighed and dropped his head, running his fingers through his dark hair. "You're right. We should have told you." He raised his head. His red-rimmed eyes fastened on mine. "I didn't want to upset you. . . . Actually, there's nothing to be upset about. It's just a precaution." He hesitated. "I've seen some footprints around the place. A man's boot print and it's not mine."

"Has Donnie been over there? Or Matt or anybody?"

He shook his head. "Sheriff Byron is working on it. Most of the prints are around the barn—coming from the woods. It could be someone just needed a place to get in out of the rain."

"Or it could be the guy who wants you dead."

He shrugged and shook his head unconvincingly. I instantly understood the reason for his bloodshot eyes.

"So you shipped TJ off to Lindsey's." My voice was calmer now, but my insides were unsettled. "What about you and Mom?"

"Well, I've asked your mother to stay at Lindsey's too. Just for now."

"Is there anything else I haven't been told?"

He smiled and shook his head. "Not that I can think of. Except that your son misses you. He doesn't fully understand this process. He thinks the hospital has hearts lined up on a shelf and the doctors are just trying to decide which one fits you. He said they'd better hurry because he wants you home for Christmas."

"That's in a few days. That would be fine with me."

He kissed my forehead and stood to reach for his coat. "That would be just fine with all of us, Samantha."

He was almost to the door before I thought to ask. "Wait a minute. Where are you going now?"

"Well, home."

"Why aren't *you* staying at David and Lindsey's? You're the one who's been threatened."

He pulled his leather gloves out of his coat pocket. "Don't you worry about that. I'm not. You just take care of yourself." He winked and walked out the door.

24

SLEEP CAME AND WENT that night. So did the nurse who checked our heart monitors and vital stats. Between my dreams, I was vaguely aware of her presence as well as Lulu's labored breathing.

I dreamed of the river all night long. And my father. In some ways they were almost intertwined. The river ran through my soul like blood in my arteries; it had for as long as I could remember. I felt its pulse, craved it somehow there in a hospital room four stories above the sidewalks of Seattle, just as I had back on the dry plains of Nevada. I thirsted for the river there, especially when the horses stirred up the red dust, causing it to swirl like ghosts at their heels. I suppose I longed for my father too—for what he had been to me as a child when I thought that his love for me was as consistent and perfect as I believed him to be.

At night in my Reno apartment the traffic on the highway two blocks away could sound like the river if I closed my eyes and visualized cottonwood trees and salmonberry bushes and the water rushing under Carter Bridge. I had to do that sometimes to keep my sanity. I had to remember how the river was in August—low on its banks from lack of rain, flowing calmly over smooth stones that twinkled in the sunlight. I saw myself wade out to where it rippled against my thighs, my strong casts slicing the blue sky. I dreamed of the sudden tug of a fish, the tension on my rod as it pulled the taut line upstream and down in the bright water. I smelled the sweetness of a trout as I slid it onto an alder switch through its gills. The river in August was like a thousand tinkling wind chimes.

I preferred these memories to the ones of spring floods. Sometimes when the snowmelt in the Cascade mountains converged with runoff from torrential Pacific Northwest rains, the river raged without warning. My river could become a stranger—dirty, ominous, thundering and unpredictable. Twice in my childhood we had to leave our home because the river escaped its banks. It pushed and spread like stampeding cattle, ripping trees up by their roots and discarding them along its path. The water invaded our backyard and the field, stranding the barn—a red island in a gray lake. We only had time to grab a few things and Lindsey sobbed, thinking our house would be carried away. My father drove slowly because of water over the road while Mom hung her head out the window, straining to see the edges of the road so we wouldn't drive into the ditch. I knelt backward on the seat and watched out the rear window as we drove away, confused and frightened. I saw Donnie's father standing knee deep between his family, who waited in the truck, and his horses, who had found a high spot in their flooded pasture. Then I knew the river could not be trusted. I loved the river, but it did not necessarily love me.

The first time I could remember my father in a torrential rage, it was by our creek that fed the river. Every odd year the pink salmon came up the Stillaguamish River to spawn. They gathered near the mouth of our little creek, waiting for a good rain. I could see them sometimes lurking beneath the dark water, tails swishing patiently, their steely bodies pointed like torpedoes ready for launch. They would not survive their mission. They never did. It was all part of the great plan.

Personally, I didn't think the plan was so great. In order to reproduce, the humpies had to die. Destiny lured them back from the deep green waters of Puget Sound to their place of birth, to lay and fertilize soft red eggs in the gravelly bottom of our shallow creek. By the time they got this far the fish had already lost their bright color and their flesh was slowly turning to mush. The pinks got the name humpies because of the hunchbacks they got when they spawned. My father said they were beautiful in the big water. He said their jaws weren't hooked like that and they were smooth and sleek, and he went on about them like he was describing a Rembrandt. He got that gleam in his eye that I saw sometimes in the middle of a worship service or when a big fish was bending the end of his graphite rod.

Which may have had something to do with his reaction when we found the piles of dead fish strewn along the edges of our little creek. We smelled them first. My father had been coaching me in fly-fishing finesse down at the river that afternoon. We came up the trail by the creek, which would eventually bring us to the field behind the barn. I wrinkled up my nose. "Pee-yu!"

"What in the . . . ?" He tossed his rod to the ground and crossed to the creek bank in huge strides.

"What happened to them?" There were shoe prints going in every direction. Different sizes and different treads. The prints at the very edge had filled up with water. A thick stick lay in the mud next to the mutilated carcass of a salmon. I answered my own question. "The James Gang."

My father seemed in shock at first. He looked like someone had punched him. Like his best friend had just hauled off and smacked him in the face. The fish had been clubbed or kicked, their huge bodies dragged up onshore. My father stared down at a fish as it shuddered. Its gills flinched slightly and he nudged it back in the water with his boot. The current prodded it gently until it rolled belly up and drifted downstream. The culprits could not be long gone, though we knew by the smell that some of the fish must have been lying in the October sun for at least a day. My father's fists went tight. His jaw clenched and the blood came to his face like when you blow on a hot coal.

Taking huge strides, he followed the overlapping footprints upstream to where they veered up the hill on the other side of the creek. I didn't hear what he sputtered as he splashed across the stream. I couldn't follow where he crossed because the water came up to my waist there. I backed out and found a wider, shallower crossing. He was way ahead of me now, crashing through salal and ferns, climbing the hill where there was no trail. He parted the vine maples like the Red Sea, but they closed in on me. Their wiry branches and scarlet leaves whipped at my face. I think he had forgotten about me. It was not until I yowled in pain from a particularly stinging branch that he wheeled to face me.

"Samantha! You go on home!"

I stopped dead in my tracks. He turned back and I heard him thrash through the thick growth until he reached the top of the hill. There was silence for a moment and then a barking dog. After a while there were voices and then shouting. The dog's barking grew frenzied. It was several minutes before I saw the shape of one of the James brothers at the top of the ravine. It was Jared, the youngest. He was a year younger than me and two grades behind.

I retraced my steps as quickly and as quietly as I could, stepping gingerly on yellow leaves, finally crawling under branches rather than call attention to my retreat. I tiptoed through the creek. Cold water squished from my jeans when I crouched behind a hollow cedar stump. They were all headed down the hillside now. My father had rounded up the entire James Gang and was herding the four brothers back to the scene of the crime. Jared seemed terrified. He ran as far ahead as he dared, apparently not willing to allow too much space between himself and his older brothers. I couldn't always see them through the trees, but I could tell when someone was going too slow because of the furious ranting and shouts of my father. The older brothers finally joined Jared in the clearing at the foot of the hill, their eyes darting nervously toward the Judge, who was on their heels. Cameron, the oldest, who was sixteen, carried a metal bucket. The other two had shovels.

"All right, you terrors of the county!" My father's eyes still flamed. "Get busy!"

The boys looked everywhere but at their piles of dead fish. Cameron dropped his bucket and crossed his arms. The others stood frozen.

I heard the soft swish of branches again. Mrs. James came into view, but she just stood there, halfway down the hill.

"Who do you think you are?" my father raged. "Are you gods? Do you in your wisdom have some better plan? Where were you when the river carved out this valley? Where were you when these fish burst from their eggs? Did you program them to make their way to the sound, to grow and then return to the exact place of their beginning to repeat the cycle of life? Was all this set in motion so that you could have a day's lark?" At this Cameron rolled his eyes. One of the brothers scoffed. I could see the veins pop out on my father's head. He yanked the fishing knife from his belt and leaned dangerously into Cameron's face. Cameron shrank away, but the Judge grabbed the front of his shirt. "What makes you think you have a right to do this? Answer me like a man! Make some sense of this destruction!"

Nathan, the fourteen-year-old, began to whimper. "Leave him be!"

Cameron's eyes got real big and his jaw quivered. He looked pleadingly up the hill but his mother stood as still as a tree stump with her arms crossed at her chest. The Judge's voice went quiet and his eyes narrowed. "It's not all about you, my friend."

He strode to the creek and began examining the salmon. "Which ones are from today?"

No one answered.

The Judge grabbed Ian by the collar and yanked him toward the creek. "Look at them! Which ones did you just kill?" The boy hesitated. "Which ones?"

Finally, Ian pointed. "That one, I think. And those over there."

"Come on." The Judge hoisted a big female by the gills. Head to tail she came up high on his thigh. "Help me here. Bring that bucket, boy!"

Cameron didn't budge for a moment. The Judge looked straight at him and started to lower the fish to the ground. Something made Cameron pick up the pail then. He brought it over just as my father poked the knife into a hole in the fish's belly and sliced it clean up to the pectoral fins. Red eggs spilled out like rubies. "Good," I heard my father say. He stirred the soft loose eggs around in the bottom of the bucket. "They're ripe. These eggs are ripe." He stood up and pronounced, "You want to be gods? Get busy, boys! This is your golden moment!"

He made them paw through the dead fish. The females were not as ugly as the males. The humps on their backs were not so pronounced and their snouts not as hooked. The younger boys began hauling the freshly killed females to my father, where their bellies were slit and the eggs harvested into the metal pail.

I wanted to come out from behind my stump to see how many eggs were in the bucket. I would have liked to take a turn at slicing the fishes' bellies. But my father's mood being what it was, I decided to stay put.

After demonstrating a few times, my father passed the knife to Cameron. He didn't look the Judge in the eye. He fondled the knife for a moment in his right hand and I thought my father was crazy for turning his back to grab another salmon. It was a heavy one. He held it up by both gills while Cameron slit the belly and scooped its jewels into the pail.

"Is that a fresh kill? Bring me that one." Ian complied, half carrying, half dragging a mottled male. "Good. Set it down there. Now get me all the fresh males you can find."

I was shocked at what he did next. My father hoisted the fish with two hands like it was a fire log. He held it over the bucket and bent it up on both ends. A jet of white liquid shot out. When it finished squirting, he repeated the process with each of the remaining humpies. Sometimes he ran his thumbs down the sides of the fishes' bellies to force the last of the milky substance out. By this time, the James brothers seemed as fascinated as I was. My father told them that the females were headed upstream to lay their eggs and it was the males' job to fertilize them. He stirred the contents of the pail gently while he told them about the mysterious pull that caused fish to fight their way back to the exact stream of their origin to repeat the cycle of life.

My hiding place was shady and cold and my clothes were wet. A flurry of golden leaves blew down from the cotton-woods. My father and four fatherless boys digging holes like nests in the gravelly streambed, pouring fertilized eggs into the man-made redds, became a scene I would carry with me forever, like one of those glass domes that you turn upside down to make it snow; but it would snow yellow cottonwood leaves.

The Judge's rage had receded back within its banks, just like the river after the flood.

Finally he stood and acknowledged Mrs. James for the first time. "Can you use some fish for your garden, Mrs. James?"

She nodded and shouted back, "That would be fine."

The James Gang had to haul the stinky dead fish all the way up the hill and bury them among their mother's pumpkins and dahlias. When my father was satisfied that the job was well under way, he washed his hands in the creek. His shirt and jeans were stained with blood. He retrieved his fly rod and the fishing vest that he had tossed aside and started up our side of the ravine.

I was inside the hollow of the old stump when I heard him trudge by. "Let's go home, Samantha," he said without break-ing stride.

THAT WAS OVER a dozen years ago.

I lay in my hospital bed, listening to the sound of Lulu's

breath. It was four a.m. I had been glad to see the Judge, glad
that he had come all by himself just to be with me. It was a
good visit, except for the part where I got upset about the secret my family tried to keep from me. It was for my own good;
I knew that. They didn't want me to worry about TJ or that the
mysterious prowler might hurt one of them. It was fun to laugh
with him—just my father and me, laughing over swaggering
penguins on the Discovery Channel as if there was nothing between us, never had been.

Why, after all these years, was I still hiding from my father?
Maybe it was safe to come out now. Maybe he'd known all
along exactly where I was.

25 ~~~~

Lulu had frog slippers with eyes that bugged out like head-lights. They were a gift from one of her friends in the Wacky Widows club, of which Lulu was president. She spoke often with the other three members on the phone, as they were planning a car trip to Monterey in June. Lulu, the only one with a convertible, was to be the designated driver. I was intensely interested in these conversations, partly because of the visual image I had of four wild gray-haired ladies partying their way south in a topless red Mustang. I asked Lulu if she wasn't worried about her hair flying off but she said she would tie it on with a scarf. The most curious thing to me, though, was that not once, in any of her dialogues, did Lulu mention the possibility that she might not be well enough to go.

So I was naturally concerned the morning that she refused to join the march of the pole people, which we normally undertook right after breakfast. I finally pushed my IV pole with all its hoses and the monitor to which I was wired out into the corridor to make my rounds. "Don't take the corners too fast!" she called after me.

It felt good to be out of that bed. I walked slowly around the block and was considering a second lap past the nurses' station when I saw Donnie exit the elevator just ahead of me. He seemed surprised to see me standing there.

"Hey," I said with a casual smile as if I had seen him just yesterday. My insides were immediately in turmoil, not sure whether to be elated or to run for cover—or at least for some makeup and a hairbrush. I adjusted my mint-green robe.

"Hey, you." He waited for me to catch up to him. The collar of his jacket was turned up and he carried heavy gloves. "How ya doin'?" He looked at me like I was an accident victim lying on the side of the road. I hated that.

"Good. I'm doing great actually. I didn't think I'd see you again. After all, you did say good-bye." Hank from 412 approached us, leaning on his pole. I reached out and touched his arm as he shuffled by. "You're it!

"Cardiac-ward tag," I explained to Donnie.

Donnie grinned. "I've come to bust you out of here."

"Hah!"

"I'm serious. Where's your room?"

I led him back to 417. Lulu smiled and nodded when we entered the room, but she did not reach for her strawberry blond hair. "Lu, this is my friend Donnie."

She left her head on the pillow. "Oh, very handsome. My goodness, girl. You been holdin' out on me." She feebly reached out her hand and Donnie took it in his.

"Hello, Lu."

"Lulu. You can call me Lulu—for long."

"Oh. Okay." Donnie didn't get her little joke.

I caught my reflection in the mirror over the sink and my hand automatically combed through my bedraggled hair. "So, what's this talk about breaking out?"

"TJ wants his mom home for Christmas."

I pushed my pole to the edge of the bed and sat down. Tears came to my eyes. "But the doctor said—"

"Forget the doctor. Your father said I was supposed to come get you." Donnie started fiddling with my wires and hoses. "How do we detach you from this thing?"

"Don't do that!" I pushed his hand away. "You can't just take me out of here!"

"Why not? Don't you want to go home?"

"Of course I do. I also want to fly."

He stopped and looked at me. "What's the worst thing that could happen? You could get sick and we'd have to bring you back. But at least you'll get to see your son open his presents." What he didn't say was that it might be my last chance. My son's last Christmas with dear old Mom. "We'll bring you back after Christmas. Your dad arranged everything with the doctor. They're sending your meds and some kind of portable gizmo with you."

"Okay." I pushed the button to summon my nurse. "My clothes are in that little closet." Donnie passed them to me, along with my cosmetic bag, and waited outside while Christopher unplugged me and helped me dress. He rigged me up with an IV pump that I could carry with me in a fanny pack or even in a purse. Its tube ran up under my shirt and down into my forearm. I could walk around like a normal healthy person again. The truth of it finally settled in. "Woo-hoo!" I yelped and then sang, *"There's no place like home for the holidays. . . ."*

Lulu stretched her hand toward me as they wheeled me by her bed. Our fingers touched. "Merry Christmas, Lulu. I'll be back in a few days," I said.

"I'll leave the light on for ya."

The December sky spread out in an infinite canopy of

smoke-colored clouds. Donnie said it felt like snow. He lifted me into his truck and tucked a plaid blanket around me before swinging into the driver's seat. We drove through the University District, where shoppers crowded the sidewalks and lights twinkled from shopwindows. Christmas was going on as usual. It happened in Reno too. I had always felt a little behind, a little out of sync with the rest of the world. Every year they repeated the ritual, flocking to malls and parties like the swallows of San Juan Capistrano, and I was a lone blackbird looking on. I did participate, if only for TJ, but always with the nagging feeling that I was a bad actor in an otherwise good play. Just the same, the thought of going home and spending the holiday with my family gave me an unexpected thrill.

Donnie whistled an unrecognizable tune as he steered with one hand, his other elbow resting on the driver's-side door. He asked a lot of questions about my treatment and seemed sincerely interested, so I told him more than I normally would. I explained the waiting process and why the next person in line did not automatically get the next available donor organ. That's why Hank had been passed up so many times. The heart was either the wrong size, wrong blood type, or, as we all suspected now, he had become too weak to withstand major surgery. For some reason, I did not remind Donnie that my type AB blood was the hardest to match or that my chances for survival were about as good as winning the lottery.

When the heater kicked in, Donnie shed his wool jacket. I pulled the blanket off my knees, not because I was warm enough but to avoid looking like an ailing grandma. I drew my knees up and sat cross-legged, wondering what Donnie thought of me now. My hair had grown longer and out of sheer boredom I had painted my nails with Lulu's Tangerine Sunset enamel. When he wasn't looking, I pinched my cheeks so I wouldn't look half-dead.

Donnie whistled quietly for a while, studying the clouds as he drove. He looked good to me. Good enough to touch. I really wanted to. I wanted to scoot up next to him, close enough to smell his skin, to feel his shoulder next to mine. I wondered what he would do if I did. My mind filled again with conjured images of Rachel, the woman he had thought I was when I tried to call. How could I compete with her? Whoever she was, she was probably a healthy specimen with a bright and active future ahead. Surely she could dance until dawn.

"Why did you come for me?" I asked.

His forehead pinched together and he smirked. "I knew you couldn't fly."

"Seriously. Why?"

"I told you. Your father asked me to bring you home. He's in court this week. Trying to wrap this case up before Christmas. It was important to him to have you home. He seemed pretty adamant about having the whole family together for Christmas. I didn't mind."

"Oh."

He studied me for a moment. "It's not that *he* didn't want to, Sam, if that's what you're thinking. By the time he gets home tonight, it will be late. He thought you'd make the trip better during the day." He looked uncomfortable for a second. "I guess you know about the threats he's had—and the prowler." I nodded. "Well, your mom and TJ have been staying over at your sister's. They're coming home today too. Your dad asked me to stay over at your place, just as a precaution. I hope you don't mind."

I smiled. "The more the merrier." As much as the Judge

liked Lindsey's husband, David, I found it amusing that he apparently didn't consider him a worthy ally in the face of danger. It was not hard, however, to imagine Donnie with his cocky confidence and burly build hurling an intruder into the next county. Anyway, so much for any romantic notions I might have had about Donnie pining away for me. It seemed my father had a lot more pull with him than I ever would.

Donnie stared at me. "Are you okay?"

"Yeah. Why?"

"I don't know. Your cheeks are all red and blotchy."

I didn't say much after that. Sometime after we passed the city of Everett I fell asleep leaning against the door and awoke only when the road began winding through our valley. Donnie turned down the political talk show he was listening to on the radio when he noticed me stretching.

"Hey. Look up there."

I followed his gaze toward the mountains, which were shrouded by heavy gray clouds. The foothills were already dusted with white. "Snow."

"And it's coming our way. Mark my words; we'll have snow before morning."

The late afternoon sky was the color of soot. Fifteen minutes after Donnie's prediction, a blinding flurry of dry crystals hurled themselves at the windshield. He drove slowly. Ours were the first tire tracks to mar the fresh snow and I was glad he knew the road so well as it was difficult to see the edges.

My relief when we pulled into the long driveway at home turned to disappointment. The house was dark. TJ did not come out and rush into my arms as I had imagined. Instead, Donnie helped me up the front steps, slid the key into the lock and pushed the door open in silence. He led me to the couch with my blanket and proceeded to turn on lights and start a fire in the river-rock fireplace. TJ's Christmas tree stood with its naked backside to the corner. I admired the homemade treasures that hung by ribbons from its boughs while Donnie made us tea. I tried to call Lindsey but got their recording. "Get your buns over here!" I demanded after the beep. "It's Christmas!" Then Donnie joined me on the sofa and we sipped the hot tea.

"I hope David knows how to drive in this snow. He's a city slicker, you know. Maybe we should go get them."

"He'll do fine. Besides, I can't fit everyone in my truck."

"I have to go to the bathroom." I pushed myself up from the sofa.

Donnie looked worried. "Are you . . . Do you need any help?"

I laughed. "No, but thanks for offering."

I combed my hair and applied powdered blush before coming out. Donnie didn't hear me when I came down the hall. His back was to me and he had the hall closet door open. I saw the handgun just as he tucked it under a hat on the top shelf.

"Is it loaded?" I asked.

He flinched and spun around. "Sam. You weren't supposed to see that."

"What's going on, Donnie? Do you really think this guy is for real?"

He shook his head. "No, I think your dad is right. Whoever he is, he just wants to make your dad sweat. If he was going to do anything, he would have done it by now. Just the same, there've been some boot prints around the place. The gun is only a precaution. Whatever this guy's beef is, sooner or later he's going to give himself away."

He headed for the kitchen and stuck his nose in the fridge. "You want some leftover spaghetti?"

"Yes, I'm starved." He microwaved the pasta while I buttered soft French bread. "What does this remind you of?" I asked as he plopped his plate down on the kitchen table and pulled in his chair.

He looked at his plate and then at me. "I give up."

"Bologna sandwiches."

He twirled a forkful of pasta and shoved it into his mouth. Now his mouth was too full for a response.

"Remember? My mom always made us bologna sandwiches with sweet pickles, no mustard because it stained the chairs. You always sat right in that chair and I sat here."

He shook his head. "I don't remember bologna. I remember those tuna things with cheese melted over the top. Those were worth coming in out of the rain for. Pass me some more bread, would ya?"

I shoved the plate toward him and watched him eat. His eulogy to me had ended, *I have loved you, Samantha.* What did he mean by that? Was it past tense? We had been friends since childhood. Was that what he meant? We had known each other for so long, he was almost family. Maybe he loved me like a cousin or, worse yet, a sister. But hadn't he wanted to kiss me last fall, the last time he took me down to the river? I turned away though. I made it clear that I was Mrs. Tim Weatherbee and he was only the boy next door. He hadn't tried since. Not even after I told him that I had signed the divorce papers and sent them in the mail.

"So"—I finally broke the silence—"what was that funeral all about? You put me in the ground and then you go dig me up again. At least one of us is confused."

He smirked and took a long drink of milk from his glass, and then set it loudly on the table. "It's you. It's always you who's confused. I had the funeral because you had given up. You kept thinking about dying, talking about dying and making plans for TJ after you were gone. Being around dead people is a drag."

"So it was psychological warfare. You did it to snap me out of it."

He shrugged. "Maybe. Did it work?"

I smiled and lifted the bottom of my sweater, revealing the pager on my belt. "I'm doing everything they tell me to do. And I haven't said anything negative all day, have I?"

He thought about it for a moment. "No, I guess not." He grinned and tweaked my nose like I was twelve. "Good girl. Keep it up."

B Y SIX O'CLOCK that night, two days before Christmas, the family was congregated in the house of my childhood. That is everyone but the Judge. TJ burst through the front door, stumbling into my arms amid the cries of my mother and Lindsey, who thought he might break me. He pulled me to the sparse Christmas tree to show off the ornaments he had made at preschool from jar lids and clothespins, while the others carried armloads of packages in from the back of David's car. At our father's request, Lindsey and David were to stay with us at the river all weekend and would sleep in Lindsey's old room.

TJ was delighted to share his room with Donnie. When Donnie produced a gallon jar of dirt he had found in the back of TJ's closet, my son looked sheepish. "That's my worms," he said solemnly.

"Well, I hope they don't make noise. I'm a very light sleeper," Donnie chided.

"They don't make no noise anymore."

"Any," I corrected him. "They don't make any noise."

Donnie shook the dry earth in the jar. "These guys are crispy critters." Then he saw TJ's face. "Hey, it's all right, buddy. Your grandpa's got plenty more where these came from. We just need to keep some moisture in there next time."

"And some garbage."

Donnie scooped him up and flung him over his shoulder like a sack of potatoes. "Come on. We'll get your worm farm going again after Christmas. Whaddya say?"

When we returned to the living room, my mother made me sit in the big yellow chair with my feet up on the ottoman. She brought a tray with mugs of hot spiced cider and played Christmas carols on the stereo while the blaze in the fireplace danced and snapped.

By the time we heard the Judge on the front porch, stomping the snow from his shoes, TJ was asleep under the Christmas tree. Mom greeted the Judge at the door, took his coat and shook it before hanging it in the closet. His face still looked drawn and tired. He smiled at me and bent to kiss my head. Lindsey threw her arms around him. "Daddy, we were worried. What took you so long?"

"I wanted to wrap up this case." He sighed in relief. "It's done. I've got my loose ends taken care of, at least the important things. Now, let's have Christmas. I just want to be with my family." He turned and stood over TJ where he slept among the colorful packages, his cherub face illuminated by the tree lights.

When he stooped to pick him up, Donnie protested. "I can do that, sir." But my father shook his head. He slid his big hands gently beneath TJ and drew him to his chest as he stood. TJ's eyes flickered. His hand went to his grandpa's face momentarily and I saw my father kiss it as he passed by on his way to the bedroom.

"Mom, is he okay?" I asked when the Judge was out of the room. "He doesn't look right."

My mother stared after him and then turned and smiled bravely. "He's just tired, I think. He's been obsessed with getting caught up on his work and hasn't been home before nine o'clock in over two weeks. That long drive to and from the city doesn't make things any better. At least he was able to stay overnight down there for the past few nights while TJ and I have been at David and Lindsey's."

"What about the bad guy? Does Sheriff Byron have any leads?"

Mom shook her head. "Nothing. They couldn't trace the calls and there haven't been any more since they put a tracer on the phone. The tracks outside were definitely not made by any of us. It was a man's boot print and it wasn't just by the barn. We found some in the garden next to the garage." She shivered. "He may have been watching us through the kitchen window."

Donnie and David were playing chess by the fire. "I hope the jerk shows up," Donnie said as he plunked his knight on the board.

David was not so cocky. "I hope he's on a one-way trip to Siberia."

"I don't want to hear another word about this!" The Judge stood as straight as a sentinel in the doorway. "He can't steal our peace unless we let him. For the next two days we will speak only of what is good and right with the world. We'll speak of life and truth and love. No man can steal these things from us. Do you understand?"

We nodded, though at the time no one really understood.

The next morning the westerly mountains held the waves of snow clouds back like a seawall for a few hours while the bright sun chased every dark thought away. Donnie took TJ with him to the ranch to do some chores. Mom diced celery and onions for stuffing while Lindsey and I rolled out our traditional Norwegian potato lefse. That night, for Christmas Eve dinner, the thin pancakes would be buttered and sprinkled with brown sugar, then rolled and cut into finger-length logs.

The Judge caught our mother beneath the mistletoe that Lindsey had hung over the arched entry to the dining room. I watched him kiss her like it was the first time. He held her until she laughed and pulled away from him, embarrassed by this show of passion "in front of the children." He never passed my chair without touching me. He brought me tea. He insisted that Donnie sit in his big leather chair because it was more comfortable for a guy as big as he, though the rest of us were subconsciously uncomfortable with the presence of another on the throne.

That evening, when the mountain dike could no longer hold back the rolling clouds, the snow fell again. We ate Cornish game hens with marmalade glaze and cranberry stuffing. There were stories and laughter and even an outbreak of song when Donnie found out that TJ didn't know the words to "Rudolph the Red-Nosed Reindeer." My son's face glowed in the candlelight, his cheeks as smooth and shiny as caramel apples.

Donnie and David brought in wood and stoked the fire in the living room fireplace. Fresh cedar branches lined the mantel, where old-fashioned kerosene lanterns glowed. The Judge read the story of Jesus' birth from the Gospel of Luke, just as he had done every Christmas Eve throughout my childhood. TJ lay on the floor near his grandpa's feet as he listened, arranging the painted figures of the old Nativity set, propping the cow with the broken leg against the thigh of a kneeling wise man. From time to time, he stopped to gaze at the Judge's face.

The Judge closed his Bible reverently and looked at each face around the room. "Let's pray." He prayed a blessing on each one by name, even Donnie. He talked to God about us like it was just him and God and we weren't even there listening in. I peeked at Donnie. His head was bowed and he wiped his eyes with his sleeve. My own eyes misted as I witnessed the exchange of love that flowed horizontally and vertically in the room. David sat with his elbows on his knees, his eyes wide open and focused on the Judge's face. I knew that Donnie would gladly risk his life for my father. David loved him too, I could tell. Though try as I might I could not picture David standing between the Judge and a loaded gun.

"Lord, direct our paths. Keep us in Your tender care. You are our light. Our hope, our joy, our strength. Thank You for sending Your perfect Son to earth as one of us, to suffer the death that we deserve for our sins so that we can live free, both now and forever. We love You. Amen."

"Amen." The room remained hushed until TJ sprang to his feet. "Now can we open a present, Grandpa? Just one!"

In our family, it was traditional to open gifts on Christmas morning, though Lindsey and I had always been successful in talking our parents into opening one or two on Christmas Eve. My mother would pass us the ones from Grandma Dodd first, which we knew would be handmade flannel nightgowns and which we donned loyally to pose for our annual photo shoot by the tree. Grandma Dodd had died three years ago while I was in Reno and I hadn't known until six months after the funeral. I found that painful now but took comfort in the circuit of life that had brought my son and me back to this place.

My father grinned. "Okay, son. Pick one."

TJ zoomed right in on the package from Donnie, which he had shaken and sniffed and fondled all day. He tore the paper from the package and we all oohed and aahed and shot questioning glances toward Donnie as TJ took aim and snapped his first slingshot.

My son hung his stocking on the hook beneath the fireplace mantel where I used to hang mine. Lindsey tried to talk him into leaving a plate of cookies and some milk for Santa but TJ shook his head thoughtfully. "No, he's too fat, Aunt Lindsey." He perused the contents of the refrigerator and finally produced a plate of salad. "But I don't think he'll eat it," he said. "He doesn't have much time."

Donnie carried him off to bed and I followed a few minutes later to tuck him in. I missed the support of my IV pole. I was weak by the time I reached the end of the hall. The bedroom door was open only a crack and I rested against the wall, smiling as I listened to their dialogue.

"Because he won't come until you're asleep, that's why."

"Then you better go to bed too. And my mom and everybody."

"Okay, bud. You talked me into it." I heard Donnie strip off his belt and the creak of the cot as he sat down to pull off his shoes. "It's been a long day."

"Hey, Don?"

"Yeah, buddy."

"Maybe we can go shoot my slingshot tomorrow."

"Sure. You come over to the ranch with me while I take care of the horses and after that we'll set up some targets. If your mom says it's okay, that is."

"And let's don't bring that lady this time."

"Who, Rachel? You don't like Rachel?"

My heart began its slow sink.

"Mm. She's okay. I just like it better when it's just you and me. So we can pee in the snow if we want to."

I heard Donnie yawn and put his full weight on the cot. "Just you and me. No girls next time. Now, let's get some sleep. Santa's probably up there hovering and it isn't nice to keep him waiting."

I returned to the living room to find Mom starting a movie. David and Lindsey were snuggled together on the sofa. "Come on, Sam. It's time for *It's a Wonderful Life*. No Christmas is complete without it."

"I'll pass," I said.

Mom came over and brushed the hair off my forehead. "You've overdone it today, haven't you? Why don't you just go on to bed now, honey?"

"I think I will. Good night, Mom." I kissed her cheek.

If Santa was up there waiting for me to fall asleep, he would be circling all night. Who on God's green earth was this Rachel person? I had become used to sleeping in an upright position against a bank of pillows, as it relieved the pressure my oversized heart put on my lungs. But that night nothing worked. I tried curling up on my left side, then the right, then on my back again, eyes open wide. Finally, I pushed myself up and pulled the curtains away from the window. There was no moon, but I could see snow falling in the soft yellow light off the back porch. I pulled the quilt from my bed and slipped my boots on without tying the laces. The movie was over and the house was quiet, dark except for the night-light in the hall and the colored lights on the tree. I tiptoed down the hall to the kitchen and slipped out the back door.

Under the eaves of the porch was the old Adirondack chair that Matthew had made for my mother using pegs instead of nails. It squeaked as I settled into it, wrapping the quilt tightly around myself. One of the pegs had broken and the left arm wiggled. Matt was a better doctor than a builder of chairs. He would be coming up tomorrow for Christmas dinner and I was happy about that. But at the moment, my Christmas joy was smothered by a dark cloud named Rachel.

New snow had turned the overlapping footprints of the day into indistinguishable dimples. The footprints converged at the back door of this house, where we all belonged, together. Including Donnie. He should be TJ's daddy. He was meant to be a part of us. Of me. But how could I think like this? I didn't even know if I would live to see another Christmas. Donnie, obviously, wasn't counting on me either. It was a pity that it took the threat of another woman to make me finally realize what Donnie meant to me. I had taken him for granted. And now, as if seeing through corrective lenses for the first time in my life, I was shocked at the clarity of what I saw. My vision had been distorted and I hadn't even known it.

I used my sleeve to stifle the cough that tore from my chest. In my abundant spare time, I had read a poem in a book from the library, an anthology of writings by organ transplant patients. It was written by a guy waiting for a donor heart. He was upbeat and hopeful and the poem stank. The only reason I remembered it was that someone had scrawled in the margin, "Dillon almost had his heart on August 1, 1988. He was, however, determined too ill to qualify. He died in his bed during his high school team's opening kickoff on September 13."

I coughed again. The cold had seeped inside my blanket. What were my chances of living happily ever after? I stood to go inside just as an eerie sound permeated the night. I froze. At first I thought it was the mournful wail of a coyote. The sound hung in the air, clung inside me like cobwebs. I pulled the blanket tight and waited. Only silence. I had thought nothing of the light escaping through the doorway and cracks in the barn until now. Didn't the Judge usually turn the lights out after he tended to the worms? The pain in my chest mounted noticeably and I began to shake. Again I heard the muffled sound, and then a shout.

It was the Judge.

27 ⟿

I WAS OFF the steps before I knew it, headed for the barn, terrified by what I might find. My untied boots scooped up snow, causing my feet to drag. I trudged in the footprints my father must have made hours ago, now half-filled with new snow. A plaintive cry from the barn drew me forward, each step too slow and labored. My heart pumped sluggishly until I was dizzy. Reason told me I couldn't be much help, but I had come too far. Too late to turn back. I should have woken Donnie. Donnie could have been there by now. I tried to call but my breathless voice came out as a hoarse whisper. Snow crystals stung my face. I paused to catch my breath and then pressed on to where the yellow light from the barn door fell on the rumpled snow.

I gripped the edge of the door, which was open slightly. My father's voice rang out clearly.

"Oh, God, my God. You always make a way. Let there be some other way!"

I was shocked to find my father alone. His back was to me and he knelt over a bale of hay. His shoulders shook and he sobbed audibly.

My throat grew tight. In a moment I found myself at his side, my own eyes welling up with tears. "What's wrong?"

He spun to look at me. "Samantha!" His face was wet and swollen, his hair a mess.

Without thinking about it I knelt and my arms went around his neck. "What happened?"

"Oh, Sammy." He pulled me to his chest in a fierce embrace. "Sammy."

I felt his arms close around me. He rocked me back and forth, his hand caressing the back of my head, and I was eight years old again. He smelled the same. Old Spice and sweat. A warm tear fell on my neck. I held him tight.

Moments later he straightened. "What are you doing out here? You shouldn't be—"

"I heard you," I gasped. "I thought you were in trouble."

"Sam, you shouldn't even be out of the house. You should be resting." He brushed the melting snow from my hair and studied my face. I lifted my chin, trying to ignore the pain that radiated from my chest.

"What did you hear?"

"I don't know. It sounded like you were dying or something."

He pulled his shirttail out and wiped his face, and then surprised me with a chuckle. "Dying? So what if I was? It wouldn't be the end of the world now, would it?"

"So," I said, suspecting that my father had lost his mind, "what are you doing out here? Just praying?"

He smiled sadly. "Just praying."

"Oh. You pray loud." Only minutes before, he had wailed like a Turkish widow; now he looked as peaceful as he had at dinner with a plate of Cornish game hen before him. He sat up on the hay bale and pulled me onto his lap, wrapping the blanket that was still on my shoulders tightly around me. I felt large. "What were you praying about?"

His eyes burned into mine. For a moment I thought he was actually going to answer my question.

"Tell me something, Sammy. What do you see yourself doing when you're thirty?"

I stared at him blankly.

"Where will you live? What will you do for fun?"

"I'm sorry. I don't know how to play this game."

"It's no game. It's dreaming. A very important part of life. I don't care, call it a game. The rules are—there are no rules. You can have anything you want, you can be anything you want, you can be with anyone you want."

"Okay. I'd be with TJ, of course. He would be . . . what? Eleven by then, fifth grade. We would live in a little house on the river." I paused to think and to catch my breath. "Since there are no rules, it will be right smack-dab in the middle of Sid Jorgenson's pasture under the old cottonwood tree."

My father was pleased with this. He closed his eyes and leaned his head back ever so slightly.

"I'm not really good at anything. So I don't know what I'd do for a living. But in my spare time, whenever I'm not doing that, whatever it is, I'd like to fish. I would teach TJ to fly-fish. I'll probably volunteer at his school a lot too."

"Will you get married?"

This one threw me. I shrugged. "I don't know."

"Well, do you want to?" He pressed my head to his shoulder and stroked my arm.

"Yeah. I guess I do. I guess I would marry Donnie. If he . . ."

"If he what?"

"Well, I'm not the spunkiest trout in the pond, you know. I think he has other options."

"Oh. Well, that complicates things. Maybe you're going to have to fight for him."

"Like I said, I don't have the spunk or the splash or the succotash that I used to. It's all I can do to walk to the bathroom gracefully. I'm too tired to fight right now."

"That will be over soon. After your surgery, you'll feel great. They'll have you on the treadmill within a few weeks. Do you know that?"

I nodded. "That's what they say. Am I getting too heavy?"

"Yes. But I don't want to put you down. It's been so long since you would do this."

"Probably because I'm a grown-up now."

"No. It started long before that."

I slid off his lap but stayed close to him. "You didn't love me like you love Lindsey. I always knew that. But it's probably because I was adopted and she, well, she's your own."

His eyes looked pained, like I had calmly slid a knife into his belly. "Samantha. Is that what you thought?"

He ran his hands through his hair. "By God, Samantha. I never loved one of you more than the other. Your mom and I loved you before we ever laid eyes on you. And when we brought you home—you were our first, you know; you were the first to take a step, the first to say my name. Your sister was always four months behind you. And the two of you together . . . well, let's just say I felt like a blessed man. But you were different. I had to treat you differently. Lindsey was happy to stay by your mother's side, learning to cook, having tea parties and the like. You, on the other hand, were more of a challenge. You

were an adventurer. Always doing the unexpected. I had to dis-
cipline you more, but that was because I loved you."

I felt myself melting into him, both from weakness and from
a strange, overwhelming need. The pressure I had felt in my
chest since the excursion to the barn mounted. I coughed reflexively. "I was a pain in the butt, wasn't I? I'm a screwup. I always have been." This gush of honesty was a surprise to me, but
I let it go. "I know what you expect from me, but I can't be
that. I can't be like Lindsey." I shrugged nonchalantly, but my
breaking voice betrayed me. "I guess I turned out to be everything you hate."

His eyes narrowed. "You know what I hate? I hate the destructive choices you've made. But I love you. I always have. I
abhor the lies that you've believed. You say you're nothing. I
say you're destined for greatness. You can do anything. Anything that you believe!"

He sighed, raking his fingers through his hair. "I know how
I am when I get angry. Like a swarm of Kansas twisters. But
you have to understand, Sammy, you're my daughter. I hate
anything that might destroy you, whether it's a diseased heart
or some lie from the pit of hell that you've chosen to embrace. I
can't just sit back and see what happens. That's against my nature."

A single bulb lit our corner of the barn. My father's shadow
covered mine so that I could see only his shape on the dusty
floor. "There is a line between right and wrong, Sam. Truth and
lies. That's all there is. There is no neutral ground." He paused
thoughtfully. "And only the truth will set you free."

It was all a bit ethereal for me. I didn't understand the words
at the time, but I felt his passion. Something stirred in my
spirit.

"The truth is," I said humbly, "if I don't get a new heart very soon, I'm going to die."

My father held my face so I had to look him straight in the eye. "You will have your heart." I couldn't look away, even if I wanted to. He said it again, his eyes ablaze, his deep voice booming with the authority of a judge proclaiming a life-or-death sentence. "You *will* have your heart, Sammy." His decree dropped inside me like an anchor. I envied his unwavering optimism. It may have been childish, but I believed him. I believed him with all my soul.

It felt good to cry. It felt good to lean into my father while he spoke of the future. My future. I had forgotten how to dream. I had forgotten that after winter comes spring; that just beyond the darkness there is light. We imagined what TJ would become, painting wonderful word pictures of the days and years ahead. And I was in every one of them.

One thing still bothered me. "Dad." It seemed right to call him that and he looked pleased. "Is something wrong? You never told me what you were praying about. Are you in some kind of trouble? You can tell me, you know."

He shook his head thoughtfully. "No trouble. It's nothing you need to concern yourself with."

I squinted my eyes at him, unconvinced.

He looked away. "Remember what I said about truth? It is an absolute and yet it is sometimes hard to see. Every time I hear a case I'm overwhelmed by the weight of my authority. My job is to make decisions that will alter the course of a person's life. Their fate. Ideally the justice system sorts truth from lies, right from wrong, according to the law. But the system is not perfect. I couldn't sleep nights if I were to make a wrong call. God and I sort it out, one piece at a time. It's always been that way. When I have my answer, I know it." He stared off into the shadows of the barn. "The answer just settles down inside me and I know it."

He became quiet and I knew that he was remembering the discussion with God that I had interrupted.

"Did you get your answer tonight?" I asked.

He touched my face tenderly and smiled. "Yes. I'm sure of it."

Maybe someday I could have unshakable faith like that—the kind that could move a mountain of trouble and cast it into the sea.

It was after midnight when my father helped me to my feet and led me toward the door of the barn. I was ready for sleep now. If I was still a little girl, I would have said, *Carry me, Daddy*, and I would have been asleep before he laid me in my bed. He turned off the light that hung over the worm bed, but as he headed for the switch near the door, he stopped short. The shadowy figure of a man leaned against the doorframe.

"I saw your light on." The raspy voice was instantly familiar and as alarming as grating gears.

"Enrich." My father pushed me gently toward the open barn door, away from the side where the man stood. "I wasn't expecting you tonight."

"But you *were* expecting me." The man pushed himself away from the jamb, swaying slightly.

I looked back at my father and he waved me toward the house, but as I slid past the opening, the man reached out and grabbed my arm. I jerked away reflexively, leaving him with a handful of blanket. My father lurched toward him. "Don't touch her!"

"Why?" the man jeered. I saw the gun in his hand. I fell to my knees and when I looked up the barrel was pointed at my head. My father pulled back, but like a cobra poised to strike. "Why, Dodd? You got a problem with seeing your kid's blood in the snow? You got a problem with looking into those pretty eyes and nobody lookin' back?" My chest was unbearably heavy, little oxygen coming to my brain. I fought to stay conscious.

His eyes were red-rimmed and liquid. "That's the way it was with my Ronnie. It looked like him, but there wasn't nobody home. He just laid there," he slurred. "The only person who ever thought I was worth a lick—boxed up like a slab o' smoked salmon ready to be shipped off to the relatives down south. He couldn't hear a word I said. And he never will."

"I'm sorry about your son, Enrich. I heard he hanged himself in his cell and I'm sorry about that. I really am. He would have been up for parole in a few more years."

The man swung the gun toward the Judge. "A few?" he cried. "He was in that hole for nine years! The prime of his life. He was the best quarterback this county ever saw. On his way to the pros. Every stinkin' day was a year! And *you* put him there."

My father's fingers moved ever so slightly. I knew he was signaling me to get up and run toward the house, but the anvil in my chest anchored me to the spot.

"Your son committed murder. He killed your wife, Enrich. Doesn't that mean anything to you?"

"She had it comin'."

"What do you mean?" Again my father glanced my way. I tried to push myself up.

"That witch . . ." Enrich looked at me over his left shoulder and I froze. "She thought she was the queen of the world. Thought she could control everything and everybody. Couldn't even divorce her. She said she would get Ronnie if I did. Said she would convince the court that I was an unfit, crazy drunk. If you were treated like a dog who was lucky to have a bed and a bowl of cold stew, you'd keep a bottle or two within reach too. I always thought I'd kill her myself, put an end to her abuse. I told Ronnie so. Don't ever trust her, I said. Told him she would destroy him in the end. I was right about that." He swiped at his wet face, tottering slightly and shaking his head. "I don't know why he did it," he whined. "I told him I would take care of it. I was going to take care of it."

"Well, you were the top button, Enrich. You had murder in your heart and you still do. You programmed it right into your boy. Ronald was so full of hatred that he was a time bomb ready to go off. I couldn't chance letting him get out and hurt someone else. Can't you see that? *You* destroyed your family. Now you want to destroy mine. The truth is *you* killed them. Both of them."

"Shut up!" he sobbed, raising the gun toward my father's face. I heard the hammer click back.

My father nodded. "Do what you have to do."

Enrich paused.

What was happening? I whimpered in disbelief.

Suddenly the gun swung toward me. I was on my hands and knees in the snow. Even in the semidarkness I could see his jaw harden. "Sorry, girl, but it's better this way. Don't you see?"

"No!" my father screamed just as my arms failed me. The shot rang out into the winter night. The sound tore through my body. I fell face-first into the snow, plunging through a terrible bottomless tunnel, helpless and very cold.

28

I REMEMBER AS IF in a dream the shouts of strangers, the slamming of vehicle doors and the glare of cruel lights—red and blue flashes on tense faces with none of the joy of Christmas. But I just wanted to sleep.

Once, when I opened my eyes, my mother's distraught face was just above mine. A warm tear fell on my forehead, trickled into my hair. When I looked again she was gone. I felt myself moving. The man with me gently held my arms down when I tried to push something off my face. I tried to ask him about my father. And Mom. He said, "They're on their way to the hospital. Now, you keep breathing. That's it. Good girl. Hang in there, darlin'." I must have slept for a long time. I heard the siren like it was only the wail of a train, miles away on a moonlit night.

In the gray light of morning I awoke to find myself between fresh sheets in my old hospital room. Tubes ran from hanging IV bags into needles stuck into my arm. The familiar electronic blipping noise of my heart monitor was comforting. I ran my hands over my body. Some kind of catheter had been stuck in my neck. I felt no pain, other than the usual nagging ache in my chest. Had it all been a dream? A vivid, horrifying dream that seemed more real than this sterile room?

The bed next to mine was empty.

"Welcome home." Christopher leaned through the partially open door, his long braid draped over the shoulder of his pale green scrubs.

Normally I would have said, "If this is home, where is hell?" or something of the sort. Instead, I weakly lifted my head from the pillow and implored, "What happened?" He walked hesitantly to my bedside but didn't sit down.

My hands continued to explore my body. "Am I shot?"

Christopher shook his head. "No. You're okay."

"It was not a dream, Chris. I remember. Some ugly lunatic hillbilly tried to shoot me."

He nodded. "So I heard. Lucky for you, he missed." He touched my forehead, pressing my head into the pillow. "Lie still. You need to rest now, do you understand? We never should have let you out of here. You've gone and worn yourself out and you have to do whatever it takes to get your strength back." He pulled the gown off my shoulder and checked the IV needles, and then did something with the bags.

"Where's my family? Is my father okay?"

"They'll be here. I guess there's quite a blizzard going on up north. Snow and ice are so bad they've had to shut down the freeway. Now get some sleep while you can. The last thing you need is a crowd bustling around here."

"Where did Lulu go?"

He patted my shoulder and turned toward the door.

"You're holding out on me! You know something, Chris. Now tell me!"

Christopher paused with a grin. "I think the old Sam's back." He slipped out the door and then poked his head back in. "I heard your boyfriend blew the lunatic's kneecap off. That ought to teach him." Then he was gone, leaving me with more questions than I had before.

In spite of it, sleep overcame me again. For how long I don't know. I awoke to find Dr. Sovold next to me, studying my chart. "How do you feel?" he asked.

"Okay."

"Do you think you can get up and walk around?" He helped me sit up.

"Where did you put Lulu?"

Dr. Sovold stepped backward and sank into the chair by my bed. He studied my face for too long and I knew. He wondered if I was strong enough to hear the truth. "Samantha . . ."

"Please say you moved her to another room."

He put his chin in his hand and shook his head. "She passed away in her sleep."

I stared at him for several moments before I could speak. "But I was gone for only two days." Her bed lay flat and white without a wrinkle in remembrance of her. She was supposed to drive to Monterey with the Wacky Widows in June. She just wanted to dine on enchiladas and watch the sea lions on the rocks below. How could she be dead? That was Lulu's tangerine nail polish on my toes.

The doctor watched me intently. "She was tired. I think she knew she wouldn't have the strength to go through the operation even if she did get a donor heart. She called her son earlier that day and spoke for some time. Her daughter too. Lulu seemed ready. At peace, you know? Are you okay?"

I nodded.

Dr. Sovold helped me out of bed. "I'd like you to take a walk down the hall. Can you do that for me?"

I felt a little shaky. "Did you guys put something in my IV?"

The doctor smiled. "Just something to help you sleep. It should be just about out of your system now. Give me a good walk around the hall now, and when you get back your nurse is going to take some blood."

When I returned from my journey, I was hungry. Christopher took blood from my arm. I had seen food trays going into other rooms, but Chris said I would have to eat later. We had to do some more tests.

"Can't it wait until after my veal and mashed potatoes? I know that's what we're having because I saw it—and I still want it. That's how hungry I am."

"Trust me," he said. "You do not want to eat on veal day." He ran me through the tests, which seemed to go faster than usual, and then wheeled me back to my room.

Dr. Sovold met us there, pretending to be jovial but coming off a little anxious. "You're looking more awake now. Are you feeling good?"

"Good?" I shrugged. "I wouldn't go that far, but I'm better. Except I missed lunch." I shot Christopher an accusing glare, which made him chuckle.

Dr. Sovold perused my test results one more time before placing the clipboard at the foot of my bed. He leaned toward me. "You need to have an empty stomach to go into surgery."

"What surgery?"

"We may have a donor, Samantha." I sat up straight. "There is an accident victim with type AB blood that may be a match. That's why we had to run the tests on you again. I think you're strong enough to undergo the surgery. What do you think? Are you strong enough?"

If I wasn't, I would have to lie. This was it. A chance—

maybe my only chance for survival. I would take it no matter what. "I'm ready."

"Your family has been informed. They're having a hard time getting here because of the snow. They've been stuck in Darlington for hours. We may have to go before they can get here, Samantha. Can you handle that?"

Tears came instantly to my eyes. I swallowed and nodded. "But I need to talk to TJ first."

Christopher jumped up. "Let me see what I can do." He left the room.

"What happened? Is it a woman or . . ."

The doctor shook his head. "You know we can't tell you that. Now, this is not a sure thing yet. The donor heart is in another city. The transplant team is flying there now. Once the heart is harvested we'll know if it's an acceptable match. Then, of course, time will be of the essence. We'll have a matter of a few hours to transport it and get it up and running again, inside you." Dr. Sovold smiled reassuringly. "I think this is going to work, Samantha. We're all proceeding accordingly. We're a team, remember? Everyone from your nurses on up to Dr. Wilhelm, who will be performing the surgery, we're all pulling for you. I think this is your big day." He started to leave and then turned back. "If by some chance this is not the one, we'll deal with that too. Right?"

"Right," I said. "Is it still snowing?"

"It's clearing up. The pilot is good. He's flown in worse weather than this. Now rest for a little bit. I'll be back."

I settled onto the bed, my mind whirling. It was happening. It was really happening. "Oh, God. Dear God. Let it be a match." Immediately I felt guilty. "I'm sorry about those other people, whose . . . person died." I pictured them wailing in disbelief over their loved one's body and then silently watching it wheeled away from them to the operating room. "Help them. Help me."

My father said that for everyone there is a time to live and a time to die. He said the secret to happiness is to live without fear and to die the same. "When you know God, you will understand this. You will know that this life is only the beginning. He has greater plans for you than your finite mind can imagine." I hoped that the dead person knew God.

It occurred to me that I should set things straight myself, just in case. At preschool, TJ had colored a picture of Jesus gathering children around him. The caption underneath read *God is Love.* I tried to imagine God loving me, but it was hard. I kept my eyes closed, and since I couldn't really imagine God, I saw myself snuggled next to my father in the barn. I pretended that it was God holding me. Talking to me about my hopes and dreams. Knowing everything there was to know about me and loving me just the same. "I'm sorry about my sins," I whispered. "I know I've been a big disappointment to You. Please forgive me." I faltered with those words. The last time I made that request of someone, I had been shot down. My sin had been too gross to forgive. "I don't want to die. Please get me through this . . . and help me change."

The ringing of the telephone by my bed startled me. "Hello."

"Sammy."

"Mom!" I began to cry. "Where are you? I'm getting a heart. I'm about to go into surgery."

"I know, we heard. We're coming, honey."

"I'm all by myself here. What happened to you guys?"

"I'll tell you all about it when I get there." I thought she was crying too. "We're coming as soon as we can. You be strong, Samantha Jean. I'm praying for you to be strong." Now she sobbed openly. "I'm not crying because I'm afraid. Do you understand that? I just want to be there with you. This is what we've been waiting for, isn't it, Sammy?"

"I love you, Mom."

She didn't answer. I thought I heard Lindsey's voice in the background. "Mom?"

"Sam, this is David. How ya doin'? We're about to lose you here. This is a bad cell zone. We're on our . . . sorry about the . . . if . . ."

"You're breaking up. Just get here." The phone went dead and I replaced the receiver.

Christopher returned to my bedside. "Okay. I've got a line on your son. Here's the phone number where he's staying." I recognized the number immediately. I had dialed it almost every day when Donnie and I used to play together. "I'll punch it in for you." He waited until it rang. "Hello. This is Samantha Dodd's nurse. Is TJ there?" I reached for the phone.

"Teej?"

"Mommy!"

"What are you doing, baby? Is Donnie with you?"

"No. Just Donnie's grandma."

"You mean his mother."

"Why did you go back to the hospital? We were s'pose to have Christmas. But when I waked up I was here."

"I'm sorry, Teej. I didn't mean to get sick again. I just got real sick and they had to take me back here. But I have good news. I think they found me a new heart! I'll probably be all better soon."

"Oh." He dropped the phone.

"TJ?"

"Mommy." His voice was so tiny and sweet and now I heard sniffles. "I want to go home. Please. Just you and me and Grandpa and Grandma. And Donnie and Aunt Lindsey. I have a present for you under the Christmas tree. I made it."

"Ooh. I wish I could have it right now. Mostly I wish I could have a hug from you right now." Christopher passed me a box of tissues. "TJ, we'll have Christmas, just a little late, that's all. We'll all—" I stopped myself. I couldn't bear to disappoint him again. I couldn't make any more promises that I might not be able to keep. "You can open your presents soon, okay? TJ?"

I barely heard his response. "Hold the phone up to your mouth, baby."

"When is Donnie coming back? I don't even have my sling-shot here."

"I don't know. I don't know where he went. I want to ask you something, Teej. Can you hear me? Good. Do you know your aunt Lindsey loves you? And David too. Do you know that?"

"Uh-huh."

"Do you love them?"

"Yeah."

"You're a lucky boy. You have a big family now. It's not just you and me anymore. You have Grandpa and Grandma—lots of people to love you."

"But I should prob'ly have a dog. Leon has a dog *and* a cat. But cats are scratchy. I just want a dog."

"What kind of dog?"

I knew exactly what his little face was doing. His fat lower lip was jutted out and he was looking skyward with squinty eyes. "Mmm . . . a fluffy one with fast legs. And a happy face."

Dr. Sovold was back, along with two other doctors. A nurse wheeled in a tray with syringes and pills on it.

"I have to go, sweetie." I longed to pull him through the phone, to bury my nose in his hair and touch his perfect skin. "I'm going to have an operation now. I love you, TJ. I love you, baby."

I rolled my face into the pillow and had a good cry. Christopher rubbed my back gently. "Are you okay now?" he asked after a respectable silence. I wiped my face on the sheet and nodded.

Dr. Wilhelm, the transplant surgeon, stood with his arms folded across his chest and smiled patiently down at me. "It looks like we've got a match, Samantha."

I managed a weak smile. "That's good. Great. Okay, let's get this over with."

I took a pill to discourage my T cells from attacking the foreign tissue while Dr. Wilhelm described the horrible things they were about to do to me. A catheter would be shot through my heart to measure pressure in the chambers; an echocardiogram transducer would be slipped down my esophagus so they could view my heart on the monitor. The donor heart had been cut out of the brain-dead body and was flying here by chopper in a beer cooler. It was time to get ready. They would have my chest sawed open and ready before the cooler hit the elevator. My sluggish old heart would be cut out while a machine took over, pumping blood and breathing for me, the new heart inserted and attached one blood vessel at a time.

"This is going to help you relax," Dr. Sovold said as he slid a needle into the IV receptor they had attached to the back of my hand. "Relaxed and sleepy. Let's just let that kick in, and then we'll wheel you on down to OR."

Christopher opened my curtains so I could see the smoky gray afternoon sky. Other families were sitting down to Christmas dinners now. I wondered if the hospital staff resented being here today. I watched their faces for clues as they came and went but couldn't tell if their quiet intensity was due to the seriousness of the pending operation, or if in their minds they were back home where music played and candles burned. I should have mentioned to them in the beginning that my timing was usually off.

My own family should have been gathering around a ham and sweet potatoes dinner right then instead of fighting their way out of a blizzard to be by my side. Was it just yesterday that Lindsey and I rolled out potato lefse, the Judge teasing me as he passed through the kitchen about the flour in my hair? My sister and I imitated the nasal voice of our high school gym teacher until we laughed too hard to function. It occurred to me that Lindsey—my annoyingly perfect almost-twin—had become my best friend. How could my thinking have become so twisted that I thought I didn't need them? I longed to see their faces now, every one of them—Mom, Dad, even David— radiant with the reflections of candlelight and love that we had shared the night before.

All too soon the doctor said it was time to go.

"Can we wait just a little longer for my family to get here?"

"We've got a healthy heart on the way, Samantha. Good tissue match, good size. We need to have that pumping in you within a few hours. Dr. Tyler's going to hook you up to his magic formula, you'll shut your eyes and when you open them again you'll see your family. It'll be like blinking. Poof! And there they are."

"Poof!" I liked the sound of that. "Poof!"

"It's working already," I heard someone say.

They were wheeling me out when Donnie came. He shouted from the elevator. "Wait!"

I rolled my face to the side and smiled. "Hi, Donnie."

He ran to my side. "Sam. I'm sorry. I tried to get here sooner. Are you . . . well, I guess you're going into . . . Hey, buddy! Can you slow down a little?"

"Ooh. Donnie's cranky."

He glanced at Christopher, who grinned and nodded. "She's feeling a little happy."

"Sammy. I'll be here when you wake up," Donnie said. "You're going to be fine."

"Maybe." I yawned. "If not, you've got a backup."

"Backup? What do you mean?"

"You know. Rachel. Plan B. Or maybe she's plan A and I'm plan B. Which is it, pray tell? Door number one or door number two? I have to warn you. Behind one of the doors is a woman with a big ugly scar across her chest."

We arrived at the swinging doors to the OR. Donnie blocked the door and leaned into my face. "Do you really care which door I pick, Sam? Tell me. Do you love me, Sam?"

"I'm sorry," Christopher interjected. "I hate to interrupt, but you can't come in here, and we've got to keep moving." Donnie stepped aside and the doors parted. The gurney pushed through.

I couldn't see him anymore. "Donnie!" I tried to shout, but my words floated out like vapor off a hot roof. "Yes. I do. I love you!" The doors closed. "Isn't that amazing, Christopher?" I yawned. "I think he loves me too."

The blue people with white masks laughed and cheered.

29 ⤸

IN AND OUT OF consciousness, in and out of the light. Voices were real and then they were a dream. I was Moby-Dick, harpooned and helplessly bound with ropes, rolling, nauseous, at the mercy of the waves. Finally, my eyes opened and focused on a middle-aged nurse with boy-cut hair. "Hello, Samantha." I could only blink. A tube had been shoved down my throat; hoses ran from my nose, my arm. I moved one hand slowly toward my chest. The tiny nurse beckoned to someone behind her. Dr. Sovold appeared, towering over her. He grinned. That was a good sign.

"Well?" I tried to say. It came out as a pathetic moan. I felt bandages, tubes, something hard.

"That's your pacemaker," the doctor explained. "They had to cut some nerves that regulate your heart rate. You'll need to wear that for a while."

I rolled my head to one side. Machines, wires and tubes all around me. There was a dull pain in my chest and the thing in my throat made me want to gag.

"How are you feeling, Sam?" Dr. Sovold asked.

I blinked. In Morse code, it was not a nice answer.

The nurse left, returning momentarily with Dr. Wilhelm,

my transplant surgeon. His reddish hair stuck straight up like tufts of mown hay, and because of the way he rubbed his puffy eyes I figured he had been catching a nap. He glanced at the monitors and then smiled at me.

"It went well, Samantha. Real well." He scratched the short wiry beard at the edge of his surgical mask. His bloodshot eyes looked kind and sincere. "You've got a beautiful, healthy heart. Good fit. We were in surgery for less than five hours; we hooked that baby up and she started running like she never missed a beat." He winked. "How about that?" A simple blink was all I could do. "I know you're feeling pretty uncomfortable right now. This tube in your throat is a ventilator. Remember us talking about that? Try to relax and let it do the breathing for you. It's only for a few days. So far there are no signs of rejection, but we'll keep a steady watch on that. Your meds are coming in through those tubes there. . . ."

A beautiful healthy heart. I didn't hear much after that. It pumped inside me now. I listened. I tried to feel the rhythm of its pulse. Closing my eyes, I imagined myself strong—Popeye after a couple of cans of spinach, bandages and tubes bursting from my body as I sprang from the bed. Soon, I reminded myself. It's almost time. I saw myself running, laughing. Chasing TJ. Flashes of brilliant energy. Like highlights from a movie preview, the images played before me and in each scene I beamed with joy. I leaped to spike a volleyball, splashed through the creek, skipped like a schoolchild. I twirled, arms outstretched, spinning like a crazy person beneath the sun.

My mother cried when she saw me. I knew she felt terrible about not being with me before I went into the OR, and now here I lay with tubes everywhere, bandaged like a mummy, unable to speak. I could not have been a pretty sight. David supported her by the arm and led her out of the room. "I'm sorry," she said over her shoulder and then I heard her sobbing in the hall.

My sister came in and stood beside me, gently touching the fingers that protruded below my IV splint. "She's exhausted," Lindsey explained. "We all are. None of us have slept." She smiled at me, but I could tell by her swollen eyes that she had cried too. It was rare to see her face without a trace of makeup. "We're so happy for you, Sam. You're going to be fine now. I just know it."

I tried to ask about my father and Donnie and TJ but Lindsey couldn't understand me. She started fussing with my pillows and covering up my toes. "Do you want me to get the nurse?" I made another attempt to communicate and then gave up. I closed my eyes and pretended to be tired. I hated the way people looked at me. Those pinched sympathetic looks annoyed me as much as the syrupy smiles of the nurses who worked so hard at keeping my attitude positive. I had read the books. I knew that my mental state played a role in my body's acceptance of the foreign heart. My mental state was fine.

I cradled my new heart, embraced it with body and soul. Even in my post-surgery condition I could feel its strong, faithful beat and wondered at the miracle of it all. With every pulse I sensed my invisible donor. Sometimes I cried for her, or him. Most of the time I found myself silently saying *Thank you*, and our heart seemed to answer in some unspoken language like glances between lovers across a crowded room. One body lay on my bed and yet I was not alone. I would never be the same.

On the third day, sometime in the morning, the doctors removed the tube from my throat. I sat up from my bed, letting the sheet fall to the floor, raised my arms to the ceiling and laughed. "I have risen!"

Christopher chuckled. He helped me take a short walk and then checked all my vitals again. "You are a new woman! You'll be on the treadmill in a few days. Time to get that skinny little behind back in shape."

"Bring it on. I can handle anything. I'm ready to see TJ now. I don't look so scary anymore. Will you tell my mother, Chris? And where is my father? He hasn't been here at all."

"Are you sure? You've been sleeping a lot." Chris tossed my cosmetic kit onto the bed. "You might want to do something with your hair first."

I looked in the mirror and smiled. "Did you notice, Chris? Look at the color in my cheeks. That's not makeup." Chris opened the curtains. All I could see was pure blue winter sky.

He returned to my bedside and took the comb from my hand. "Let's see what a French braid looks like on you." He pulled my hair back gently and began to weave.

"What's the matter, Chris?"

"What do you mean?"

"You seem preoccupied . . . or sad. You're going to miss me, aren't you? I mean, I don't think you're in love with me or anything. You've seen too many of my body fluids, not to mention my stinky moods."

He kept braiding silently for a moment. "I guess I'm just concerned about you."

"There's nothing to worry about, Chris. Trust me; my body won't reject this heart. It's mine forever. I'm going to do all the right things. I've changed. I feel it, Chris. No more pity parties. If I have to fight, I'll fight. I can do anything now. I can get a job, and a house! A house by the river so TJ can have the kind of childhood I did—fishing and building forts and climbing trees."

He grinned and hugged me. "I don't know who you are or how you got in here, but I like you."

"I like you back."

There was a light tap on the door. Dr. Sovold peered in, then motioned and was followed by my mom and Matthew.

"Hey, Matt!" I reached out and he placed the pink palm of his black hand on mine like we used to do when I was small. "Hey, Mom." She looked better. There were still shadows under her eyes, but her hair was pinned up in a French roll and she wore a clean and pressed pants outfit. They all pulled up chairs next to my bed. "What's up? Where's Dad?"

I had called him Dad again, which still seemed new to me, but no one seemed to notice. Mom was smiling. "You look wonderful." She touched my cheeks and I knew she was seeing me healthy for the first time since I left home as a teenager. Matt leaned forward, resting his arms on his knees. Dr. Sovold's chair was pushed back a little, like he was just there as an observer or something. Christopher nervously excused himself and left the room.

"Is something up?" Mom's eyes darted toward Matt as he cleared his throat. I sat up a little straighter and took a deep breath.

Matt sighed, dropping his head momentarily, and then raised his chin and let his eyes meet mine. His lower lids hung open a bit like apron pockets and they immediately filled with tears. He swiped at them and shook his head with a weak laugh. "I wasn't going to do that." Mom reached over and placed her hand on his arm. "You know I love you, Sammy. Like you were my own little girl. I'm so happy for you. You look like you've come back to life again." He placed his hand over Mom's. "Doesn't she look just like she's twelve again with her hair all pulled back like that, that sparkle in her eye. This is a happy day, Sammy." He sighed. "But we got ourselves some sadness too."

"Where's Dad?" Now my mother's eyes flooded up. I stifled a sob. "Where's my father, Matthew?"

He broke down. His forehead dropped to his clenched hands and he cried right out loud. "I'm sorry. I'm sorry."

My body fell against the pillows propped behind me.

Mom took a deep breath and squared her shoulders. "Sammy, we're going to tell you the truth now. The doctor says you're strong enough and I believe you are. I don't know what you were doing out in the barn that night." She shook her head. "I thought you were asleep in your bed. Dwight Enrich is the one who's been prowling around, harassing us. Do you remember, honey? Do you remember anything about that night?"

I nodded. It was all coming back to me. It seemed so unreal. I had been whisked into surgery so fast afterward that it seemed like a bad dream. "I was on my knees. His gun was pointed at my head."

Matt wiped his face and cleared his throat. "Your father took the bullet, Sammy. They found him on top of you." He began to stroke my hand.

It was supposed to be me. Enrich wanted to kill me. "I asked Christopher that next morning. He said Dad was alive!"

Matt shook his head. "The bullet went right up through here"—he pointed to his jaw—"and lodged in his head. He was unconscious. An ambulance took him into Darlington. Another one took you on down here, where they could take better care of you."

"So it wasn't just the snow that kept you from getting out of Darlington."

"No. It wasn't the snow. The surgeons were trying to get the bullet out . . . but where it was—it was just no good, Sammy. They couldn't save him."

My eyes were fixed on my mother. She sat there like the queen of England, regal and strong, half smiling at me with moist eyes. My father was the only man she had ever loved.

"Mom," I managed to croak, "I'm so sorry." It was a while before any of us spoke. I used my bedsheet as a tissue. The sky was still so blue beyond my window, like any ordinary day. "Where is he now?"

Mom smiled. Matthew reached out and took my hand, gently placing it on my chest. "He's here, Sammy. He's right here."

MAY CAME AGAIN. Purple lilacs bloomed on the bush outside my mother's bedroom window, and their scent combined with the spicy fragrance of the new cottonwood buds was almost more than I could bear. Goldfinches the color of buttercups twittered from the branches of the old apple tree and then scattered in a flurry of wings. I swear there has never been a spring, before or since, that was so intense. So perfect.

The river, swollen from melting mountain snows, flowed peacefully, musically, from places I had never seen to places I hoped I would. My possibilities were endless.

Donnie climbed the grand old cottonwood that stood near the intersection of our creek and the river and tied one end of a rope to a thick limb; the other end he triple-knotted around a tire we found behind the barn. TJ wanted to go first, but Donnie insisted that the maiden swing be his. He held the tire in the crook of his elbow as he climbed the nearby slope and then with a running start and a sickly Tarzan yell swung out over the creek. He and TJ went double next, laughing like two little boys, while I pinched off a sticky, aromatic cottonwood bud and held it beneath my nose. They wanted to go again, but I wrestled the tire away from them and ran up the hill. The rope creaked when I hoisted my body onto the tire and pushed off. I swung wide over the creek and then back to the bank and pushed off again with my feet. The tire began to spin as I lay back, holding on to the knot, admiring the kaleidoscope of waving leaves and shards of sky above me.

When I was a child I hung by my knees from the lower branches of that very tree. Sometimes I sprawled like a cheetah on a fork of heavy limbs and watched my father fish the mouth of the creek where it spread to join the river. He would turn his head from time to time and look at me there among the big leaves that flapped like laundry in the breeze.

I never went to his grave and I never will. He is not there.

The Judge's memorial service was held at the Darlington Community Church, where I had sat between my parents every Sunday as a child. The service had been delayed for several weeks so that I would be well enough to attend. The place was packed, with people standing along the side and back walls. Friends and relatives gave glowing tributes, including Matt, who broke down and cried twice, as we all did right along with him. When he came down from the pulpit and sat with us in the front row, Mom rested her hand on his arm. Everyone made a big deal about Blake Dodd living on because his heart still beat inside of me. It was a terrible thing that happened: the father of a convicted killer taking his revenge on the judge who sentenced his son. But Enrich's rage had turned on me. What better way to repay the Judge? An eye for an eye, a daughter for a son. (The news media loved it. They were out in full force, even though Matthew threatened to smash the first camera he saw in the church.) And then, how ironic, my father threw himself on me. He saved me twice. Once by taking my bullet and then by giving me his heart so that I could live to raise my son. So that come spring I could swing on the tire swing down by the river with Donnie and TJ, planning and dreaming about the log house we would build on the other side. It was a great story, but they really didn't get it. How could they? They didn't know what I knew—what Matt told me while I was still in the hospital—which I couldn't comprehend for some time. In fact, there are still days when I am so overtaken by the whole truth that I fall to my knees and cry.

After the service a lot of people came to our house with food. It was still too cold outside to use the deck, so they milled about with overflowing plates, dripping coffee onto the carpet, reminiscing and chatting, even laughing right out loud. Aunt Lilse kept saying it should have been her that died. "Blake was so young and strong," she said. "Who would have thought he'd go before me? God knows, *I've* been on the verge of death for twenty years." People said a lot of nice things to me about my father. They said they were happy for me and that I must be proud to have his heart beating inside me. They said they were sorry that we lost him, but wasn't it fortunate the way things turned out? Like it was all a fluke. An accident with a lucky twist. After the hundred and fiftieth person asked me how it felt to have my father's heart, I ducked down the hall to the refuge of the Judge's study.

The room had not changed. I settled into my father's leather throne and pulled my feet up. There was a gap on the bookshelf where several law books had been removed. The Judge had willed them all to Donnie, but Donnie removed only a few at a time and later replaced them in the exact same spots on the shelves. My mother had dusted the worn leather Bible on the Judge's desk, an antique brass fishing reel, a glass display case of tied flies. Everything was left in its place like she expected him to return any day, lean back in that big chair with the capillary cracks in the brown leather and plop his feet up on the mahogany desk.

My father knew that he had type AB blood, just like mine. I was not his daughter by blood. I was the offspring of a cheating husband and a wild-haired woman with big orange lips. But still, we somehow ended up with the same blood type. The hardest to match, they say. Matthew said the Judge called him one day last fall and asked him to come up; he had something serious to discuss. He needed Matt's medical expertise, he had said. Matt said his first thought was that something was wrong with my father. He drove all the way from the city, worried by the sober tone of my father's voice. Then the Judge confided in his trusted friend his knowledge of our blood match and pumped the doctor with questions about other factors necessary for a good match. He asked Matthew to run tests on his heart. My father wanted to know if his heart was strong.

I was still in the hospital when Matt told me these things. "I'll be honest with you, Samantha," Matt had said. "I told him he was crazy. I told him it's not like giving blood, or even a kidney. You've only got one heart and when it's gone, so are you. He understood all that and yet he kept probing. He wouldn't let it die. Wouldn't let *you* die."

I thought it must be the residue of painkillers and other drugs in my brain that made this information so hard to process. "What on earth did he have in mind? How could he have planned what happened? He couldn't—could he, Matt?"

Matt shook his head. "He didn't really have a plan. He wanted me to help him come up with one. I just couldn't, Sam. I'm a doctor. To him it was a necessary sacrifice; to me it was suicide. I told him to wait it out. I told him I would have no part in helping him arrange his own death."

I remembered that day in early November when Matt had stormed out of that very study, leaving the Judge to brood alone. My father probably sat there in his leather chair, running his hands through his dark hair. Maybe he leaned back and stared at the ceiling for a long time as he did when he was considering a case.

He was thinking about me. He must have seen me differently than I saw myself. How else could he even consider giving up his own life for mine? I was a loser. A failure as a daughter, a mother, a wife. I had rejected my father and all that he stood for. I worried my family for years while I screwed up my life. I killed my unborn child, betrayed my husband, danced half-naked for strangers while my son ate and slept under the care of people I hardly knew. If it was Lindsey who was dying, the Judge's sacrifice might make sense, but even then it would be a stretch.

I closed my eyes and snuggled into the leather chair, pretending that its arms were the arms of my father, holding me as he did that snowy December night in the barn. I understood his prayer now. It was like the prayer of Jesus—I remembered it from Sunday school—when he cried out to God in agony, knowing that the time had come to do what he came to do. It was the prayer of a man, not God. A man who knew his destiny, had already embraced it, but was having second thoughts. *Let there be some other way!* My father pleaded with God, but God didn't make another way. He let Dwight Enrich sneak through the woods to carry out his twisted plan.

My father had not been shocked to see Enrich. Not really. He must have figured out who was making threats on his life. I

wondered how long he had known. I wondered if he was waiting, maybe even hoping for Enrich to come, before I surprised
him in the barn.

When they found us lying there in the snow, I was covered
with my father's blood. This was not the judgment I had expected from him, certainly not what I deserved. And yet by his
willing wounds I was healed—in more ways than one.

My heart beat strongly now. My father's heart, I mean. I
placed my hand on my chest and with every beat I heard his
message to me. *I love you . . . love you . . . love you.* He knew just
what I was and yet he loved me all along. I let my body slide to
the floor, turning to kneel at the foot of his leather throne, my
face in my hands.

I finally understood.

"Oh, Daddy," I wept, "I love you too."

READING GROUP GUIDE

1. *Where Mercy Flows* is set in the lush, green Stillaguamish River Valley. In what way is the setting important to the story? What does the river represent to Samantha?

2. What were the things that tormented Samantha?

3. The author uses many analogies throughout the story. Which ones stand out in your memory? Is it possible that the entire work is a metaphor? If so, what is the author trying to say?

4. If the major characters are symbolic in any way, what or whom might each represent? Judge Blake Dodd? Lucy Dodd? Lindsey? Samantha? TJ? Dwight Enrich? What word clues does the author use to convey any subliminal identities?

5. In chapter ten, the night of the Fourth of July celebration, Samantha has a recurrent dream. What is particularly haunting about the dream this time?

6. Most of Samantha's childhood memories are idyllic. At what point do you think her perspective on life begins to change?

7. How does the revelation of the character of Samantha's biological mother affect her?

8. Would Samantha have felt guilty about her abortion if not for the influence of her father's strong conviction?

9. Why does Samantha always refer to her father as the Judge? What causes her to finally call him Daddy? Who changes: Samantha or her father—or both?

10. Why do you think the author chose to have the Judge die in the manner in which he did as opposed to some other plan?

11. Samantha says she was covered with her father's blood. What is the significance of that?

12. Would this story make a good movie? If so, what actors would you choose to play the major characters? What were your favorite scenes?

13. In the last chapter, Samantha pinches off a cottonwood bud and breathes in its scent. What is the significance?

14. Has the reading of *Where Mercy Flows* impacted your life in any way? If so, how?